States of Desire

States
OF
Desire

Wilde, Yeats,

Joyce, and

the Irish

Experiment

VICKI MAHAFFEY

New York ◆ Oxford

Oxford University Press

1998

Oxford University Press

Oxford   New York

Athens   Auckland   Bangkok   Bogotá   Buenos Aires   Calcutta
Cape Town   Chennai   Dar es Salaam   Delhi   Florence   Hong Kong   Istanbul
Karachi   Kuala Lumpur   Madrid   Melbourne   Mexico City   Mumbai
Nairobi   Paris   São Paulo   Singapore   Taipei   Tokyo   Toronto   Warsaw

and associated companies in
Berlin   Ibadan

Copyright © 1998 by Oxford University Press, Inc.

Published by Oxford University Press, Inc.,
198 Madison Avenue, New York, New York 10016

Oxford is a registered trademark of Oxford University Press

Library of Congress Cataloging-in-Publication Data
Mahaffey, Vicki.
States of desire : Wilde, Yeats, Joyce, and the
Irish experiment / by Vicki Mahaffey.
p.   cm.
Includes bibliographical references and index.
ISBN 0–19–511592–9
1. English literature—Irish authors—History and criticism.
2. Yeats, W. B. (William Butler), 1865–1939—Criticism and interpretation.
3. Wilde, Oscar, 1854–1900—Criticism and interpretation.
4. Joyce, James, 1882–1941—Criticism and interpretation.
5. English literature—19th century—History and criticism.
6. English literature—20th century—History and criticism.
7. National characteristics, Irish, in literature.
8. Ireland—In literature.   I. Title.
PR8750.M34   1997
820.9′9415′09041—DC21   96–54631

Portions of *States of Desire* were published elsewhere in an earlier form. I am grateful to the
James Joyce Quarterly and The University of Michigan Press for permission to reprint revised
versions of these articles:

"Fantastic Histories: Nomadology and Female Piracy in *Finnegans Wake*," in *Joyce and History*,
ed. Mark Wollaeger, Victor Luftig, and Robert Spoo (University of Michigan Press, 1996),
157–76.

"Heirs of Yeats: Eire as Female Poets Revise Her," in *The Future of Modernism*, ed. Hugh Witemeyer (University of Michigan Press, 1997), 101–17.

"Fascism and Silence: The Coded History of Amalia Popper," *James Joyce Quarterly* 32
(Spring/Summer 1995): 501–22.

"Père-version and Im-mère-sion: Idealized Corruption in *A Portrait of the Artist as a Young Man*
and *The Picture of Dorian Gray*," special issue of *The James Joyce Quarterly* 31 (Spring 1994),
"Joyce and Homosexuality": 189–206. Reprinted in *Quare Joyce*, ed. Joseph Valente (University
of Michigan Press, 1998, 121–36).

"'Minxing Marrage and Making Loof': Anti-Oedipal Reading," *James Joyce Quarterly* 30 (Winter
1993): 219–37.

"Wunderlich on Joyce: The Case Against Art," *Critical Inquiry* 17 (Summer 1991): 667–92.

1 3 5 7 9 8 6 4 2

Printed in the United States of America
on acid-free paper

◆ *To Chris*

Preface

Small things matter, and that's where the leakage begins.

—Virginia Woolf, *Night and Day*

When I was working on the issue of authority in the writings of James Joyce,[1] I attempted to define an exercise of authority that was unoppressive, dynamic, and even joyous, which I associated with the authority of experience (as opposed to the more tyrannical authority of power or force). This is the kind of authority I had come to enjoy in the classroom, and it offers all the rewards that are usually associated with mastery of one's discipline and the ability to restage that mastery for students. What I also came to recognize was that this kind of authority is by definition backward-looking, even nostalgic, since it depends upon a re-presentation or belated staging of discovery; moreover, the authority of experience produces a feeling of widening distance between teacher and students, who are cast primarily as audience. I found it increasingly disturbing, for example, to teach the works of Samuel Beckett, and especially *Waiting for Godot* and *Endgame*. These two plays were uncannily beginning to resemble, in the relation between characters and audience, the relation between myself and my students. Like teachers, Beckett's characters are experienced at playing the same scenarios day after day, and at moments they succeed both in entertaining and in being entertained, but the ennui of repetition frays their patience to the point that they long for ending, and they question the meaning of such rituals even while performing them. Despite their preoccupation with routines authorized by experience, with behaviors randomly repaid by carrots or sticks, Beckett's characters sometimes recall the allure of "beginning," which is not an idealized or fetishized youth, but the process of discovery that precedes the formation of habit. In *Endgame*, Hamm asks Clov, as Clov pushes Hamm's wheelchair toward the light, "Do you remember, in the beginning, when you took me for a turn? You used to hold the chair too high. At every step you nearly tipped me out. (*With senile quaver.*) Ah, great fun we had, the two of us, great fun. (*Gloomily.*) And then we got into the way of it."[2] Or, as Vladimir expresses it in *Waiting for Godot*, "We have time to grow old. The air is full of our cries. (*He listens.*) But habit is a great deadener."[3] Beckett exposes mastery as a disguise of habit, intermittently ludicrous and delightful, but also excruciatingly boring. As Vladimir explains, "All I know is that the hours are long, under these conditions, and constrain us to beguile them with proceedings which—how shall I say—which may at first sight seem reasonable, until they become a habit" (*Godot*, 51).

The only sparks of vitality in *Godot* are associated not with experience but with experiment, with the kind of discovery that becomes possible when we abandon the intentions, goals, and expectations born of experience. Didi and Gogo agree that it is more difficult to discover something if you are looking for it:

> VLADIMIR: When you seek you hear.
> ESTRAGON: You do.
> VLADIMIR: That prevents you from finding.
> ESTRAGON: It does. (*Godot*, 41)

Moreover, our desire to discover is handicapped by our tendency to set our sights too high, to situate ourselves in a frame of reference that is too large. Because they are expecting Godot, Didi and Gogo fail to learn anything from the arrival(s) of Pozzo and Lucky. They are so preoccupied by their appointment with the unknown, which they faithfully await, that they miss the opportunity to analyze or learn from the events of the present. The problem with such a universalizing or generalizing approach is that it never delivers the promised revelation because, as Clov puts it in *Endgame*, you "need a microscope to find [a telescope]" (76).

One of the most important tools for registering the energies of buried desire, then, is a microscope. As Woolf writes in *Night and Day*, "Small things matter." James Joyce famously makes a similar point in *Dubliners* by emphasizing the vital importance of local control, the loss of which constitutes paralysis, Joyce's ruling figure for dis-ability in *Dubliners*. In a similar way, William Butler Yeats redefines the national as the local, and especially the rural; he is invariably less interested in resisting the British empire than in rediscovering the history, mythology, and speech patterns of individual Irish communities. Although Yeats is known as a propagandist of nationalism, he is actually what I call a micronationalist, since all of his fulminations against cosmopolitanism are rooted in his Blakean conviction that you can find the whole universe in a grain of sand.[4] As he suggested in an article for the *Providence Sunday Journal* in 1888, national experience is only ever realized as local experience. He envisions a "nation" as something small and personal, a glove on the hand with which one reaches out to the universe:

> To the greater poets everything they see has its relation to the national life, and through that to the universal and divine life: nothing is an isolated artistic moment; there is a unity everywhere; everything fulfills a purpose that is not its own; the hailstone is a journeyman of God; the grass blade carries the universe upon its point. But to this universalism, this seeing of unity everywhere, you can only attain through what is near you, your nation, or, if you be no traveller, your village and the cobwebs on your walls. You can no more have the greater poetry without a nation than religion without symbols. One can only reach out to the universe with a gloved hand—that glove is one's nation, the only thing one knows even a little of. (*LNI*, 78)

Although Yeats's credo partakes of the rhetoric of nationalism, what he is actually endorsing is not an abstract category (which is how "nation" is usually understood), but micronationalism, the poetic concreteness of the local, the particular. What we know is what we can touch, but we can only touch the world through our knowledge of local detail. For Yeats, too, only a microscope gives access to more telescopic perspectives.

Several decades later, the value of microscopic attention also forms the basis of Gilles Deleuze and Félix Guattari's insistence on the importance of what they call "micropolitics," as well as informing their advocacy of "minority" literature. Micropolitics is a version of what Oscar Wilde called "individualism," a resistance to all forms of coercion at the microlevel of an individual's private thoughts and desires. It is the antithesis of imitation, which Wilde unambiguously condemned as a mode of unnatural and barbaric conformity: "All imitation in morals and in life is wrong."[5] Wilde extravagantly criticized all forms of authority and government, especially those forms "accompanied by prizes and awards," as demoralizing and degrading. They make

> People . . . less conscious of the horrible pressure that is being put on them, and so go through their lives in a sort of coarse comfort, like petted animals, without ever realising that they are probably thinking other people's thoughts, living by other people's standards, wearing practically what one may call other people's second-hand clothes, and never being themselves for a single moment. (*A as C*, 267)

Wilde's interest in crime and his declaration that "disobedience is the original virtue" both stem from his appreciation of individualism. Importantly, Wilde sees the epitome of individualism not in Satan but in Christ. He warns that protest is not an end in itself but simply a means to its own antithesis, for "[t]he note of the perfect personality is not rebellion, but peace" (*A as C*, 263). Wilde's appreciation of Christ as the supreme individualist shows that his stance is not one of unthinking resistance to authority. On the contrary, he intimates that peace is only possible through an acceptance of paradox, through an embrace of incompatible extremes.

These three Irishmen's insistence on recovering local control was rendered all the more urgent by their acute awareness of Ireland's impoverishment under foreign rule, although each focused his attention on the microcosms of local language, customs, and individual identity. Wilde centered his campaign for greater artistic, personal, and national autonomy on the multifaceted individual personality, celebrating its real contradictions and inconsistencies rather than an unnatural, socially acceptable coherence. Both Yeats and Joyce trained their microscopes more consistently on the individual moment—in life and in language—building a symbolic system and a verbal world out of the complex interplay of moments (instead of taking a world and dividing it into arbitrary units, as a clock does to time). Through painstaking revision and elaboration (Joyce's books took anywhere from seven to seventeen years to complete, and Yeats revised his poems intensively for subsequent editions), both Joyce and Yeats honed the precision of their words and the art of their arrangement, making it imperative for their readers, too, to exercise precise local control in their reading. The object is to restore to reading and thinking the unpredictability of desire together with the agility, strength, and dynamism of athletics, thereby developing the reader's resistance to uses of language that sedate rather than energize independent thought and expression. In some respects, both Joyce and Yeats were trying to reinvent the politically effective, sinewy poetic language extolled by Percy Bysshe Shelley in 1821, language that strengthens the "faculty which is the organ of the moral nature of man, in the same manner as exercise strengthens a limb." It is facility with such language that, in Shelley's famous phrase, makes poets "the unacknowledged legislators of the World" ("A Defense of Poetry").

In choosing to focus on three Irish writers, I have sought to illustrate the importance of attending to the local, the concrete, and the historically and geographically specific. Ireland is a concentrated symptom of the contradictions of modernity, poised between economic shortage and imaginative richness, riven by seven centuries of violence, invisibly divided by different branches of the same creed, and forced to articulate its protests in English, the language of the colonizer. As a symptom of modernity, Ireland allows us to see the outlines of the larger condition, while condensing what is finest and most volatile in that condition. In the twentieth century, Ireland has also produced a disproportionate number of successful experimental writers for the size of its population. The predominance of Irish writers was recently brought home to me once again when I was teaching a large lecture course on British experimental writing. At the end of the course, one of the students complained with what I believe to be genuine naivete, "Are all British writers Irish? Why don't we read Wilde, or Shaw?"

Irish literature and history provide a particularly rich terrain for study not only because they are layered and densely concentrated, but also because they bear traces of two dramatically different narratives: the story of a long and bitter oppression by the English interwoven with an ancient mythic tradition of underground life, in which the power of the unconscious is given vitality, specificity, and history. Tir na n-Og, the "Land of the Young," is according to Irish mythology both a parallel world and an afterworld. Its perfection is the mirror image of the real Ireland, corresponding with and countering it at every point. Ireland and Tir na n-Og are simultaneously identical and opposite—if it is autumn in Ireland, it will be spring in Tir na n-Og; Tir na n-Og is the shadow land that haunts and completes the imperfect life of mortals. As James Stephens describes it in his book, *In the Land of Youth*, Tir na n-Og "is within the world you have left, as an apple is within its skin, and all who die in your world come to this one."[6] But as the Irish poet Nuala Ní Dhomhnaill points out, the Irish otherworld ("an saol eile") "is not simply an anticipated joyful afterlife; it is also—even primarily—an alternative to reality."[7] To enter the otherworld is to pass through the looking glass, to leave the world of rational constraint for the more vivid and threatening world of imagination and desire.

In Ireland, desire, forced underground and dammed up by a long and bloody history of colonial oppression, pours forth again in exuberant language, a dynamic, everchanging language that seeks to spend itself on the richly layered landscape of history. Such language, while playful, is trivial only in the most literal sense of "trivia," as a place of magical insight where three roads cross; as Wilde implied a century ago, the "trivial" activity of play is earnest as well as pleasurable. Moreover, Ireland—which produced the finest playboys of the western world—is a place where everyone recognizes that play is political. Like childhood, Ireland became a green world animated by fairies in response to a very real oppression—its often violent domination by England—but the impulse that produced the green world was not simply escapist. Play, as any child knows, is the language of outlawed desire, a subversive expression of resistance when rebellion fails. Like Puck, play unobtrusively drains the pleasure out of arbitrarily exercised power, drawing pleasure to itself. Play unleashes the principle of excess to sport with the law of oppressive denial, until denial finds itself exhausted. The desire that fuels play is both exuberant and corrosive, violent and prolific. It riddles prescriptive, unified images of self, text, and nation, breaking up categories and setting the shards dancing in unexpected ways. The resulting combinations and recombinations of "meaning" continue to change, dramatizing at every moment both the importance and the inadequacy of each constituent part.

Verbal invention is implicitly political because it challenges hardened ideas, ideas that have grown into communal ideals, which are the mental equivalent of institutions. Ideals can be inspiring, but when the number of socially acceptable ideals is relatively small, and when we idealize accidents of birth (such as sex, race, or class) instead of qualities of mind, ideals become a means of encouraging conformity, of standardizing a population. Conformity comes to seem highly desirable despite—perhaps even because of—the fact that it is impossible for many people to meet the privileged standards by virtue of their sex or their skin color. Play—animated by outlawed desire—dispels the aura of idealized standards, exposing it as artificial. In other words, play interrupts the conformist's desire to belong to a privileged group, replacing the passive desire to belong with the more active, concrete pleasures of invention.

It is because aesthetic play encourages potentially political independent thinking that the Puritans closed the theaters during the Reformation and the Nazis confiscated experimental art. I am writing this book partly as a reminder of the destructive power of idealism and the dangers of idealizing conformity in particular. As George Bernard Shaw (an Irishman) said of the Golden Rule, "Do unto others as you would have others do unto you? Hell no, they might be different!" This book is designed to illustrate an alternative to imperialist idealism, an alternative available to everyone because it is rooted in language and thought. This alternative goes by many names in the pages that follow—play, experimentation, micronationalism, subversive desire—but what differentiates it from idealism is its emphasis on active questioning rather than passive admiration. What disciplined play enables us to discover are the hidden affinities that connect even the most apparently disparate subjects. Ireland has been a successful laboratory for such verbal play (which is never divorced from social and historical contexts) because of its intertwined legacies of imaginative richness and real violence. In Ireland, where the majority of the population was deeply critical of imperialism, and where traditional political and military strategies of resistance had repeatedly failed, both writers and talkers used words to subvert and expose the hollowness of values that do not abide our questioning.

Modern Irish literature is engendered in the rich linguistic furrow where imagination and history, pleasure and politics commingle. In the hands of the Irish, English is no longer a language of mastery but a field of play, where what has been undergoes rearrangement, metamorphosis, and multiplication. It becomes a "jinglish janglage" (FW, 275.F6), a jingle-jangle of letters that breaks the spell of convention and habit; it takes as its basic unit not meaning, but the alphabet, with which it invites us to rearrange—and respell—a badly jangled world. What experimental writers offer is a revolutionary way of reading that has the power to expose—and therefore change—what we desire, which makes it quite literally "revolitionary" (FW, 234.11). Such reading proceeds by way of shattering or bypassing or only partially appropriating the interpretive categories licensed by experience. Gender, nationality, and belief are exposed as expedient fictions that produce friction; they survive as partial truths that are disabling to the extent that they demand conformity. Words, too, are shattered—broken into pieces and re-membered differently, variously, humorously, in ways that map the underground logic of the pun. To see the word as malleable is to see the meanings established by habit as mean, and our categories of sense-making as unnecessarily impoverished. In contrast, the process of redefining language in precise but provisional ways sets meaning in motion, and churns up (instead of palliating) desire. The technique of punning, in particular, is subversive in intensely personal ways; the pun brings an awareness of the underground (and of undertones) into the sanctuary of private thought. The rhetorical and political power of the pun, recognized early and widely by the Irish, has since been employed by critics as diverse as Mary Daly, Jacques Lacan, and Jacques Derrida in ways that highlight the potential of punning to serve as a "language" of the repressed and oppressed.[8] If the pen is mightier than the sword, Irish experimental writers might reply with "revolitionary" fervor that the pun is mightier than the word.

Of course, not all play is subversive. Often, play is simply a diversion, a form of entertainment that beguiles the hours of waiting for life to take its course. This is the kind of play that Beckett dramatizes as fatal in Endgame (Fin de Partie). The games played by Hamm and Clov are too repetitive to be fun; they play husband and wife, master and servant, father and son, actor and audience, king and pawn. What Hamm imagines to be a huge creative effort—the composition of his story—is simply an effort to remember his history, which will also be the pattern of Clov's future, and so on in perpetuity. As Hamm tells himself, "The end is in the beginning and yet you go on" (Endgame, 69). Both Hamm's "creative" play and his games with Clov are a response to an isolation so extreme that it feels like the end of the world; they "babble, babble, words, like the solitary child who turns himself into children, two, three, so as to be together, and whisper together, in the dark" (Endgame, 70). In Endgame, everyone dies of darkness, like Mother Pegg, but before they go they rehearse, repeating "the old questions, the old answers" (*Endgame,* 38). Such endless rehearsal is a losing game, inspired by loneliness and fatigue, what Hamm wearily calls "Old endgame lost of old, play and lose and have done with losing" (*Endgame,* 82).

Is there an alternative to the old, overregulated chess games that seem to be contests of power but proceed through slow attrition? Biologically, no; growing old is an endgame. Morally, maybe; Hamm had some oil he could have given Mother Pegg so that she would not die of darkness. In *Waiting for Godot,* Didi and Gogo hear cries of help, addressed to "all mankind," and Didi exclaims, "at this place, at this moment of time, all mankind is us, whether we like it or not. Let us make the most of it, before it is too late!" (*Godot,* 51). The point of training a metaphorical microscope on local, particular details is that it enables us to make a personal connection with some small aspect of reality, to take responsibility for individual moments, and to renew that responsibility in vital and pleasurable ways. Instead of replaying the past, we can learn to be more responsive to particular aspects of the present. As Ralph Waldo Emerson once wrote, "The invariable mark of wisdom is to see the miraculous in the common." What Emerson does not say is how we can learn to see the miraculous in the common: through thoughtful play that remains responsive to the multiple, changing states of desire.

Acknowledgments

The main premise of this book is that desire, usually considered a private and individual emotion, has an important and often overlooked relation to the public state or nation. I argue throughout that one of the main functions of language is to forge subtle but perceptible links between personal and national—or even global—concerns, between the world of the mind and the larger world of political maneuvering. Language performs that function in a way that seems playful, thereby allowing us to deny both the seriousness and the scope of its hidden ramifications. I focus on Ireland as a place with a rich linguistic heritage that is also haunted by a history of failed resistance to colonial rule, a "mad" [angry, insane] country that, to paraphrase W. H. Auden, "hurt" its writers into poetry. Yet "Ireland has her madness and her weather still, / For poetry makes nothing happen" ("In Memory of W. B. Yeats"). Poetry is simply "a way of happening"; it expresses the fearful symmetry between nations "sequestered in [their] hate," on the one hand, and "the seas of pity" that "lie / Locked and frozen in each eye," on the other. Poetry makes nothing happen except the kind of healing that, if it begins at all, must start "In the deserts of the heart":

> Follow, poet, follow right
> To the bottom of the night,
> With your unconstraining voice
> Still persuade us to rejoice;
> . . . .
> In the deserts of the heart
> Let the healing fountain start,
> In the prison of his days
> Teach the free man how to praise.

My debts in the preparation of this manuscript are many. Without the generosity of Paul Wunderlich, and the inspiration his art has provided, this book would be much diminished. Roland McHugh, by publishing his *Annotations* to *Finnegans Wake*, has transformed the experience of reading the *Wake*. I would like to thank the Guggenheim Foundation for the fellowship that made this book possible. I am also grateful to the Research Foundation at the University of Pennsylvania for a grant to help cover publication costs. Many people read portions of the manuscript and judiciously isolated the sections that most needed revision. I am deeply appreciative of the time, effort, and intelligence that shaped the responses of Ronald Bush, Marian Eide, Marjorie Levenson, A. Walton Litz, Deborah Luepnitz, Nicholas Miller, Jean-Michel Rabaté, Natania Rosenfeld, and Joseph Valente. My thanks are also due to Sue Sun Yom for providing me with the epigraph.

Finally, I am left with an old question that always seems new: how can I possibly give adequate thanks to those who have had to share their lives with this book? To my husband, Christopher Dennis, and my daughters, Amanda and Laura, I can only offer my heartfelt gratitude for their patience and encouragement. Thanks are also due to my parents, Nancy and Jack Mahaffey, and my siblings, Jack, Mindy, and Tim, for their unwavering faith in the abstract value of my efforts. To all of my family, I would say in the words of Louis MacNeice that although "Sunlight on the garden / Hardens and grows cold, [and] We cannot cage the minute / Within its nets of gold," I am "glad to have sat under / Thunder and rain with you, / And grateful too / For sunlight on the garden" ("The Sunlight on the Garden," 1938).

Contents

Abbreviations

For more information see Selected Bibliography

A	*The Autobiography of William Butler Yeats*
AasC	*The Artist as Critic*, ed. Richard Ellmann
CW	*The Complete Works of Oscar Wilde*
CWY	*The Collected Works of W. B. Yeats*, ed. Richard Finneran and George Mills Harper (general eds.)
DG	Oscar Wilde, *The Picture of Dorian Gray*, ed Donald Lawler
E&I	William Butler Yeats, *Essays and Introductions*
FW	James Joyce, *Finnegans Wake*
GJ	James Joyce, *Giacomo Joyce*
Mem	William Butler Yeats, *Memoirs*, ed. Denis Donaghue
NS	Giambattista Vico, *The New Science*, 3d ed., trans. Thomas Goddard Bergin and Max Harold Fisch
P	James Joyce *A Portrait of the Artist as a Young Man*
SR	William Butler Yeats, *The Secret Rose*
TP	Gilles Deleuze and Félix Guattari, *A Thousand Plateaus*
VSR	Yeats, *The Secret Rose, Stories by W. B. Yeats: A Variorum Edition*, ed. Phillip L. Marcus, Warwick Gould, and Michael J. Sidnell
U	James Joyce, *Ulysses*, ed. Hans Walter Gabler
UP	William Butler Yeats, *Uncollected Prose*, ed. John P. Frayne
VP	*The Variorum Edition of the Poems of W. B. Yeats*, ed. Peter Allt and Russell K. Alspach
VPl	*The Variorum Edition of the Plays of W. B. Yeats*, ed. Russell Alspach

States of Desire

We lose ourselves in violent forms of dances in our ballrooms. The faces of the white world, looking on in wonder and curiosity, declare: "Only the Negro can play!" But they are wrong. They misread us. We are able to play in this fashion because we have been excluded, left behind; we play in this manner because all excluded folk play. The English say of the Irish, just as America says of us, that only the Irish can play, that they laugh through their tears. But every powerful nation says this of the folk whom it oppresses in justification of that oppression.

—Richard Wright, *12 Million Black Voices:*
A Folk History of the Negro in the United States

A man isn't what he seems but what he desires;
Gaieties of anarchy drumming at the base of the skull.

—Adrienne Rich, "The Blue Ghazals"

The coexistence of two states of movement, two states of desire, two states of law, doesn't signify hesitation but rather an immanent experimentation that will open up all the polyvocal elements of desire.

—Gilles Deleuze and Félix Guattari,
Kafka: Toward a Minor Literature

One

Introduction

Reading and "Irish" Desire

The broad background of this study is the twentieth century itself, throughout which people have seesawed between the impulse to idealize powerful images and an equally strong determination to resist their alluring and subtle power. Over the course of the century, the ideal images against which we typically measure both individual and collective value have emerged as both seductive and horrifying. These dominating ideals range from the individual to the global in scope; they include the notion of an impossibly "pure" or coherent self, the assumption of male superiority, the concept of a master race, and the ideal of an imperial nation. Such symbols of desirability—representative standards of what is ostensibly best and purest—swelled in power in the years preceding World War II, reaching their epitome in the glorification of the Aryan race; like the graven images proscribed in the Hebrew Bible, they gained numerous adherents, but they also provoked attacks from without and were subject to corruption from within. The insistence upon the authoritarian power of the master provoked the cruelest genocide in the history of the world, but it also galvanized massive military resistance. In this book, I argue that ordinary objects of desire in literature correspond to these powerful forces on a much smaller scale. In Joyce's *Dubliners*, for example, the wedding ring that Maria unconsciously pines for in "Clay," or the small gold coin that Lenehan and Corley pursue in "Two Gallants," are highlighted as deceptive images, promising a satisfaction and closure they can never deliver or sustain. By focusing on the idiosyncratic but intense yearnings of specific characters, such as a boy's desire to buy a trinket for a young girl, Joyce is able to demonstrate the futility and often the destructiveness of any desire directed toward a single end. The reductive desires for absolute truth, for a transcendent romantic or erotic climax, for purity and coherence of being—whether personal, racial, or national—and for a perfectly rounded narrative that makes human life seem transparent and utterly reasonable are all interrelated, and they all depend upon a repression that shades into potentially violent oppression.[1] This book traces an experimental movement in twentieth-century literature to puncture such images and reroute desire at the most private level, in the mind of the reader. This movement was especially strong in Ireland.

Ireland endured seven hundred years of English rule, a lengthy domination punctuated by highly emotional, often brutal episodes such as Cromwell's massacres, the abortive revolutions of 1798 and 1848, the Penal Laws, the act of union with Britain and the dissolution of the Irish Parliament, the potato famine, and the ill-fated Easter Rising of 1916. In the first half of the twentieth century, Ireland produced a profusion of politically aware, subversive writers (including Oscar Wilde, George Bernard Shaw, William Butler Yeats, John Millington Synge, James Joyce, Sean O'Casey, Flann O'Brien, and later Samuel Beckett) who had learned from Ireland's history that political opposition is often inadequate when the difference in power is great and long-standing. Moreover, in Ireland, the painful contrast between a mythic legacy of imaginative richness and a more recent history of domination was concentrated in the dominant language: English, the language of the oppressor. The writings of Wilde, Yeats, and Joyce are politically subversive in the most local and dangerous sense of the term, since they aim to take apart the assumptions and verbal practices that make dominance possible. They take categories such as manhood and nationhood and shatter them into their component parts, revealing the interplay of forces that produce such categories. Since any coherent category is produced by a suppression (and if necessary an oppression) of divergent elements, the unmaking of such categories also involves a tapping of submerged energy.

The book illustrates how, in a highly verbal set of responses to a long history of political and economic oppression, Irish writers such as Wilde, Yeats, and Joyce developed an experimental, politically devious model of desire. The kind of desire—or motivation—that propels their writings is local rather than global, concrete rather than abstract; instead of accelerating toward a climactic self-annihilation, the desire that animates their language works to keep itself alive through rhythmic metamorphoses and fortuitous interconnections with alien images and ideas. The experimental writing shaped by playful desire is an ingenious and constructive individual response to the experience of national oppression; it is more associative than teleological, and it relies on a view of language as a means of periodically achieving an energizing contact with the unknown. The book details how these three writers use language to riddle or puncture the everyday idols that dominate public and private life. Their demanding practice of writing trains receptive readers to develop a more flexible politics and a more complex and vibrant mode of perception and interaction.

In the chapters that follow, wordplay emerges as a local, germicidal version of a larger, more overtly political iconoclasm. Because wordplay (like dreams) both reveals and conceals meaning, it acts as a code that clothes the joy of alterity in a protective disguise. Riddling conventionally formulated truths that are billed as impervious to change is both a playful and resistant way of restoring flexibility to petrified systems of thought. Because it works through inclusion rather than opposition, because it offers readers (or audiences) choices among possible meanings, play is both radically democratic and potentially threatening to the established order. A riddling method of writing discourages a channeling of desire toward a single end; instead, it promotes a profusion of desires, an open network of potential connections. To riddle is not only to puzzle, it is also to explain (akin to the Old English *raedan,* to interpret; Webster's New Collegiate Dictionary, 1974 ed.). Moreover, to riddle is to fill with holes, to puncture often and thoroughly, to corrupt: this meaning of riddling illustrates how hierarchies of gender, sexual orientation, and imperial power may be corrupted through an infiltration of intentional meanings with incongruous associations that become meaningful in unexpected and unauthorized ways. If we riddle a container, it will spring leaks, and imperialism, patriarchy, and highly conventional art forms all represent attempts at containment.

The central argument of the book is that the most productive and far-reaching dislocations are paradoxically produced by an intense and precise concentration on the local. I offer a theory of micronationalism that bypasses the predictable opposition of nationalism and internationalism. Micronationalism is a concentration on highly local and sometimes submerged features of a country, a person, or a text that are never taken as "representative," but which instead initiate an expansive and energizing process of connection (as opposed to a movement of consolidation).

This introductory chapter outlines a subversive way of reading that is also a mode of desiring, arguing that such reading/desiring was promoted by historically specific conditions that were present in a highly concentrated form in Ireland. The mode of thought characteristic of Irish experimental writers is driven not by imitation and the desire for mastery but by the desire for fortuitous and transitory connections, by play against a stable object or attitude that resists play. Gilles Deleuze and Félix Guattari offer a range of models for how such experimental thinking operates: their theories of micropolitics, schizoanalysis, and rhizomatic thought provide a pragmatic way of mapping "alternative" flows of desire. The three chapters following the introduction turn from theory to a practical demonstration of how Irish literature in particular constitutes an intervention in the larger politics of domination. Wilde, Yeats, and Joyce provide three very different models of how language may be used to riddle dominant assumptions by destabilizing and metamorphosing conventional sequences of ideas, images, and letters.

Oscar Wilde, for example, challenged proprieties of thought by expressing a proliferation of ideas that were often in conflict with one another. His playful virtuosity was most apparent in the whiplashes of wit that score his writings, although he was increasingly unable to sustain a comparable openness in his life: in his later years, Wilde found himself caught in the cross fire between two different models of desire. I read the history of his trials and his disastrous fall from eminence against the richly varied evidence of his writings—his plays, fairy tales, stories, novel, and criticism—to highlight the tragic discontinuity between his intellectual stance and his emotional commitments. Emotionally, Wilde lives out the contradiction epitomized by his love of green, which signifies both the principle of growth and its opposite, a state of arrested unripeness. Wilde's fall was precipitated not by his ability to entertain and set into motion a rich panoply of ideas, but by his "purity," by his denial of any realities that would sully his ideal of youthful beauty. Wilde shattered ideals in his writings, but worshiped them in his life; this inversion of the typical relation between art and life transformed Wilde from an irreverent aesthete into a corrupt image that society felt obliged to obliterate.

For much of his poetic career, Yeats was hampered by a less tragic version of the contradiction that ruined Wilde. Instead of destroying Yeats, however, his inconsistency prevented him from being taken entirely seriously by his contemporaries. Like Wilde, Yeats remained emotionally tied to a nineteenth-century model of desire, and, like Wilde, the way he wrote was very different from the way he lived and loved. Instead of idealizing youth and beauty, Yeats was entranced by passion, which he initially defined as an escape from the world into a vortex of private love and suffering. The unusual fixity of Yeats's feelings is apparent in his famous, persistent obsession with Maud Gonne. In contrast, his literary technique is not marked by the imperative to possess and destroy but works instead through a constant transformation of images (as opposed to ideas). Even when the mood of his poems is stormy and apocalyptic, his technique is playful, reveling in the dynamic power of language and imagination. He repeatedly explores multifaceted images such as a rose or tower from a range of perspectives, only to expose their incompleteness and to translate them into related images, beginning the process again. Yeats eventually brings his idea of love into startling and powerful alignment with the subversiveness of his poetic technique. That alignment is most vividly illustrated when he speaks in the voice of a poor old woman, Crazy Jane, who famously affirms a love that has pitched its mansion in the place of excrement. Yeats's passion for the purity of possession and destruction has given way to a vision of desire as powerfully inconsistent, magnificently adulterated, built upon refuse and waste, and stronger than death.

James Joyce's desire is only briefly at odds with the dynamic inclusiveness of his technique as a writer. In the years when he was finishing *A Portrait of the Artist as a Young Man,* he privately recorded his passion for a young Jewish student of his in a notebook he never published during his lifetime, *Giacomo Joyce.* It shows how Joyce learned to identify the conflict between a possessive, destructive passion and the comic, inclusive, and exhilarating operations of desire that shape *Ulysses* and *Finnegans Wake.* Perhaps because he diagnosed his tendency toward emotional hypocrisy so early, understanding its complicity with racism and oppression in very specific terms, Joyce was never shattered, like Wilde, or scattered, like Yeats; the outrage of his readers was directed primarily at his books. Joyce enacted a dynamic model of desire less through a transformation of ideas (like Wilde) or images (like Yeats) than by rhetorically transforming the relation between his texts and the reader's expectations. *Finnegans Wake,* in the extremity of its challenge and its resistance to readers' appropriations of it, provides the fullest practical demonstration of what is at stake in the conflicting impulses to subsume or to engage difference. The contradiction of *Finnegans Wake* is that it offers an unexpected access to the unknown that is thoroughly wrapped up in inaccessibility, incomprehensibility. Because *Finnegans Wake* is made of up entirely of puns, many of which are in different languages, and because it attempts to model the movements of the subconscious mind in sleep, it stages an encounter between the reader and a verbal and psychological universe that is mostly buried; it brings the reader into alienated proximity with traces of the unknown and the submerged. *Finnegans Wake* is only accessible (and accessible only in part) through its puns; it shows how very local recombinations of units as small as individual letters and words both exhume and reinter the buried vitality of mythic, social, and political history.

Reading as "Habit"

The writings of Wilde, Yeats, and Joyce are products of a way of reading that I will later associate more concretely with micropolitics and subversive desire. These associations serve to underscore the view that a politics and a climate of feeling are importantly implied in the way we read; despite popular assumptions to the contrary, reading is not the politically neutral, "private" activity that it is often taken to be.[2] Techniques of reading are carefully if invisibly regulated by rules of interpretation that have come to seem natural: readers are taught to concentrate attention on the plot; to read for general meaning or the overall "message"; to align signs with the denotations allocated to them by convention. As we learn it, reading is the most conventional of activities—both figuratively and literally, since we define the meaning of a sign as that which has been agreed upon by convention. We have struggled to make language *representational,* to make it typify the world as we know it and as we would like it to be. Words have become icons that, in their conventional usages, are sacrosanct, and language as it is socially regulated serves subtly to enforce the purity of other socially regulated categories, ranging all the way from the State to differences of gender.[3]

The practice of reading as an automatic or habitual activity is a highly artificial enterprise, one that has to be carefully taught. This mode of reading corresponds to a way of desiring, one that is possessive in nature and tilted toward the past rather than the present or future. When we reify words by turning them into counters for exchange, ignoring their suggestiveness and concentrating instead on the meanings assigned them by convention, we create a linguistic economy driven by the desirability of possessing and accumulating knowledge, not one that prizes the plasticity, the virtually infinite retranslatability, of meaning. And as Wilde emphasized in his last work, *The Ballad of Reading Gaol,* the desire to possess something contains a desire to kill it, an insight underscored by the poem's repeated insistence that "each man kills the thing he loves."

In addition to expressing and reinforcing a desire for possession, which is comparable in political terms to microimperialism, the practice of reading habitual to most of us also plays out an ambivalence toward the past which reflects and reproduces a corresponding ambivalence toward the self. Later in this chapter, I use the theories of Gilles Deleuze and Félix Guattari to argue that what they call "oedipalization" is actually a habit of reading the self through a past that is split—like Oedipus's two parents—into incompatible components unconsciously charged with love and hate, desire and repulsion. It is essential to emphasize that Deleuze and Guattari use the figure of Oedipus differently than Freud: Freud used the story of *Oedipus Rex* to illustrate the unconscious conflicts in a child at a particular developmental stage that is usually completed by the age of five and undergoes a resurgence in adolescence,[4] whereas Deleuze and Guattari suggest that the Oedipus story serves as a blueprint for habits of mind that are endemic to society as a whole, especially in adulthood. As they see it, the Oedipus story is a narrative of social programming; it illustrates a deeply rooted prescription about how the self should be constructed. The myth of Oedipus suggests that the self is a mirror of the unknown past, personified as both parents, which must suffer radical division. The drama implies that we repress, deny, or symbolically expel that half of the self that is superficially most similar (the father, if we are male), and that we fetishize and eroticize that part of the self that seems most different (for a son, the mother). What the Oedipal drama produces is not only a hopelessly divided and alienated self, but also a mode of desiring that precludes a love of *wholeness,* of diversity, of change as a process of continuing adulteration and transformation. Moreover, such a construction of desire relies upon a view of sexuality as the *principle of division* itself; sexual difference is the clear, biological marker that allows the subject to distinguish desirability from undesirability. Because sexual difference is the foundation upon which the subject's self-division depends, the subject cannot ever "know" or enter into meaningful relation with either men or women: if the subject is male, men will represent the half of the self that must be discarded as "waste," and women will be impossibly romanticized, forced to embody a promise that they cannot possibly fulfill, since the individual's buried desire is really for a more heterogenous self that is not predicated on a halving of the past.

Starting Again: Experimental Reading and Desiring

In the pages that follow, I attempt to outline a way of reading that is neither automatic nor habitual, which once again corresponds to a mode of desiring. As I suggested in the preface, the value of this alternative mode of reading is measured not by the accumulation of knowledge based on experience, but by its suggestiveness as *experiment,*[5] its freedom to "try" the meaningfulness of unexpected connections. Experimental reading is also, as I indicated earlier, more intensive or microscopic in its focus than the dominant reading practices. An experimental approach to reading refuses to regard words and images primarily as "icons" whose main function is to represent an object or concept assigned to it by convention. Instead, the experimental reader sees words as temporary "assemblages"[6] capable of being taken apart and assembled differently, plugged in elsewhere, recontextualized; such assemblages are sites of multiple interconnections and potential recombinations. To use yet another of Deleuze and Guattari's analogies, one might say that experimental thinkers see words not as having deep roots—like trees—but shallow roots that can send out offshoots in many different directions. Changing the metaphor again, one might say that meaning is no longer regarded primarily as the cumulative product of a linear

process—grammar—but as selectively omnidirectional. Not *all* words are omnidirectional, nor do they go in *every* possible direction at any one time, but certain "key words" have the capacity to extend themselves in dynamic and unpredictable ways that produce fresh *and demonstrable* patterns of meaning. As
Deleuze and Parnet point out in *Dialogues*, experimental thought is akin to
humor, in which "principles count for little, everything is taken literally" (68).
Experimentation facilitates not a representation or confirmation of being, but
an ongoing process of becoming, of growth and change. Language most effectively promotes such becoming through "'indefinite' plays on words" (69).

Since the motive behind experimental reading and writing is to promote
growth through encounters with a language rich in metonymic connections
and constantly undergoing transformation, some readings and writings will inevitably be more suggestive than others. Experimentation does not result in an
interpretive or literary relativism in which all attempts are equal, even if it does
challenge the authority of stable and absolute distinctions. The quality of a
reading is determined not by its adherence to a tradition or to a set of established values, but by the intensity of its focus (its command of local detail and
its ability to use detail in exponentially enlightening ways), and also by its capacity to inspire connections with other sets of ideas. A "good" reading is one
that is unexpected, rich in local insights, and capable of being translated into
new contexts in ways that produce fresh understanding; it is not so much inde-
terminate as multideterminate.

The political implications of experimental reading have been loosely characterized as antifascistic—by Michel Foucault, Fredric Jameson, and Guattari.[7] Especially in the United States, however, the writing of Deleuze and Guattari has
been impressionistically misread as a kind of intellectual terrorism that would
ultimately abolish all distinctions whatsoever and usher in a conceptual free-for-
all. As Alice Jardine points out, "Their books are often categorized and then dismissed as but frivolous by-products of 1968."[8] Such misconceptions arise from
the assumption that Deleuze and Guattari's work is primarily iconoclastic, when
in fact, after *Anti-Oedipus*, their stance is actually icon-*elastic*. Although their
philosophy is clearly antirepresentational, when they begin elaborating alternative flows of thought their aim is not so much to attack the status quo as to evade
its power to colonize and predetermine thinking. They concentrate instead on
the *elasticity* of thought and language, the reach and capacity for metamorphosis inherent in constructs that have been unnaturally stabilized by the rules governing interpretation. Like the work of Irish experimental writers, their thought
is not merely a reaction against domination; it evolves into a clearly articulated
system that encompasses the desire that they began by criticizing: the power to
dominate and possess—and ultimately to define—the other.

Verbal Experimentation in Ireland

The new ways of reading and desiring that I am calling experimental were fostered more successfully by some historical conditions than others; unexpect-

edly, the colonial situation in Ireland stimulated not only a powerful tradition of physical resistance, but also a richly complex artistic response. What factors turned Ireland into a fertile ground for conceptual icon-elasticity? Of course, not all Irish writers are experimental, nor is all experimentation Irish. What made Ireland particularly hospitable to experimentation was a long history of political resistance curiously reinforced by an equally strong adherence to Christianity, and a linguistically oriented, six-thousand-year-old culture that was never really unified; for reasons that were partly geographical and partly historical, Ireland was always a country with many "centers."

As I argue earlier in this chapter, experimental thought is not the same as political resistance, but is instead a reaction to the futility of such resistance, combined with a recognition that protest is simply the inverted image of obedience; rebellion does not constitute a structural alternative to the power structure it challenges. In Ireland, the legacy of failed uprisings is daunting, as the revolution of 1798, to take just one memorable example, illustrates. When the American colony successfully threw off the yoke of British control to proclaim itself the United States, and when France overthrew its rulers in a bloody rage, Ireland, suffering under the Penal Laws that prevented Catholics from owning land, holding office, or voting, prepared to follow suit with promised aid from the French.[9] Through a combination of bad weather, unfortunate timing, and intelligence leaks, the Irish effort ended in disaster. After the rising in Wicklow, in particular, the yeomanry and the militia, "without any attempt being made to stop them by their leaders, perpetrated dreadful atrocities on the peasantry. They made hardly any distinction, killing every one they met: guilty and innocent, rebel and loyalist, men and women" (P. W. Joyce, 469). Giovanni Costigan recounts that "[i]n the opinion of Lord Morley, the excesses committed by the British authorities in Ireland in 1798 exceeded in horror the September massacres in Paris in 1792, which had so revolted and alarmed the people of England."[10] Protestants were spitted upon spikes, Catholic peasants were hung on their own market crosses in the center of town, scalding pitch was poured on peasants' heads (Costigan, 127). While the French and the Americans were celebrating democracy and independence, Ireland was undergoing its own private reign of terror in a revolution that was not only futile but which triggered exceptionally violent reprisals.

The rebellion of 1798 is just one example of Ireland's repeated attempts to free itself from British rule through resistance to its authority; the Irish have ample instances of revolt, all of which can be read as testifying either to the glory of resistance (through heroic martyrdom) or to its futility (because the effort repeatedly failed). Catholicism, too, has served to support the ethos of protest. Since Christ was a Jew who campaigned on behalf of the downtrodden and poor in a society ruled by the Romans, his example served to legitimate martyrdom as a protest against oppression. The Irish often associated the English with the pragmatic, materialistic Romans, as well as with the Egyptians who kept Moses's people in bondage, as Joyce shows in the "Cyclops" episode of *Ulysses*.[11] In fact, the identification of the English with the Romans is the most important basis of the parallel between the Hebrew and the Irish races that underlies *Ulysses.* Padraic Pearse's dedication to blood sacrifice, which climaxed in the Easter Rising of 1916, is yet another famous example of how Christian precedents seemed to sanction Ireland's resistance to British rule, even at the cost of the rebels' lives. Like Christ on Easter, Ireland would rise again out of the blood of its martyrs, and its spiritual kingdom would have no end.

It is the sheer excess of martyrdoms that prompts Irish thinkers to interrogate the political effect of heroism. Could heroic resistance be a response that empires have anticipated, a response that doesn't effectively challenge imperial control? Additional questions about the legitimacy of colonial control and its capacity to absorb resistance were sparked by the similarity of Ireland to England. Ireland was not just a colony of England, it was a "twin colony," a mirror island whose inhabitants were Celtic, like the inhabitants of western England and Scotland. The Irish were not dramatically different in appearance from Anglo-Saxons, which made it more difficult to justify the severe measures that the British sometimes used to control them. As L. P. Curtis points out, the British went to some lengths to represent the Irish as simians, or more generally as primitive, wild, and animalistic. Even the difference of religion that divides Ireland from England was initially slight, resulting as it did from an English king's lascivious whim. Because Ireland so closely resembled England, it was difficult for either country to account for the dramatic differences in privilege and economic prosperity that divided the two nations, differences that were particularly marked in the nineteenth century. Furthermore, the lower class in Ireland was not an industrial proletariat but a peasant class with a long history of poetic and heroic accomplishment, and the upper class—or Ascendancy— was primarily composed of former settlers and conquerors, both English and Norman, who had been assimilated. With a native population whose mythic traditions rival Arthurian legend and with an immigrant ruling class that was partly British, the Irish could see no reason for Britain's characterization of them as socially and even racially inferior.

The readiness of the Irish to question the structure and legitimacy of established authority also stems from a history in which power was exercised regionally, by several different kings. Some historians have attributed the high degree of autonomy enjoyed by these kings to the geographical features of the island. As Karl Bottigheimer argues, "The political particularism so notable a part of the history of Ireland is related to its topographical variety and the absence of a single large and easily inhabited area that could have served as the cradle of a dominant civilization."[12] Oliver MacDonagh also relates Ireland's resistant stance to its geography, but instead of focusing on topographical variety as something that discouraged a unified civilization, he attributes Ireland's characteristic intransigence to the autonomy it enjoys as a sea-ringed island.[13]

Even if it can be proven that Ireland was uniquely situated as a site of futile resistance to colonial domination by Britain, how did it happen that a less active resistance came to be expressed in language? The answer to this question is rooted in the highly literate culture of Ireland, a tradition that values language as a repository of local customs and traditions. The writings of Irish literary revivalists such as Douglas Hyde and W. B. Yeats promoted a popular image of

Ireland as an island of saints and scholars. Furthermore, because Ireland is a small country that has been inhabited for over six thousand years, because it contains large bogs with extraordinary preservative properties at its center, because different periods have left highly visible marks on the landscape (from cromlechs and passage graves to market crosses, burned churches and sites of British reprisal), the land itself serves as a powerful reminder of the coexistence of living and dead, past and present. And as the Irish look back over the history etched on their landscape, they can see the "written" marks not only of different times but also of different nations—of the waves of invasions that brought Partholonians, Firbolgs, Milesians, Vikings, Normans, and of course the English to Irish shores. Not only the landscape, but also the languages spoken in Ireland bear traces of her various invaders.

One of the languages to have left visible traces throughout Ireland is Ogham, the language of the Druids. Even before the advent of Christianity, when Ireland became famous as a center of monastic learning, the Irish had a native system of letters that they conceived as an extension of the landscape. As John Toland wrote in the early eighteenth century,

> The use of letters has been very ancient in Ireland, which at first were cut on the bark of trees, prepared for that purpose; or on smooth tables of birch wood, which were called *Taibhe Fileadh,* poets' tables; as their characters were in general named *Feadha,* twigs and branch letters, from this shape.[14]

Alphabetical letters, which were themselves shaped like twigs, were named after trees ("b" or *"Beth"* was a birch, etc.) and were often written on trees, although they were sometimes etched on stone.[15] Ogham writing was apparently closely connected to the Druid religion, since the Druid sun god was annually reborn from the offshoot of a tree (Bonwick, 311). As Nigel Pennick claims, Ogham was

> far more than merely a system of writing. Each ogham character was assigned correspondences within the animal and plant kingdoms, with colours, and even with tones in harp tablature. Certain famous Irish fortresses were known by its letters, and ogham still has a place today as a divination technique.[16]

Long before the advent of Christianity, language in Ireland had been regarded as a natural, artistic, and spiritual system that facilitated a "magical" resolution of personal and political dilemmas.

The important relation of language and land is also vividly dramatized in Brian Friel's *Translations* (1981), in which the progressive British military control of Ireland is enacted through the process of renaming Irish places, a literal imposition of English upon the Irish language and landscape. The play celebrates the exuberant vitality of the Gaelic tradition while also endorsing a practice of constant retranslation, negotiation, exogamy, multinationalism—to help us "interpret between privacies." When the English lieutenant falls in love with Ireland's landscape, language, and an Irish woman, the hedge schoolmaster extols the indigenous beauty of the Irish language while warning the lieutenant

of the inevitability of adulteration and change: "Yes, it is a rich language, Lieutenant, full of the mythologies of fantasy and hope and self-deception—a syn-
tax opulent with tomorrows. It is our response to mud cabins and a diet of pota-
toes; our only method of replying to . . . inevitabilities.[17]

It is hardly surprising, in view of the fine linguistic traditions from Ogham
and Irish Gaelic, enriched by an influx of Latin, Danish, French, and English,
that language and literature should be seen as appropriate venues for innovative variation. Moreover, Ireland's linguistic traditions feature the letter as wor-
thy of being celebrated in its own right, whether that letter is conceived as part
of a sacred tree, or whether it is an initial letter, elaborately illuminated by the
monks at Kells. Even in Irish Gaelic, letters are more nomadic than they are in
most languages; because of lenition and eclipsis, sounds and letters frequently
change depending upon their position in the sentence.[18] The decomposition or
rearrangement of words is a logical experiment for writers to try in a highly
verbal, antiauthoritarian culture that has long featured the letter, not the word,
as the primary unit of composition.

Iconoclasm as De-siring

Subversive reading (such as that practiced and encouraged by Wilde, Yeats, and
Joyce) proceeds by successive trials, attempts to recontextualize familiar semantic units, or to rearrange the sequence of words, letters, and syllables. Both
writers and readers learn to approach the building blocks of language almost
as if they were numbers, producing a complex mathematics of richly interconnected signs that is further enriched by changing combinations of images and
sounds. Yet another metaphor for how readers and writers treat language is
provided by musical performance: they *play* language as if it were a finely tuned
instrument, and in so doing, they "finish making [it]; complete its construction" (*Oxford English Dictionary;* one of the meanings of "perform").

As an example of how subversive reading works, consider the word "desire,"
which most often denotes a longing or craving. Read literally, "desire" reveals
the word "sire" lodged within it (a connection unsupported by etymology). If
we see this connection between desire and sires as an example of the illegitimate bonds that language is continually forging between very different concepts, it becomes possible to explore the buried relation between the two words.
For example, if we read "desire" as de-sire, so that the prefix "de-" means "to de-
prive, divest, free from" (*OED,* "de-" 2.), desire emerges as the process that frees
an individual from sires, or fathers, as well as from the responsibility of "siring,"
or reproducing the self upon the body of another. The word "sire," more familiar in the abbreviated form of "sir," comes from the Latin for "senior," so that to
de-sire can also mean to divest oneself of seniority, or authority, as well as to
free oneself from external authorities. Sires are accorded the respect of their ju-
niors (hence the use of the term "Sir" in polite address); de-siring, in sharp contrast, stresses not the privilege of age but its helpless isolation. Etymologically,
"desire" comes from the Latin *desiderare,* to miss or long for, which *Webster's*

New Collegiate Dictionary (1974 ed.) derives in turn from *de* + *sider-, sidus* (from a star). Such a meaning emphasizes the distance between the desirer and the object of desire, a distance that in youth is erotic and idealized, but with age shades into alienation and despair. If a sire *is* an idealized image, de-siring *requires* an idealized image, and at a certain point the two fictions of potency (which locate privilege in the self and in the other, respectively) collapse into each other as complementary deceptions, which may be comic or poignant.

Alternatively, we could divide "desire" differently, reading it as "des-ire." As a prefix, "des-" is a form of "dis-," which has as its primary meaning "two ways, in twain" (*OED*, "dis-"), but which can also reverse or negate the action of the verb. As a result, desire can designate two forms of ire, or wrath, or—more literally and punningly—"Dublin (doubling), Eire," and finally it can designate the power that destroys wrath (*OED*, "dis-" 6.), or frees one from Ireland ("dis-" 7.a).

Many readers would see my reading of the narratives suggested by the word "desire" as counterfeit—the misleading waste products of our reliance upon a limited alphabet to produce meaning. Wilde, Yeats, and Joyce, however, along with many other Irish writers over the last hundred years, entertained the possibility that to insist upon a separation between two words that sound similar, to define a word without hearing its alienated echo in similar words, is a form of cognitive narcissism. Divorced from its Echo, each word—like Narcissus—becomes an unnaturally reified image, still, silent, and destructive of both self and other (as Narcissus destroyed himself and Echo). Images do not age, as the word itself suggests if we disregard its etymology in order to hear the "age" in it (the prefix "im-" means "not"). The image, in its imperviousness to time, differs markedly from both siring and de-siring, which both grow and decline in the medium of time. To de-sire, in fact, is to declare war on the tyranny of images, to practice iconoclasm.

In *The Importance of Being Earnest,* Oscar Wilde implicitly contrasts siring and de-siring in order to dramatize how each produces the other in a set of reciprocal reactions that does not end. Both Jack and Algernon are pulled between the responsibility of fatherhood (associated with earnestness) and the fecklessness of pleasure (that which is in-valid, like the imaginary invalid, Bunbury). For Jack, the site for de-siring is the city, whereas the urge to sire is born in the country (where both Jack and Algernon are seized with the sudden desire to be Ernest). The play presents earnestness as a somewhat provincial quality that women idealize, an attitude that goes hand-in-hand with responsibility and "a very high moral tone on all subjects."[19] As Gwendolen informs Cecily, "Ernest has a strong upright nature. He is the very soul of truth and honour. Disloyalty would be as impossible to him as deception" (*CW,* 362).

In the country, both Gwendolen and Cecily conceive an irrational passion to marry men they believe to be Ernest, whereupon Algernon and Jack hasten to rechristen themselves. In so doing, Jack inadvertently adopts the name of his father, who was also (as he discovers) named Ernest. Earnestness emerges as the mark of what society associates with fatherhood and the moral authority that accompanies it, despite Jack's earlier attempts to dramatize a countertruth, that Ernest is really the name of a profligate.[20]

De-siring, in sharp contrast to earnestness, is a denial of the father-function; as Algernon comments, "Fathers are certainly not popular just at present" (*CW,* 335). To deny one's sire is to pursue pleasure, which is why Jack bets that "there is not a single chap . . . who would be seen walking down St. James' Street with his own father" (*CW,* 335). Jack is forced into the siring role when he is in Woolton, since there he acts as Cecily's guardian or father-substitute, but he is able to de-sire when he goes to town, where he adopts the identity of his invented brother, a hopeless rake named Ernest. What Jack does in town is what Algernon does in the country: "Bunburying." To Bunbury is to revel in the pleasures of unpredictability and uncertainty, which the play associates both with heterosexual flirtation and with same-sex companionship (instead of earning, they are engaged in the activity of "urning"). When Jack tells Algernon that he has come to town to propose to Gwendolen, Algernon reproves him:

> I thought you had come up for pleasure? . . . I call that business. . . . I really don't see anything romantic in proposing. It is very romantic to be in love. But there is nothing romantic about a definite proposal. Why, one may be accepted. One usually is, I believe. Then the excitement is all over. The very essence of romance is uncertainty. (*CW,* 323)

As Algernon defines it, romance, like desire, depends on an awareness that "[t]he truth is rarely pure and never simple" (*CW,* 326); romance is predicated on a concern for what is in-valid.

Another way of articulating the relation between siring and earnestness is to define its relation to labor. The position Wilde associates with siring sees labor as profitable, whereas from the perspective of the de-sirer, it is idleness that is enriching. In terms of political economy (as Cecily understands it), we could say that siring stresses the dependence of capital on labor (specifically labor for others), whereas desiring illustrates "the relations between Capital and Idleness." When Cecily claims to know all about the relations between Capital and Idleness, or the moneyed privilege of amusing oneself, she shocks Miss Prism (*CW,* 342), who warns her that such thinking leads to Socialism. Cecily replies that Socialism leads in turn to Rational Dress (such as Miss Prism now wears), concluding that if a woman dresses rationally, she will be punished by being treated rationally. What Cecily implies is that her own whimsicality is a prelude to rational primness, that if she continues on her present path she will eventually resemble Miss Prism, exiled from the wayward pleasures of desire. Cecily has deconstructed the oppositions between idleness and labor, decorative whimsy and rationality, herself and her governess, comically revealing that, contrary to popular belief, each extreme *produces* its apparent opposite: pleasure and earnestness are implicated in one another.

Although it is possible to see Prism as merely prim, a more precise account of her relation to desire would accent her function as prism: her rationality and restraint serve to refract and thereby multiply desire. From such a perspective, men become earnest and women turn prim *in order* to intensify the need for desiring, since, as Algernon remarks, "one must be serious about something, if one wants to have any amusement in life" (*CW*, 367); what makes people "trivial" is an insistence on being serious about *everything*. In other words, the social origin of *all* families and persons is—like Jack's—a Terminus. Desire plays against the resistance, earnestness, or primness that fosters it.

The Importance of Being Earnest ends as the world of the country and the world of the city comically collide. By the end of the play, the audience has been prompted to see that responsibility and play are not mutually exclusive. "Earnest" means "serious" as well as what we would now call "gay," but such meanings only become accessible through play—the puns on the name "Ernest" (an earnest is a pledge, which is what the women want Algernon and Jack to offer, and urning is engaging in less binding homosexual activities). Wilde's play is designed to produce and celebrate the agile operations of laborious play. Labor-intensive—or highly skilled—play can best be understood in contrast to what it is *not:* humorous labor. The play of the rude mechanicals in *A Midsummer Night's Dream* exemplifies play so belabored and serious that it becomes ludicrous, "very tragical mirth" (*MND*, V.i.57). Wilde's play, in contrast, is "A Trivial Comedy for Serious People"; if people take its apparent triviality seriously, they will come to appreciate the hidden value, not of virtue, but of virtuosity. In Wilde's play, not only is Jack's origin a Terminus, but every Terminus is also an origin: the play demonstrates the paradoxical coincidence of extremes—and the importance of recognizing that convergence. Every Ernest is also not Ernest; to put it another way, every young man is both more and less than earnest, and every sire is also, inevitably, a de-sirer.

While Wilde presents marriage as a narrative crux where desire humorously intersects with its opposite, the urge to sire, Yeats spotlights a different meaning of desire. Instead of focusing on the interdependence of siring and de-siring as different attitudes toward fatherhood, Yeats concentrates on desire's capacity to express the idealism of youth, and also the disillusionment of age. Yeats concentrates on the etymological meaning of desire as "from the stars," showing how the considerable distance between the desirer and the stars highlights the hopelessness of desire. In "When You Are Old," Yeats dramatizes his reading of desire as "star struck" when he relates that Love, disregarded and spurned by his beloved, "hid his face amid a crowd of stars." As this conceit intimates, idealism is a refuge from disappointment, but it is one that Yeats eventually disavows. In "Among School Children," Yeats presents himself simultaneously as public sire and secret desirer; he feels keenly the discrepancy between how the children perceive him and how he sees them. To the children, he is "a sixty-year-old smiling public man," a comfortable scarecrow, whereas to him they are a startling reembodiment of the birdlike freedom and beauty of youth that drives his heart wild. The children bring the older man's losses back to life; they point the contrast between the "Ledaean body" of his beloved in childhood and her present image, "Hollow of cheek as though it drank the wind / And took a mess of shadows for its meat." And as the speaker realizes the vitality he has lost, the poem focuses on the way his desires de-sire (or de-authorize) him. He falls from his eminence as a famous public figure; he regresses sixty years to become a shape on his mother's lap, questioning whether his life's achievements justify even the pain of her labor; he attacks his own present status. The poem criticizes the impossible perfection of ideal images, stressing that they "break hearts"; they are "self-born mockers of man's enterprise." Ideals of perfection or success prompt us to disdain or abuse our changing and imperfect bodies; such perfectionism promotes what the poem describes as the bruising of the body "to pleasure soul." The nuns are teaching the children a masochistic or mechanical labor that trains them to "be neat in everything / In the best modern way," to approach an impossible perfection. In contrast, Yeats would show the children the joys of a labor that moves and changes, "blossoming or dancing." Yeats's alternative labor does not dissociate the worker from his or her work; the producer and the product are linked as part of a performance in time. As Yeats famously inquires at the end of the poem, "How can we know the dancer from the dance?"

In "Among School Children" Yeats endorses "de-siring" over the tyranny of tragic desire by refusing to idealize images—whether artistic or natural—over those who produce them, and by refusing to see art or nature as static instead of in motion—"blossoming or dancing." Read this way, desire is a return from the stars and not a longing for them. Instead of wishing for a telescope to see stars that they can never reach, those who appreciate worldly desire employ its opposite and counterpart, a microscope.

As Yeats suggests, images are most destructive when they are reified, offered as permanent representations of entities that in reality change, such as people or nations. In *Finnegans Wake,* Joyce extends this line of thought by insisting that the nation is not an abstract category. On the contrary, *imagination* is a "nation." When Anna Livia Plurabelle is awakened in the night by her son, who is having nightmares about his father, she reassures him that there are "No bad bold faathern" in the room, that it is "Sonly all in [his] imagination . . . Poor little brittle magic nation, dim of mind!" (*FW,* 565.19–20, 29–30). Like the threatening sire, the magic nation is a construct, a phantom that seems to exist only (or sonly) in the minds of the disenfranchised. A more realistic (if inaccessible) record of the past is not the father, the image, or the nation, but the sights and sounds of a constantly mutating, richly adulterated language, what *Finnegans Wake* punningly identifies as the "sound seemetery" of the past (sound and sight; sound sleep; sound cemetery, cemetery of seeming, *FW,* 17.36).

Wilde, Yeats, and Joyce all wrote in a way that challenges idealized norms. Their playful language, which re-members shards of broken ideals, constitutes both a critique of and an alternative to conformist imperatives. To rearrange available possibilities of meaning is a political act in the most basic sense. Instead of supporting violence, these writers worked to tease apart the idealized images they saw as limiting, whether those images were aesthetic, sexual, or national. The metaphor of teasing captures the complex political ramifications of using language to promote revisionary thinking. Teasing is not only a form of playfulness, simultaneously expressing affection for and resistance to the object being teased, but it also denotes diametrically opposed processes: to tease is both to tear apart and to coax into acquiescence. To tease can mean to disentangle fibers, thereby reducing their volume (wool, for example), or it can mean to increase fullness by tangling (as in teasing hair). When we "tease" an image, whether of a person or a nation, it produces a comparably contradictory effect. Teasing challenges the integrity of what is being teased, exposing its capacity to be both bigger and smaller than it currently is and underscoring its propensity to change. In contrast, idealized norms—whether of people, races, or nations—appear relatively stable and unconflicted.

A work of art can "tease" reality or seek to stabilize it through representation. The problem with representation, as we almost always recognize in theory and forget in practice, is that in spite of our deepest desires and fears, an image is not a replacement for the danger and rapture of the flux it temporarily masks. In the popular imagination, representations—of what is human, what sociocultural, what divine—harden and seem to take on the appearance of naturalness and permanence; over time, and until the return of the repressed, they become indistinguishable from reality. Even in representative government, representatives too often forget that they are not really substitutes for their constituency. A constituency is far more various than its representative can even know, much less represent; many of the constituents do not speak and perhaps cannot articulate their political desires. If they did, their voices would not, in all likelihood, be heard, because a representative represents not the whole of his or her constituency, but a crude caricature of its majority. The representative does not reflect the variety and lack of consensus within the constituency itself.

If mimetic representations serve to stabilize and unify a much more various and vital range of cognitive possibilities, then it is possible to gain greater access to such possibilities by changing the way we read—by reading less for a coherent meaning than for clues as to how to tease apart the sacrosanct verities and to forge fresher, more dynamic connections between the past and the future, between experience and experimentation. By attending more closely to *how* we read from moment to moment, and especially by defying social prescriptions against attending to the play of words and to the insights encoded within language itself, we become better able to interrogate the assumptions that shape intention, thereby sharpening and accelerating the play of difference among jostling possibilities.[21]

In theory, becoming more receptive to wordplay, to experimental possibilities of local (rather than universal) meaning, will change our understanding of discourse. Discourse will appear more polyphonic, humorous, and dynamic, *more* collaborative and *less* consensual. The barbarity in popular conceptions of authority—even democratic ones—lies in their subtle insistence on consensus, a consensus that short-circuits resistance and derails imaginative freedom: Gilbert in "The Critic as Artist" argues that "[a]nything approaching to the free play of the mind is practically unknown amongst us" (*CW*, 1057).

The overall project of experimental art is to disassemble images instead of reifying their wholeness as integral and definitive, to shatter them and then to map the interplay of the forces that animate and at the same time disintegrate the whole. Interestingly, it is this extreme particularity of nonrepresentational art that allows it to ramify in so many different directions. Words and ideas, instead of being commodified and hoarded, begin to work like a musical score: the author serves as composer, arranger, conductor, and even a performer of language, and the challenge to the reader is to play skillfully and imaginatively as many of the melodic and rhythmic patterns *and variations* as possible. As Wilde intimates, when we imaginatively engage with a novel or play we do not restrict our identification to the protagonist alone; at a deep psychic level, we are *all* the characters, Iago as well as Desdemona, and it is the interplay in art, and not any moral or narrative overcoding of that interplay, that offers rare if troubling insight (*A as C*, 209); (Stephen Dedalus makes a similar argument in the "Scylla and Charybdis" episode of *Ulysses*). Wilde, Yeats, and Joyce saw language as a dynamic, richly adulterated system that condensed multiple contradictions in a form that was at once definite, easily manipulable, and accessible through prismatic reading practices.

A Micropolitics of Experiment

The most common impediments to a freer circulation of language and desire are institutions, prescriptions, external directives of all kinds—what Gilles Deleuze and Félix Guattari refer to as "territorializations." Deleuze and Guattari have argued at length that territorialization (which is akin to what I referred to as representation above) has greatly dominated our cognitive and social processes. Their project was to demonstrate, to practice the antidote of deterritorialization, which can be accomplished through violence, but also through what I refer to as play. In *A Thousand Plateaus*, they aim to highlight possibilities of connection, unpredictable and transitory, and show how it is possible to make provisional "assemblages" out of these coincidental connections. Such encounters produce multidirectional energy, "lines of flight," that lead in turn to new encounters. Deleuze and Guattari argue that we produce desire through an intensive labor that is also play.

The writing of Deleuze and Guattari models not viscosity but velocity of thought; it shows how quickly words and metaphors may be translated into closely related variants, and how energizing and creative the process of continual retranslation and subtle modification can be. Their thought is not centripetal in its organization but centrifugal, and the thought processes they demonstrate are much more uncommon and less well understood than those needed to decode viscous language. What they display, especially in *A Thousand Plateaus*, is not the absorptive capacity of language, but its virtuosity, its plasticity and the speed with which its components can be put into dynamic and revealing play.

Subversive writing—especially when read in an experimental way—is intended to produce what Deleuze and Guattari call *mille plateaux*, a thousand intensities. The Lacanian idea of *jouissance*—of productive, terrifying, or pleasurable excess—is related; moreover, in French the double entendre of *jouissance* and *j'ouïe sens* ("I hear meaning") suggests that the specular emphasis of phallocentric logic is being supplemented by a gynocentric attention to the ear and to the multiple possibilities of sound and signification.[22] Again, the importance of training the *ear* as well as the eye to the process of reading was emphasized one hundred years ago by Wilde (in the wake of Walter Pater) in his role as Gilbert in "The Critic as Artist":

> Since the introduction of printing, and the fatal development of the habit of reading amongst the middle and lower classes of this country, there has been a tendency in literature to appeal more and more to the eye, and less and less to the ear which is really the sense which, from the standpoint of pure art, it should seek to please, and by whose canons of pleasure it should abide always. . . . I have sometimes thought that the story of Homer's blindness might be really an artistic myth, created in critical days, and serving to remind us, not merely that the great poet is always a seer, seeing less with the eyes of the body than he does with the eyes of the soul, but that he is a true singer also, building his song out of music, repeating each line over and over again to himself till he has caught the secret of its melody, chaunting in darkness the words that are winged with light. (*A as C,* 350–51)

Emphasizing the music of language naturally directs greater attention to more local effects and rhythms, drawing significance away from the more comprehensive design of plot. Both Yeats's reliance on accentual rhythms and verbal echoes to give a musically associative coherence to his poetry and Shem's defense of "earsightedness" in *Finnegans Wake* are part of a similar effort to counterpoint the visual with an equally strong measure of "sound sense."

Both the structure of a text and the expectations with which a reader approaches it are interwoven with different threads of desire. The conventionally plotted novel, which moves toward a climax and then resolves the different strands of plot, is an expression of fantasy and wish fulfillment; it satisfies the "rage for order," reassuring its readers of the ultimate coherence of what initially seem to be random events. As Hayden White argues in *The Content of the Form,* "narrative strains for the effect of having filled in all the gaps, of having put an image of continuity, coherency, and meaning in place of the fantasies of emptiness, need, and frustrated desire that inhabit our nightmares about the destructive power of time." A narrative that achieves closure gives "to reality the odor of the ideal."[23]

What is exciting about writing that is not oriented toward a single revelatory and unifying climax is that it is not invested in excluding meanings. This does not mean that all meanings are operative at all times; it simply means that writers and readers alike are engaged in constructing patterns of meaning that must be reshaped in response to changing circumstances. Transgression, since it is neither impeded nor celebrated, loses its erotic and violent charge, and the familiar polarizations of subject and object, male and female, are drained of meaning. Like narrative, subversive desire is dynamic rather than static, but unlike narrative it is omnidirectional rather than sequential. This centrifugal desire is produced by the cumulative interaction between reader and text as the reader confronts the slippage between her expectation and her actual experience of reading. The gap between expectation and experience leaves a space for the antic participation of the unconscious, and the prolongation of the reading

process, which is errant and often unpredictable,[24] allows some of that unconscious energy to be discovered or real-ized in ways that can produce vertigo and
exhilaration. The effervescence of unconscious desire in response to an errant
disregard for plot or to an exaggeratedly artificial plot is disruptive, but what it
stands to offer is not the consoling enervation of textual closure, but an accelerating vitality energized by the discovery of coincidental connections. Instead
of a single climax, the reader will unexpectedly encounter many apparently
gratuitous moments of intellectual and erotic intensity.[25] And instead of interpreting or representing a perspective that is in turn a representation of some
transcendent truth, the reader is asked only to participate—not passively, but
actively, with precision of thought, a ragbag of knowledge, and a receptivity to
others and to the unknown that is difficult to sustain. As readers, our challenge
is to establish conditions whereby we can have an unpredictable dialogue with
the text, a dialogue that we have not written a script for beforehand. Instead of
colonizing or using or subordinating the text, as experience teaches us to do, we
have to grant it a limited power to remake us to the extent that we remake it.

Fretting Nationalism and Masculinity

Wilde, Yeats, and Joyce are most productively understood as writers who neither discarded nor endorsed but rather *fretted* the proud ideals of nationhood
and manhood. Like many citizens of colonized countries, they took the full double imprint of colonizer and colonized. Instead of conceiving of themselves as
purely Irish, they saw themselves as hybridized, with allegiances both to Ireland
and to other nations. As Joyce suggests in *A Portrait of the Artist as a Young Man*,
the Irish individual's attitude toward English is symptomatic of his or her orientation toward all norms that have been culturally coded as superior. As Stephen
Dedalus suggests, one's very fluency in the language of an oppressor is rooted
in estrangement from it:

> The language in which we are speaking is his before it is mine. How different
> are the words *home, Christ, ale, master,* on his lips and on mine! I cannot speak
> or write these words without unrest of spirit. His language, so familiar and so
> foreign, will always be for me an acquired speech. I have not made or ac-
> cepted its words. My voice holds them at bay. My soul frets in the shadow of
> his language. (*Portrait*, 189)

When Stephen claims that his soul "frets" in the shadow of the Englishman's
language, he means that it restlessly chafes or worries, but "fret" also has an
opposite meaning that suggests how Stephen's soul is divided. To "fret" is also to
"adorn," especially with crisscrosses and jewels, and a fret in music is a piece of
wood that affects the vibration of the strings by crossing them; fretting is a kind
of beauty drawn from the intersection of opposed lines. The paradox of fretting
is like the paradox of articulation, which is both a breaking up of pure sound
and a way of rendering it meaningful. The situation of the Irish writer whose
native language is English illustrates how it is possible to be both inside and out-

side a defining boundary, to be stamped with an identity that is both familiar and foreign, to be fretted (both worried and made musical) by two incompatible states.

These three writers' double relation to language and to the Irish nation is replicated in their relation to gender. Just as they found themselves marbled with Irish and English influences, and unable to disentangle the two, they also saw their maleness as ineluctably bound up in femaleness,[26] a femaleness that both supplements their masculinity and exposes its categorical inadequacy. Wilde, editor of *The Woman's World*, sporting a flower and garbed in velvet, was the most flamboyant of the three in flaunting a stylishly hybrid gender, but Yeats and Joyce also—more subtly—signaled a strong and serious identification with women that rivaled their identification with men. Yeats in his love-stricken passivity and his poetic insistence on the centrality of the hearth, or home, plays a role closer to the one traditionally accorded to women, in sharp contrast to his counterpart, Maud Gonne, whose advocacy of violent revolutionary action placed her in a stereotypically male role. Of course, as a male writer Yeats also struggled, more conservatively, to limit Gonne to the role of inspirational Muse and national symbol. Moreover, Yeats and Gonne were apparently comfortable in reenacting the traditionally gendered opposition between "masculine" intellect and a "feminine" pragmatism made irresistible by courage and beauty; as Gonne insisted from the outset, "I was not intellectual."[27] What makes the relationship between Gonne and Yeats unusual, however, is the dramatic instability of their assumption of masks, as well as their willingness to assume in highly public ways attributes traditionally associated with the opposite sex. James Joyce's identification with women is apparent not only in his decision to end his last two books with powerful female monologues, but also in his insistence that "Joyce" was a woman's name. He projects his dual gender identification—as "James" and as "Joyce"—onto the protagonist of *Ulysses*, Leopold Bloom, describing him in "Circe" as "the New Womanly Man" and giving him a woman's middle name: Leopold Paula Bloom.[28]

The ability of male writers to shift into perspectives that they denominate "female" has often been read as a desire to appropriate or annex female experience. Although such a view might seem to uphold the very categories of gender difference that these writers would undo, the problem grows more complicated if we argue that such categories were fictional in the first place. If, as Jacques Lacan has suggested, in our system of signification everything tends toward oneness, a oneness that Lacan identifies with the phallic function, then his conclusion that the woman (as a separate category) does not exist makes sense, given that what we call womanhood is defined as whatever kindles man's desire. It follows that "the whole of [man's] realisation in the sexual relation comes down to fantasy."[29]

The argument that male writers such as Wilde, Joyce, and Yeats are not actually subverting the hierarchy of gender but only indulging in a fantasy of identity with the cause of their desire holds or breaks depending on how they construct their masculinity. Lacan argues that men only have a chance of experiencing *jouissance* of being by saying "no to the phallic function," by constructing themselves as "not all" (*Feminine Sexuality*, 143, 144). It is precisely by asserting themselves while stressing their own inadequacy that the male writers treated here fret masculinity, displaying in their works a mastery that importantly, often humorously, undermines its own potency. In the moments when male writers or characters confess their insufficiency or impotence, what makes their confessions either striking or pathetic depends not only upon who is revealing the inadequacy or exposing the *lapsus*, but also on their lack of defensiveness in doing so; Wilde remembers thinking during his trial, wouldn't this be grand if I were saying it all about myself? What would make such self-revelation grand is the act of publicly assuming responsibility for one's own behavior, misjudgments, and self-interest, and all the writers here discussed share a commitment to the importance of a disciplined awareness of what they do and do not know, which acts as a rudder for the giddier motions of the imagination.[30]

Whether we are talking of their approach toward gender or toward nationality, it should be stressed that the writings of Wilde, Yeats, and Joyce demand supplements that are not simply complements. As a category or "class" ("gender" means "class," according to the *OED*), gender is always either incomplete—in perpetual need of provisional, carnivalesque supplementation—or excessive, having been supplemented by an erotic energy that exceeds normative, reproduction-oriented heterosexuality. The problem with manhood as a category is that at any one moment men necessarily experience themselves as more or less than a man; the boundary separating the masculine from the nonmasculine is constantly under siege. A similar set of pressures—from within and without—serves to destabilize the idea of a nation (what Joyce calls the imagination). We tend to think of nations as stable entities clearly defined by geographical boundaries, when in fact nations are always becoming bigger (through imperialism, for example) or smaller (as through the partition of Ireland). A micronationalist approach recognizes this instability in the definition of a nation, seeing also that both imperialism and the vulnerability to colonization depend upon a view of the nation as locked in opposition to the foreign. If we abandon the antagonism to foreignness, and if we envision the nation as a dynamic entity that is both intensely local and yet oriented toward international contacts, this reorientation produces a new way of reading. Such revisionary reading involves combining attention to local detail with a flexible willingness to register shifts in context; a multinational—or telescopic—context is as vital as the local one, and integrally related to it. Whether the subject is reading, gender, or nationalism, the boundaries that define a text, an individual, or a country are simply less important than the energy of the diverse components to be found inside (and outside) those boundaries.

Micronationalism refers to more than just a concentration on the local, then. It also refers to an attitude toward internationalism that is not focused primarily on one country—a more powerful opponent, such as England—but which is multinational in scope. Just as the characteristics of a country appear more various when it is viewed not as a nation but as many specific locales, so it is necessary to admit a host of foreign cultures to answer to the richness of local diversity. Wilde, Yeats, and Joyce move beyond the opposition of Ireland

and England when constructing their national identity, extending offshoots into ancient Greece (Wilde, Yeats, and Joyce), Norway (Yeats and Joyce), Egypt (Wilde and Joyce), and Italy (Wilde and Joyce). This list could go on and on, especially if we tried to categorize the national influences on *Finnegans Wake*, but the general point may be best illustrated by focusing on a single country that all three embraced as an "alien" alternative to England and Ireland: France.

The writers in this book have particularly strong and significantly ambivalent relationships with England and France, in particular (although Greece often figures as another, more remote point of reference). England is typically cast in the role of the repressive, authoritarian father, in contrast to France, which seems to offer refuge and even comfort. When Oscar Wilde was celebrated by English society and then broken by English law, it was to France that he went in exile, under the alias of Sebastian Melmoth (an echo of *Melmoth the Wanderer*). Maud Gonne fought British law—particularly its evictions of Irish tenant-farmers—in England and Ireland, yet centered her private and erotic life in France. Joyce and later Beckett were both drawn to France as a place that allows freedom of expression: *Ulysses,* its serialization having been stopped and certain issues of the *Little Review* in which it was appearing confiscated in America, was finally published in book form in Paris. It would soon be banned in most English-speaking countries. Beckett, after having lived in London for several years, moved to France and began writing in French.

The Irish-French axis is more than a trajectory of desire, though; the Irish view of the French is also troubled by subtle distrust, even suspicion. The Irish word for a Frenchman, "francach," also means "rat," and in *Ulysses* Joyce plays on a confusion in French between *"irlandais"* and *"hollandais,"* or cheese (*"non fromage,"* U, 3.220). If the French are rats and the Irish cheese, the trajectory of desire is disturbingly reversible, and the French can represent the threat of domination as well as the promise of emancipation. The relation between Ireland and France, troubled by the historical relations of each with England, serves as a miniature model of multinational relations, in which each culture, language, and geography serves as a differently distorted reflection in a house of mirrors, where the only center is where one happens to be standing, and where the object reflected is the momentary product of time and circumstance.

Beyond Radicalism

I have been arguing that representation as a mode of substitution is a stabilizing, definitive process that is at odds with wordplay, which demands greater intellectual agility and attentiveness from its practitioners. Moreover, I have suggested that the pun is an economical linguistic operator of what is essentially a political enterprise: that the logic of representation works to contain or suppress difference, in sharp contrast to a micronational or experimental logic, which sharpens and animates an interplay of differences. Punning facilitates movement; it is the nomadic element of language, that which provides slippage, allows adaptation, fosters experimentation, and connects different elements without reconciling them. Puns and related forms of wordplay, including narrative synchronicity, serve not only as indices to the secret operations of desire but stimulate the reader's desire as well, a desire to explore the often untested limits of thought and language. The relation between representation, which tends to calcify into law (or at least authoritative prescription), and punning, which awakens the urge to stray, is economically captured in Jacques Lacan's pun on *"les noms du père"* (the names of the father) in *Television.* The names of the father are always associated in Lacan's work with law, especially the law of signification, but when he renders the phrase homophonically as *"les non-dupes errent"* (those who are not dupes wander), he evokes the movement of desire in the very shadow of patriarchal law.[31]

Subversive textual desire makes itself felt in the dynamic, potentially explosive undercurrents that run through works of literature, currents that are produced, intensified, and multiplied by the very energies designed to mask them. Although numerous writers utilize antirepresentational or destabilizing techniques in their work, the writers who have done most to theorize the operations of antirepresentational thought are, in my view, Gilles Deleuze and Félix Guattari. Deleuze and Guattari position themselves as strongly resistant to what they call rooted or arboreal thought, Oedipal paradigms, and "fascist" or totalitarian tendencies, in order to expose the political ramifications of representational logic when it is privileged as the dominant mode of discourse. As an alternative to rooted or stable forms of thought, they celebrate what they call rhizomatic movement, an associative, omnidirectional, ever-changing process of exploration without a set goal. And in providing a set of models for how such thinking operates, they also, without ever mentioning the pun, articulate a theory of punning.

Deleuze and Guattari are certainly not the first to oppose a stable, vertically oriented ontology with one that is dynamic and horizontal, nor are they unique in seeing this opposition as political and gendered. William Faulkner, in *As I Lay Dying,* ridicules the value system that he explicitly associates with trees, men, and property by identifying it with the shiftless, culpably self-absorbed character of Anse Bundren. Faulkner has Anse himself explain the difference between men and women as axial, suggesting that men are vertical and are meant to stay in place (like trees), whereas women are horizontal. Like roads, women wander, bringing evil into man's arboreal "garden." In his first monologue, Anse, in indignant lassitude, delivers a ranting diatribe against roads, which highlights his moral objections to movement, wandering, or exploration of any kind: "Durn that road. . . . A-laying there, right up to my door, where every bad luck that comes and goes is bound to find it. I told Addie it want any luck living on a road when it come by here, and she said, for the world like a woman, 'Get up and move, then.'"[32] Anse's point is that he is against movement on principle, which is why he resists women. His view of men as treelike leads him to valorize human inertia as part of the divine plan:

the Lord put roads for travelling: why He laid them down flat on the earth. When He aims for something to be always a-moving, He makes it longways, like a road or a horse or a wagon, but when He aims for something to stay put, He makes it up-and-down ways, like a tree or a man. . . . Because if He'd a aimed for man to be always a-moving and going somewheres else, wouldn't He a put him longways on his belly, like a snake? (34–35)

The snake in Anse's garden is anything that moves, which is how he can rationalize attributing all the misfortune and inconvenience in his life—including the death of his wife—to a road. By casting himself as a tree, Anse can protest his innocence while indulging in righteously comic complaint against a mobile world: "I have done no wrong to be cussed by. . . . But it seems hard that a man in his need could be so flouted by a road" (37).

In *Anti-Oedipus, Kafka: Toward a Minor Literature,* and especially *A Thousand Plateaus,* Deleuze and Guattari take an importantly different view of the opposition that plagued Anse. They are equally concerned with the contrast between stasis and movement, but instead of reading human stasis as part of a natural and divine plan, they see it as the combined product of a desire to interpret (instead of experiment) and a complementary willingness to submit to *being* interpreted (literally "put between") or interpellated by a series of culturally defined institutions ranging from the family and the office to religion and the state. They use the tree-image to show how interpretation serves to root and stabilize the individual in society, contrasting it to the rhizome, which (like roads) traces the possibility of lateral movement and contiguous connection (as opposed to hierarchical dominance). They argue that movement is integral to any experience of human vitality, creativity or collective power.[33]

Unlike even "radical" thought, which attempts to penetrate to the root of oppressive social or literary practices, rhizomatic thought eschews deep roots altogether. Instead of anchoring itself vertically so that the branches above ground mirror the radical system below ground, the rhizome extends itself via lateral shoots that proliferate from interconnective "nodes." Unlike a tree, "[t]he rhizome is an anti-genealogy" (*TP,* 11); it is an "acentered system" (*TP,* 17), "a map" that is "entirely oriented toward an experimentation in contact with the real. . . . The map is open and connectable in all of its dimensions; it is detachable, reversible, susceptible to constant modification. . . . [I]t always has multiple entryways" (*TP,* 12–13). Definition, then, is never absolute but always temporary and provisional; rhizomatic thought, like the associative property of language, "grows between" other things, like weeds or grass (*TP,* 19); "[i]t has neither beginning nor end, but always a middle (*milieu*) from which it grows and which it overspills" (*TP,* 21). In principle, the idea of a lateral, associative thought process that stresses neither beginnings nor endings but what lies between seems simple enough, but, the authors warn, "It's not easy to see things in the middle, rather than looking down on them from above ["overdetermining" them] or up at them from below [literally "under-standing" them], or from left to right or right to left: try it, you'll see that everything changes" (*TP,* 23).

Oedipal Desire

In "Everybody Wants to Be a Fascist,"[34] Félix Guattari expresses his desire to "put in place new theoretical and practical machines, capable of sweeping away the old stratifications, and of establishing the conditions for a new exercise of desire" (88). To do this, Guattari argues, it is necessary to engage "in a political struggle against *all* machines of the dominant power, whether it be the power of the bourgeois state, the power of any kind of bureaucracy, the power of academia, familial power, phallocratic power in male/female relationships, or even the repressive power of the super-ego over the individual" (which produces guilt) (88). Guattari sets up his "micro-politics of desire" as a guerrilla force against the infiltrations of fascism. He defines fascism as a totalitarian system that can take a variety of forms and operate on many levels, detecting the fascist machine in Stalinist Russia as well as in Nazi Germany. His most important point, though, is that since World War II fascism has been molecularized, so that "it passes through the tightest mesh"; it "seems to come from the outside, but it finds its energy right at the heart of everyone's desire" (97).

The machines Guattari urges us to dismantle are those that invisibly program individual desire, but how does an individual go about becoming conscious of such structures in daily practice? As I argue earlier in this chapter, one pragmatic solution is to train ourselves to read differently. The objective of experimental reading is to loosen the stranglehold that the user of language would have over meaning, to reduce the power of conscious intent. To do this, we must make the division between the subject, object, and means of representation less absolute, as Guattari argues in "Everybody Wants to Be a Fascist":

> Subject and object are no longer face-to-face, with a means of expression in a third position; there is no longer a tripartite division between the realm of reality, the realm of representation or representativity, and the realm of subjectivity. You have a collective set-up which is, at once, subject, object, and expression. The individual is no longer the universal guarantor of the dominant meanings. Here, everything can participate in enunciation: individuals, as well as zones of the body, semiotic trajectories, or machines that are plugged in on all horizons. (91)

Deleuze and Guattari argue that the story of Oedipus crystallizes in mythic form the way we as social subjects are taught to constitute or colonize the self, so that we learn to desire our own repression. We "colonize" the self by defining ourselves as individual subjects through the exclusion and repression of undesirable elements. By carving out a self, we transform ourselves into art objects that are simultaneously more stable than living reality and also less comprehensive. By fashioning ourselves artistically, we produce a lack, which is nothing more than all the contradictory, fluctuating possibilities that we have excluded from our self-representation. In this sense the very act of defining a self also constitutes a "castration" of sorts for both sexes. The subject's lack is a mere by-product of the need to construct a unified and stable self condemned always to be in conflict with what has been designated the not-self, the "other"—whether mother, father, lover, or brother.

Deleuze and Guattari identify Oedipus with the principle of self-division, which is then projected onto society in various divisive forms—patricide, fratricide, misogyny—all of which are mapped onto a system of kinship and love. Love and hate are produced in the same act of self-division: *"everything divides, but into itself"* (*Anti-Oedipus*, 76). Everything is a facet of the ego attempting to *express* itself (to press itself out) through a simultaneous repression (pushing itself back). What results is infinite regression, an orientation toward the past, not the future; toward lack, not plenitude; toward fantasy, not materiality.

One way of explaining the significance of oedipalization as an explanation of unconscious desire is to say that Oedipus uses history (the past, the parents) to dramatize and account for self-conflict (the nightmare of history from which Stephen Dedalus is trying to awake). The conflict between that which we have designated as the self and its residuum, the not-self, gets personified as two parents, who together represent the self's ambivalence—attraction and repulsion—toward that which engendered it. The oedipal triangle, then, is a way of diagramming the self's ambivalence about the mode in which it was constructed, or more accurately, the way in which *it constructs itself* in conformity to a culturally dictated model.

The theory about Shakespeare that Stephen Dedalus expounds in Joyce's *Ulysses* is predicated upon a similar view that we *create* or father the ghostly selves that haunt us. If *we* construct the self through the act of self-representation and its corollary, exclusion and repression, we can truly say that the child is himself his own father (*and* mother). What we think of as the father is simply the *ghost* of the self; the mother is its too too solid/sullied reification.[35] Tradition teaches us to *prefer* the dead father, to revile the sullied mother; an antioedipal view underwrites these commands with their antitheses: our preference for the father's ghost is a reaction against forbidden jealousy and hate; the reviling of the mother's flesh is powered by an equally illegitimate love. The model self need not be defined as dead and male, like Hamlet's father; instead, it can be construed as comprehensive and internally conflicted, like Hamlet himself for most of the play. Shakespeare's *Hamlet* suggests that if an individual's conflicting realities are externalized—projected upon various family members and friends—they can be horribly destructive, as the end of the play dramatically attests. The alternative is to manage conflict internally, as Hamlet does by expressing his many minds through a dazzling play of words and actions that simulates madness.

In a sense, Deleuze and Guattari continue Hamlet's project of trying to avoid the externalization of psychic conflict, which in their view produces violence. They begin by suggesting that we replace representation with production, with multiple sites of enunciation. They propose a view of the subject, not as locked in stable opposition to its object, but as peripheral and nomadic, as something that is always passing through different systems.[36] They ask us to admit internal conflict, which they call schizophrenia, leaving behind the need to root our selves in the ambivalence of mother and father, or the mutually exclusive operations of gender.

According to Deleuze and Guattari, the logic of desire as we have constructed it is all wrong—we are asked to choose *either* to produce or to acquire. If we choose to acquire, we make desire idealistic, locating its source in the *lack* of an imaginary object. But, they argue, desire does not lack anything; it is the *subject* that is missing in desire. In other words, the subject constructs an identity by splitting off or repressing contradictory elements—there is no fixed subject without repression—but all of those alienated elements are still in some sense "there"; the only thing that is missing is a more comprehensive definition of personal subjectivity. As a result, the means of immense productivity are theoretically available, since production comes out of the plenitude of an unterritorialized unconscious to which we all have access. Breaks and disjunctions are all potentially productive.

None of the oedipal narratives—the story of the fall, the holy trinity, *Hamlet*, to name just a few—actually *legislates* oedipalization, although they may be said to normalize it. Depending on how resistantly we read, such narratives also allow us to see the form and pressure of oedipalization: they stage and thereby expose its operations and limitations. *Hamlet*, read in such a light (in which Shakespeare himself plays all the parts), dramatizes the social consequences of projecting conflicting internal impulses outward, of embodying them in different people. In *Hamlet*, patricide, fratricide, and misogyny all support and perpetuate each other: Claudius's jealous murder of his brother and his marriage with Hamlet's mother, produce a situation—fueled by Hamlet's repulsion at his mother's sexuality—in which both stepfather and son want to kill each other, and a new "brother," Laertes, wants to kill Hamlet, who has inadvertently killed *his* father and sister. All the characters in *Hamlet* are, in some sense, Hamlet himself: King Hamlet is a ghost with the same name as prince Hamlet; Hamlet is also reflected in Laertes, who is in Hamlet's own position of trying to revenge himself against the man who killed his father. As Hamlet says of Laertes, "by the image of my cause I see / The portraiture of his."[37] The mad Ophelia, drifting to her death, is another alter ego for Hamlet; both Ophelia and Hamlet are pulled between desire and death, represented by two men: for Hamlet, the two men are his father and Claudius, whereas Ophelia is pulled between Hamlet and *her* father, Polonius. Hamlet is also Gertrude, a "beast" whose flesh is both solid and sullied, and Claudius (like Claudius, he desires preferment). The proliferation of Hamlets, all fighting with and loving one another, is reflected in narratives of the fall of Troy and the founding of Rome: Hamlet and Ophelia are also Aeneas and Dido, telling and hearing of the murder of Priam by Pyrrhus.

An antioedipal reading of Pyrrhus would see him as a counterpart to Paris (a similarity reinforced by the similar sounds of their names). Paris is Priam's son whose adulterous lust for Helen *started* the Trojan war; Pyrrhus, as a version of Paris, finishes Troy by killing its "father," Priam. So when Hamlet asks the players to resume the account of Pyrrhus' murder of Priam, he is describing his own situation, as well as echoing that of Everyman, in his account of Pyrrhus' transformation after he emerged from the Trojan horse and fought on the streets of Troy:

'The rugged Pyrrhus, he whose sable arms,
Black as his purpose, did the night resemble
When he lay couched in the ominous horse,
Hath now this dread and black complexion smeared
With heraldry more dismal. Head to foot
Now is he total gules, horridly tricked
With blood of fathers, mothers, daughters, sons,
Baked and impasted with the parching streets.'
II.ii.440–47.

Like Pyrrhus, Hamlet by the end of the play is "total gules, horridly tricked / With blood of fathers, mothers, daughters, sons." He has betrayed the passion of Paris and the deadliness of Pyrrhus, which is also the legacy of his parents. We inherit the blood of our fathers and mothers in two senses—we have their blood in us but also on us, and we pass down the guilt to our children.[38]

History, then, is indeed a ghost story, haunted by insubstantial fathers and the bodies of mothers importuning us to "List, list, O list!" (*Hamlet*, I.v.22; *U,* 9.144). To list is not only to listen—to suffer "poison" to be poured into our ears via words—but also to desire (to list is to incline toward, or want). The ghosts of the past tell us to listen to them, which is also to *desire* the lack, the substance-lessness they represent and seek to propagate. How can we resist that call? One way is by parenting *them,* by understanding the pun on "heir" and "air."[39] We are their heirs, but they are simply *air;* we can remake them, insofar as they are, after their death, simply the precondition of our being. In addition, we can understand the parents' call to "list" as an example of one among many uses of language; the parents treat language as a hierarchical and imperative system designed for "a transmission of orders, an exercise of power or of resistance to this exercise" (*Kafka,* 23). Another way of evading the pressure to submit to (or resist) an external power is to dismantle the dominant conception of language as an imperative system by letting it dissolve into sound, into non-sense, into "a cry that escapes signification . . . a sonority that ruptures in order to break away from a chain that is still all too signifying" (*Kafka,* 6). By focusing on the particles that *make up* language—sounds, letters, stray associations, and inappropriate "meanings"—we can avoid the necessity of either submitting to or resisting the parental order. And what is at stake in the pressure to submit is nothing less than the social order itself.

Hamlet, by simultaneously submitting to and resisting his two fathers, eventually reenacts the destructiveness of the oedipal narrative, but he also exposes its foundations. He shows how inextricably intertwined are all the oppositions that the social order has staked itself on separating—good and evil, spirit and body, sanity and madness, love and hatred. He dramatizes the necessary interdependence of extremes within the individual by painting *himself* black as well as radiating "son-light"; he puts an antic disposition on and portrays himself not as heroic, but as impotent in his self-division. He resists the flattery of others—reminding Polonius that the desert of all men is a whipping; he depicts himself as womanly *as well as* manly (which prompted Vining to argue that Hamlet was a woman brought up as a man);[40] in short, he flaunts the logical inconsistencies of productive desire. He tells Ophelia, "I loved you . . . I loved you not," accurately recording conflicting feelings, a conflict that corresponds to the half-truth of the imagination that Beckett expresses at the end of *Molloy*, which Deleuze and Guattari quote in *Anti-Oedipus:* "It is midnight. The rain is beating on the windows. It was not midnight. It was not raining" (77).

Territorializing and Deterritorializing Desire

The theory of Deleuze and Guattari illuminates the argument of this book in three main ways. First, their description of how rhizomatic desire operates and undergoes repeated metamorphoses serves as a correlative for the way that Wilde, Yeats, and Joyce enrich and animate their works with encoded or "minor" meanings. To see the complex techniques of these three writers as an expression of desire, specifically a desire at odds with the status quo, produces a fresh way of reading their works that is simultaneously political: it highlights minority perspectives that are loosely associated with Ireland.

The second aspect of the theory of Deleuze and Guattari that underpins *States of Desire* is their analysis of oedipalization as a socially constructed blue-print for constructing the self upon gender division. If, as I am arguing, the writing practices of Wilde, Yeats, and Joyce cumulatively produce a model of the self that revels in contradiction and change, their revisionary view of the self renders the patriarchal view of male superiority a useless fiction.[41] Instead, all three writers portray themselves as occupying dramatically different subject positions at different times, including female ones.

Finally, Deleuze and Guattari's argument in *Kafka* that two models of desire are always intertwined—straining in opposite directions and conditioning very different responses—is illustrated by my depiction of all three writers as torn between a possessive desire that their culture endorses and the experimental desire that drives their writing. Oedipalized desire is a subcategory of what Deleuze and Guattari call territorializing desire, which aims to govern rather than release the volatile energies of thought and action. Territorializing desire aims to contain and isolate these energies; this is the function of law, the effect of which is comparable to that of a photograph. A photograph, they explain, "capture[s] desire in an assemblage that neutralize[s] it, reterritorialize[s] it, and cut[s] it off from all its connections. It mark[s] the defeat of metamorphosis" (*Kafka*, 61).

What the metaphor of the photograph suggests is that—as subjects—we are subject to the reductive image-making power of social and historical forces. We, in turn—identified with our images, framed by overly static and simple definitions, and separated from one another by reductive categories—compensate for such subjection (or subjectification) with fantasies of resistance or escape; we admire heroism (the principle of doomed resistance) and long to transcend our constricting circumstances. What Deleuze and Guattari call territorialization is at bottom the power of representation.

Deleuze and Guattari imply that territorialization is something that is *done* to desire, by social forces and institutions, whereas I am treating it as a *form* of desire that is powerfully influenced by social forces. Despite what Deleuze and Guattari suggest, individuals as well as institutions desire stability; an individual must accede to and even actively participate in the territorialization of desire. Wilde did this by idealizing youth and beauty and abhorring ugliness and pain; Yeats worshiped a kind of passion that offered an escape from the world; Joyce favored control, which is how he briefly found himself identifying with the desire of men to dominate women and of Christians to dominate Jews when he was composing *Giacomo Joyce*.

For Wilde, Yeats, and Joyce, though, their tendency to idealize was countered by an experimental impulse that became stronger with each generation. Deleuze and Guattari describe this impulse as an energy that seduces us to *participate* in the production of desire, to *realize* the power that is always potentially available to us, to multiply our connections, transform ourselves through constant and dynamic metamorphosis. The minoritarian is an individual who can be a stranger in his or her own language by apprehending minor tensions within a dominant meaning (see *Kafka*, 16–27). A minoritarian sees desire as self-propelling, immanent, unfolding in many directions under the lenient direction of chance. When desire is unleashed, allowed to overrun and recharge the social field, what is produced at the same time is a general erotic force, a sense of collective energy, a polyvocality of enunciation, and a redefinition of what used to be called individuality, or subjectivity, as "an ensemble of states, each distinct from the other, grafted onto the [hu]man insofar as [s]he is searching for a way out" (*Kafka*, 36). In place of the articulation, analysis, and segmentalization of ideas is the energy of questioning, or questing—traveling without a known destination. In place of the guilt, sentencing, and judgment endemic to the majoritarian system, what we are promised is a less mediated engagement with justice, a justice that is compatible with both desire and power.[42] As Deleuze and Guattari contend, "There is nothing to judge vis-à-vis desire; the judge himself is completely shaped by desire. . . . Justice is the continuum of desire, with shifting limits that are always displaced" (*Kafka*, 51). And our response to the minoritarian strains of our experience is diametrically opposed to our reaction to the majoritarian tendencies: instead of longing to transcend or flee the world, we experience a determination to "'grasp the world' to make it take flight"; instead of fleeing it, we try to caress it (*Kafka*, 60).

The challenge, then, is first of all to perceive the operations of two different movements within society, language, and thought:

> We can simply say that there are two coexistent movements, each caught up in the other. One captures desire with great diabolical assemblages, sweeping along in almost the same movement servants and victims, chiefs and subalterns, and only bringing about a massive deterritorialization of man by also reterritorializing him, whether in an office, a prison, a cemetery. . . .[43] The other movement makes desire take flight through all the assemblages, rub up against all the segments without settling down in any of them, and carry always farther the innocence of a power of deterritorialization that is the same thing as escape. (*Kafka*, 60)

These two movements are so deeply entangled in one another that it is impossible to determine in advance which forces will capture desire and which ones will unleash it, which is why Deleuze and Guattari put so much stress on the necessity of *practice* over theory:

> we cannot say in advance, 'This is a bad desire, that is a good desire.' Desire is a mixture, a blend, to such a degree that bureaucratic or fascist pieces are still or already caught up in revolutionary agitation. It is only in motion that we can distinguish the 'diabolism' of desire and its 'immanence,' since one lies deep in the other. (*Kafka*, 60)

Nonoedipalized desire must be an expressive practice rather than an organizing theory[44]—a performance rather than a product. To translate the concept yet again (and constant retranslation, renaming, recontextualization are all linguistic activities that operate like puns to help release and propel desire), desire *"doesn't take place as a punctual ending but is already at work in each limit and at every moment"* (*Kafka*, 88; my emphasis).

Experimental desire, then, "is not form, but a procedure, a process" (*Kafka*, 8), an explosive, dynamic praxis founded on the verb and working—like the pun—in subatomic units. Subversive desire is a mode of reading that is not driven by what we expect to find. Moreover, because it "is already at work . . . in every moment," there are no units too small to be part of the productive political process, and "everything in [minor literatures] is political" (*Kafka*, 18). Deleuze and Guattari define minor literature as "that which a minority constructs within a major language" (*Kafka*, 16); it is that "whole other story" that vibrates within an individual concern (*Kafka*, 17). A primary concern is to be able to hear the vibrations of the minor within the major, which means not only that small things matter, but that they are what we are trying to train ourselves to apprehend. Specifically, when we listen for the "subversions" within an authorized account, when we concentrate attention on the miniaturized elements of individual words and letters as they reverberate in a wider linguistic and intra-referential context, we are performing a political act. We are actively looking for "points of underdevelopment" within major institutions—political, social, linguistic, interpretive—not to "develop" them, but to escape through them. What Deleuze and Guattari call "points of underdevelopment" are comparable to what Stephen Dedalus in *Ulysses* calls volitional errors: they are "portals of discovery" through which we can pursue a more collective, heterogenous, and uncharted journey propelled by joyful desire.

The search for "minor literatures" leads us away from "universals," paradigms, established truths and familiar concepts, and pulls us instead into the world of detail, where we scrutinize with microscopic closeness the smallest components of language and experience. The goal is to alienate the familiar in order to hear the faint hum of vitality within the still forms, "to become a nomad and an immigrant and a gypsy in relation to one's own language" (*Kafka*, 19). We can accomplish this by investigating the world of "subrepresentative matter" (*TP*, 218-19) within the smallest semantic units—words; to examine the operations of letters, even syllables, and experiment with their re-combination, as Joyce does in *Finnegans Wake*. We can attune ourselves to the *sound* of language, learning to experience a "language torn from sense, con-quering sense" (*Kafka*, 21), which is what we are doing when we learn to listen for the homophonic connections in the pun. Finally, we can learn "to make use of the polylingualism of one's own language" (*Kafka*, 26). Although Deleuze and Guattari do not integrate these suggestions to produce specific experimen-tal reading "methods," it is essential to have a methodology of reading, and that is what the pun provides, along with its analogues: palimpsestic verbal rela-tions, strings of appositives, acrostics, anagrams, portmanteau words, syn-chronic narrative accounts, multiple perspectives in time and space. Learning to register the strain of incompatible referents within a single verbal unit is a way of destabilizing established "meanings," and in that respect punning is both a subversively micropolitical activity and a means of psychological re-lease: "a simple joke can derout [*sic*] repression" (*Kafka*, 49). Punning becomes a way of highlighting the internal fissures that always lie beneath the surface of apparently unified categorical units, whether those units be words, secretly di-vided in-dividuals, or nations.

Whether we focus on language, subjectivity, or nationalism, the emphasis is on the local, the minor, the "small" cogs or gears that make up the assemblages of apparent power. And just as a macroscopic focus on a universalized "hu-mankind" tends to display not human diversity but instead to produce and privilege a "normative" sameness, so when we focus on microscopic particles, it produces a similar but opposite inverse effect, highlighting the color and variety within even the smallest units. This accords with Deleuze and Guattari's view of the effects of molecularization. To molecularize is to produce "the continuous variation of free action, passing from speech to action, from a given action to another, from action to song, from song to speech, from speech to enterprise, all in a strange chromaticism with intense but rare peak moments or moments of effort that the outside observer can only 'translate' in terms of work" (*TP*, 491). Molecularization of perception is the first stage of "becoming," which also pro-ceeds through bursts of effort and moments of exhilaration. The aim of becom-ing, though, is to realize or make real the incomparable versatility of what could perhaps be called—not the subject or the individual—but the "multiple-dividual." Paradoxically, to become is to experience one's affinity—perhaps even identity—with "everybody else." According to Deleuze and Guattari,

> Not everybody becomes everybody [and everything: *tout le monde*—TRANS.], makes a becoming of everybody/everything. This requires much asceticism, much sobriety, much creative involution. . . . For everybody/everything is the molar aggregate, but *becoming everybody/everything* is another affair, one that brings into play the cosmos with its molecular components. Becoming everybody/everything (*tout le monde*) is to world (*faire monde*), to make a world (*faire un monde*). (*TP*, 279–80)

Finally, to become is not only to learn to *be* everybody/everything through the supreme effort of remaking it internally, but it is also to grow away from the standardized norm, which in our culture is decidedly male. Manhood, socially defined as the ideal standard, is majoritarian rather than minoritarian, whereas "women, children, . . . animals, plants, and molecules, are minoritarian. It is perhaps the special situation of women in relation to the man-standard that accounts for the fact that becomings, being minoritarian, always pass through a becoming-woman. Even blacks, as the Black Panthers said, must become-black. Even women must become-women. Even Jews must become-Jewish" (*TP*, 291). Micropolitics, then, necessitates a radical proliferation of all sexual, racial, and national identities. Instead of rigidifying and stratifying the sexes, micropolitics aims to liberate the erotic energy of a sexuality that is not dual, but multiple, and that changes from moment to moment in response to different, richly various stimuli. (See chapter 4, "Joyful Recoveries.")

As the following chapter shows, Wilde's writing deterritorializes desire not only through the exercise of wit, but also through a principled inconsistency that emerges through his insistence on paradox, through his use of dialogue not only in plays but also in critical essays, and through a technical virtuosity that revels in change. Yeats's experimental desire is most apparent in the way that he arranges poems to simulate a panoply of voices, in his constant revisions and retranslations of the images that govern different volumes of his poems, and in the evolution of his poetic corpus as a whole, which becomes increasingly more inclusive of logically incompatible positions. Joyce's virtuosity reveals itself not only in the proliferation of styles that characterizes *Ulysses*, but in the obscure mutations of language that make up *Finnegans Wake*. Partly under the pressure of the rise of the Third Reich, Joyce's last and least understood work is his most extreme verbal experiment; it was designed to counter territorializing forms of desire, which had gained immense power through the incursions of fascism and Nazism in the 1930s. Joyce once told Jacques Mercanton that people should stop concerning themselves about the prospect of a Nazi invasion of Poland and instead "occupy themselves with *Finnegans Wake*."[45] I read this not as a symptom of megalomania but as an indication that the bizarre techniques he used in *Finnegans Wake* were politically inspired. Joyce believed—with a faith that was either unrealistically utopian or too farseeing for his contemporaries to credit it—that for individuals to lose their susceptibility to authoritarian systems, they must learn to read, to see, to hear, even to think differently, and *Finnegans Wake* is an extended exercise in such retraining.[46]

The main objective of this book is to problematize the implied claim of an interpretation to *represent* (speak for, replace) its subject. Accordingly, I have refused to privilege any single theoretical frame of reference, preferring a methodology that traverses different contextual discourses—historical, psychoanalytic, feminist, political, literary—in order to show how the unraveling of plot and the fall of the image result from a host of different pressures, all of which revolve around the expression, suppression, oppression, and repression of desire. *States of Desire* explores the poisonous potential of ideal and static images, as well as the relationships between interpretation, metaphor, plot, and social "norms," all of which attempt to contain the fluxes of textual and social experience. One alternative to representative substitution is a mode of precise, localized experimentation that I identify on the verbal level with punning—a performative, metonmymic, subversive activity driven by a desire for provisional connection rather than domination. The aim of experimentation is to tease out nonadaptive habits of mind, to tap the energy of the unconscious through an active pursuit of difference and a vigilant respect for the power of coincidence to forge unexpectedly productive connections.

Two

Wilde's Desire

A Study in Green

> Oh I was young and easy in the mercy of his means,
>   Time held me green and dying,
>   Though I sang in my chains like the sea.
>
> —Dylan Thomas, "Fern Hill"

Oscar Fingal O'Flahertie Wills Wilde used wit to tease apart his Irish nationality, his image, and the prescriptive power of authority in ways that are widely misunderstood. To appreciate Wilde's extraordinary inventiveness and to see how it was propelled and derailed by a tendency toward "greenness" that is both lushly verdant (in an intellectual and national sense) and grotesquely naive (in his understanding of the power of age and class), it is first necessary to peel away the image of Wilde that was disseminated through the popular press, an image that he did little to dispel and sometimes actively embroidered. Wilde's fall came about largely because of the way he was troped (and trapped) by caricatures, but Wilde's writings express values that are diametrically opposed to such labeling; they endorse a methodology that is antirepresentational, self-contradictory, and dynamic. His exuberant comedies demonstrate his command of vertiginous wordplay, most immediately apparent in his "earnest" punning, yet his fairy tales emphasize an equal awareness of the importance of humility, a quality that simultaneously affirms the insufficiency and the compassion of the individual. Although they differ sharply in mood, what punning and humility have in common is an exultation in the necessity of supplementation. Wilde's sense of the vital importance of the supplement is also apparent in his critical writings, in his theory of an "individualism" that is paradoxically multinational and socialist.

Wilde's attitude toward sexuality was problematic, but not in the way it is most often represented as being. Wilde was not a libertine, but a hybrid, and his hybrid nature resulted in an attitude toward sex that was remarkably close to the traditional Victorian desire to dissolve sexuality into the spiritual. Wilde was deeply ambivalent about adult sexuality, an ambivalence that is apparent in his pattern of self-identification. He identified with women as well as men, which helps to explain the sharp contradiction in his writings between, on the one hand, compassion for women and outrage at the double standard (most strongly apparent in *Lady Windermere's Fan* and *A Woman of No Importance*), and, on the other, an airy dismissal of women as intellectually vapid. (Frank Harris quotes him as saying that "[girls] have no minds, and what intelligence they have is given to wretched vanities and personal jealousies."[1])

It is slightly misleading to say that Wilde identified with "men" and "women," however, since it is more precisely "boys" and "girls" with whom he felt special kinship; more important than the cross-gender identification (which it subsumes) is his cross-generational identification. These two kinds of identification become fused in a preference for sexual ambiguity, not only a male/female ambiguity, but more important, for the ambiguity characteristic of children before they reach sexual maturity. Wilde's attraction to the carelessness of youth and his revulsion at sexual ripeness is best illustrated by Frank Harris's account of Wilde's changed attitude toward his wife Constance after she became pregnant. Harris purports to quote Wilde's own words:

> When I married, my wife was a beautiful girl, white and slim as a lily, with dancing eyes and gay rippling laughter like music. In a year or so the flowerlike grace had all vanished; she became heavy, shapeless, deformed. She dragged herself about the house in uncouth misery with drawn blotched face and hideous body, sick at heart because of our love. It was dreadful. I tried to be kind to her, forced myself to touch and kiss her; but she was sick always, and—oh! I cannot recall it, it is all loathsome . . . I used to wash my mouth and open the window to cleanse my lips in the pure air. Oh, nature is disgusting; it takes beauty and defiles it; it defaces the ivory-white body we have adored, with the vile cicatrices of maternity; it befouls the altar of the soul. . . . How can one desire what is shapeless, deformed, ugly? Desire is killed by maternity; passion buried in conception.[2]

Wilde's attraction to youth is primarily an aesthetic preference, although it is fraught with powerfully erotic overtones; ironically, the erotically charged image of innocence is appealing precisely because it is asexual. The erotic object is also, paradoxically, a representation of the desire to escape sexuality. This contradiction—an eroticization of children because of a fear of mature adult sexuality—is not an idiosyncrasy peculiar to Wilde, but a disturbingly widespread cultural phenomenon that is still powerful today among homosexuals and heterosexuals alike.

What makes Wilde controversial, even now, is this double-edged appropriation and idealization of youth. It is important to understand the complex mechanisms at work in his attitude toward unripeness and growth, toward greenness (his urbane pastoral), because without such an understanding, his spectacular and excessive disgrace will continue to obscure the powerfully innovative and forward-looking character of his thought.

The possibility of a misprision that for Wilde eventuated in imprisonment can be glimpsed in the boldly experimental complexity of his thought. As a man who affected feminine styles of dress and a citizen of a colonized country, Wilde understood, more vividly perhaps than anyone in his age, that the tension between being a subject and being an object, between identification and alienation, instead of being what it appears to be (a way of differentiating self from an external other) is actually internal to the self, a consequence of living in society. That is one of the many implications of the Narcissus myth—especially Narcissus' rejection of Echo—that Wilde uses so variously in his writings: the beautiful images that we love (like the hideous ones we hate) signify our naive preference for a selectively constructed, flattering self-image, a denial of the divided and inconsistent self that is in psychic terms both Narcissus and Echo, male and female, image and voice, joy and sorrow. In his Paterian appreciation of music and sound, Wilde knew that the challenge posed by the Narcissus myth was to avoid exclusive admiration for the beautiful image and to attend as well to the haunting echo; he also knew that the beautiful image and the sorrowful echo were representations of the unequal privilege of men and women in a narcissistic, patriarchal society.[3] Nevertheless, in *De Profundis* he suggests that he committed a version of the crime of Narcissus toward Echo when he pursued joy to the exclusion of sorrow, and when he preferred unmarked youth to age. (*CW*, 916; see also 917–22). Wilde's later, chastened view is that joy and sorrow (which he also associates with Hellenism and Christianity, respectively), need to be kept in a more perfect balance, a balance that he, by his own account, violated.[4]

Here is where Wilde's case becomes most intricate. On the one hand, Wilde demonstrated a sophisticated understanding of the split within the self, which he read as a version of the Cartesian mind/body dichotomy, in which the mind is free, individual, and dynamic, whereas the body and its actions are subject to social regulation. He insisted that thought—and its corollary, art—should be daringly vital, knowing no restrictions but those of style. Where restrictions and laws were necessary was in the realm of action, where the individual is inevitably subjected to (and to some extent objectified by) the needs of a larger social unit. It is Wilde's acute sense of the difference between the privileges accorded to thought and action that is refracted in Frank Harris's condemnation of him as "incapable of action" and "easily led in action, though not in thought" (141, 140). Similarly, Wilde's view that restrictions on action are legitimate and necessary explains George Bernard Shaw's insistence that "Wilde was a conventional man; his unconventionality was the very pedantry of convention; never was there a man less an outlaw than he" (340).

In *De Profundis*, Wilde accused himself of being too conventional, too constrained by social values, and too dependent upon the approval of the outside world. He explained,

> People used to say of me that I was too individualistic. I must be far more of an individualist than I ever was. I must get far more out of myself than I ever got, and ask far less of the world than I ever asked. Indeed my ruin came, not from too great individualism of life, but from too little. (*CW*, 937)

Even in *De Profundis*, though, Wilde is more concerned with the mystery of his own inadequately developed individualism than with the unknowability of others: "[T]o recognise that the soul of man is unknowable is the ultimate achievement of Wisdom. The final mystery is oneself" (*CW*, 934). What he never fully appreciated was the mystery of others, particularly those who were even more vulnerable to social pressure than he was—such as children and working-class men. The reason he was blind to these differences is that he loved children and "ignorant people" with a love that relied too heavily on identification. As he said on the second day of his first trial, "I like people who are young, bright, happy, careless and original. I do not like them sensible, and I do not like them old; I don't like social distinctions of any kind" (Harris, 126), but in the generosity and openness of his spirit, Wilde elided the fact that his disapproval of social distinctions and of maturity did not erase them. What makes Wilde such an important case study are not his sins of the flesh (as he says in *De Profundis*, "Sins of the flesh are nothing" *CW*, 899), but the very purity of his love, a purity that did not admit or take into account the pressures of society on the less empowered. The greenness he loved was, like a green carnation, artificial; his ideal was ultimately more aesthetic than real. As in his native Ireland, green became a sign for oppressed life that is abundantly verdant and free only in retrospect and in the imagination. Green is also a code for the oppression of homosexuals, then known as "inverts," which I would argue that Wilde heard in French as "en vert," or "in green." During his imprisonment, the greenness he worshiped took on its traditional connotation of unfaithfulness as he castigated Lord Alfred Douglas for neglect and opportunism. Finally, his last years were tinged with the green of the absinthe he drank in France, which we now know to be a poison.

A reappraisal of Wilde's strengths as an experimental thinker and performer of social and literary roles can only take place through a reassessment of Wilde's weaknesses, and particularly through an awareness of how his "goodness," not any unnatural "wickedness," led to his demise. The first section of this chapter focuses on Wilde's reputation, its resolution into mutually incompatible caricatures that represent, not Wilde, but the fears and desires of society toward freer and more precise expressions of individual desire, expressions that are inevitably (and with some reason) confused with enactments of that desire. Wilde broke the rapier of his wit against the blunt strength of the social and legal system; an account of that battle, unequal on both sides, follows. Second, what happened to Wilde is a particularly shocking illustration of the case against representational art (a case that Wilde himself made repeatedly in his writing), since part of what brought Wilde down were the crude representations of him. As Lord Henry once exclaimed in *Dorian Gray* when refusing the title of "Prince Paradox," "From a label there is no escape!" (*CW*, 147). My main goal throughout this chapter is to show exactly how dangerous a confusion between life and textuality can be. It is not that art and life are different in kind, but that they are different in scope and are subject to different laws. Wilde made fun of such confusions in *The Importance of Being Earnest*, when he had Miss Prism absentmindedly swap a baby with a three-volume novel. In some respects, Wilde came to resemble Miss Prism, not only by privileging the complexity of art over life, which he read too simply, but also by being prim: it is not only Miss Prism's love of literature but also her unacknowledged fear of sexuality that prompts her to "lose" the baby named Ernest. Ironically, it was a comparable conflation of life and textuality, grafted onto a distrust of sexuality, that devastated the man who had so wittily parodied similar tendencies in his plays.

A Scary Wildman, or Nothing Wilde?

One of the many song parodies that sprang up in the wake of Gilbert and Sullivan's *Patience* (1881), which had famously lampooned the aesthete—who in some respects resembled Oscar Wilde—in the character of Bunthorne, was "The Flippity Flop Young Man." In one of its refrains, the aesthete sings,

I'm a very aesthetic young man,
A non-energetic young man;
I'm a bitter and mildy,
Naturey Childy,
Oscary Wildy man . . .[5]

The triple rhyme of "mild," "child," and "wild" builds to the image of the aesthete—identified with Wilde through the plays on his name—as a scary wildman ("O-scary Wildy man"), but by the time this phrase is produced, its threat has already been defused by the earlier descriptions of the speaker as a bitter but mild nature-child. In his aesthetic phase, Wilde was troped as tame, a personification of the artist as bogeyman (and as bogus man).[6] It was only during his three trials—technically for homosexual offenses,[7] and more generally for successfully unconventional "poses"—that the suggestion of Wilde's wildness became seriously threatening to the social and legal system that would incarcerate—and break—him.

Not only was Wilde lampooned as nonthreatening, he was also—largely through his association with *Patience*[8]—cast as a man who lacks "manhood," or wildness, insufficiently differentiated from woman—a characterization that helped to define subsequent stereotypes about male homosexuals.[9] The subtitle of *Patience* is "Bunthorne's Bride," which is ironic since Bunthorne is the one male character left at the end without a bride. Moreover, Bunthorne's name—especially in combination with his description as a "fleshly poet"—delicately alludes to sodomy, so when he is upstaged by Grosvenor, first in the guise of "idyllic poet," and then as an everyday, commonplace young man who wins Patience, and when the maidens pair off with the dragoons they formerly scorned, what is being simultaneously parodied and confirmed is a "norm" of ordinary, soldierly masculinity that does not include poets, and a heterosexual community that triumphantly excludes Bunthorne.

What ruined Oscar Wilde was, ultimately, an image, a representation, a stereotype (disseminated largely through satirical plays and the popular press, especially the cartoons in *Punch*); he was *textualized* in a way that framed him as the representative of fleshly indulgence in a world that valued sublimation and self-denial; as a flamboyantly feminine man in a culture that celebrated hypermasculinity; and as the epitome of poetic individualism in a society regulated by conformity. In this sense, he was literally an "invert"; in his own person, he deliberately and aggressively inverted the values of the culture at large.[10] He was also, insofar as the values he inverted were culturally dominant, seen as a subversive force, potentially dangerous if not constantly ridiculed. Ironically, the plot of *Patience* would forecast the trajectory of Wilde's own career: the initial success and fame of the poet would trigger a backlash, in which the flamboyant, the iconoclastic, and the individualistic would be ritually purged in a choric reaffirmation of the mundane and communal. The tragedy of Wilde's career is that he who so determinedly set out to shatter the stasis and unreality of stereotyped images in his writings, himself became a shattered image. He gained notoriety early by marketing himself as a human work of art, a living "character," which in turn set him up to be caricatured, and he was—at first humorously and then viciously. By violating the distinction between author and character, life and art, in his own person, by claiming an extravagant aesthetic license in his appearance and conduct that served to expose the mandated conformity of more ordinary lives, he inadvertently magnified an already widespread confusion between art and artists, creativity and ethics, texts and people. Such a confusion helps to explain the extraordinary fact that, during the first trial (when Wilde was suing the Marquess of Queensberry for libel), *Dorian Gray* was repeatedly interrogated for evidence against Wilde himself, to the point that Wilde's counsel insisted, "Judge no man by his books," and the judge had to remind the jury to keep their disapproval of Wilde's books out of the judgment (Hyde, *OW,* 254, 265). The tendency throughout the trial was to treat Dorian the character and Wilde the author as fully equivalent and interchangeable; the boundary between published and private, imagined and enacted, had been dissolved. To read Dorian as Wilde is to mistake a part for the whole, and to fetishize both character and author, rendering both as equally repulsive.

It is clear from Wilde's writings, however, that intellectually he never confused the realms of art and ethics; on the contrary, he insisted that life and art were essentially and necessarily incommensurable. This is also to say that art, although it is concerned with the same issues that we confront in life, enjoys an exemption from the consequences of action; art, unlike life, is reversible, subject to revision and erasure. Art's value, like that of thought, is its freedom from irreversible consequences. Art, like thought, has and must have a license for excess, unlike active life, which is necessarily hedged round by restrictions and taboos. His dislike of journalism grew out of his conviction that journalism, by probing into the private lives of public figures, was eroding the crucial distinction between imagination and lived reality, between creativity and morality, between play of mind and regulation of behavior.[11]

The issue that sets the narrative of Wilde's life so dramatically at odds with his own writings is the issue of representation. Wilde was tried and found guilty under a different set of assumptions about representation than the ones that inform his drama, his criticism, and his fiction: Queensberry provoked the sequence of trials by accusing Wilde of *posing as,* or representing, a sodomite (or "somdomite," in Queensberry's misspelling), so that the whole first trial—Wilde's suit against Queensberry for libel—revolved around the question of what Wilde represented. Wilde's suit for libel (like all such suits) was filed to protest a label; it was designed to disrupt the implied resemblance between himself and a word, to expose the crudeness of consigning Wilde's writings and his affections to a single humiliating and criminal category. In sharp contrast, Wilde's writings, especially *Lady Windermere's Fan, A Woman of No Importance,* and *The Picture of Dorian Gray,* mount a clever and principled attack on the reductive premises of representation as a whole, interrogating the seriocomic absurdity—even hypocrisy—of labeling a woman as "fallen" or a man as evil, since everyone is by definition both good and evil.[12] In *The Picture of Dorian Gray,* Dorian brutally murders Basil for representing him too naively—first as ideal, then as corrupt. Wilde, unlike Dorian, held himself subject to most legal and ethical restrictions, except those pertaining to his private life, his sexuality, and used only his wit and his writings—not a knife—to register his protest against idealizing and degrading caricatures. Wilde appealed to the law for protection against Queensberry's representation of him, forgetting, perhaps, that the law is structured around mutually exclusive characterizations of guilt and innocence; in a trial, the goal is to label a defendant, to pronounce a verdict and, if necessary, to "sentence" (or textualize) the offender, and as Wilde writes in *De Profundis,* "all sentences are sentences of death" (*CW,* 955). The law brings the authoritarian power of language to bear on a more chaotic human reality, using language to distinguish black from white; this, in a much more primitive sense, was also Queensberry's method—but it was not Wilde's. Not surprisingly, Wilde's appeal to the law backfired, and in a matter of weeks the Crown had taken up Queensberry's charge. As a result, Wilde, who had made a career out of fashioning sentences, was himself sentenced; he was reduced to a text to be censored. What makes Wilde a strangely moving object lesson in the politics of representation is largely the divergence between his own writing—which is a prescription for joyous self-production, an acutely intelligent celebration of diversity and change that refuses to be framed or unnaturally stabilized—and the social plot which wrote him in, first as trivial jester (nothing Wilde) and finally as transgressive villain, a "scary wildman."

Before his trials, and in response to attacks on his works, Wilde was quick to protest the operations of censorship on the grounds that words and thoughts, unlike actions, should never be policed, because *words and thoughts are not equivalent to actions* in their scope and implication, which is to say that the potential exceeds the actual. In defense of *The Picture of Dorian Gray,* Wilde, echoing Kant's "What Is Enlightenment," wrote to the editor of the *St. James Gazette* (27 June 1890) to reprimand him for having apparently countenanced

> the monstrous theory that the Government of a country should exercise censorship over imaginative literature. . . . So far from encouraging it, you should set yourself against it, and should try to teach your critics to recognise the essential difference between art and life. The gentleman who criticised my book is in a perfectly hopeless confusion about it, and your attempt to help him out by proposing that the subject-matter of art should be limited does not mend matters. It is proper that limitations should be placed on action. It is not proper that limitations should be placed on art. (*The Artist as Critic,* 243)

Remembering always that the same logic Wilde refutes here would be used to censor him, we can see Wilde's statement as an acute analysis of what is at stake in censorship, which he sees as an indefensible abuse of authority: he insists that freedom in a social context is a freedom of thought, feeling, and expression that is akin to excess (as Wilde has famously quipped, "Nothing succeeds like excess"), and *not an unlimited freedom of action*.[13] To affirm an ethos that encourages one to express to excess, to respect no boundaries of thought and feeling except those dictated by style, but to abide by limitations placed on action, is also to affirm at one stroke the necessity for law *and* lawlessness, the difference between them being roughly equivalent to the disjunctions between body and mind, the social and the psychological, action and conception.

In Wilde's view, censorship, like many related forms of abuse, should be outlawed, and it should be outlawed precisely because it represents an attempt to weld thought and action together in an unnatural union rather than an ambivalent tension. The popular conception of individuality is staked on such a vision of mind and body, thought and action, as indivisible (this is what the word "individual" literally means—incapable of being divided further). Wilde's view of individuality is exactly opposed to the popular view, however; if the default position is to *fear* a division between mind and body as a violation of the principle of individuality, Wilde's position is to portray the insistence on uniting expression with action—which denies the productive liminal space between the two—as a violation of individuality. He represents such a violation as a decapitation, a lethal and horrifying division or symbolic castration of the individual. Wilde's position is dramatized most graphically in *Salomé,* where he shows how Herod's conviction that his word binds him to action and Salomé's determination to enact the desires she has expressed produce lethal results, a literal division of the individual in the person of John the Baptist.[14] John the Baptist, or Iokanaan, becomes a prophetic image of what happens to a censored text. The alternative to censoring texts, individuals, and nations (remembering that to censor is to create an unnatural unity or "transparency" of meaning through violent self-division and selective suppression), is to foster productive rather than destructive self-division and inconsistency. It is because he advocated this latter strategy that Wilde, like Joyce after him, believed that a nation—like an individual—must foster competing discourses about itself in order to remain vital; this is why, to anticipate and revise a phrase of Stephen Dedalus's, both Wilde and Joyce came to see internationalism as the highest form of nationalism.

In *Salomé,* Iokanaan (John the Baptist) emerges as the embodiment of a certain kind of text—elusive, beautiful, and above all *incomprehensible*—over which Salomé struggles for mastery. Imprisoned in a cistern, he emerges first as a pure, riddling voice; the first soldier comments, "Sometimes he says things that affright one, but it is impossible to understand what he says."[15] His discourse is internally fractured, literally resonant (he speaks from a well), and split off from action, since he has no power to enforce what he says. Salomé longs to converse with this voice, which comes from a black hole like a tomb, but even when Iokanaan is dragged forth, he will not speak *with* her; like Lacan's *saint homme,* whose saintliness derives from the capacity to desire without directing that desire toward any single object, he *speaks* but not *to* anyone or for anything. Similarly, unlike Salomé, who looks at *him* with insatiable hunger, he will not look at her; even in death, his eyes are closed. Nor can he tolerate being the object of *her* gaze. He asks:

> Who is this woman who is looking at me? I will not have her look at me. Wherefore doth she look at me, with her golden eyes, under her gilded eyelids? I know not who she is. I do not desire to know who she is. Bid her begone. It is not to her that I would speak. (*S*, 76)

Iokanaan's refusal to address his interlocutors directly or to engage in intercourse with them helps to identify the category of text he produces; his is a public or "published" discourse, resistant to appropriation and marking out its difference from conversation. Iokanaan's textuality is evoked more materially through Salomé's appreciation of him as a collage of black and white slashed with red; she lovingly details his white body, his red mouth, and black hair.

If Iokanaan is an embodiment of one kind of text, one which controversially attempts to articulate the unspeakable, Salomé is another. Wilde accents their potential similarity by using the moon as an image of both, but the moon that prefigures the appearance of Salomé is likened to a dead woman rising from a tomb, "looking for dead things" (*S*, 44). Not only is she portrayed as one of the living dead; her search for dead things appears as a determination to commodify others, as is apparent when *she* sees the moon as "a little piece of money," a virginal, economic counter that has never been circulated (*S*, 62). Her textuality is that of sign, not symbol, but she would exempt her textual signs from the economy of exchange; when she demands Iokanaan's head on a piece of silver, she is, in addition to killing him, turning him into a literal representation of what she desires: a dish to taste (which cannot satisfy her appetite), and a stamped coin (that she cannot circulate). Her self-defeating pursuit of Iokanaan resembles Lord Illingworth's description of a fox hunt in *A Woman of No Importance:* "the unspeakable in full pursuit of the uneatable" (*CW*, 437).

Salomé's divergence from Iokanaan is further marked by the different way she responds to the man who is hunting *her,* her stepfather Herod. When she asks to look upon Iokanaan, he protests against the direct gaze as well as the immorality of the gazer. When Herod begs to look upon her, however, she agrees to dance for him in order to make him give her his word to *act* in a way that conforms with her desire. By gratifying Herod's desire, she puts him in a position in which he is "a slave to his word" (136); she makes him suit his word to a deed, limiting the possibilities of verbal excess, eliminating the "play" in language (this is yet another form of censorship). By ordering Iokanaan's death, she has also realized (limited) her words through action. As she nibbles at the dead lips of Iokanaan with her teeth, she tells his severed head, "Yes, I will kiss thy mouth, Iokanaan. I said it; did I not say it? I said it. Ah! I will kiss it now . . ." (*S*, 160). Wild with unsatisfied, uncontrollable desire, Salomé, kissing the head of her coin and eating the fruit of dead lips, becomes an emblem of the grotesque results of censorship, here depicted as the authoritative decapitation of a textual and bodily corpus in accordance with a principle of desire that insists on an authorized equivalence between action and expression. Her victory is a pyrrhic one, however; she succeeds insofar as she does what she said she would do, but fails insofar as she finds herself more unsatisfied than before: she is left only with the fetish—Iokanaan's head—that she had confused with the man. Finally, she herself falls subject to the very logic she used to obtain the object of her desire: the last "act" of the play is a brief tableau of the destructiveness of equating word and deed—Herod sentences her to death, as she had sentenced Iokanaan. Censoring, she herself is censored. She had literally constructed a sentence of death—a mode of construing textuality, or constructing sentences, that is fatal, and which results not only in her sentencing Iokanaan to death, but in her own death sentence.

Censorship, then, is also sentencing—sentencing the sentences or even the life of the other. It is an evaluative judgment that limits, as opposed to a play of thought and language that multiplies with a potentially comic abandon;[16] to censor is to maim or destroy the mediated possibilities of sexual or textual interplay. *Salomé* and *Dorian Gray* were themselves censored (public access to them was restricted), which is especially interesting in view of the ways they proleptically comment upon the very processes that were used to suppress them. The fact that *Dorian Gray* was virtually put on the stand in Wilde's trials reinforces our awareness of the vertiginous and dangerous slippage between the personal and the textual. In *The Picture of Dorian Gray*, Wilde limned the horror of interchanging life and art through the medium of Dorian's portrait, and he later dramatized the humorous side of confusing written and human characters in *The Importance of Being Earnest*, when Miss Prism mistakes a novel for a baby.

The dangerous side of the slippage between the personal and the textual is also garishly apparent in Wilde's life, especially when seen in counterpoint to the life of his fellow Irishman, Charles Stewart Parnell. In the 1890s, within five years of each other, both men were censured for the same thing that books are usually censored for—indecency—with a severity that proved fatal to both. It is difficult in such cases not to hear the "sin" in "censured"; Parnell's sin was adultery, Wilde's homosexuality, and the unsettling parallels between the two cases are highlighted by a coincidence that unites them via a name shared by two of their respective enemies: "Pigott" (a name that fortuitously blends "pig" and "bigot"). Richard Pigott is best known for what he had tried to do to Parnell in 1887, which is alluded to again and again in Joyce's *Finnegans Wake*: he forged a letter to the London *Times* attempting to implicate Parnell in the Phoenix Park murders, a forgery eventually exposed (in 1890) through Pigott's misspelling of the word "hesitancy" (as "hesitency"), a mistake shown to be characteristic of Pigott, but not Parnell. Parnell was exonerated only to be found vulnerable in another direction; instead of a fanatic Irishman, he was revealed as a literally unfaithful one, which cost him the leadership of the Nationalist party and, shortly thereafter, his life.

Wilde also suffered a reversal at the hands of a Pigott, E. F. Smyth Pigott, a licensing official for the lord chamberlain who in 1892 censored the performance of *Salomé* (which Sarah Bernhardt had already begun rehearsing at the Palace Theater) on a technicality, that it used biblical subject matter. Shaw later described this Pigott as "a walking compendium of vulgar insular prejudice"

(Hyde, *OW,* 142 n). This coincidental convergence in the lives of Parnell and Wilde serves to highlight a larger issue: the interdependence of forgery and censorship as complementary ways of interfering with authorship and authority. The roles played by the two Pigotts represent diametrically opposed strategies for interfering with writing: Parnell's Pigott was a forger, attributing to Parnell letters he did not write, whereas Wilde's Pigott was a censor, who prevented Wilde's most foreign work from being performed (*Salomé* was the only work Wilde wrote in a foreign language). In both cases, the interference with the writing of the two men serves as a prophetic prologue for the more lethal attacks on the men themselves.[17]

What the pairing of the fortunes of these two Anglo-Irishmen shows is that their "unpardonable" offenses—homosexuality and adultery, respectively— were neither as simple nor as purely sexual as they appeared to be. That sexual licence was selectively granted to public figures is shown by the popularity of Victoria's son Edward, Prince of Wales (later Edward VII), a notorious libertine.[18] The similarity in the falls of Wilde and Parnell allows each to be illuminatingly read in terms of the other. The fact that Parnell was disempowered by a frenzy of moral outrage similar to that which would later ruin Wilde suggests that Wilde's offense was not only a matter of sexual orientation, although the issue of sexual orientation was certainly important. The fact that Wilde was similarly broken five years after Parnell suggests that Parnell's fall was not purely a function of national politics, although his politics were relevant, and it is significant that both were Irish. Although undone by a different arm of society—Wilde was denounced from the bench, Parnell from the pulpit—both men were utterly ruined, and died at a young age as a direct result of their fall: Parnell was forty-five, Wilde forty-six.

Contemporary treatments of Wilde and Parnell as forged or censored texts alternated with accounts that relied upon the metaphor of sport, casting Wilde and Parnell as "wild" or undomesticated animals that sportsmen—or "men of action"—derive pleasure from pursuing and slaughtering. The master-trope of the hunt may be found in several anecdotal, sympathetic narratives of both men's undoings, and lurking behind the sporting overtones of the hunt lie memories of animal sacrifice, a slaughter of the innocents that carries with it suggestions of crucifixion. James Joyce, among others, saw Parnell as devoured by the Irish: in "The Shade of Parnell" (1912; written in Italian for *Il Piccolo della Sera*), after describing Parnell's peregrinations "from county to county, from city to city," as those of a "hunted deer," he concludes with mock satisfaction, "[His countrymen] did not throw him to the English wolves; they tore him to pieces themselves" (*Critical Writings,* 227–28). In contrast, Wilde's supporters portrayed him as hounded by the English, a metaphor reinforced by the fact that Douglas's father, the Marquess of Queensberry, was an avid British sportsman. Robert Sherard amused Wilde by referring to "Die Wilde Jagde" (the Wild(e) hunt);[19] Frank Harris presents Wilde as a "defenceless quarry" being closed in upon by "hounds with open mouths, dripping white fangs, and greedy eyes" (*OW,* 223). Joyce describes Wilde, after his release from prison, as "hunted from house to house as dogs hunt a rabbit" (*Critical Writings,* 203). It is the parallel between Queensberry's hunting down of his "Wilde" animal and the English sport of fox hunting (which Queensberry loved) that prompts Joyce in *Finnegans Wake* to turn Wilde's epigram about fox hunting into a refrain that describes Queensberry's pursuit of Wilde: "The unspeakable in full pursuit of the uneatable."

The fact that Wilde was hounded by the English also makes him a troubled emblem of England's historical mistreatment of Ireland; in *De Profundis*, Wilde's letter from prison to Lord Alfred Douglas,[20] Wilde conflates Douglas's family with the English as a whole when he refers to "the ruin your race has brought on mine" (*CW*, 947). Both Frank Harris and George Bernard Shaw also see Wilde's witty defiance as a decidedly Irish form of resistance to British control. Harris compares the feeling against Wilde with that against the Irish revolutionaries who perpetrated the Phoenix Park murders: "I had seen enough of English justice and English judges and English journals to convince me that Oscar Wilde had no more chance of a fair trial than if he had been an Irish 'Invincible'" (163).

Shaw insists that Wilde's "fierce Irish pride" compelled him to stand trial when all his friends were counseling him to leave (Harris, 337). In reality, however, Wilde was no more a "pure" symbol of Irishness than Parnell was; what propelled both stories out of the political arena, giving them a mythic and even sacral aura, was the fact that they were decried by *both* sides—by Irish and English alike.[21] Harris exposes the bipartisan vituperation against Wilde by recounting the strong bias of English journalists against Wilde, followed by an account of an Irish gentleman's even more violent hostility: "'Oi'd whip such sinners to death, so I would,' cried the Irishman; 'hangin's too good for them'" (150). In Wilde's first trial, the leading counsel for the defense (who opposed Wilde and brought about his arrest after he had withdrawn his charge of libel) was a former classmate of Wilde's at Trinity College Dublin, Edward Carson. (In the second trial, another Irishman, Charles Gill, led the prosecution, and only in the third trial was the prosecution led by an Englishman, the solicitor-general for the Crown, Sir Frank Lockwood.)[22]

If the sins of Wilde and Parnell may be said to converge, producing an oddly similar catastrophe in the lives of statesman and aesthete, if the charges of sexual misconduct leveled against them can be seen as symptomatic of a more comprehensive threat, then what is this more serious crime for which both were condemned by public opinion? I would argue that this "crime" is cosmopolitanism, hybridization, a crossing or "pollution" of categories, in which the sexual, the political, and the textual all come to reflect and abrade each other. In the case of Parnell, adultery comes to figure a double betrayal; not only does it signal a love of otherness (as in adulteration), but it also perversely constitutes a betrayal of Irishness in the sense that Parnell, by not following the moral dictates of the Catholic church, marked himself as "foreign," despite never having professed to be a Catholic.[23]

Wilde's "crime" was to love regardless of gender divisions (and, more problematically, to love across generations). Intellectually, his nonpartisan "catholicism" was expressed through his witty defense of what he calls socialist individualism, but which could also be called cosmopolitan "nationalism." At the heart of his system was the paradox, bolstered by the radical nonequivalence of verbal and physical expression, and by an awareness that productive, internal contradictions are illuminated by encounters with what is alien. In "The Critic as Artist, II," Gilbert insists that "it is only by contact with the art of foreign nations that the art of a country gains that individual and separate life that we call nationality" (*A as C,* 373).

Given what happened to Wilde and Parnell, it is easier to see why Joyce showed an almost neurotic fear of returning to Ireland after the printer destroyed the proofs of *Dubliners* in 1912. He said that he had been crucified once by proxy and worried that if he returned he would be crucified in person. The fates of Wilde and Parnell also cast the stylistic difficulties of *Ulysses* and *Finnegans Wake* in a new light: the strangeness of the new is not only an assertion of the value of cosmopolitanism but also, at the same time, a defense against reprisal. To some extent, the defense worked: *Ulysses* was banned, but Joyce himself never went to trial, and *Finnegans Wake,* which is at once the most cosmopolitan and the most indecent book ever written, has never even been attacked. It can be asked to what extent this is a pyrrhic victory, since *Finnegans Wake* is also seldom read, but what is less controversial is the real power and violence of the clash between nationalist and cosmopolitan impulses (a clash that, when intensified, would lead to World War II). Censorship is a tool of the extreme I am calling nationalist, although nationalism should really be defined more broadly as any group's stake in the simplicity and faithfulness of the individual, whether that faith be sexual or political. Forgery, in contrast, represents the extreme to which the internationalists sometimes tend: not a decapitation, limitation, or "castration" of a text, but its inappropriate extension, its propensity to encompass—or appropriate—too much.[24]

From the point of view of a cosmopolitan like Wilde, public opinion is also a tool of those who would legislate conformity; it would have us read truth and novelty as immorality and unintelligibility. As Wilde writes in "The Soul of Man under Socialism,"

> A fresh mode of Beauty is absolutely distasteful to [the public], and whenever it appears they get so angry and bewildered that they always use two stupid expressions—one is that the work of art is grossly unintelligible; the other, that the work of art is grossly immoral. What they mean by these words seems to me to be this. When they say a work is grossly unintelligible, they mean that the artist has said or made a beautiful thing that is new; when they describe a work as grossly immoral, they mean that the artist has said or made a beautiful thing that is true. (*A as C,* 273)

Wilde's position on censorship is that it will outlaw truth and novelty in the name of morality and readability. Joyce, after watching what happened to an Irish politician and an Irish writer in the 1890s, adopted a more internationalist stance. He saw that those who successfully censure censorship are themselves censored, and he used novelty (what the public calls unintelligibility) to disguise truth (what the opposition calls immorality). That was his triumph and his failure.

Flowers of Green: Ireland, Crime, and Youth

Wilde's investment in free thought and his fervent opposition to censorship is admirable to the extent that a clear boundary can be drawn between thought and action. Artistic self-expression, however, as a realization of thought falls somewhere between the two. Wilde's immersion in the world of theater may have made it more difficult for him to keep thought and action apart, since in the theater, action does not have irreversible consequences. Wilde realized that free, creative thought, if translated into action, constitutes crime, since both creativity and crme depend upon a bold transgression of boundaries. And sometimes, his appreciation of art shaded into a fascination with crime, especially when the perpetrator was an artist, like Charles Lamb's friend Thomas Griffiths Wainewright. To change the frame of reference slightly, we can say that at his best, Wilde celebrated the lush verdancy of personal growth, with all of its productive inconsistencies. What Wilde did not always see, however, was how easily an emphasis on one's own creative development can preempt or even terminate the growth of others. The proximity between personal creativity and crime is illustrated for Wilde in the career of Wainewright, the urbane poisoner whom Wilde associates with the color green in "Pen, Pencil and Poison: A Study in Green" (first published in January 1889 and revised for *Intensions*, 1891). Wilde interprets "that curious love of green" in individuals as "the sign of a subtle artistic temperament," although he points out that "in nations [it] is said to denote a laxity, if not a decadence of morals" (*A as C*, 324). In this brief memoir, by painting his prose-portrait of a stylish murderer in shades of green, Wilde not only highlights the interdependence of Wainewright's many roles—as poet, painter, art critic, antiquarian, prose writer, forger, and poisoner—he also advances a theory of greenness as a principle of both productivity and corruption that is revealingly applicable to Wilde himself.

Wainewright was a highly cultivated dandy, famous for his pale, lemon-colored kid gloves, who wrote chatty articles on art for the *London Magazine* under the name Janus Weathercock (in which he refers to his two-faced self as "we"). In one of his articles, he describes himself in the company of Lamb and several other men, walking through Covent Garden after a dinner party, "returning from a high court-plenary of literature and French wines—one might see at a glance that they were famous in puns, poetry, philosophy, and exalted criticism! Briefly, they were the *wits* of London!"[25] After poisoning his uncle, mother-in-law, and sister-in-law for money, elegantly dispensing strychnine from "one of the beautiful rings of which he was so proud, and which served to show off the fine modelling of his delicate ivory hands" (*A as C*, 333), Wainewright was charged with forging his trustees' signatures in order to liquidate his inheritance, and he was transported to Van Diemen's Land (Tasmania) for life, where he developed an addiction to opium. He began his sentence with the hard labor of working on a chain gang and eventually graduated to painting portraits of society women.

Wilde's view of Wainewright is revealingly selective, almost a self-portrait. He presents him, first and foremost, as a refutation of the popular image of the artist as narrowly focused, offering him as a modern example of a Renaissance man, an artist whose nature is whole and complete, who "followed many masters other than art" (*A as C*, 320, 321). Second, he praises Wainewright as someone who (like himself) "tried to revive style as a conscious tradition" (*A as C*, 327). Third, Wilde proposes that we may see in Wainewright "an intense personality being created out of sin," whose story makes the important point that "There is no essential incongruity between crime and culture." Near the end of the essay, Wilde gently faults him for having always lacked "the self-restraint of the true artist" (*A as C*, 338, 339). Perhaps for polemical reasons, Wilde fails to condemn the extremity of Wainewright's narcissism, with its outrageous license for self-indulgence at the expense of others, even at the cost of their lives; as he writes in the *London Magazine*, last, but "not least in our dear love, [are] *we*, myself, Janus!" (Norman, 23). Nor does Wilde comment on the destructiveness of Wainewright's fetish for perfection, which allows him to brush off criticism for murdering his sister-in-law by saying, with finical delicacy, "Yes; it was a dreadful thing to do, but she had very thick ankles" (*A as C*, 337). Finally, Wilde has nothing to say about Wainewright's pathological conviction of his own innocence in the face of abundant evidence of his guilt. Wainewright exulted in an almost Wordsworthian sense of his own self-sufficient simplicity, as he reveals in a discussion of how "blessed Art" could refresh him:

> by [the] pure and high influences [of Art] the noisome mists were purged; my feelings, parched, hot and tarnished, were renovated with a cool fresh bloom, childly, simple, beautiful to the simple-hearted. The writings of Wordsworth did much towards calming the confusing whirl necessarily incident to sudden mutations. I wept over them tears of happiness and gratitude. (Quoted by Norman, 14)

Wainewright constructed his innocence as a "natural" phenomenon (as Wilde wrote, "Like most artificial people he had a great love of nature," *A as C*, 332), and he protested that innocence to the very end, initially pleading not guilty to the charges of forgery, and presenting himself in a 1842 letter to the lieutenant-governor of Van Diemen's Land as an unswerving *"follower of the Ideal"* (Norman, 161).

Wainewright, in some respects like Wilde, constructed himself as many people and at the same time as an innocent nature child. Wilde's deliberately outrageous admiration for Wainewright is symptomatic of his propensity to collapse innocence and guilt in a way that makes psychological sense but not social or judicial sense. But it also reveals much about the contradictions that were magnetized for Wilde by the color green. When associated with Wainewright, green suggests not only the "subtle artistic temperament" and "laxity of morals" that Wilde mentions, but also a love of nature and an intense individualism that seduce him to equate originality and crime. Green is the principle of intellectual fertility and of social infidelity. During Wilde's career, the associations surrounding the color green continued to exfoliate. In 1897, Wilde described green as the color of the underworld—or hell; interestingly, he applied the color to many colonized or subservient groups, including the Irish, young women, male homosexuals, criminals against society, and children. As Wilde is quoted as saying, "Believe me, love the green, love Hell; the colour green and Hell are both made for thieves and artists."[26] Green is the color of resistance to authority and the price paid for such resistance; it denotes any inversion or subversion of established norms. In a subtle way that has gone largely unnoted, Wilde used green as a code through which he expressed his sense of Irishness, which he saw as a celebration of individualism over centralized authority. Wilde also associated green with eroticized asexuality in young men and women and children; green is the color of process not product, and accordingly Wilde links it with unripe fruit and with the flowering (as opposed to the fruiting) stage of growth. Finally, the very innocence of greenness turns it (as in the case of Wainewright) into a poison, such as the absinthe Wilde drank in his later years in Paris. The glory of green—its disdain for and incompatibility with the regulating functions of society—is also its shame; the pastoral ideal, seen from another angle, is Hell. Innocence and youth can become the very type of corruption, as Wilde illustrates most memorably in *The Picture of Dorian Gray.*

The Emerald Isle

Green is also a color associated with Catholic Ireland. Although Wilde, who loved Oxford, lost his Irish accent, and took English society as the subject of his comedies, has typically been read as an Englishman, his whole life, including his deathbed conversion to Catholicism, could be productively reread as an object lesson in what it means to be Irish. George Bernard Shaw was one of the few contemporaries who insisted upon the importance of Wilde's Irishness: "it is not to be forgotten that though by culture Wilde was a citizen of all civilized capitals, he was at root a very Irish Irishman, and as such, a foreigner everywhere but in Ireland" (cited by Hyde, *Oscar Wilde,* 37). What tends to obstruct an appreciation of how deeply his Irishness affected Wilde are the simplistic constructions of what Irishness meant to him, together with a tendency to brush over his much-admired mother's famous participation in the nationalist agitations of 1848.[27]

For Wilde, Ireland was a complex constellation of attitudes and circumstances, both historical and personal. First of all, Ireland—as signified by the color green—connotes a radically antiauthoritarian stance (as Wilde proclaims in "The Soul of Man under Socialism," "all authority is equally bad," *A as C,* 282). The Irish principle of radical self-determination inflects Wilde's view of greenness as connoting an uncompromising, subtle, and subversive individualism that can produce both crime and culture. Related to the view of Ireland as a land of intractable individualism and resistance to authority is the insistence that Ireland is multinational, a country produced and defined by the transgression of national boundaries, speaking a conqueror's language in a way that cleverly violates the boundaries of conventional meaning and usage. Furthermore, Wilde viewed Ireland's colonized status not only in relatively familiar gender terms, as a feminized country, but also in generational terms. His vision of Ireland is not critical—a nation infantilized by long colonization—but loving; he sees it as a country whose beauty is unnaturally preserved in a green and frozen youth. As the Wilde/child rhyme might suggest, Wilde *is* and loves the idea of the child. Wilde's love of youth is also, metaphorically, a love of Ireland, the place of his own youth and that of his much-grieved sister, Isola (another "island" whose youth was simultaneously truncated/preserved, in this case by an early death).

In addition to evoking Wilde's own childhood, Ireland also becomes identified with the mythical land of wish-fulfillment, Tir na n-Og, the Land of the Young that is also the Irish underworld, its heavenly "hell." Greenness in this sense comes to connote escapism, as well as the intuitive realization that heaven and hell are mutually constructing, that desires *produce* fears and vice versa. Finally, youth for Wilde is a state of equality between the sexes because sexual difference has not yet ripened. It is a time/place where he and Isola are virtually interchangeable, since she "hardly knew / she was a woman, / So softly she grew" (see Sherard, 79). Wilde's homosexuality—famously represented by the green carnation—grows naturally out of his love for youthful indeterminacy, and the contemporary term "inversion" comes to denote not only greenness (through the macaronic French pun), but also Ireland's relation to England as a whole. Despite his personal extroversion, Wilde devoted all his sympathies to the invert—to the Irish, whose extreme individualism and particularism inverted the imperialism of the English; to women, as devalued and commodified inversions of a dominant masculinity; to men who inverted the "normative" practice of heterosexuality and who were also historic lovers of youth. Homosexuality represents the love, not of reproduction, but of generation—a younger generation together with a love of youth for its capacity to represent potential growth ("green" derives from a word meaning "grow," *OED*). The poignancy of a love for youth, as Wilde argues in "The Portrait of Mr. W. H.," is that the principle of generation, or change, wars against the beauty of youth, or stasis. In the case of Ireland, the opposite is true: its luxurious verdancy, or capacity for growth, is curtailed by colonial infantilization (producing involuntary arrested development), so that the full, paradoxical meaning of "generation" may be realized only briefly and lives on only in the imagination. As Wilde wrote of Celtic myth and legend in *De Profundis*, "the loveliness of the world is shown through a mist of tears, and the life of a man is no more than the life of a flower" (*CW*, 924).

It is hardly surprising that Wilde's thought is so distinctively Irish in its clever but intractable resistance to social and moral systems of domination, or that it resists the blandishments of simple propaganda. His mother, Jane Francesca Elgee (whose pen name was "Speranza"), was well known as a somewhat intemperate patriot associated with the Young Ireland movement of Thomas Davis, Charles Gavan Duffy, and John Blake Dillon.[28] Speranza began submitting patriotic verse and poetry translations in 1846, as well as letters to the editor under the pseudonym of John Fanshawe Ellis. One of her more effective efforts was a poem on the Famine printed in 1847 called "The Stricken

Land" (reprinted as "The Famine Year"), in which she threatens that the bones of the famine-starved Irish will rise up against their British oppressors:

> But our whitening bones against ye will rise as witnesses
> From the cabins and the ditches, in their charred, uncoffin'd masses,
> For the Angel of the Trumpet will know them as he passes.
> A ghastly, spectral army, before the great God we'll stand,
> And arraign ye as our murderers, the spoilers of our land.[29]

The nationalist fervor of the Young Irelanders reached its zenith in 1848, and in May Speranza published a poem in which she urged the Irish to defy the English tyrant and wreak "manly" vengeance for the wrongs to Ireland. She clearly implies that Ireland has become a weak and feminized country, using her scorn for the feminine to lash her countrymen into resistance: "What! Are there no MEN in your Fatherland / To confront the Tyrant's stormy glare, / With a scorn as deep as the wrongs ye bear?" (from *The Enigma*, quoted in T. White, 98)

Two months later, in July, when the editor of the *Nation*, Charles Gavan Duffy, was in prison for sedition (he was arraigned six times from 1846 to 1849), Speranza published two incendiary articles in his absence, "The Hour of Destiny," and "Jacta Alea Est" ("The Die is Cast"), in which she announced that Ireland was at war with England and urged the Irish to take up arms against the British. The issue of the *Nation* that contained "Jacta Alea Est" was seized by the police, and when Duffy came up for trial, it was mentioned in the indictments, forming part of the Crown's case against him. By Speranza's own account, when her articles were mentioned she stood up in the courtroom and declared, "I, and I alone, am the culprit, if culprit there be" (Ellmann, *OW*, 8).[30]

Wilde's own published statements about Ireland, if less extravagant than his mother's, are invariably critical of English rule. In a review of "Mr. Froude's Blue Book [on Ireland]" (April 1889), Wilde writes that Blue Books on Ireland are interesting because

> They form the record of one of the great tragedies of modern Europe. In them England has written down her indictment against herself, and has given to the world the history of her shame. If in the last century she tried to govern Ireland with an insolence that was intensified by race-hatred and religious prejudice, she has sought to rule her in this century with a stupidity that is aggravated by good intentions. (*A as C*, 136)

In "A Chinese Sage," he sharply criticizes Britain's current Irish policy with a reference to Balfour's "coercion and active misgovernment in Ireland" (*A as C*, 226). It is clear, moreover, that Wilde considered Ireland more broad-minded in artistic judgment than England. When he was interviewed by the press about the imminent censoring of *Salomé*, he replied by reviling England's artistic provincialism and proudly asserting his Irishness: "I will not consent to call myself a citizen of a country which shows such narrowness in its artistic judgment. I am not English. I am Irish—which is quite another thing" (Hyde, *OW*, 140). Wilde intimates that to be Irish is to be intensely imaginative, arguing that "the imagination is the result of heredity. It is simply concentrated race-experience" (*A as C,* 384). Wilde concludes that "the Celt leads in art" (*A as C,* 396).

The Celt, then, is for Wilde the epitome of intense imagination, dynamism, and resistance to centralized authority, all of which figured prominently in his own personality. Wilde half-seriously typed the Irish as clever and the English as stupid, as is clear from the similarity of a quip from *A Woman of No Importance* to one in *An Ideal Husband.* In *An Ideal Husband,* Mrs. Cheveley complains that the English can't talk and the Irish can't listen: "If one could only teach the English how to talk, and the Irish how to listen, society here would be quite civilised" (*CW,* 533). In *A Woman of No Importance,* Mrs. Allonby dismisses the people who do not talk (identified as the English in the other play) as stupid, and those who do not listen (the Irish, according to Mrs. Cheveley) as clever: "[At London dinner parties] The clever people never listen, and the stupid people never talk" (*CW,* 441).

From an Irish perspective, cleverness and even unfaithfulness can be highly individual and artistic expressions of subversive resistance. Wilde identified the cause of Ireland with respect for autonomy, as he made clear when explaining his admiration for Jefferson Davis and articulating his odd identification of the Irish cause with that of the American South:

> The case of the South in the Civil War is to my mind much like Ireland today. [In Ireland] it is not a struggle to see the empire dismembered, but only to see the Irish people free, and Ireland still as a willing and integral part of the British Empire. . . . We in Ireland are fighting for the principle of autonomy against empire, for independence against centralisation, for the principles for which the South fought.[31]

Wilde's stance is invariably antiauthoritarian. He refuses to recognize *any* restrictive principle other than style, and even style, he insists, is both multiple and variable: "properly speaking, there is no such thing as Style; there are merely styles, that is all" (*A as C,* 97). He sets himself vehemently against government—"*The form of government that is most suitable to the artist is no government at all*" (*A as C,* 282)—and against what he calls "the barbarous conception of authority," proclaiming that "all authority is equally bad" (*A as C,* 275, 282). In addition, his disposition is equally hostile to parental authority, the authority of the mother as well as that of the father (see the discussion of *Dorian Gray* later in this chapter); his fervent championing of youth, like his endorsement of individualism and his defense of the unconscious, reveals the extent to which he has taken sides against the exercise of authority, whether familial, social, political, or psychological.

Green Girls and Youth

Wilde recoils not only from explicit and established forms of authority, but also from presumptive authority, from prescriptive "standards" bolstered by unthinking consensus, from the tyranny of convention. His distrust of such authority ranges from contempt for patriarchal dominance—what Deleuze and Guattari later called the "man-standard"—to his famous dislike of moralism, often confused with a disdain for morality. What Wilde dislikes about moralism is its complacency, its reductiveness, and its incompatibility with charitable love. Wilde's subversion of the male, rational, heterosexual, law-abiding citizen takes the form of a resistant preference for irrationality, ignorance, women, children, and, finally, male homosexuals.[32] The greenness he loved took the form of gullibility, especially the gullibility of young women, which served as an antithesis to the complacent authority and sociolegal privilege enjoyed by men. Wilde exulted in the less educated and more sheltered condition of women not because he supported the patriarchal status quo, but because he saw women and children as less contaminated by the carefully schooled tenets of those who stood to profit by the current system (see, for example, the jokes about educating women in *An Ideal Husband*). In *The Importance of Being Earnest*, Miss Prism startles Dr. Chasuble by asserting that "[y]oung women are green" (*CW*, 345). She hastens to explain that she means they are unripe and therefore untrustworthy, but it is precisely such unpredictability—the unpredictability that comes of innocence and gullibility—that Wilde values under the sign of green.

Wilde's subversion of the dominant male order begins with a deliberately shocking affectation of feminine attributes to signify his own "green" unfaithfulness to conventional constructions of masculine identity.[33] During his early aesthetic period, he created the effect of sexual ambiguity through the studied contrast between his physique and his dress. With his striking height of six feet three and his unexpected strength (especially in the early years, at Trinity, at Oxford, and in America), Wilde conveyed the impression of physical masculinity, which he contradicted, transforming himself into a living paradox, through the "feminine" decorativeness of his attire: he wore his hair to his shoulders, donned the famous velvet coat, knee-breeches, and flowing green tie, and sported a large flower (usually a sunflower or lily, later a green carnation) in his buttonhole.[34] Wilde's success in associating himself with women through dress (and his interest in interior decoration) is confirmed by his appointment as editor to the *Lady's World* in 1887 (he changed the title to the *Woman's World*).

Interestingly, a significant number of Wilde's friends and acquaintances attributed his downfall to a possession of feminine qualities that they considered unnatural. Julian Hawthorne described Wilde in his second year at Oxford as having "a sort of horribly feminine air about him" (Ellmann, *OW*, 59). Frank Harris, too, describes Wilde as "curiously feminine" in his "abnormal receptivity of character," his "love of courtesies and dislike of coarse words" (167). Harris clearly construes Wilde's "femininity" as synonymous with weakness; when Wilde refuses to continue his attacks on Whistler after Whistler has won what Harris calls their "second paper war," Harris asks, "Was it magnanimity or weakness or, as I think, a constitutional, a feminine shrinking from struggle and strife" (170). Harris describes Wilde as weak-willed and irresolute in ways that make him seem to Harris debilitatingly "feminine."

The most outrageous condemnation of Wilde, however, mirrors Harris's, yet castigates Wilde not for femininity but for unbridled masculinity. Written by a woman, Countess Anna de Brémont (a protegée of Wilde's mother), *Oscar Wilde and His Mother: A Memoir* (1911) begins with an unconventional, if somewhat mystical *appreciation* of Wilde's identification with both genders and gradually escalates into an attack on Wilde for disrupting the balance between the "male" brain and the "female" soul in his psyche. The fact that Wilde is castigated by men for being too feminine and by women for being too masculine dramatizes the extent to which anyone who attempts to integrate extremes is subject to attack by both sides; however, what is most insidious about de Brémont's diatribe is its scorn of intellectual energy, its insistence on seeing intellectual productivity as the corollary to sexual vice, both of which she decries as "masculine."

De Brémont begins her argument by asserting that genius can always be attributed to a "hybrid state wherein the soul and brain are bound in sexual antithesis":

> The feminine soul in the masculine brain-building creates the genius of man—while the masculine soul in the feminine brain-building creates the genius of woman. Therefore, to the soul in the wrong brain-building is due all that is great in art and wonderful in the world's progress. (De Brémont, 15)

So far, this argument, although strange, is intriguing for its unconventional acceptance of hybrid states, even if it insists on displacing sexual differences onto the more numinous qualities of soul and intellect. Where the argument becomes poisonous is in its attribution of Wilde's fall to the shriveling of the feminine soul and gradual predominance of the "brute force of his powerful masculine brain structure," in league with his masculine body, which in the countess's hackneyed view is always plotting to degrade the soul (86, 69). Although she is quick to appreciate the logic of Wilde's preference for drama, which she calls a "hybrid realm of literature" (112), her argument quickly degenerates into an anti-intellectual diatribe in which she denounces Wilde's "masculine" brain for producing "intellectual monstrosities, . . . unnatural problems born of a perverted literary instinct, abortions of inspiration" (106). She asks, "For what are paradox, epigram and retroversion of thought and expression, but monstrosities of the intellect?" (106). For the countess, Wilde's tendency toward sexual vice is a natural corollary of his unbridled intellect, which makes him "a juggler of words, an acrobat of expressions," and a man "addicted to plagiarism" (110, 111). What she fails to see is that the paradoxes she reviles in the intellectual sphere, and the perversities she decries in Wilde's sexual behavior, are the precise equivalents of the hybridization she so appreciates in the cross-gendering of his identity.[35]

The countess's castigation of Wilde for what she calls the "masculine" cleverness of his writing is misguided, since Wilde's writing is strangely ethical in its agile precision, but it does to some extent replicate Wilde's own tendency to categorize the difference between culture and nature in terms that are loosely gendered. What the countess does not see is that this opposition between culture and nature is defined not only in terms of gender, but also in terms of age, so that culture in his writings is associated with mature men and nature with young women (and with young people in general). What he appreciated in "green," uneducated young women was not intellectual cleverness but naturalness. Wilde is so commonly thought of in his aesthetic pose that his even more pronounced love of nature's greenness has been virtually erased. (See, for example, Gilbert's exposition of the opposite view in "The Decay of Lying.") Characters such as Lord Illingworth, Lord Henry, Lord Darlington, and even Lord Goring are as charming as young women in their unpredictability, but their freshness is limited to ideas and locutions; the daring and mesmerizing talk of such characters allows them to upstage their younger, greener female counterparts, as well as the characters who receive Wilde's strongest endorsement: those who have taken the risk *and paid the price* of following their "natural" instincts and desires in a system that prohibits such self-realization: Mrs. Erlynne, Robert Chiltern, Mrs. Arbuthnot, the Duchess of Padua, Sibyl Vane.

Wilde loved beauty, both natural and cultural, but his highest admiration was reserved for the beauty of nature, which he identified with youth and represented most often as a flower. Art and religion he saw as wonderful because literally *super*natural; he viewed them as products of the iconoclasm and originality characteristic of a higher nature. Wilde's sense of art as supernatural is most clearly and playfully presented in "The Canterville Ghost," where the ghost is described as an actor with a propensity for changing costumes and props. He is also a painter who changes the color of his signature bloodstain by stealing paints from Virginia's palette, and at one point he even paints the stain a bright emerald-green (*CW,* 198). Wilde's conflation of art with religion is apparent when the sinful old actor is saved by the sympathetic love of a child; her higher nature transforms his supernatural art, thereby causing the withered almond tree to burst into sudden blossom (in an echo of Wagner's *Tannhäuser*) (*CW,* 208, 211). Innocence renaturalizes the supernatural, producing a rejuvenation that is expressed through flowering.

Nature's Art: The Child-Flower

> The force that through the green fuse drives the flower
> Drives my green age; that blasts the roots of trees
> Is my destoyer.
> And I am dumb to tell the crooked rose
> My youth is bent by the same wintry fever.
>
> —Dylan Thomas

The idea of flowering provides a metaphorical nexus through which many of the different associations of greenness, nature, and youth pass for Wilde. As they do somewhat differently in Yeats's early poetry, flowers represent the full range of love, from desire to the charity that costs no less than everything, but for Wilde the emphasis always falls on love's blossoming, never its fruit. The beauty of love is not in what it produces, but what it is. In *De Profundis,* Wilde wrote that to him "flowers are part of desire" (*CW*, 955), and throughout his life he famously used his lapel to speak a visual language of flowers. He began his career with the lily (in partial tribute to Lillie Langtry) and the "gaudy leonine sunflower" (*CW*, 821), which was most often identified with Wilde himself. In the early 1890s, however, Wilde began to wear instead a green carnation.[36] He wore one to the opening of *Lady Windermere's Fan* in February of 1892 (along with several of his friends whom he had asked to adorn themselves similarly), and he wore another to the opening of *The Importance of Being Earnest* (Ellmann, *OW*, 365, 430).

There are two separate versions of how Wilde came to sport a green carnation in the early nineties. H. Montgomery Hyde writes that, as Wilde knew, a green carnation was the "distinguishing mark of homosexuals in Paris," and that Wilde was responsible for extending the custom to England (Hyde, *OW*, 187). However, in a letter to the *Pall-Mall Gazette* (1 October 1894) in which Wilde denies having authored that "middle-class and mediocre book" *The Green Carnation*, he takes credit for having "invented that magnificent flower . . . [which is] a work of art" (Ellmann, *OW*, 424–25). When at the opening of *Lady Windermere's Fan* Wilde's friend Graham Robertson asked him what the green carnation meant, Wilde replied, "Nothing whatever, but that is just what nobody will guess" (Ellmann, *OW*, 365). However, the green carnation does mean something: it is a pun on the French *en vert* in "invert"—Havelock Ellis's term for a homosexual—meaning "in green." The word "carnation" already suggests flesh through its derivation from the Latin *carnem;* the flower received its name originally from its pinkish flesh-color. A green carnation suggests a carnation in *vert*, carnal inversion or inversion incarnate; greenness becomes a code for sexual opposition and a preference for youth.[37]

In its last metaphorical incarnation, greenness evokes the same associations as a flower: it is a sign of youth. Wilde's worship of youth is troublingly complex; it is obvious that, on one level, his obsession with youth contributed to the exploitation of lower-class boys—some of them as young as thirteen—for which he was censured in the trials. Wilde seems to have idealized such exploitation by focusing not on the dissimilar levels of agency that make poor boys less free than brilliant and successful middle-aged dramatists, but by consulting instead his personal feelings of tenderness and admiration for "greenness": his interest in ignorance as preferable to learned stupidity (see *De Profundis, CW*, 932); his attraction to the sexual ambiguity associated with prepubescence ("The Portrait of Mr. W. H.," *A as C*, 191). In the trials, Wilde's prosecutors played on the difference in age between himself and Lord Alfred Douglas to insinuate an accusation of pederasty. Ironically, however, Wilde's association with Douglas was not unequal in the sense that Queensberry suggested; despite his boyish appearance, his initials (LAD), and his nickname, "Bosie," which according to Hyde was a contraction of "Boysie" (142), Douglas was not a twelve or thirteen-year-old boy but a sexually active undergraduate already committed to a range of illicit activities when he first met Wilde.

Wilde's infamous love of youth was also, like his hermaphroditic public persona, an appreciation that includes and subsumes his respect for young "green" women. Wilde's fascination with gender ambiguity is unmistakable in "The Portrait of Mr. W. H.," which locates such a fascination in the work of the great playwrights: "Of all the motives of dramatic curiosity used by our great playwrights, there is none more subtle or more fascinating than the ambiguity of the sexes" (*C as A*, 191). Such ambiguity is epitomized by the boy actors who played female roles in Shakespeare's time. The narrator of "The Portrait of Mr. W. H." argues that the reason Shakespeare rails against the passage of time in his sonnets, fashioning a "wild appeal to time to spare the beauty of his [male] friend," is because his friend was a boy actor, whose sexual ambiguity—or beauty—would be erased with maturity (*C as A*, 195).[38]

Wilde's appreciation of the greenness and flowerlike perfection of youth is particularly apparent in his plays and his fairy tales. Three of his plays (*Lady Windermere's Fan*, *A Woman of No Importance*, and, less seriously, *The Importance of Being Earnest*) revolve around the redemptive power of the child, who in all three plays has reached maturity (Lady Windermere, Gerald Arbuthnot, and Jack Worthing). Wilde presents young women, too, as beautifully gullible, and as natural in their inclinations as flowers. In *A Woman of No Importance*, Lord Illingworth tells Mrs. Arbuthnot, whom he had impregnated and abandoned many years before, "no woman ever loved me as you did. Why, you gave yourself to me like a flower, to do anything I liked with" (*CW*, 480). In *An Ideal Husband*, Mabel Chiltern is described in similar terms, but with even more enthusiasm. The stage directions specify that

> *She has all the fragrance and freedom of a flower. There is ripple after ripple of sunlight in her hair, and the little mouth, with its parted lips, is expectant, like the mouth of a child. She has the fascinating tyranny of youth, and the astonishing courage of innocence. To sane people she is not reminiscent of any work of art. But she is really like a Tanagra statuette.* (*CW*, 483)

Dorian describes Sibyl Vane in almost exactly the same way in *The Picture of Dorian Gray:*

> Harry, imagine a girl, hardly seventeen years of age, with a little flower-like face, a small Greek head with plaited coils of dark-brown hair, eyes that were violet wells of passion, lips that were like the petals of a rose. . . . There is something of a child about her. . . . She knows nothing of life. (*CW*, 50–53)

When Dorian spurned Sibyl for spoiling her art because it had become nothing more than a pale shadow of her love, she flung herself at his feet "and lay there like a trampled flower" (*CW*, 76).

Wilde typically conjoins tenderness for youth's brevity and fragility with a passionate insistence on the kind of love that accepts and pays the costs of human imperfection, an imperfection that is universal. People who see each other as perfect, as Basil sees Dorian in *Dorian Gray*, or as the Chilterns see each other in *An Ideal Husband*, are depicted as unintentionally cruel in their refusal to "make sufficient allowances" (*CW*, 511). As Lord Goring remarks, "All I do know is that life cannot be understood without much charity" (*CW*, 511).[39] Wilde most fully endorses characters who have erred and paid for their error;

taking responsibility for one's own natural imperfection is what makes an individual capable of love, as Wilde shows most dramatically through the contrast between Mrs. Arbuthnot and Lord Illingworth in *A Woman of No Importance*.[40]

Wilde's fairy tales also pay tribute to a "flowering" of love for which the lover pays full cost, which they oppose to an artificial finery bought with someone else's labor. In place of Lord Illingworth, the charming gentleman of *A Woman of No Importance* who would enjoy the fruit of Mrs. Arbuthnot's suffering without sharing the responsibility for producing it, is the miller in "The Devoted Friend" (*The Happy Prince and Other Tales*). In the contrast between the miller and his friend, little Hans, Wilde plays out not only the difference between the theory and practice of love, but the concomitant difference between exploitation and personal labor. This difference is highlighted by an implicit pun on flour and flower, which the miller subtly calls attention to when his son suggests that he give little Hans some flour. The miller has just been anticipating the coming of spring, when he expects little Hans to give him a large basket of primroses, but at his son's suggestion he cries,

> What a silly boy you are! . . . if Hans came here, he might ask me to let him have some flour on credit, and that I could not do. Flour is one thing, and friendship is another, and they should not be confused. Why, the words are spelt differently, and mean quite different things. Everybody can see that. (*CW*, 303)

The miller grinds flour, whereas little Hans grows flowers, and in these rhyming ways both men gain a very different livelihood. The miller grinds others, and will not share the fruits of his labor with his friend, whereas little Hans freely offers the flowers he has grown himself to the miller when he could have sold them for food. The miller convinces Hans, with the concurrence of popular opinion, that his own position is morally superior, and he assures him that "At present you have only the practice of friendship. Some day you will have the theory also" (*CW*, 306). To have the theory without the practice is exposed as monstrous, and part of its monstrosity is that little Hans's acts of devotion contribute substantially to the miller's already considerable prosperity, whereas the miller's purely theoretical friendship drains Hans of his livelihood and eventually his life.

"The Young King" (*A House of Pomegranates*) also dramatizes the contrast between adorning oneself at the expense of others and "flowering" through a counterworldly love of nature that becomes supernatural in its luminous integrity. Like little Hans, the young king intuits the high cost of beauty, culture, friendship, and love and determines to bear such costs himself rather than sentimentally or snobbishly deputizing others to bear the costs for him. Although the sixteen-year-old king who was raised as a country shepherd discovers a "strange passion for beauty" (*CW*, 225) when he first comes to the palace, the night before his coronation he has three dreams that show him who has borne the cost of the beauty that will adorn him the next day: the sickly underfed weavers, the black slaves sent to risk their lives diving for pearls, the men who sought for rubies in the jungle and were felled by disease. The next morning he refuses to wear his king's raiment, proclaiming that "on the loom of sorrow, and by the white hands of Pain, has this my robe been woven. There is Blood in the heart of the ruby, and Death in the heart of the pearl" (*CW*, 230). Instead, he dons the leather tunic and sheepskin coat he had worn as a goatherd, carries a shepherd's staff instead of a sceptre, and crowns himself with a spray of briar. His nobles, his people, even the bishop revile him, but he is miraculously vindicated by what is literally a supernatural adornment: the sunbeams weave for him a tissued robe; his dead staff puts forth lilies in place of pearls, and his crown of thorn blossoms with roses redder than rubies. In refusing to wear in joy "what Grief has fashioned" (*CW*, 232), the young king eschews the "sentimentality" of privilege, thereby taking on the aspect of divinity. The supernatural comes to figure the fairest blend of art and nature, one that is absolutely incompatible with pride or condescension.[41]

In "The Selfish Giant," "The Happy Prince," and "The Nightingale and the Rose," Wilde again expresses an appreciation of the love that flowers through selfless passion. "The Selfish Giant" emphasizes the spiritual importance of children, who for Wilde embody not narcissism (a failure to distinguish self from others) but charity (an attempt to overcome the interested differences between self and others), a charity that Wilde identifies both with Christ and with the seasonal renewal of spring. As long as the giant refuses to let the children play in his garden, his castle is dominated by winter, but when he lets the children enter, his garden bursts into bloom and he is kissed by a child we later recognize as Christ. Under the tutelage of a loving child, the giant has learned to discard narcissism and practice charity, for which Christ rewards him.

"The Happy Prince" and "The Nightingale and the Rose" simultaneously demonstrate the beauty and the waste (in worldly terms) of self-sacrifice. In "The Nightingale and the Rose," a student covets a red rose to offer to his beloved. The nightingale takes it upon herself to make him that rose. She sings all night with a thorn in her heart to build a rose out of music and stain it with her heart's blood, and in the morning she is dead. Ironically, her martyrdom is wasted; the student's beloved disdains the rose as not costly enough, and the student casts it out on the street. The dying nightingale's song, which paradoxically makes a rose arise out of her own decline, traces the evolution of love from its birth to its climax as "the Love that is perfected by Death, . . . that dies not in the tomb," whereupon the rose turns crimson to the heart. It is to such a flowering that the fairy tales pay tribute, to a (com)passion that is also suffering.

When Wilde constructs youth as a value, it illustrates the ideal of an almost supernatural balance of extremes: a conjunction of art and nature, male and female, beauty and fairness, joy and compassion, simplicity and complexity, wonder and honesty. Youth, like the flower, epitomizes for Wilde the union of body and soul through the heart. In *De Profundis*, Wilde writes that

> What the artist is always looking for is that mode of existence in which the soul and the body are one and indivisible: in which the outward is expressive of the inward: in which Form reveals. Of such modes of existence there are

not a few: youth and the arts preoccupied with youth may serve as a model for us at one moment. . . . Music, in which all subject is absorbed in expression and cannot be separated from it, is a complex example, and a flower or a child a simple example of what I mean. (*CW,* 919–20)

"The Fisherman and the Soul" (*A House of Pomegranates*) is a more despairing account of the attempt to unify body and soul. The fisherman casts away his soul in order to love a little mermaid, whereupon his soul—because it is detached from the human heart in his body—becomes evil. The soul keeps trying to reenter the heart of the fisherman, but it is only able to do so when the little mermaid dies and the fisherman's heart breaks. The union of mermaid and fisherman, and body and soul, is pronounced unholy by the priest, who declares them as accursed in death as they were in life. However, the priest is unexpectedly humbled when a profusion of strange and odorous white flowers from the lovers' unmarked grave appear on his altar; the flower here, like the child elsewhere, marks the supernatural beauty of body and soul united through the heart.

The fact that the fisherman loves a mermaid, who is by definition incapable of reproductive sexuality, points to one last feature of Wilde's love of children: it is a love of asexuality that betrays a hidden aversion to sexuality itself, a sense of it as sinful, dirty, in need of cleansing or sterilization. The sterility of homosexual love serves as one such method of cleansing; Wilde pursues its time-honored association with Platonic love, which he defines, following the *Symposium,* as "sex in soul" (*A as C,* 184). Over and over again, he tries to dissolve the sexual in the social and spiritual, eulogizing male "friendship" in his eloquent appreciation of the relations between David and Jonathan and the poetry of Michelangelo and Shakespeare. His poems, however, express a conventional Victorian sense that bodily activities are at best shamefully animalistic and at worst lethal.

Wilde's disapproval of physical and especially sexual contact emerges most prominently in poems such as "The Harlot's House" (1885, written 1883), in which lust and death, the physical and the spectral are instantly conflated when the prostitutes are likened to "slim silhouetted skeletons" whose dancing shadows race across the blind of the harlot's house. In "Wasted Days" (1877), an early sonnet about a "fair slim boy" that was later rewritten as "Madonna Mia," its subject transformed into a "lily-girl," Wilde renders the mark of a kiss as a "stain," recording his appreciation of "Pale cheeks wherein no kiss ["love" in "Madonna Mia"] hath left its stain." "The Sphinx" (1894) also equates the sensual, the bestial, the promiscuous, and the lethal. The speaker berates the sphinx:

> Get hence, you loathsome mystery! Hideous animal, get hence!
> You wake in me each bestial sense, you make me what I would not be.
> You make my creed a barren sham, you wake foul dreams of sensual life,
> And Atys with his blood-stained knife [after having emasculated himself for
>   infidelity] is better than the thing I am.

The poems as a whole yield abundant evidence that despite Wilde's propensity to pose as a connoisseur of sinfulness, he idolized innocence. In "Taedium

Vitae," the speaker proclaims that the lowest pastoral abode is better "Than to go back to that hoarse cave of strife / Where my white soul first kissed the mouth of sin" (*CW,* 788).

For Wilde, carnal knowledge was evidence of guilt. Even in a poem like "Charmides," which seems to applaud Charmides's daring as an "overbold adulterer" and "dear profaner of great mysteries" when he violates the temple of Athena, undressing and caressing her image, Wilde stresses the payment exacted for such joyous transgression: Athena drowns Charmides.

In *Teleny,* the erotic novel authored by a group of men that many assume included Wilde,[42] the swiftness with which punishment attends illicit pleasure is even more pronounced. Several episodes conclude with a grotesque *liebestod,* an orgiastic climax punctuated by sudden death: in the brothel, while two whores are stroking each other in erotic fury for the pleasure of their audience, one of them (who is consumptive) breaks a blood vessel and dies as her partner achieves climax: "Thus it happened that the death-rattle of the one mixed itself up with the panting and gurgling of the other" (*Teleny,* 67). Again, after Des Grieux's dalliance with a chambermaid, who with "the slender lithesomeness of a young boy" (87) had seemed somewhat attractive to him, she is surprised by the coachman, who has been waiting in her room in a way that briefly evokes and roughly dispels "The Eve of St. Agnes." He brutally rapes her, whereupon she, "who now knew what the love of men was" (99), jumps to her death from the casement. The third instance in which death grotesquely figures as the wages of pleasure occurs during Briancourt's "symposium," which has turned into a male orgy. A man who had enlisted in the Algerian Spahis, whom Des Grieux describes as "lust incarnate" and "past-master in lewdness" (146), proposes to sodomize himself with a broad flask, overriding his companions' smiling protests that this is "a crime against nature," that "worse than buggery, it would be bottlery" (153). After a climactic experience of pain mingled with intense pleasure, the Spahi emits "a loud scream of pain and terror," and the onlookers realize in horror that "The bottle had broken; the handle and part of it came out, cutting all the edges that pressed against it, the other part remained engulfed within the anus" (155). The Spahi shoots himself shortly thereafter.

The inexorable "truth" that Wilde represents again and again in his works is that sin brings its own punishment, and that sexual activity is sinful. The experience of love, as he presents it, is inextricable from the anguished consciousness of crime, as he shows in "Panthea." The speaker begins by accepting the deadliness of illicit desire, proposing to his auditor, "Nay, let us walk from fire unto fire, / From passionate pain to deadlier delight,— / I am too young to live without desire, / Too young art thou to waste this summer night." He goes on to characterize himself and his beloved as inconsolable:

What balm for us in bruised poppy seed
Who crowd into one finite pulse of time
The joy of infinite love and the fierce pain of infinite crime.
(*CW,* 781)

The only hope in "Panthea" is the hope of a postmortem dissolution into nature, "beast and bird and flower," a pantheistic freedom whereby "We shall inform ourselves / Into all sensuous life" (*CW*, 783), a general greening. Carnal knowledge, for Wilde, *is* crime; even what he considered the higher Platonic love of men for men was stamped as criminal. In the end, the love of green does become a deadly poison, and "crime" emerges as an inevitable result of growth.

Mature Individualism

Although on one level Wilde feared sex, conflating maturity with a criminality that results from growth, on another level he gloried in the capacity of mature, "fallen" individuals to refresh and even modify the world by skillfully agitating it. One carefully chosen image of the privilege Wilde accorded to maturity is the fan Lord Windermere gives his wife when she comes of age in *Lady Windermere's Fan*. The fan's function is partly decorative, but its power to agitate also figures a greater disruptive power, the power to defy social convention while simultaneously fanning the winds of passion: anger, shame, and the reckless desire for change at any cost. When Lady Windermere's fan is found in Lord Darlington's rooms, it would seem to signal her disgrace, but the infamous woman she does not know to be her mother draws the disgrace onto herself by claiming that it was *she* who left the borrowed fan in Lord Darlington's rooms, thereby saving her daughter from scandal. The importance of the fan as an image of potentially self-destructive power is echoed in the name "Windermere," which means fan-mother (*winder* is another word for winnow, or fan, and *mère* is French for mother). But to fan is not only to agitate air; a fan is also a winnow or winder, which can reduce something in volume through the application of movement (as a stream might winnow the rocks in its bed or as breezes may winnow sand). Mrs. Erlynne is also an effective Winder-mère in this less familiar sense of the term, since by claiming the fan she manages to deflate and simplify a situation that has grown quite complex.[43]

Wilde, too, proved himself capable of producing extreme social agitation, but Wilde's most impressive contribution was in the power of his art to winnow modes of thought that society had clumped together. Wilde offers to his readers a vision of comprehensiveness that is realizable only in part at any one moment, but that achieves a kind of wholeness through constant, vertiginous movement, through continuous invention, translation, and self-criticism.[44] Such deft, unceasing verbal movement restlessly violates and redefines stale categories; it destabilizes habitual formulations and stimulates the desire to reinvent language, society, gender, and even dress in fresh and antic ways. Wilde's thought replicates the power of greening, or growth, without evoking the poisonous connotations of sexual corruption. Wilde's verbal and conceptual play is micronational and multinational in its disregard for national borders. Its ethic is to remember at all times the insufficiency of the individual, the inadequacy of a single performance, and the creative (as well as criminal) potential of dissatisfaction. In short, individual morality and social justice cannot be assured by a universally applicable principle, but are instead—like word-play—the results of insightful and self-aware readings of discrete texts, contexts, and subtexts as they inform a wide range of situations.

Where the verdant productivity of Wilde's thought breaks down, and even betrays itself, is when the green of growth becomes a preference for its opposite, arrested development; when his love of beauty and joy prompts him to recoil from and deny the realities of age, ugliness, and sorrow; when his Hellenism eclipses what he will later identify as its countertruth, Christianity. Wilde's addiction to beauty fostered a partial blindness, so that Wilde, ringmaster of paradox, became caught in a self-contradiction that was *not* deliberate: he who insisted on recognizing the partiality of experience became strongly partial to half of it. Wilde confesses this partiality in *De Profundis*, presenting the dark deprivations of prison as a painful righting of the balance.

Although Wilde instinctively and perhaps shamefully recoiled from age and ugliness, the enemy that he fought deliberately and well was stasis, repetition, habit. His famous disdain for the Philistine stems from a conviction that the Philistine is the henchman of society, bent on arresting movement or change: "He is the Philistine who upholds and aids the heavy, cumbrous, blind mechanical forces of Society, and who does not recognise the dynamic force when he meets it either in a man or a movement" (*CW*, 938). "Individualism"—a courage to experiment powered by desire and compassion—is Wilde's prescribed antidote for the deadening effects of habit, the potential for rationalization latent in an overdependence on reason, the merely reflexive or reactive qualities of action, and the oppressively conformist tendencies of society. Again and again Wilde highlights the potentially pernicious effects of unparadoxical logic, which, he suggests, may produce a kind of culturally programmed stupidity. As he writes in *De Profundis*, "The fatal errors of life are not due to man's being unreasonable: an unreasonable moment may be one's finest moment. They are due to man's being logical" (*CW*, 894). Action, Wilde contends, is similarly programmed; in "The Critic as Artist," Gilbert argues that "when man acts he is a puppet" (*A as C*, 361), asserting that "[a]ction . . . is always easy":

> It is a blind thing dependent on external influences, and moved by an impulse of whose nature it is unconscious. It is a thing incomplete in its essence, because limited by accident, and ignorant of its direction, being always at variance with its aim. Its basis is the lack of imagination. It is the last resource of those who know not how to dream. (*A as C*, 359)

Action is blind for the same reason that consciousness is unreal: both are programmed, the former by unconscious compulsions and the latter by the constructs of reason.

Society is the expression of such willful blindness on a larger scale; it also regulates and programs, inhibits imagination and experimentation. Wilde saw society as promoting "sentimentality," a lack of personal responsibility characteristic of those who are regulated. In *De Profundis*, Wilde, with some pain, addresses Douglas as a typical sentimentalist: "For a sentimentalist is simply one who desires to have the luxury of an emotion without paying for it" (*CW*,

946).[45] The individual regulated by society not only tends toward sentimentality (or irresponsibility), but he or she is also predictable, artificial, and interchangeable with others: "Most people are other people. Their thoughts are someone else's opinions, their life a mimicry, their passions a quotation" (*CW*, 926). Wilde had put a similar observation in the mouth of Gilbert in "The Critic as Artist": "it is not our own life that we live, but the lives of the dead" (*A as C*, 383). In "The Decay of Lying," Vivian launches a comparable attack on Life— "poor, probable, uninteresting human life"—as mere imitation, mechanically copying forms of expression from the glorious lies of Art (*A as C*, 305).

In *De Profundis*, Wilde underscores his lifelong hatred of philistinism, arguing that his life had "been a complete protest against it, and from some points of view a complete annihilation of it." Philistinism, like ordinary life, is entropic, tending toward a stasis reinforced by repetitiveness, and Wilde insists in *De Profundis* that "all repetition is anti-spiritual" (*CW*, 929). Art, spirituality, and even crime, as he defines them, seek, by contrast, to promote growth, change, development—what he elsewhere celebrated as a socialist individualism. Part of Wilde's appreciation of Christ in *De Profundis* grows out of the conviction that Christ saw life as "changeful, fluid, active" (*CW*, 931); the artist, too, if imbued with the critical spirit, can give us a heightened sense not only of being, but of *becoming* (*CW*, 384). Art, Wilde contends, is a passion made fluid by emotion (*CW*, 392). Individual artistry provides an alternative to life's slavishness and acts as a "disturbing and disintegrating force. Therein lies its immense value. For what it seeks to disturb is monotony of type, slavery of custom, tyranny of habit, and the reduction of man to the level of a machine" (*A as C*, 272). What Wilde proposed in place of habit and involuntary action was social change—a double resistance to oppression and repression—enhanced by responsible invention: the joyful, imaginative designs that facilitate change and growth.

In "The Soul of Man under Socialism" Wilde endorses a nonauthoritarian socialism as that which would make self-realization—what he calls individualism—accessible to a greater number of people. He proposes eliminating the class system in order to make the flexible boundary-crossings of individualism available to everyone; he advocates a sudden, even revolutionary emancipation of desire through the institution of a nonhierarchical, nonoppressive social system. Like Deleuze and Guattari after him (and like Shelley and Blake before him), he addresses social and psychological constraints in tandem; what he pursues in the name of individualism is an (impossible) degree of self-determination in which the self is free to develop its uniqueness unmarred by external circumstances; it is an imagination of individual potential unlimited by insufficiency or want, an expression that is only conceivable "on the imaginative plane of art" (*A as C*, 262). Wilde's vision of individualism may not be fully attainable or even completely desirable, but as a corrective to overdetermined social and historical constructions of competing and hierarchically organized human categories divided by class, age, race, and creed, it promises greater appreciation of diversity as well as a more widespread experience of the joy of invention and self-realization.

Wilde imagines individualism as resistant not only to authoritarian social governance, but also as decidedly *voluntary*, which means that the individual must be exceptionally attuned to unconscious determinants as well as institutional and economic ones; as Wilde cautions, "It is only in voluntary associations that man is fine" (*CW*, 260). Interestingly, Wilde's insistence on individual choice makes him technically a heretic, since "heretic" comes from a Greek word meaning to choose (*OED*).[46] Choice is only meaningful, though, if the individual remembers the limits of his or her awareness.

If Wilde's vision of individualism could be fully realized, he argues that it would produce a wonderfully diverse and tolerant form of society, one which is based not on competition but on non-consensual cooperation, one which predicates love not on a potentially intrusive identification with others (narcissism) but on an appreciation of the novelty and autonomy of otherness:

> the true personality of man . . . will not be always meddling with others, or asking them to be like itself. It will love them because they will be different. And yet while it will not meddle with others it will help all, as a beautiful thing helps us, by being what it is. The personality of man will be very wonderful. It will be as wonderful as the personality of a child. (*A as C*, 263)

To be an individual is to resist influence, to privilege impulse over everything that would determine or channel it—history, society, language, custom, heredity.[47]

Since Wilde's main complaint against life is that it is slavishly imitative, one of the most important methods he prescribes for realizing individualism is through what he calls "Romantic" or nonrepresentational art, art based on invention rather than imitation or realistic representation ("Romantic art deals with the exception and with the individual," *A as C*, 240). In "The Decay of Lying," he implicitly identifies individualism with what he approvingly refers to as an "Oriental" disdain for realism when he has Vivian argue that "As a method, realism is a complete failure. . . . [The history of the arts in Europe] is the record of the struggle between Orientalism, with its frank rejection of imitation, its love of artistic convention, its dislike to the actual representation of any object in Nature, and our own imitative spirit" (*A as C*, 303). Wilde makes a similar argument in a letter to the editor of the *St. James's Gazette* in defense of *Dorian Gray*, when he responds to the charge that Wilde's characters have no counterpart in life. Wilde concurs: "Quite so. If they existed they would not be worth writing about. The function of the artist is to invent, not to chronicle. There are no such people. If there were I would not write about them. Life by its realism is always spoiling the subject-matter of art. The supreme pleasure in literature is to realise the non-existent" (*A as C*, 240). Representational art, like Basil's portrait of Dorian, promotes narcissism and its opposite, self-hatred—"the rage of Caliban seeing his own face in a glass" (preface to *Dorian Gray*). One after another, Wilde's works aim to shatter the mirror of "realistic" representations, because such representations seem to justify the status quo.[48]

In his writings, Wilde tries to provide a practical, dynamic illustration of a freer and more politically responsible exercise of desire that a reader can approximate through invention, not imitation. The most important feature of Wilde's writing is its flexibility, its capacity to adopt and discard a dizzying variety of positions, positions unified only by Wilde's momentary but fully engaged commitment to them. Like Yeats after him, Wilde wrote all of his works not from the unified and elevated position of the authoritative narrator, thereby producing an internally coherent corpus of works controlled by a distinctive and stable authorial perspective, but with the fractured, often contradictory allegiances of the dramatist. As a result, each of his perspectives is animated by a different spirit, is spoken by a different persona; as Wilde says through Gilbert in "The Critic as Artist," "to arrive at what one really believes, one must speak through lips different from one's own" (A as C, 391). In Wilde's writing, no master narrative arranges and orders the divergent, often conflicting voices; no teleological frame urges a mechanical development and climax. Even his criticism is often framed as a dialogue (see, in particular, "The Portrait of Mr. W. H.," "The Decay of Lying," and "The Critic as Artist"). When, in his dramas, Wilde uses the conventions of plot, the plots are delightfully absurd, exaggerated, or self-consciously melodramatic; Wilde does not employ plot as the narrative equivalent of a fate overshadowing the characters' lives, nor does plot come to signify the oppressive determinism of heredity or history. Instead of representing the forces of restriction, plot is invariably decorative, even frothy.[49]

The freedom to cross boundaries, to choose one's allegiances voluntarily and to change them in a way that expresses a more complex truth and sustains the momentum fueled by difference emerges not only through Wilde's orchestration of the dramatic medium, but also through his presentation of national "identity" as always already adulterated. Wilde described his own nationality as significantly mixed; in a letter to the *Echo de Paris*, Wilde described himself as "French by sympathy, . . . Irish by race," and English by speech: "the English have condemned me to speak the language of Shakespeare" (Hyde, *OW*, 133).[50] Irishness, though, encompasses and promotes these other national allegiances: to be Irish is to be simultaneously micro- and multinational. The logic of this formulation, which Shaw clearly understood and which would later be accepted by Joyce, Beckett, and, to a lesser extent, Yeats, is simply that a colonized status is itself a form of domestic exile; to be Irish under British rule is to be simultaneously native *and* foreign. In addition, the Irish had always historically favored particularization over centralization, ruling themselves regionally by micronational clans rather than through a unified nation-state. It is a culture founded on individualist principles, in which each extended family conceived itself as a separate nation. The Irish pursuit of an individualism that courageously encounters—and has repeatedly assimilated—foreignness is the exact opposite of the patriotic xenophobia so characteristic of much of Europe in the late nineteenth and early twentieth centuries. It is also an attitude that— in theory—promotes openness to sexual difference, which perhaps explains one reason why the Catholic church has had to work so hard to discourage such openness.[51]

If a socialist multinationalism—which happens to coincide with a peculiarly Irish understanding of national identity as incorporating many kinds of foreigness—is one way of promoting precise, revisionary thinking, yet another method is through criticism. Wilde defines criticism as a wide-ranging, eclectic mode of intellectual translation and *performance* that (like multinationalism) aims to refresh our perception of a work of art by remaking it in an alien mode: "the critic is he who exhibits to us a work of art in a form different from that of the work itself, and the employment of a new material is a critical as well as a creative element" ("The Critic as Artist," II, *A as C*, 374). Intellectual criticism is also that which promotes internationalism. Wilde argues that it is only the exercise of intellectual criticism that eradicates prejudice, thereby making us cosmopolitan:

> emotions will not make us cosmopolitan, any more than the greed for gain could do so. It is only by the cultivation of the habit of intellectual criticism that we shall be able to rise superior to race prejudices. . . . Criticism will annihilate race-prejudices, by insisting upon the unity of the human mind in the variety of its forms. (*A as C*, 405)[52]

Criticism, multinationalism, individualism, and even aestheticism are all, in Wilde's view, practices that erode prejudice and promote a more agile, pleasurable, and productive exercise of thought. All of these practices, in their revisionary boundary-crossings, may be defined as exercises of humor—literally, in the sense that humor means "whim" and therefore suggests the active and conscious operation of desire, and also figuratively, since the structure of humor is dependent on the unexpected violation of categories and expectations. Verbal humor, in particular, is cosmopolitan in the sense that it accents the unexpected congruities among apparently incongruous elements. Like joy, it is unstable and transitory, and its function is to liberate the reader or listener momentarily from learned, oppressive habits of mind.

De Profundis: Taming Wilde

In *De Profundis*, Wilde wrote to Lord Alfred Douglas, "Everything about my tragedy has been hideous, mean, repellent, lacking in style. Our very dress makes us grotesques. We are the zanies of sorrow. We are clowns whose hearts are broken" (*CW*, 937). Although the tone of Wilde's revisionary account of his life betrays a raw anguish uncharacteristic of his more public writing, his metaphors for what he and Douglas had, in his view, become—zanies of sorrow, brokenhearted clowns—are characteristic of the paradoxical mode of self-representation he had always adopted. Wilde's defense against the social pressure to construct an artificially coherent, necessarily simplistic but adaptive identity was to present himself as a contradiction, a human oxymoron, an embodied paradox and an avatar of perversity, but he had never before allied himself with *sorrow*. What makes his depiction of himself in *De Profundis* particularly wrenching is that in calling himself a clown he simultaneously relinquishes any claim to class privilege and authoritative control; instead of a dandy, whose very self-presentation is designed as an artistic affront to the widespread conformity of those who consider themselves "natural,"[53] Wilde depicts himself as a zany, a foolishly imitative servant whose power to amuse is inextricably bound to sorrow. This despairing description of his own artistry denies the possibility of autonomy and reduces his own power to that of a broken-hearted, popular entertainer, but it also balances humor and pain with an enhanced understanding of their inevitable interdependence.

Wilde's prison view of the role he had played in society bleakly reflects his feeling that his artistic efforts had proven futile, even laughable, in the light of his disgrace, but it also eloquently expresses a renewed appreciation of the function of sorrow, ugliness, and solitude as the necessary counterpart of joy. Although he had earlier expressed compassion for pain and even ugliness in his writings, most memorably in his tribute to "The Happy Prince," the statue who gave away his gold and jewels to the poor and was consequently pulled down and discarded, Wilde's friends record many instances of his disgust for ugliness in ordinary life. Robert Sherard records that Wilde had a

> sheer horror of physical ugliness, and avoided the society of those who appeared to him ill-favoured. . . . This repulsion was an idiosyncrasy—part and parcel of his artistic temperament. I have heard him refuse to meet people who were ugly, however sympathetic to him, because of the real distress which their appearance caused to him. I have heard him excuse himself on such occasions in accents which left no doubt of his sincerity. "I cannot do it—I really cannot." (55–56)

Sherard quotes Wilde as saying, "Ugliness . . . I consider a kind of malady, and illness and suffering always inspire me with repulsion. A man with a toothache ought, I know, to have my sympathy, for it is a terrible pain. Well, he fills me with nothing but aversion. He is tedious. He is a bore. I cannot stand him. I cannot look at him. I must get away from him" (57).

Wilde's inability to tolerate the sight of ugliness and pain also accounts for his dismissal of Christianity—with its emphasis on suffering—in "The Soul of Man Under Socialism," where he famously recommends a joyful Hellenism as the philosophical inspiration for the future, rather than an agonized and lonely Christianity. In the conclusion to "The Soul of Man under Socialism," Wilde commends Christ's individualism, but argues that *"Christ made no attempt to reconstruct society, and consequently the Individualism that he preached to man could be realised only through pain or in solitude"* (C as A, 286). He argues that the individualism of the future, in contrast, will express itself through joy, proclaiming that the new individualism is the new Hellenism (C as A, 286–87).

In *De Profundis*, Wilde's perspective on suffering has changed; he now sees his earlier preference for joy and dream and his avoidance of sorrow and realism as tragically one-sided. He upbraids himself for having disrupted the balance of extremes by misrepresenting the interdependence of sorrow and joy, realism and fantasy:

> My only mistake was that I confined myself so exclusively to the trees of what seemed to me the sungilt side of the garden, and shunned the other side for its shadow and its gloom. Failure, disgrace, poverty, sorrow, despair, suffering,

tears even, the broken words that come from the lips of pain, remorse that makes one walk in thorns, conscience that condemns, self-abasement that punishes, the misery that puts ashes on its head, the anguish that chooses sackcloth for its raiment and into its own drink puts gall—all these were things of which I was afraid. And as I had determined to know nothing of them, I was forced to taste each one of them in turn, to feed on them, to have for a season, indeed, no other food at all. (*CW,* 922)

By accusing himself of a one-sided preference for joy, Wilde is implicitly indicting himself for an "innocence" that he sees in retrospect as denial.[54] Despite his brilliant insights into the inevitability and productive potential of adulteration, despite his insistence on hybridity and on the vitality produced by violating and reshaping categories, Wilde's ultimate self-criticism was not that he was too dissolute but that he was too pure: in practice, he recognized only half of experience—the more pleasing and innocent half. Ironically, he confirms Mrs. Allonby's whimsical definition of "a bad man" in *A Woman of No Importance* as "the sort of man who admires innocence" (*CW,* 441).

De Profundis shows Wilde reviewing the paradoxical design of his life, and focusing on the departures from that design that made him vulnerable to social reprisal. He isolates four painful failures: not only did he pursue joy in disregard of sorrow—"I thought life was going to be a brilliant comedy" (*CW,* 892)—he also underestimated the power of hate, particularly Douglas's hate for his father, to overcome love. He tells Douglas, "In you Hate was always stronger than Love. Your hatred of your father was of such stature that it entirely outstripped, o'erthrew, and overshadowed your love of me. . . . You did not realise that there is no room for both passions in the same soul" (*CW,* 893). Third, he failed to respect the strength of society's opposition to his own attack on conventional values, a failure for which he was made to pay when he asked the law to protect him against Douglas's father. He writes Douglas, "The one disgraceful, unpardonable, . . . contemptible action of my life was [to appeal] to Society for help against your father . . . once I had put into motion the forces of Society, Society turned on me and said, 'Have you been living all this time in defiance of my laws, and do you now appeal to those laws for protection?'" (*CW,* 938). Finally, like Wagner's Tannhäuser and Joyce's Stephen Dedalus (fashioned in the same tradition), he proved himself unable to keep spirituality and sensuality, control and abandon, in interdependent balance, and instead alternated wildly between the two:

> I let myself be lured into long spells of senseless and sensual ease. . . . I became the spendthrift of my own genius, and to waste an eternal youth gave me a curious joy. Tired of being on the heights I deliberately went to the depths in the search for new sensations. What the paradox was to me in the sphere of thought, perversity became to me in the sphere of passion. . . . I forgot that *every little action of the common day makes or unmakes character,* and that therefore what one has done in the secret chamber one has some day to cry aloud on the housetops. I ceased to be Lord over myself. I was no longer the Captain of my Soul [reference to Henley's "Invictus"], and did not know it. (*CW,* 913, my emphasis)

In short, Wilde castigates himself for not knowing himself and the nature of his social protest thoroughly enough, for not regarding it seriously. Significantly, however, although Wilde deplores the furtiveness of his passionate acts, he does not question either his conventional assumption that thought takes place on the heights and sexuality in the depths, or the vexed issue of the extent to which sexuality is an *act* subject to limitation, and to what extent it is expressive and therefore free.[55]

Père-version and Im-mère-sion: Parental Corruption

Wilde's idealization of childlike purity does not exist in isolation, but instead forms part of a complex generational politics in which child-love serves as a psychic counterbalance to a more or less direct condemnation of parental influence. Wilde's contempt for fathers is conveyed throughout his writing with relative straightforwardness, but his attitude is too dismissive to serve as a revealing critique of the paternal role in educating progeny; for a subtle and nuanced analysis, it is more rewarding to examine Joyce's *A Portrait of the Artist as a Young Man* (which is in several respects a response to *The Picture of Dorian Gray*). Wilde's distrust of fathers is closely bound up with his antiauthoritarian convictions, as is most apparent in his early play, *Vera, or The Nihilists* (1880). The protagonists of the play are a group of Russian nihilists who engage in a simultaneous act of regicide and parricide when they kill the cruel czar, since the czar is "the father of his people" (*CW*, 656) as well as Alexis's father. The nihilists are sworn to destruction, on the grounds that "whatever is, is wrong" (*CW*, 677) (contrast the refrain of *De Profundis*, "Whatever is realised is right"); and they advocate the annihilation of the family, which they condemn "as subversive of true socialistic and communal unity" (*CW*, 675). The connection between regicide and parricide is underscored when Alexis warns his father the czar that "from the sick and labouring womb of this unhappy land some revolution, like a bloody child, may rise up and slay you" (*CW*, 671).[56] Unexpectedly, however, the play builds to the discovery of an anarchic force greater than nihilism: the force of passion. The love between Vera and Alexis (who becomes czar after his father's death) has the power to make them betray every other allegiance; Alexis breaks his nihilist oath and wears his father's crown for love of Vera, and Vera kills herself to save the czar (now Alexis), in violation of *her* sworn duty. The "children" revealingly discover that their love for each other is stronger than their resistance to patriarchal tyranny.

When Vera and Alexis experience love in the wake of rebellion, the sudden conjunction of extremes has the effect of highlighting the ambivalence of the subject in a realizable form. Vera and Alexis are forced to relinquish any illusion they may have had that they are whole or self-consistent, and discover in themselves instead an intoxicating flexibility, a volatile capacity for complex self-realization and betrayal. The dynamic sense of range and motion that they unlock when they realize the ambivalence of the self corresponds to the revolutionary aspect of Wilde's thought, but their imaginative versatility is shadowed by an equally powerful incapacity: they cannot achieve their desire. They are debilitated by the persistence of the very nihilism that also liberated them; they are unable to salvage any viable principle of containment (however provisional) from the wreckage of their hate or from the intensity of their love.

In short, Wilde's ambivalence is both revolutionary (as a minority critique of the status quo) and unresolvable; he is locked in an internally oppositional stance—a paradox—in irremediable oscillation between extremes. Because Wilde refuses to recognize any external, resistant force or principle of containment beyond those of taste and aging, his writings, although dazzling in their wit and brilliance, seem oddly weightless, unbearably light. His epigrams seem to have as much force as Whistler's butterfly; what seems to be missing, as his last play half-seriously concedes, is the name of the father—law—which turns out to be earnestness: can anyone who is not Ernest ever hope to be taken seriously?

Wilde is acutely aware that the political system that prevents the realization of an antic individualism begins in the oedipal family, where ambivalence produces paralysis. Wilde's most overtly oedipal drama is an early revenge tragedy, *The Duchess of Padua*, which is also a rewriting of *Hamlet*. The Hamlet of the play is Guido Ferranti, whom Count Moranzone searches out in order to give him what the ghost of King Hamlet gave his son, an "awful message from the grave" (*CW,* 578), the tale of a father betrayed, "on the public scaffold murdered" (*CW,* 579). Moranzone incites Guido to revenge, and Guido hotly pledges "to forswear / All love of women, and the barren thing / Which men call beauty" (*CW,* 587) until he has revenged the murder in blood. It turns out, however, that Guido falls desperately in love with the wife of the man he has sworn to kill: Beatrice, the Duchess of Padua. Unlike Hamlet, whose conflicted obsession with his filial duties drives Ophelia to madness and suicide, Guido abandons his mission on the grounds that murder would drive out love:

> if bloody murder
> Knock at the Palace gate and is let in,
> Love like a wounded thing creeps out and dies.
> (*CW,* 609)

Beatrice—like Shelley's Beatrice Cenci—takes exactly the opposite position, that murder would be an indubitable *expression* of her love, and she accordingly kills the evil duke, her husband. The tragedy is in the interdependence of the opposite truths embraced by Guido and Beatrice; together, they demonstrate the hopelessness of a binary frame of reference, in which every truth is balanced and negated by an incompatible countertruth, and no solution is possible; Beatrice and Guido will be unable to satisfy their desire *whether or not* the Duke is murdered.

Guido has said that women's love turns men to angels, and the Duchess rejoins that "the love of man / Turns women into martyrs" (*CW,* 613). It is only in a posthumous world that angels and martyrs can be united, and the play moves toward a pyrrhic "union" in death, a double suicide, Guido and Beatrice having exchanged positions. Guido, who had charged Beatrice with murdering love, concludes that she is guiltless—"They do not sin at all / Who sin for love" (*CW,*

613, 645)—and Beatrice, who had presented her act as a selfless sacrifice for love, dies hoping to wipe out, Lady Macbeth-style, the sin she had earlier disavowed:

> Oh, I have been
> Guilty beyond all women, and indeed
> Beyond all women punished. Do you think—
> No, that could not be—Oh, do you think that love
> Can wipe the bloody stain from off my hands,
> Pour balm into my wounds, heal up my hurts,
> And wash my scarlet sins as white as snow?—
> For I have sinned.
> (*CW*, 645).

Wilde's treatment dramatizes the insolubility of love's ambivalent construction as the sum of equal, opposite (and reversible) attributes: purity and crime, renunciation and expression. At the same time, it both asserts and problematizes the "oedipal" move to polarize the two parents as "good" in conflict with "evil." Like Hamlet, Guido has two men in the father position—a "good" father (who is dead) and the evil "father" who killed him. The wife of this new "father" is, by virtue of her marriage to the evil authority figure, a kind of mother, but she, in contrast to her husband, is good—until she calls her goodness into question by murdering him. Guido is "good" in the sense that he gives up his revenge for love, but in so doing he tempts the woman he loves to murder, and everyone dies, unsatisfied and riven by an unresolvable moral ambivalence.

To a large extent, Wilde fell victim to the oedipal temptation to demonize the father and idealize the mother, but in *The Picture of Dorian Gray* he trained his analytical sharpness at the idealized and idealizing mother. When coupled together, Joyce's *A Portrait of the Artist as a Young Man* and *The Picture of Dorian Gray* (from which Joyce drew the first part of his title[57]) expose the complementary parental mechanisms by which children are corrupted, offering critiques that are precise enough to distinguish between specific, harmful exercises of authority and authority in general (which need not be synonymous with corruption). Revealingly, in both cases the child is corrupted not by homosexuality, but by homophobia; not by openness, but by secrecy; not by the real, but by the objectifying force of the ideal.

In *A Portrait of the Artist as a Young Man*, it is the father whose voice coaches Stephen's simultaneous education and corruption, instructing him in homophobia and in misogyny, thereby producing in him the socially acceptable norm of perverse masculine desire, what Jacques Lacan calls *père*-version: "Perversion [*père-version*] being the sole guarantee of [a man's] function as father."[58] *Portrait* shows how a male child is inducted into patriarchy: schooled in homosocial bonding, chastised for expressing such bonds sexually (thereby learning homophobia), and displacing his ideal onto women, seen not as subjects but as displaced objects of desire (what Lacan refers to as "La femme," the universalized woman who does not exist).[59] Joyce identifies the heterosexual father as the driving force behind Stephen's initiation into "normal" heterosexual perverse desire;

like Daedalus, the father thinks he is giving his son wings to escape the labyrinth of sexual despair, but for Stephen, as for Icarus, these wings of "escape" are instead the agents of a disastrous fall: he learns that the pursuit of an ideal precludes interpersonal relationship, that paternal authority is isolated and strangely disembodied.[60] *Portrait* shows Stephen turning from his biological father to the celibate fathers of the Church, to God the Father, and finally to the idea of a disembodied author, without ever being able to experience relation; although he grandly says no to God in the tradition of Lucifer, he has not learned to say no to the phallic function, to experience and accept his own insufficiency and self-division. Only in Leopold Bloom does Joyce develop the model of a father who lacks the self-protective and disabling delusions of omnipotence.

In *The Picture of Dorian Gray*, Wilde explored another model for the operation of perverse desire, one I have labeled "Im-mère-sion" because it is presided over by the mother and because it affects the child in an opposite and yet comparable way: instead of raising the child above the real, it uses repression to situate him below it, to lock him in the cordoned-off room of the mother's unconscious. *Immersion* comes from the Latin *immergere*, "to dip, plunge, sink (into)"; in astronomy, it refers to "the disappearance of a celestial body behind another or in its shadow"; with reference to a title or an estate, to immerge is "to become merged or absorbed in that of a superior, so as no longer to have separate existence" (*OED*). If the father's exercise of desire isolates the child, directing him to transcend the real, the mother's exercise of "immersed" desire denies the child a separate existence, condemning it to live in the shadow cast by her own repression.[61] If the father unconsciously subordinates social intercourse to the principles of magnetism, teaching the child to polarize the sexes in a literal sense, so that unlike poles attract and like poles repel (thereby constructing heterosexuality as compulsory), the mother who idealizes her child and sacrifices her own pleasure in the process subordinates *herself* in a way that ties the child helplessly to her. Like Yeats in "Among School Children," Wilde's target is the "nuns and mothers" who "worship images," and Wilde's reply to those mothers is to expose their unnatural constraint and self-denial, a self-stifling that resembles the unnatural closeting of homosexual desire. Wilde conflates the amorous and maternal tendencies to construct the lover/child as an impossible ideal (or, in Lacanian terms, as the "phallus" that everyone wants but no one can have), showing that the fruit of "im-mère-sion" is not sterile detachment, but corrupt enslavement. Furthermore, by conflating closeted homosexual love with idealizing maternal love, Wilde suggests that such enslavement—im-mère-sion—is the danger that haunts homosexual love, in sharp contrast to heterosexual love, which is haunted by the opposite, mirror intimation that "there is no sexual relation."

A Portrait of the Artist as a Young Man and the Prohibition of Desire

When, in "A Love Letter," Lacan asserts that "[t]he soul is conjured out of what is *hommosexual*, as is perfectly legible from history" (*FS*, 155), he seems to be using his neologism "hommosexual" not to mean homosexual in the usual sense, because he has just said that this conjuring of the soul by men is a sexless process. Instead, the emphasis is on the intertwining of "homme" and "homo" in "hommosexual"; the "normal" attitude of men (*hommes*) toward desire precludes the sexual, and at the same time it is a love of men for men—it is the reflection of a social structure that Eve Sedgwick more clearly identifies as "homosocial."

In *Between Men: English Literature and Male Homosocial Desire*, Sedgwick isolates and questions the asymmetry between what she calls the homosocial-homosexual continuums for men and women. She argues that for women, we see the relationship between female bonding on the one hand, and lesbianism, on the other, as a more or less seamless progression, whereas for men, homophobia produces a radical discontinuity between male homosocial bonds and homosexual intimacy.[62] Homosocial bonding is the basis of patriarchy (as Gayle Rubin and Luce Irigaray have influentially argued), but that bonding is upheld, not by an understanding of its continuity with male homosexuality, but by a violent denial of such kinship, a denial that takes the form of homophobia.[63]

It is well understood by theorists who work on sexual politics that misogyny and homophobia are the twin children of patriarchy, that both women and male homosexuals must be recreated as objects of desire and loathing, respectively, for patriarchy to work. In fact, it is the necessary construction of women as desirable objects and men as forbidden objects that defines the "compulsory heterosexuality" prescribed by patriarchy. The problem, of course, is that under such a system only heterosexual men are granted the status of subjects; moreover, this privileging of male subjectivity ensures a stultifying sameness in sexual and social politics.

I am fully in sympathy with Sedgwick's antihomophobic and feminist inquiry. On the structural level, it is absolutely clear that women and male homosexuals have been (differently) commodified; you could almost say that they have been cast as the fuel and waste products, respectively, of the patriarchal system of social production. But I'd also like to call attention to the ways in which certain practices of women and male homosexuals either effectively resist or else unconsciously replicate the objectifications to which they themselves have been subject. Effective resistance to objectification involves a huge burden of consciousness, a constant vigilance over one's behavior as well as that of others toward one, a refusal to succumb, in theory or in practice, to the seduction of stereotypes. Unconscious replication of oppression, however, tends to be enacted upon the least empowered members of a patriarchal system—children. Joyce's famous illustration of the ease with which disempowerment in adults can be translated into tyranny over children is "Counterparts," but he also exposes the ways in which both mothers and gay men may objectify children. Mothers may objectify their children in one of two ways, by capitalizing on their "use value" (turning them into mere instruments of the mother's own will), or by turning them into ideal love objects. Joyce dramatizes the maternal tendency to turn children into passive instruments of maternal will in "Eveline," "A Boarding House," and "A Mother." Moreover, he explores the tendency of adult men to treat children (both male and female) as sexual objects in "An Encounter." It is interesting, parenthetically, that Joyce has the man in the field respond erotically to *both* the softness of young girls *and* the disobedience of young boys, a disobedience that seems to justify the pleasure of whipping them. The story is carefully constructed around the man's *two* monologues—on girls and boys, respectively—which has the effect of discouraging or complicating any knee-jerk homophobic response. By constructing the story this way, Joyce makes it clear that the focus of his implied critique here is *not* a critique of sexual orientation, but the sexual abuse of children, which includes incest as well as other forms of pedophilia.

Joyce demonstrates that *all* love relationships, gay and straight, are haunted by a tendency toward perversion, defined by Jacques Lacan in the first seminar as desire that "finds its support in the ideal of an inanimate object."[64] Interestingly, although Lacan notes in passing that "the intersubjective relation which subtends perverse desire is only sustained by the annihilation either of the desire of the other, or of the desire of the subject," he is less concerned in this seminar with the deleterious effect of perverse desire on the object of desire than he is with exploring its effect on the *subject*. He argues that the *value* of perversion is that *because* "it can find no way of becoming grounded in any satisfying action" (Seminar I, 221), it allows one to experience human passion more profoundly. The perverse lover is in search of *himself*; therefore his experience of desire opens up a gap within himself within which "all manner of nuances are called forth, rising up in tiers from shame to prestige, from buffoonery to heroism, whereby human desire in its entirety is exposed, in the deepest sense of the term, to the desire of the other" (Seminar I, 221).

Lacan makes it clear that perverse desire ensures "a reciprocal relation of annihilation," because such desire cannot be satisfied by possession of the object—the object is lost through its realization. Moreover, Lacan argues, such a relation also dissolves the being of the *subject:* subject as well as object are eroded by perverse desire.

In perverse desire, then, the object is also an ideal, which is why no lasting satisfaction can be obtained simply by possessing the object. Possession of the object simply displaces the ideal onto some other object. This is important because it helps to explain Stephen's failure to achieve maturity—defined as the ability to achieve intersubjective relation—in *Portrait*. Stephen, as a young man, learns the rules of perverse desire, but never experiences or learns to appreciate his own fractured subjectivity, a subjectivity that may not even be compatible with rigidly defined gender categories at all.[65]

The first two chapters of *Portrait* show Stephen undergoing a socialization process with boys and then girls which initiates him into the world of perverse (insatiable) desire by way of the attitudes that are imposed upon him: the necessity of homosocial bonding, homophobia, and misogyny. Homophobic and misogynistic attitudes are frequently intertwined in *Portrait;* moreover, it is the voice of Stephen's father which is the most authoritative proponent of these attitudes. He is infecting Stephen with his *père*-version. The law of the Father is here, quite literally, to bond with men without sexual intimacy and to objectify women through the desire for sexual intimacy. More precisely, male bonding is accomplished *through* the commodification or fetishization of women.

The first voice in the novel is the voice of the father, telling the child a "fairy tale" story of his origins. The father is the author and narrator of the story; he is not represented within it, which along with his position as first speaker gives him his authority. Those represented within the story, as characters rather than narrators, are Stephen, played by baby tuckoo, and his mother, who appears as the moocow. "Once upon a time and a very good time it was there was a moocow coming down along the road and this moocow that was coming down along the road met a nicens little boy named baby tuckoo . . ." To cast the mother as a moocow—even before she meets baby tuckoo—ranges from the humorous to the appalling, but the child accepts it, charmed perhaps by the rhyming link between the names for mother and child ("moo" and "koo"), and apparently oblivious of the devolution of the mother to a milk-giving animal (a devolution familiar from children's stories).

When Stephen goes to Clongowes, he overhears many sexual innuendoes that he records but fails to understand, many of which are associated not with food (as in the case of the moocow) but with bathrooms or lavatories, which trigger homosexual associations. First, Stephen recalls the fellow who tells Simon Moonan that he is McGlade's suck; Stephen recoils at the ugliness of the sound (11) and remembers the draining of the sink water when his father pulled up the chain in the lavatory of the Wicklow Hotel. There is of course "smugging" in the square, where the boys' waterclosets are located, as well as the square ditch into which Wells has pushed Stephen. Stephen draws attention to the place where the smugging took place by asking, "But why in the square? You went there when you wanted to do something. It was all thick slabs of slate and water trickled all day out of tiny pinholes and there was a queer smell of stale water there" (43).

Stephen's fear of the "warm turfcoloured bogwater" at Clongowes represents a fear of sexuality in part because of the association of male homosexuality with lavatories; but in *Ulysses* Stephen also explicitly associates the water he fears with women. Again, the threat of sexuality from men and women is presented as equivalent.

Even Eileen puzzles Stephen with sexual metaphors when she puts her hand into his pocket where his hand was, says that "pockets [are] funny things to have" (43), and runs away laughing. It is clear from *Stephen Hero*, in which Stephen refers to women as "marsupials," that Joyce associated pockets with female genitals, as would Flann O'Brien after him in *At Swim-Two-Birds*. The sexual threats from men and women are commensurate, although at Clongowes the threat from Eileen is remembered (when Stephen is puzzling over the smugging) rather than immediate.

In the midst of the vague sexual threats represented by the older boys in the square, Stephen is buoyed up by his father's warning: whatever he did, never to peach on a fellow (21). As his father primed him for misogyny by introducing his mother as a moocow, he here uses slang to send Stephen a double message about boys. He legitimates homosocial bonding through the dominant meaning of the phrase—never betray or inform on a fellow. But a now obsolete meaning of "to peach" is also to breathe hard from exertion, to pant; deeply encoded in his father's language is the injunction not to pant on a fellow, not to have sexual feelings for a male friend, not to be what is now called, more generally, a "fruit."[66]

Interestingly, the word "smugging" also carries a meaningful constellation of associations. Smug is a form of snug, which is associated with privacy and snuggling. A snug is also a hard knob, and snugging is a nautical term for the operation of rubbing down a rope to give it a smooth finish (OED). It is apparent how the word came to be associated with male arousal, but the meanings of the word smug are also relevant to an understanding of the sexual politics at work here. Smuggy also means "grimy," "smutty" (it is related to smoggy), an association reinforced by the fact that the smugging takes place in the oozing square (which in turn encourages Stephen to consider the activity "dirty"). But the primary meaning of smugging is to steal, and in fact this is what the boys think at first that Simon Moonan and Tusker Boyle's gang has done—stolen cash from the rectory or wine from the sacristy (40). The connection between homosexuality and stealing serves to point up the commodification of sexual exchange. If homosexual activity is "stealing," then it is logical that Stephen decides in the next chapter to pay to gratify his sexual desires, which he does in his encounter with the female prostitute. What he has been taught is that sexuality, whether homo- or heterosexual, circulates via an economic exchange; the difference is that patriarchal law designates one as unlawful—stealing—and the other as compulsory, which is why Stephen must always be in pursuit of a prostitute or Mercedes, a temptress or a bird-girl. Joyce, however, goes on to associate female sexuality with orality and male homosexuality with elimination, thereby positioning them as opposite but equal extremes in a bodily (oral/anal, or prereproductive) system of production. Chapter 2 ends with the pressure of the prostitute's tongue between Stephen's lips, an emphasis that puts him in the female position. Gender identity, then, like sexual orientation, is fluid. Furthermore, the similarity between heterosexual and homosexual desire, as both have been socially constructed, is underlined by the image of the doll in the prostitute's room, sitting on the easychair with her legs apart (101). This doll recalls Bertie Tallon, dressed as a girl for the Whitsuntide play, of whom a prefect asks, "Is this a beautiful young lady or a doll that you have here, Mrs Tallon?" (74). It turns out to be neither a lady nor a doll, but a painted boy. Once again the expected gender categories have been subverted, and at the same time the undressing of the prostitute has been imagistically linked with the cross-dressing of boys. Both in this context represent an imitation of sexuality, an appearance of sexuality that bears the same relation to lived sexuality that a doll bears to a person.

Stephen, however, doesn't really take the imprint of perverse desire in a way that is satisfactory to his father: his ultimate acceptance by his schoolfellows at Clongowes is too mythic, and his pursuit of female sexuality too literal and fetishized. Both of these relatively exaggerated expressions of homosocial bonding and compulsory heterosexuality threaten by their very excess to expose the principle of objectifying and thereby distancing the sexuality of the other—both male and female—on which they are built.

Stephen learns his lesson somewhat superficially because all his actions and discoveries are overcoded by the voice and fortunes of his father, who serves as a disembodied guide. This role is later taken over by priests, only to take its most congenial form in the ideal of the triumphantly transcendent author (a view of authorship that differs significantly from Joyce's). It is his father's voice, directing Stephen to be a gentleman in all things and never to peach on a fellow, that inspires Stephen's victory at Clongowes, and it is his father's misfortunes that prompt him both to begin writing (he tries to write a poem to Parnell on the back of one of his father's second moiety notices, 70) and to pursue women. As Stephen begins to brood upon Mercedes at the beginning of chapter 2, his meditations are repeatedly interrupted by the realization that his father is in trouble (64): "he became slowly aware that his father had enemies and that some fight was going to take place. He felt too that he was being enlisted for the fight" (66). Later, Stephen is haunted by the hollow-sounding voices of his father and masters urging him to be a gentleman and a good Catholic above all things (83), and he perceives a likeness between his father's mind and that of a smiling well-dressed priest that seems to desecrate the priest's office (84).

The problem with his father's voice, like the desires it authorizes, is that it is disembodied. Stephen's mother, who is not yet disembodied, becomes audible to him only after her death. What this disembodiment seems to mean to Stephen is a lack of full commitment, an incipient if unintentional hypocrisy in which precepts aren't backed up by physical enactments. It is easy to see why Stephen's second father, Bloom, had to be so very physical—to the point that Mulligan sees him as a sexual threat to Stephen: "He is Greeker than the Greeks! Get thee a breechpad!" One implication is that more typical relationships between men—including between fathers and sons—aren't physical enough.

Wilde Im-*mère*-sions of Desire

Initiated into the transcendent sterility of perverse desire by his father in *A Portrait of the Artist as a Young Man,* alienated from the fuel and waste of bodily production, as represented by women and homosexual men, respectively, Stephen only becomes subject to the dangers of im-mère-sion (or "in *mère* son," the son locked in the mother/horse, like Ulysses in Troy) in *Ulysses,* after his mother has died. Perversion unnaturally ages a child; in *Portrait*, Stephen, watching his father and his cronies, thinks, "His mind seemed older than theirs: it shone coldly on their strifes and happiness and regrets like a moon upon a younger earth" (95). Im-mère-sion, in contrast, makes a child younger than he is: in *Ulysses* Stephen is associated with an embryo (an association made explicit in the schema of "The Oxen of the Sun"), and in *The Picture of Dorian Gray* Dorian keeps an appearance of unnatural youthfulness. Perverse desire, authorized by the father, designates the woman as the male fetish; immersion, authorized by the mother, fetishizes the child itself, who in turn looks for his own image as love object (these are two different forms of narcissism). What is corrosive about immersion comes not only from the mother's limiting idealization of the child, but also from the mother's idealization of her own desire, her denial of the sexual overtones of that desire and of the fact that she idealizes the child in order to buttress her own repression, a process that keeps the child tied to her.[67]

In *The Picture of Dorian Gray*, Basil is depicted not only as a man who secretly desires Dorian, but also as his "mother," the creator of his physical image: the portrait that Basil has painted and labeled his masterpiece. Basil's fear of exhibiting the finished portrait betrays the extent to which he has identified it both with himself and with the secret of his desire. When he tells Harry that "every portrait that is painted with feeling is a portrait of the artist, not of the sitter," that "[i]t is not he who is revealed by the painter; it is rather the painter who, on the colored canvas, reveals himself," he betrays the extent to which he has appropriated Dorian, thereby revealing "the secret of [his] soul."[68]

Basil's picture represents the merging of the beautiful self-image Basil desires and Dorian's (real) body; by painting it, he has, at one stroke, repainted himself as he would like to be and frozen Dorian as that which—at a distance—mirrors and supports his own desire.[69] What Basil doesn't know is that only at the level of appearances can Dorian mirror Basil's ideal; by annexing Dorian to his own needs, Basil ensures that Dorian will reflect *all* of him, which means that Dorian must also secretly act out the desires Basil has repudiated and denied. The portrait is what integrates Basil's noble intentions and his subterranean desires, made corrupt through secrecy; just as Basil fears that it will betray the secret of Basil's soul, it will later reveal the secrets of Dorian's. Basil's "secret" is his love for Dorian, a love that dare not speak its name; Dorian's secret is that he is Basil's counterpart and his progeny—Basil and Dorian not only mirror each other's submerged desire, but Basil has also, like Dr. Frankenstein, *produced* Dorian, who, like Frankenstein's creature, is maddened at the monstrosity of his creation out of repressed desire. Basil *refuses* to express his socially unacceptable love for Dorian; Dorian, whose image Basil has literally created, is doomed, in sharp contrast, to realize every impulse that Basil would deny, thereby revealing the corruption implicit in beauty.

What Basil failed to do—what he never even attempted to do—is to try Lord Henry's prescription for living. While Basil is painting Dorian's image, Lord Henry's musical voice advises,

> I believe that if one man were to live his life out fully and completely, were to give form to every feeling, expression to every thought, reality to every dream,—I believe that the world would gain such a fresh impulse of joy that we would forget all the maladies of medievalism, and return to the Hellenic ideal,—to something finer, richer, than the Hellenic ideal, it may be. But the bravest man among us is afraid of himself. The mutilation of the savage has its tragic survival in the self-denial that mars our lives. We are punished for our refusals. Every impulse that we strive to strangle broods in the mind, and poisons us. (*DG*, 185–86)

Dorian tries to do what Henry has suggested, but with disastrous results, since his impulses are not his own. Dorian's libertinism, his sensual self-indulgence, are the *products* of Basil's repression, his obedient goodness, his commitment to sublimation, and his love of secrecy. There is no physical contact between Dorian and Basil; their common—and interdependent—secrets meet only through the mediation of the portrait, hidden away in the room of Dorian's childhood.

What is fascinating about the helpless complicity of Basil and Dorian is that it conflates the sublimation, the idealized closeting of homosexual desire, and the grotesquely repulsive product of such denial with another highly idealized, sublimated relationship ringed round with taboo: the relationship of mother to child. Here, the prohibition against incest serves the same function as the ban on homosexual intercourse: it prompts the mother to idealize and thereby hide or deny the highly erotic and ambivalent nature of the relationship, a repression that sentences the child to take up psychic residence in the cordoned-off room of the mother's unconscious desires, as well as awakening in the child a forbidden desire for the mother, who through repression has made herself unavailable, a mere *representation* or portrait of femaleness. (Incidentally, the overlap between injunctions against homosexuality and those prohibiting incest helps to explain the humorous appropriateness of Joyce's conflation of the two in *Finnegans Wake*, where he describes buggery as "insectuous.")

Dorian Gray, then, is a powerful indictment against the corrupting piousness of compulsory heterosexuality *and* virtuous motherhood. Basil is at once Dorian's would-be lover and his mother, as is even clearer in the 1890 edition of *Dorian Gray* published in *Lippincott's* (which Wilde revised—toned down—in response to the furor over its publication in England, where the publishers had to withdraw it from the newsstands). In the *Lippincott's* version, Wilde clearly implies that Basil and Lord Henry are lovers. In the garden scene, immediately before the two men together produce Dorian's consciousness of himself (Basil producing consciousness of the body through his mirror-portrait, Henry producing consciousness of the mind—generating thought—through words), Wilde relates that "the two young men went out into the garden together, and for a time they did not speak" (176). Wilde suggests that they not only produce Dorian's self-image, but that they also jointly "parent" him in this encounter in the garden before Dorian appears. Wilde again reinforces the identification of Basil with motherhood in another deleted passage, in which the narrator explains that "there was something in Basil's nature that was purely feminine in its tenderness" (230).

The ostensible villain of *Dorian Gray* is Lord Henry; it is he, with his musical voice and magical words, who kindles in Dorian a wild curiosity, who plays the role of the devil in this modern morality tale. He is the snake in the garden, explicitly associated with evil, who inspires Dorian to yearn for immortality, for eternal youth. His temptation, like that of Satan to Eve, is for man to be as God, to eat the forbidden fruit of the knowledge of good and evil, which Dorian accordingly does. Henry *is* irresponsible in his friendship with Dorian; he toys with him, views him with the fascinated detachment of a scientist toward a specimen. But nothing happens to Henry; it is Basil—the "good" mother, the champion of conventional morality propped up by Victorian repression—whom Dorian brutally murders in a fit of uncontrollable loathing. Dorian is seized with an irresistible need to *confront* Basil with the rotten fruit of his idealism; Basil is the only one to whom Dorian ever shows the portrait of himself once it has begun to express the corruption of his soul, and as he invites Basil into the locked room to see the painting, Dorian taunts, "Come: it is your own handiwork" (259). When the picture is revealed, Dorian asks bitterly, "Can't you see your ideal in it?" (122). Dorian's one despairing attempt to make Basil understand his mistake of denying the chiaroscuro of the soul is his insistence that "Each of us has both heaven and hell in him, Basil" (122).[70] Basil doesn't get it; all he sees is that once Dorian was good and now he's bad—he begs Dorian to repent. It is for this Dorian kills him.

Later, Dorian struggles to explain his action by saying to Alan Campbell, "You don't know what he had made me suffer. Whatever my life is, he had more to do with the making or marring of it than poor Harry has had. He may not have intended it, [but] the result was the same" (270). Wilde's account of the moral of *Dorian Gray* reinforces the implication that the original sin was *Basil's*, and that it inhered in Basil's poisonous combination of excessive love with renunciation (this is what idolatry *is*). The moral, according to Wilde, is that "All excess, as well as all renunciation, brings its own punishment" (*A as C*, 240).

One way of articulating the problem of Basil's relationship to Dorian that also defines both the institution of motherhood as it is traditionally defined and repressed homosexual desire is suggested by some lines that Wilde deleted in the manuscript of *Dorian Gray*. Originally, when Basil confesses his idolatry to Lord Henry, Lord Henry protests against the wickedness—and even worse the silliness—of "making yourself the slave of your slave" (180 n.7). What makes motherhood potentially more invidious than even fatherhood, Wilde suggests, is that it is a slave–slave relationship, a state of being dependent on one's dependent. Wilde is one of the few writers I know of to explore the destructiveness, not of master–slave relationships, but of slave–slave relationships. The problem crops up again in *Teleny*, the anonymous erotic novel attributed by some to Wilde and others, that was published in 1893 (two years after *Dorian Gray* appeared in book form). The book tells the story of an all-encompassing, passionate love between a man with Dorian Gray's initials, Des Grieux, and a Hungarian pianist (not a painter) named Teleny. Initially, Des Grieux resists his attraction to Teleny with all his power, and interestingly his resistance is both expressed and unconsciously resolved in a nightmare in which Teleny is not a man but a woman, and the prohibition he breaks is against not sodomy but incest. Des Grieux dreams that Teleny is his sister and that he is discovered having intercourse with this "sister" by his mother. Des Grieux is completely unaware of his anger towards his mother (whose promiscuity he blames not on her but on his father, who had gone mad). Promiscuity, like motherhood, might also be described as an addiction to slave–slave relationships, and Des Grieux defends such relationships to the end. What makes his relationship with Teleny so wonderful, however, once he can allow himself to yield to it, is that theirs is a *reciprocal* and unbelievably fulfilling master–slave relationship, in which each takes turns being master and slave. Unfortunately, what interrupts the bliss of Des Grieux's relationship with

Teleny is, as in his dream, his mother. He surprises Teleny having intercourse with a woman for money to pay his debts, and when she turns around, Des Grieux discovers she is his mother. Because he is so deeply identified with Teleny, Des Grieux experiences this as both betrayal *and* incest, which results in another instance in the novel of death's intrusion in pleasure: Des Grieux tries, unsuccessfully, to drown himself and Teleny succeeds in stabbing *himself.* The mother, here, is both Des Grieux's conscience, which will not let him have his illicit love, and the personification of that illicit desire, which breaks all taboos and, in the process, destroys the self. She is a version of Bella Cohen in *Ulysses:* the mother who is also a whore, who generates an unbearable ambivalence in her son by combining, like Basil, excess love and renunciation. She is the whore who becomes impossibly conflated with the virginal ghost of May Dedalus, whose bridal veil disguises rotting flesh, and who simultaneously asks her son to yield to the sins of the flesh and to repent them.

When read as background to *Portrait* and *Ulysses,* Wilde's novels help to expose Stephen's helpless, angry dependence on the woman who depends on him. He both absorbs a vision of woman as virginal whore and loathes her for accepting that role by agreeing to be pure in a way that casts a shadow of corruption that will haunt her child. Stephen's self-contradiction, his bondage to a disintegrated soul and body that produces "a realism that is bestial, and an ideality that is void" (*DG,* 180), is his mother's legacy. Moreover, one reason Stephen can't stand Mulligan is that Mulligan threatens Stephen's own repression. Not only does he quote Wilde frequently and twit Stephen about the homosexual overtones of Bloom's concern for him, but the intimacy between them also triggers Stephen's own defenses against homosexual desires, repeating his mother's sin of repression in a different key. Finally, Mulligan's callous indifference to Stephen's mother's death threatens to bring Stephen's own anger at her to consciousness, which would confirm his fear that he has killed her by acting out her unconscious desires as well as her conscious ones.

One sobering fact about both Wilde and Joyce is that the artistic framing of their bondage to their mothers failed to contain the problem. Wilde, who indicted mothers for putting their sons on pedestals in *Dorian Gray,* and who again cried out against women's idealizations of men through the character of Sir Robert Chiltern in *An Ideal Husband,* asking, "Why can't you women love us, faults and all? Why do you place us on monstrous pedestals?" (*CW,* 521), replicated the pattern in his relationship with Lord Alfred Douglas, who told him devastatingly, "When you are not on your pedestal you are not interesting" (*De Profundis, CW,* 887). Similarly, Joyce, who represented Stephen's anguished resistance to his mother's ghoulish purity, establishes a relationship with Nora in which, once again, he fans the flame of his lover's innocence with his guilt. And as Wilde explains in *De Profundis,* "It is a very unimaginative nature that only cares for people on their pedestals. A pedestal may be a very unreal thing. A pillory is a terrific reality" (*CW,* 937).

Joyce seems to have seen *Dorian Gray* as Wilde's *Hamlet;* both ghost stories have to do with the way that parental ignorance and denial overdetermine the lives and loves of their children. This may be economically illustrated if we ex-

PARALLEL.

Joe, the **Fat Boy** in Pickwick, startles the **Old Lady**; Oscar, the **Fad** Boy in Lippincott's, startles Mrs. Grundy.

FIGURE 2.1. The *Punch* perspective on the publication of *Dorian Gray* by *Lippincott's*

plore the previous life of something John Eglinton says about Stephen in "Scylla and Charybdis": "He will have it that *Hamlet* is a ghoststory. . . . Like the fat boy in Pickwick he wants to make our flesh creep" (*U*, 9.141–43). When the *Lippincott's* edition of *Dorian Gray* appeared in July 1890, *Punch* published a cartoon caricaturing the event (Fig. 2.1). Oscar is represented not as the *fat* boy but as the "Fad" boy, holding out a copy of *Dorian Gray* to Mrs. Grundy, arbiter of middle-class values. The caption reads, "Oscar Wilde's Wildest and Oscariest work . . . a weird sensational romance." What the Fad boy says as he hands his dangerous book to the middle class is what Stephen is imputedly saying as he proffers his *Hamlet* theory to Lyster, Russell, Best, and Eglinton, "I want to make your flesh creep!" (*AOW*, 208). Such an aim is, in one respect, a valuable antidote to the operations of père-version and im-mère-sion, both of which authorize flows of desire that attempt to transcend or deny the painful and complex orientations of the flesh.

Three

"Horrible Splendour of Desire"

The Will of W. B. Yeats

At the height of his success, Wilde confused his life with his art, acting as if his deeds were free from real consequences. William Butler Yeats began his career with an attitude similar to the one that derailed Wilde's; to the young Yeats, everything was art. Life was simply a responsibility-laden distraction from the richness of an imagination inflamed by natural beauty. If Wilde worshiped youth, innocence, and even criminality, organizing his preferences as a love of green that was rooted in his identity as a homosexual and an Irishman, Yeats idealized passion, women, and a vision of heterosexual bliss uncomplicated by personal experience. Unlike Wilde, who insisted that his flowers be "green" or young, Yeats paid homage to flowers by personifying them to form an eroticized and divine woman who was also Ireland. Under the influence of the pre-Raphaelites and Tennyson, in the 1890s Yeats initially imagined woman as incarnated lily and rose, alternating between purity and passion, but gradually he dropped the lily and developed the rose into an image as capacious and complex in its symbolism as Wilde's verdancy. Eventually, and much less traumatically than Wilde, Yeats achieved a richer understanding of the life he had deprecated in youth. He came to appreciate the intensity generated by the fact that life is terminal and unrepeatable, and he heeded the ethical imperative to respect the uniqueness and unknowability of others, while experiencing a powerful desire to discover an artistic mode of translating between privacies.

Both Wilde and Yeats used their fantasy of living aesthetically to great advantage: by imaginatively projecting themselves into a world free of consequences, governed only by its own, internally generated, laws (what in chapter 1 I called disciplined play), they were able to learn the principles of constant transformation generated by the movements of desire. Wilde discovered the intellectual exhilaration that comes from a constant reformation of ideas, and Yeats experienced the emotional richness attendant upon a perpetual retranslation of images. Yeats, however, had a whole lifetime to adapt the technical skill he had learned in his youth to an art that acknowledged life's poignant limitations and its insistent possibilities.

Interestingly, Yeats—like Shaw—deeply understood Wilde's Irishness, which he associated with the bite and inventiveness of his work, although he had little understanding of the inner conflicts of the man. Nine years younger than Wilde, Yeats portrayed his countryman as an audacious, nonviolent terrorist whose weapons were wit and humor,[1] and whose shield was his inscrutable Irishness, which the British could not penetrate. In his 1891 review of *Lord Arthur Savile's Crime and Other Stories*,[2] Yeats presents Wilde as animated by the "spirit that filled Ireland once with gallant, irresponsible ill-doing." He argues that this mischievous Irish spirit is principally apparent in Wilde's irreverent intellect; in Wilde, the spirit has taken "its right place making merry among the things of the mind, and laughing gaily at our most firm fixed convictions" (*UP* I, 205). For Yeats, Wilde was a cipher whose politics of excess could be decoded only by the Irish; the English, he argues, were incapable of understanding the subversiveness of his verbal and intellectual play. Yeats's Wilde is an Irish Robin Hood of wit, who occupied himself by deftly and almost imperceptibly puncturing the stupidity and self-importance of the British:

> 'Beer, bible, and the seven deadly virtues have made England what she is,' wrote Mr. Wilde once; and a part of the Nemesis that has fallen upon her is a complete inability to understand anything he says. *We* should not find him so unintelligible—for much about him is Irish of the Irish. I see in his life and works an extravagant Celtic crusade against Anglo-Saxon stupidity. 'I labour under a perpetual fear of not being misunderstood,' he wrote, a short time since, and from behind this barrier of misunderstanding he peppers John Bull with his pea-shooter of wit, content to know there are some few who laugh with him. There is scarcely an eminent man in London who has not one of those little peas sticking somewhere about him. (*UP* I, 203–204)

Yeats saw from the outset that Wilde's humor was both a shield and a subversive political practice, played out in the ebullient spirit of Irish resistance to the complacency of British power.

Yeats's appreciation for the exuberance of Wilde's wit underscores a kinship between them that Yeats frames in terms of their common nationality, but which actually extends beyond their colonized status into their subversive practice as writers. Yeats's writing is characterized by a volatile complexity similar to that of Wilde: read as a whole, his corpus has a comparable deftness, a similar command of a dizzying array of internally inconsistent perspectives, an analogous love of peculiarity, and a persistent, precise retranslation of images. The similarities between Wilde and Yeats reside in their restless determination to tease apart prescriptive categories of being, and to replace such static categories with fresh strategies for *becoming*, for encountering the buried and alien possibilities that catalyze change. But the registers in which Wilde and Yeats perform these operations are different, although overlapping: Wilde's humor works primarily in the intellectual register, through a scintillating play of ideas, whereas Yeats's greatest flexibility is demonstrated through a complex interplay of *images*, which evoke a variety of emotional responses.

Yeats's twin arenas are the imagination and the heart, which he anxiously contrasts with Wilde's mastery of wit and intellect. Yeats sees Wilde as a hero, a man of courageous action and strong intellectual integrity,[3] whereas he depicts himself as a fearful and irresolute dreamer, "without industry and without will":

> I was always conscious of something helpless and perhaps even untrustworthy in myself; I could not hold to my opinions among people who would make light of them if I felt for those people any sympathy. I was always accusing myself of disloyalty to some absent friend. I had, it seemed, an incredible timidity. (*Memoirs* 33)[4]

Yeats constructed Wilde not only as a fellow Irishman whose family was loosely linked with Yeats's own,[5] but also as a work of art. He recounts the wonder of his first impression of Wilde, who arrived on the scene "talking in perfect sentences": "I think he seemed to us, baffled as we were by youth, or by infirmity, a triumphant figure, and to some of us a figure from another age, an audacious Italian fifteenth-century figure" (*A*, 87). Wilde was literally and figuratively bigger than life, which made his catastrophic fall all the more shocking and unbelievable.[6]

Unlike many of Wilde's contemporaries, Yeats remembers Wilde not for moral turpitude but for moral fiber, as well as for an intellectual brilliance he identified with "coldness." That Yeats admired such coldness is clear from the determination voiced in "The Fisherman" to write one poem "as cold / And passionate as the dawn." If Wilde's was the note of coldness, Yeats's was the note of passion, and the driving ambition Yeats expresses here is to unite the two in powerful tension. Yeats writes, "I knew the greatest kind of literature is passion. I sought passion, religious passion above all, as the greatest good of life" (*Mem*, 36). What makes Yeats's desire to unite Wilde's coldness with his passion both possible and credible is that although played in different keys, the two attitudes were similar. Wilde's exuberant skepticism toward the social pieties, although different in mood from Yeats's dreamy and sensual poetic meditations, proceeds from a similar determination to *entertain* (and be entertained by) a plethora of possibilities, a stance antithetical to unthinking obedience. For Wilde, nothing was unthinkable, and for Yeats nothing was unbelievable; Yeats maintained a strategic credulity, an openness to all forms of belief, that is ultimately as unsettling and energizing as Wilde's insistence that no limitation should be placed on thought. What is not always apparent, however, is that Wilde's playfulness is serious, and that Yeats's dreaminess is also playful.[7]

Yeats's method of using words and images to resurrect latent possibilities and bring them into a complicated and ever accelerating interplay is, in the larger analysis, a version of Wilde's clever transgression of intellectual boundaries, but it differs from Wilde's subversion in its immediate aim. Wilde is a wickedly funny satirist in irreverent dialogue with the authority of convention; Yeats, in apparent contrast, seems blissfully (even naively) unaware of the bite of social and intellectual prescriptions. If Wilde tends to erode boundaries (and expose their artificiality) by repeatedly transgressing them, Yeats undoes and enlarges categories by carefully selecting and revising romantic images, such as the rose, the wind among the reeds, boughs of trees, wild swans, dancers, a tower, or a winding stair.

In his poetry, Yeats initially aims to construct multivalent, apparently comprehensive symbols by examining them from unexpectedly different perspectives, only to expose, in a subsequent composition, the incompleteness and artificiality not of society's *but of his own* constructions. His symbols work like a Deleuzean rhizome, and the volumes they govern have the temporary stability and momentary comprehensiveness of a Deleuzean plateau. By restlessly revising his own symbols, Yeats unleashes a host of new and unexpected perspectives, all of which are tangentially related to the discarded symbol. Yeats's images *yeast*; they increase in volume and they ferment, becoming part of new imaginative configurations, the "images that yet / Fresh images beget" ("Byzantium"). Because Yeats's images speak to each other across different volumes of his poetry, his work is most meaningful when read as a whole. Although the lyric poem is the unit of composition with which he works, his poems clash, reply to one another, and gradually develop a vision of desire that changes, like mortal life itself.

Yeats's volumes of poetry are at once dramatic—in the sense that the poems express competing perspectives, sometimes told in different voices—and lyrical in their richly varied relations to a single point of reference, the symbolist image, which is itself compounded of several traditions. Not only do the poems *within* a volume illuminate each other, so that one poem lights up another, but the volumes were assembled and revised so as to orchestrate a polyphonic dialogue with one another. The poems, journal entries, stories, folklore, and plays Yeats wrote in a given period were also closely intertwined. Over the course of his career, Yeats engaged in a lifelong "play" of images that, in its restless appetite for new points of view, has the effect of enlarging his capacity to feel and to embody those feelings, so that he rushes into an extraordinarily passionate and engaged old age. Words are the counters that give this play of images its precision, and their capacity to suggest unexpected connections and to be translated into new words (that are both related and different) reflects and exercises the adaptive elasticity of the imagination.

Despite the apparent differences that divide Wilde and Yeats—Wilde's ironic technique versus Yeats's expansive and revisionary one, Wilde's humiliation and early death in contrast to Yeats's success and longevity—both were driven by a restless desire to experiment and a refusal to present any of their constructions as a "truth" that is not also—in the very next moment, given the changes of time and circumstance—a lie. Their attitudes toward Ireland, too, seem at first glance to be diametrically opposed: Wilde lost his brogue at Oxford and was so easily assimilated into polite society that his Irishness was often forgotten, whereas Yeats insisted upon his Irishness to the point that loyal readers tend to forget his Protestant background and his long residence in England.[8] But as we have seen, if Wilde's Irishness was buried, it nevertheless became the "green" ground of many subsequent allegiances. Wilde's nationality is the foundation of his self-definition, which is true for Yeats as well, although it might be more accurate to say that his self-definition evolved in relation to his successive redefinitions of Irishness. Yeats's Ireland, although almost always present in his writing, was not the dominant and static ideal that it might seem to be, since he constructed Ireland in the same way that he constructed any other image—as ultimately incomplete, in need of constant revision. That revision takes place not only through contemplating Irelands of the past, particularly the Ireland of the druids and the Red Branch kings, but also by regarding Ireland through the lens of other national mythologies, especially ancient Greece.

The most significant link between Yeats and Wilde, however, is that their youthful passions were at odds with the dynamism and comprehensiveness of their writings. On one level, both Yeats and Wilde entertained all perspectives with a destabilizing but wildly productive inventiveness, but on a more personal level, that comprehensiveness was—in the 1890s—belied by partial and one-sided passions, Wilde's for art, masculinity and youth, Yeats's for art, femininity, and death. Although Wilde's partiality for "green" youth might seem diametrically opposed to Yeats's taste for passionate death, the differences between them are more a matter of style than substance, since both are fueled by idealism and by a yearning to escape the present. The idealism of Wilde's love of youth is apparent in the nostalgic identification of youth with a lost pastoral, an impossible green world associated both with ancient Greece and with Ireland. Wilde's intellect played brilliantly upon the interdependence of extremes, but his desire was more tragically partial: he loved youth and joy to a self-destructive surfeit.

Yeats is driven by a comparable tendency toward self-contradiction. Although, like Wilde, he strove always for a comprehensive and dynamic vision,[9] in the 1890s and the first years of the new century that vision was threatened by the predictable, even obsessive tenor of Yeats's emotional life and love for Maud Gonne. If Wilde's intransigent skepticism was shadowed by a secret desire for simple faith, Yeats's propensity to believe in everything is haunted by an apocalyptic pessimism, a magnificent or "decadent" despair. Such ambivalence affects not only faith but also passion, so that at the beginning of Yeats's career it is difficult to disentangle his profession of a flaming desire for love from an implicit but equally powerful dread of love. That the "hunt" for love is actually a flight from love is illustrated most memorably through the stories of Red Hanrahan; Hanrahan is the lover driven by a misogyny he denies even as he seeks ideal women who elude him: he both pursues and is pursued by the *sidhe* (pronounced "she"). Hanrahan is the poet hopelessly enamored of an ideal that can be realized only in death; he is a human exemplum of the "horrible splendour of desire." Years later, when the older Yeats interrogates and dismisses him in "The Tower," Yeats is, like Wilde in *De Profundis*, simultaneously confessing and relinquishing his own willful blindness to the flawed but human beauty of the real. The apparent changeability of Hanrahan, who goes where the wind goes, driven by the *sidhe* who are in the wind, is exposed as superficial; because he pays homage to an unchanging image, Hanrahan—despite his itinerancy—renders himself incapable of imaginative change.

In the pages that follow, I trace the evolution of Yeats's representations of desire from the semiautobiographical figure of Hanrahan, who is in full flight from human love, to Crazy Jane, with her implacable resistance to any vision of the divine or the ideal that would deny the tawdry glory of time and change. Between these two very different, wandering lovers lies a trail of symbols in constant metamorphosis—the rose, the wind among the reeds, the tower, the winding stair—that show, through the logic of their successive transformations, how and why Yeats eventually came to embrace the mortality from which he initially fled. With a linguistic playfulness comparable to (if less apparent than) Wilde's, Yeats devised a technique that celebrated the versatility of time and change long before he was willing to accept the full implications of his poetic method. By bracketing Yeats's transformation of symbols with the human characters of Hanrahan and Crazy Jane, I hope to highlight the underlying humanness of Yeats's treatment of the rose and other symbols that tend to seem archaic, esoteric, or clichéd to many readers of his early poetry. Detached from her antecedents in Red Hanrahan and the Rose, Crazy Jane loses the fullness of meaning that comes from her evolution through Yeats's successive poems. As Yeats famously suggested in "The Circus Animals' Desertion," his "masterful images" served as ladders; to understand how and why they were employed, we have to go back to the beginning, "where all the ladders start / In the foul rag and bone shop of the heart."

Hanrahan's Passion: Hunt as Flight

Owen or "Red" Hanrahan significantly embodies the self-contradiction that makes Yeats's early poetry, despite its brilliant virtuosity and rhizomatic play of images, seem unreal. As the figure who represents romantic desire made eloquent by learning and poetic inventiveness, his shortcomings are also those of an entire tradition of poetry and romance to which Yeats at least partly subscribed. As an itinerant poet and hedge schoolmaster, Hanrahan seems to be a character whose experiences are as rich as his imagination is fertile, but in fact he is a figure who—like many of the Irish he sang to—is always driven and dominated not by life but by a static vision: the patriotic, erotic, and poetic eighteenth-century *aisling*.[10] Although in *The Secret Rose* Yeats seems to be celebrating the romantic power of that vision, in the 1905 revision of the Hanrahan stories that he did with the help of Lady Gregory, and especially in his evocation of Hanrahan in "The Tower," Yeats increasingly exposes the predictability and futility of pursuing a shadowy ideal. Hanrahan seems to be a traveling poet, but he dies in the arms of the vision with which his journey began; in an imaginative sense, he never really goes anywhere.[11]

Near the end of his poetic career, Yeats replaces Hanrahan with Crazy Jane as his embodiment of desire. Like Hanrahan, she is itinerant and resistant to authority, but the desire she personifies does not know where it is going, and, unlike Hanrahan (and Wilde), she has not cursed ugliness and old age. Far from setting herself against the changes of mortality, as Hanrahan did, Crazy Jane sees beauty in the most disfiguring changes of the real. In waging passionate argument against the bishop, Jane directs her anger not at the changes of mortality, but at his moralistic insistence on privileging obedience and decorum over the chaotic ferment of reality. In replacing Hanrahan with Jane, Yeats suggests that his early poetic vision was unsatisfactory not because it was "womanish," as he once claimed,[12] but because it was too male—and too limited—in its understanding of what it means to be female.

The character of Hanrahan is based on the eighteenth-century poet Eoghan Ruadh Ó Súilleabháin (c. 1748–84), who specialized in *aisling* (or "vision") poems, in which the poet sees a *spéir-bhean* (or sky woman), a vision of "the spirit of Ireland as a majestic and radiant maiden."[13] Although as Daniel Corkery relates in *The Hidden Ireland, aisling* poems were characteristically political laments over the exile of the Jacobite Pretender (Corkery, 129), Yeats does not use them in this precise political sense;[14] for the stories in *The Secret Rose*, he takes the subject of Hanrahan's vision from an *aisling* poem in which the poet sees not Erin sorrowing for her "true mate" in exile, but Cliodhna (Cleena), the banshee queen of the Munster fairies.[15] (In "Kathleen the Daughter of Hoolihan and Hanrahan the Red," Yeats shows Hanrahan in the more typical stance of an *aisling* poet commiserating with Ireland and her sorrows.) Moreover, one of Ó Súilleabháin's most famous poems, "Ceo Draoíchta" ("Magical Mist"), in which Ó Súilleabháin is comforted by the appearance of a *sidhe*-girl after he has been led through the deep night by "a magic mist,"[16] serves as the inspiration for "The Vision of Hanrahan the Red," in which Hanrahan, too, watches a grey mist, out of which come processions of dead lovers.

Hanrahan's character is defined by two grand renunciations that return to curse him: in pursuit of an impossible and eternal beauty, he idealistically spurns both mortal or fleshly love and old age. In "The Book of the Great Dhoul and Hanrahan the Red," Hanrahan calls up his ideal vision, Cleena of the Wave. She appears to him "like the women of ancient Ireland" (*SR*, 134), but at first he cannot hear her. She then reappears as a version of the Rose; he can see the "embroidered roses that went round and about the edge of her robe" (*SR*, 135; compare *"To Ireland in the Coming Times"*). Finally, Cleena dares to become human out of love for Hanrahan, whom she admires as "fierce and passionate, and good and bad, and not dim and wave-like as are the people of the Shee" (*SR*, 138). When she takes on "the tender substance of mortality," she explains her metamorphosis as an act of compassion, telling him, "I have come to you and taken on mortality that I may share your sorrow" (*SR*, 137). But Hanrahan is incapable of compassion, and therefore of full life. He tells her in anger, "I have had enough of women. I am weary of women. I am weary of life" (*SR*, 137). When he spurns her mortality, saying he preferred her as a woman of the Shee (much as Dorian Gray spurned Sibyl Vane), she condemns him to a life of unquenchable desire for phantoms because of his failure to recognize the miraculous blossoming of the real:

> Owen Hanrahan the Red, you have looked so often upon the dust that when the Rose has blossomed there you think it but a pinch of coloured dust; but

now I lay upon you a curse, and you shall see the Rose everywhere, in the noggin, in woman's eye, in drifting phantoms, and seek to come to it in vain; it shall waken a fire in your heart, and in your feet, and in your hands. A sorrow of all sorrows is upon you, Owen Hanrahan the Red. (*SR*, 139)

After Cleena's curse, Hanrahan seeks the companionship of women but is never able to find rest or fulfillment in such company; he is made unquiet, as he indicates when he puns on his desire to see (and to be) "Maid [made] Quiet": "I never have seen Maid Quiet, / Nodding her russet hood" (*SR*, 145).

Hanrahan spurns mortality not only by rejecting incarnate love, but also by cursing old age in "The Curse of Hanrahan the Red." That curse returns on his own head in "The Death of Hanrahan the Red" when he is attacked by the creatures he had cursed. He grows weak, and Whinny Byrne appears to care for him, a crazy, wrinkled woman with black, broken teeth who shares Hanrahan's denial of mortality, crying, "I am beautiful; I am beautiful . . . I am young" (*SR*, 186). At the end of the story, Yeats suggests, perhaps unintentionally, that the ideal and the real are inseparable, that Hanrahan's attempt to deny the flesh is a foolishly romantic gesture that deflects and reduces life's possible consummations to one eroticized, apocalyptic, and pyrrhic climax at the moment of death. As Hanrahan's death approaches, the white arms of Cleena come out of the "withered earthen arms" of Whinny Byrne and embrace him,[17] and Cleena assures him that he and she will be married in death. Cleena identifies herself not as the transcendent ideal he took her for, but as a symptom of his madness. She tells him that she is of those "who dwell in the minds of the crazy and the diseased and the dying" (*SR*, 196), and she claims him for her own. By conflating Cleena and Whinny Byrne, Yeats shows that Hanrahan's "ideal" inhered in the real, aging, even crazed peasants of his native land, although Hanrahan did not realize it.

Yeats's attitude toward Hanrahan as a poet figure is crucially ambivalent. On the one hand, Hanrahan is a great songmaker, a learned man, and an effective writer of patriotic verse, like Yeats himself. On the other hand, Hanrahan is a romantic failure, comically deluded, burning with an insatiable and meaningless lust, and incapable of intimate compassion or commitment. His transience is poetic, but empty. Yeats is careful to delineate both sides of Hanrahan, but despite his awareness of Hanrahan's inadequacies, Yeats cannot fully dissociate himself from Hanrahan's fatalism, which pervades *The Secret Rose*. With the bitterness of the disappointed idealist, Yeats depicts all his poet-prophets as either impotent (like Hanrahan), castrated (like Aodh), or crucified (like Cumhal).

In *The Secret Rose*, Hanrahan, like Yeats himself, is riven by contradictory impulses. On the one hand, he is at war with mortality and change, pursuing instead a beauty that erases difference and is incompatible with life, but he is also, paradoxically, seduced by the very admixture of extremes that he would escape. Hanrahan, like his creator, is inconsistent; although he pays homage to an ideal of impossible purity (comparable to Wilde's ideal of youth), he also appreciates the beauty of adulteration, as heaven and earth, spirit and body commingle and achieve a momentary balance. Yeats emphasizes Hanrahan's desire for the fullness of comprehension rather than a simple, unreal purity in "The Twisting of the Rope and Hanrahan the Red," when Hanrahan is traveling westward into the Celtic Twilight:

> day by day as he wandered slowly and aimlessly he passed deeper and deeper into that Celtic twilight . . . in which heaven and earth so mingle that each seems to have taken upon itself some shadow of the other's beauty. It filled his soul with a desire for he knew not what, it possessed his body with a thirst for unimagined experiences. (*SR*, 142–43)

As Yeats depicts it here, twilight is both an even-ing of extremes, a moment of balance, and a half-light that allows for a softening or evasion of reality through the erasure of difference. Yeats—like Hanrahan—remained caught in that contradiction for years, but in most accounts of his early work, the romantic vagueness of twilight rubs out its other meaning—a precision of balance. Appropriately, Yeats's twilight period has *two* contradictory meanings, one a celebration of balance and the other a disruption of balance through idealization, a blurring of boundaries. In his Celtic Twilight period, the poet at his best is not one but two people, straddling two worlds: he is male and female, head and body, fool and queen, painter and image, dance and dancer. His subsequent poetry represents repeated attempts to discover a truer balance of extremes, one that does not deny half of reality even in the act of asserting its equality with the other half.

When Yeats rewrote the Hanrahan stories he accented Hanrahan's short-comings as lover and as idealist even more strongly, presenting his strengths and weaknesses as parallel. In "Red Hanrahan" (which replaces "The Book of the Great Dhoul and Hanrahan the Red"), Hanrahan wants to marry his sweetheart, Mary Lavelle, but finds himself instead chasing an illusory destiny, represented by a pack of cards that has been magically transformed into a hare and a pack of hounds. Hanrahan has been dealt not domestic happiness but a hunt in which both the pursuers and the prey are unreal. Hanrahan's hunt leads him to a fairy mound on Slieve Echtge where he is unable to unlock the secrets of the symbolic (and the political power it promises) any more than he was able to access the pleasures of the real by joining Mary Lavelle. Hanrahan is presented with the Irish equivalent of the symbols of the Holy Grail (from which the four suits of cards also derive): a cauldron, stone, spear, and sword. Hanrahan's challenge (which he fails to recognize) is to awaken the sleeping queen (a representation of Ireland) by asking about her four treasures and the pleasure, power, courage, and knowledge they represent. Through a lack of curiosity and a propensity to chase phantoms, Hanrahan fails to respond to the needs of his country, just as he failed to keep faith with his sweetheart earlier.

In "Red Hanrahan," the real (Mary Lavelle) and the ideal (the sleeping fairy queen) are not in conflict, for Hanrahan is equally unsuccessful with both. Yeats accents the futility of Hanrahan's idealism by dramatizing the way that Hanrahan confuses escape with pursuit. Hanrahan thinks he is pursuing his prey, like a pack of hounds, but his phantom hunt is actually a flight—not only from the love of a mortal woman, but also from the kind of courageous and engaged questioning that could awaken his sleeping country.[18] Hanrahan reveals himself as powerless to help anyone, be they mortal or divine.

"It Was the Dream Itself Enchanted Me"

Hanrahan was Yeats's champion of the imagination, and in this respect he embodies not only Yeats's fear of mortal, human love but also his youthful aversion to action. In the edition of Blake that Yeats prepared with Edwin Ellis, the editors hail the power of imagination as "the Saviour, whose symbolic name is Christ."[19] In the preface, Ellis and Yeats argue that conduct only has any importance, or "existence," in so far as it affects imagination (*Blake* I, xii); later they paint imagination as a kind of panacea for the ills of the world, as well as a principle of escape:

> Imagination is eternal—it knows not of death—it has no Western twilight and Northern darkness. We must cast our life, thought after thought, desire after desire, into its world of freedom, and so escape from the warring egotisms of elements and years. (*Blake* I, 273)

Although as Wilde had done in *The Picture of Dorian Gray*, Yeats sometimes demonstrated the commensurability of thought and action,[20] he, like his countryman, clearly preferred the wildness of the inner world over the servility demanded by the outer one.[21] Yeats's suspicion of action is apparent in his reservations about Maud Gonne's activism, but it also appears throughout his youthful writings.[22] In his early poem "The Priest and the Fairy," the priest asserts that action is the source of evil in the world: "the only good is musing mild, / And evil still is action's child" (*The Wanderings of Oisin*, 1892). In an early version of *The Speckled Bird*, the virginal heroine Margaret Leroy quotes her father as saying that "everybody would be idle if they could and that all the evil of the world was done because people did things instead of doing nothing."[23]

The view that alienation from worldly life produces a higher virtue and a sterner beauty was influentially promulgated in Yeats's "Sacred Book": Villiers de l'Isle-Adam's *Axël*.[24] *Axël* is a powerful renunciation of life, "swollen like a brilliant bubble with misery and deceit" (171), that builds to a climactic double suicide in a burial vault. The treacherous, shallow Commander presents himself as a personification of "real life," which Axel challenges and kills (83). The most famous line in the play is Axel's contemptuous denigration of the quotidian—"as for living? our servants will do that for us" (170)—which Yeats significantly chose as the epigraph to *The Secret Rose*. Daily living is little more than serving; for Yeats as for Wilde all freedom is in thought. As Axel exclaims, "I have thought too much to stoop to act!" (170).

In his review of a performance of *Axël* in the *Bookman* (April 1894), Yeats insists that the final love scene among the tombs dramatizes the importance of renouncing the immediate pleasures of life and love, a progressive renunciation that eventually repudiates life itself:

> The marvellous scene prolongs itself from wonder to wonder till in the height of his joyous love Axel remembers that this dream must die in the light of the common world, and pronounces the condemnation of all life, of all pleasure, of all hope. The lovers resolve to die. They drink poison, and so complete the fourfold renunciation—of the cloister, of the active life of the world, of the labouring life of the intellect, of the passionate life of love. The infinite is alone worth attaining, and the infinite is the possession of the dead. Such appears to be the moral. (*UP*, 324)

What Yeats does not accent is that the poison that the lovers drink is stored in a ring that they refer to as their "engagement ring." What they escape by a "marriage" in death is "the sordid and jangled utterance of daily life which has saddened the world" (*UP*, 325). According to Yeats, "death" in this context serves as a metaphor for being dead to the world,[25] and thereby alive to the life of the imagination and poetry, "the only things which are ever permanent" (*UP*, 323).

As critics have noted, it was the shadowy world of dreams—not Maud Gonne—that was the real object of Yeats's early passion. What makes this dreamlike twilight world most appealing is its potential to intensify nature to the point of transcendence. Like Wilde's "green" world, the world of Yeats's dreams is quite literally supernatural: it is based on nature as opposed to society, a nature cleansed of time and change; it is a spiritual realm where "God goes by with white foot-fall"; it is the secret world of mysticism and magic, permeated by the desire to transform the mutable into the eternal; and it is the world of the emotions or "moods," personified by the Tuatha Dé Danaan, the ancient kings, queens, and perhaps even gods, who when defeated by the Milesians were driven underground—into the hillsides—to become seductive and treacherous spirits of place. What Yeats once said of Rossetti is even truer of Yeats himself: "drunken with natural beauty, [he] saw the supernatural beauty, the impossible beauty, in his frenzy."[26]

Yeats's insistence on the superiority of dream to daily life, which he represents as banal and chore-laden, is vividly dramatized in *The Land of Heart's Desire* (1894). In this play Mary, a new bride, is torn between the faery world of "maddening freedom and bewildering light" (*Variorum Plays*, 193) and the world of work and responsibility where she will be defined as a wife and mother. She resents having to choose between the hearth and the heart, yet fearing that she will grow "old and bitter of tongue" under the weight of daily chores, she chooses to join the fairies in the wild, "where kind tongues bring no captivity" (*VPL*, 206). She seems to have chosen nature and art over human contact, saying that she will "marry / The spirits of wood and water" (*VPL*, 203)[27] and dance "until the reeds / And the white waves have danced themselves asleep" (*VPL*, 198), but what she has elected as the epitome of imaginative freedom is that which Axel and Sara also embraced: death.

In *The Shadowy Waters*, Yeats again celebrates the deathlike superiority of dream as more "real" than the world of banal convention that the world calls reality. In both the play and the narrative poem, Yeats adopts the platonic view that the world of dreams *is* the hidden reality, and the so-called real world is in fact insubstantial and unstable. In the play, Forgael, like Mary in *The Land of*

Heart's Desire, elects to abandon the ordinary world in favor of pursuing the un-heard of passion at the end of the world. He does this by capturing Dectora, subduing her with his harp music, and drifting out to sea with her alone, "fol-lowing the birds, awaiting death and what comes after, or some mysterious transformation of the flesh, and embodiment of every lover's dream" (1906 note, *VPL*, 340). The apocalyptic climax comes when Dectora covers her lover with her hair, so that they "will gaze upon this world no longer"; for Forgael, her hair becomes the golden net in which the "Ever-living" hold them and in which they grow immortal (*VPL*, 329, 339). In the play, Forgael's harp (which may, like Aengus's, be strung with his lover's hair[28]) begins to burn, as the shadowy world of mortality gives way to the fiery world which, in a neoplatonic scheme, it darkly mirrors. Like Sara and Axel, Forgael and Dectora spurn what the world calls love in favor of flamboyant self-destruction.

In "Baile and Aillinn" (1903), Yeats once again promotes the passion that consummates itself in death. Aengus, the god of love, tricks the two lovers into mutual suicide so that they may escape the ravages of domesticity, age, and "the savage heart of love" (*VP*, 193). When Baile and Aillinn die, they become swans linked together by a golden chain. The heart of the poem is a lyrical cele-bration of the "wonders" and "undying things" that the lovers come to know in the world beyond, where "They eat / Quiet's wild heart, like daily meat" (*VP*, 196). For the early Yeats, death represents a wildness akin to that of nature, whereas life means captivity. He demonstrates again and again that in his view, the desire to sustain the wildness of passion is incompatible with the mundane responsibility of ordinary life.

Yeats's conviction that a passionate death is preferable to the compromises of domestic life is pressed into the service of nationalism in his powerful and in-fluential play *Cathleen ni Houlihan* (1902). When Cathleen pressures Michael to choose between the careful husbandry of marriage and the glorious immor-tality promised to those who die in the service of Ireland, it is clear that death and immortality constitute the only heroic course of action.[29] Those who would live fully and forever must paradoxically renounce life and human love.

Ironically, then, although Yeats's early poetry is usually classified as love po-etry, it is actually based on a dramatic rejection of love as a mutual exchange compatible with life. In *Axël*, Axel proclaims to Sara that the erosion of time makes him long to kill (and thereby preserve) the thing he loves, a position that Yeats adopted more metaphorically in the 1890s.[30] Axel proclaims,

> I am *he who wills not to love*. . . . My dreams know another light!—Doomed creature, you were the temptress whose magic presence reawakened their old hopes.—From now on, my senses tell me, knowing you are alive would keep me from living! That is why I crave the sight of your lifeless body . . . And—whether or not you understand—I am going to become your executioner so that I may forget you! (*Axël*, 154)

Sara, in turn, threatens to kill Axel by veiling him in her hair, warning him that "Flowers and children have died from [her] shadow" (*Axël*, 155). Yeats, how-ever, marks her as more dangerous than Axel by calling her a "Medusa"; he seems to share Axel's view of her as someone who, instead of turning him to stone, would awaken his sensual desires, tempting him to enter the world of mutability (her first name is "Eve"). As a living woman, she—like the consummation of love she invites—threatens her lover's dream.

Yeats sees romantic desire as a small, petty affair in comparison to the glory of the natural and supernatural worlds, as he shows in "Who Goes with Fergus." This is a classic antilove poem, in which the speaker directs two lovers to lift up their eyes to a nature governed by the imagination, which is larger and full of sharper contrasts than the "fallen" world of personal emotion:

> . . . no more turn aside and brood
> Upon love's bitter mystery;
> For Fergus rules the brazen cars,
> And rules the shadows of the wood,
> And the white breast of the dim sea
> And all dishevelled wandering stars.
> (VP, 126)

Like the narrator of "Who Goes with Fergus," who urges his listeners to "brood on hopes and fear no more," Hanrahan also searches for a quiet maid who personifies his desire to be "made quiet," to be purged of the storms of desire:

> Where has Maid Quiet gone to,
> Nodding her russet hood?
> The winds that awakened the stars
> Are blowing through my blood.
> (VP, 171)[31]

The Quiet Hanrahan desires is at once virginity (she is a maiden) and an absence of consciousness (Quiet is "hooded" and "nodding"); it is the freedom of the unconscious that precedes and (in death) succeeds the tempests of passion.

What is decadent about Yeats's early advocacy of dream is his insistence that the only alternative to daily drudgery is idealized self-sacrifice, an insistence consonant with many contemporary expressions of nationalist and religious fervor. Yeats was similarly reductive in his treatment of women, whom he treated merely as sites for imaginative projection, as if they were in themselves empty, devoid of content. He projected onto women either the emotional state of the men who contemplated them (Maid Quiet, for example, embodies Hanrahan's own tranquil oblivion, which he has recently lost) or the attributes of a dead (and therefore immortal) ideal. If, as Yeats suggests in *The Secret Rose*, "where there is nothing there is God," Woman (as virgin) marks the origin of man's journey towards God by adumbrating God's nothingness. In "The Lilies of the Lord" version of *The Speckled Bird*, Yeats presents his view of virginal women as "blank slates" who represent the pure potential of God and death, the "white pages" on which male artists may learn to inscribe and recognize their desires. John Leroy teaches his son Michael that all things are subject to the Virgin, even God, that she is the beginning and end of all life: "she is beauty, and that beauty is the ancient stillness from which all labouring things, the maker of the world and the saviour of the world and the ministering angels, have come and wither [*sic*] they shall return at the consummation of days" (*Yeats Annual* 7,155–56). Margaret Leroy personifies the Virgin for Michael, initiating his quest for spiritual life; she awakens in him not only "a vague impatience with near and common things, a sense of dim and distant things" (164), but also represents for him the death of shallow mortal passions, which he sees as an intimation of "the passion of God" (165).

In "The Lilies of the Lord," Yeats explores a vision of woman as a particular kind of flower: not the Rose, a national and erotic muse, but the lily, a chaste religious inspiration. "The Lilies of the Lord" defines the inspirational woman as a pure and passive instrument, occupied or possessed not by man or herself but by eternity. Yeats's treatment of the lily-woman reveals the extent to which his early work is not about women at all. The personified female lily is valued not for herself but for the effects she produces in the man who adores her; she's merely a catalyst, a means for her lover to gain for himself a desire and knowledge that she does not and cannot possess if she is to fulfill her function. Michael stipulates that

> [b]ecause he was to desire all things, it was needful that she who awakened his desire should desire nothing, and Deirdre and Grania had a stillness that was like hers[?]. They had endured all things and their beauty had awakened armies before the dawn . . . but they had done nothing, they had planned nothing, they had thought nothing, but eternity had laboured and planned and thought in their dim eyes. (171)

In his early period, the lily-woman marked for Yeats the principle of nothingness, the ancient stillness that represents not only the birth but also the much-desired death of consciousness. Michael specifies that pure lily-women stimulate the imagination, awaken the senses, and transform "all life and nature" into a passion ("Lilies," 170). Moreover, he unambiguously declares that Margaret is an aperture through which his own desires might harmlessly escape; he reflects that her beauty "was not a passionate [?] wonder, as lesser beauty may be, but a gate through which his dreams rushed into an eternal [?] and shadowy stillness" ("Lilies," 170). In short, the Lily is a vacuum that exposes the emptiness and deathly peace of Yeats's ideals.

Michael, like Axel and Red Hanrahan, evades women in all their erotic reality (Margaret is only a child when she visits); all of these characters worry that a woman would be a siren or Medusa who (like life) would try to confine them, whereas what they admire is really the power of their own passion. Michael stresses that

> his love, that did not know that it was love, was not for a woman, who would have bound [?] his soul to definite [?] hopes and dreams, but for that absolute of emotions, as it is in eternity, and which [we] seek and find for a moment in the paintings of the old [and] modern Pre-Raphaelites . . . in the deep colours of sunrise and sundown, in the greatest verse of the great poets, and in the music of birds and of instruments, and which we seek and do not find in the bed of love. (170)

Michael prefers women in the roles of religious icon and objet d'art, so that their sexuality may serve as a mere portal to a safer, unreciprocated passion for eternity.

As the lily, woman signifies the virginal inertness that stimulates a man's imagination to move.[32] As the Rose, however, she is no longer merely a vehicle of the poetic imagination, but instead an embodiment of its capacity for abundance, dynamic change, and a principled balance of opposite extremes. The poetic system that Yeats dedicated to the Rose is complex and dynamic; it traces the movements of desire not as desire is known in the world (after "reason came to set bounds to it," making it a devouring flame), but as it lives in the imagination: "joy seeking its own infinity" (*Blake* I, 248). Yeats's early symbolic system, loosely modeled on Blake's, aims to produce "the sympathetic will or love that makes us travel from mental state to mental state and surround ourselves with their personified images" (*Blake* I, 276). To read Yeats, or Blake, it is necessary "[t]o be able to follow the changes of symbol" (*Blake* I, 370), for the changing symbol performs changes of mood, and such changes of mood constitute the "countless little reflections of our own image" (276) through which we perceive a much more various and constantly modulating world. Yeats's kaleidoscopically changing symbol of the Rose is a model of subversive, dynamic, precise play, one which treats male and female principles not as antagonistic, but as equal and interdependent.

The Rose

Yeats loosely gathered his diverse and vibrant perceptions around multifaceted symbols, symbols that intertwined personal, occult, mythic, literary, Judeo-Christian, and nationalist elements. These symbols were never totalizing, because they were dynamic and unstable, constantly metamorphosing into new images. What it is sometimes difficult to recover from the early poetic volumes, though, is the sharp specificity of the symbolic context, which was typically veiled. Taken at face value, the symbol of the rose is almost a literary cliché, but what lies behind its vaguely romantic referential surface as it metamorphoses into the lakescape of *The Wind Among the Reeds* is an often unexpected and coherent constellation of emotional, literary, religious, occult, and sexual references.

What relates and animates the different perspectives in Yeats's corpus is the fact that their errancies are driven not by socially channeled desires, but by the vibrant and inconsistent currents of outlawed passion. It is essential that Yeats's passion be at odds with the law—whether it is the law that subjects his nation or the rejection that forbids his union with Maud Gonne—because such resistance to desire allows the waywardness of that desire to be felt in all its complexity. The thread through the labyrinth of Yeats's poems is his use of the heart as a metamorphosing and redefined center. The heart takes many forms and is transposed into many keys before that famous moment in "The Circus Animals' Desertion" when the speaker proposes to "lie down where all the ladders start, / In the foul rag-and-bone shop of the heart." In the same poem, the speaker asks how masterful or complete images begin. Yeats's entire poetic corpus is a series of answers to that question: they begin in the refuse of feeling and desire, or, to change the image, at a crossways; in the crucified rose; in a lakescape where the wind stirs the reeds; in a half-ruined tower built around a winding stair. Yeats's poetic corpus is unified by interconnected and dynamically changing *super*-natural images that double as fragments of spiritual and emotional truth; as Yeats says of Blake, "As natural things correspond to intellectual, so intellectual things correspond to emotional" (*Blake* I, 239), and the emotional life is the "poetic genius" that inspires all.

Yeats's first important symbol of the heart is the Rose, which he used to gather together a group of poems from *The Countess Kathleen and Various Legends and Lyrics* (1892) for *Poems* (1895),[33] and also to unify the tales in *The Secret Rose*. The Rose, which stresses the fire of passion, mediating between the divine and the sexual, gives way to an image that emphasizes its watery depths and its production of music and poetry in *The Wind Among the Reeds*. The rood of the earlier cluster turns via verbal proximity into the reed of the 1899 volume, although "rose" is in the reed as well, since the French word for reed is "roseau." The lakescapes of *The Wind Among the Reeds* are anticipated in *The Rose* by such poems as "The Lake Isle of Innisfree"; and poems such as "The Secret Rose" in *The Wind Among the Reeds* refer back to *The Rose*. But images dominating the later volume (1899) are more local and less general than in *The Rose*; the mood is restless and incipiently cataclysmic. The location is Sligo, and the heart is split between the ideal and the real in the persons of Maud Gonne and Olivia Shakespear. The implied view of Ireland shifts, too; Ireland is not only the land dedicated to the love of the dark rose (Rosin Dubh or Dark Rosaleen), but it is also a world haunted by the murmurs of dead voices and threatened by the seductions of the *sidhe*.

The successive shocks of the real, registered in such subsequent volumes as *In the Seven Woods, The Green Helmet, Responsibilities, The Wild Swans at Coole*, and *Michael Robartes and the Dancer*, eventually produce *The Tower* and *The Winding Stair*, which both revisit and revise the earlier emphases of *The Rose* and *The Wind Among the Reeds*. In these later volumes, the violence of history has displaced the imaginative unity of myth, and instead of the love of the heart Yeats explores its destructive and creative *power*. If *The Rose* focused on the female sexual organ, *The Tower* answers with an antiphonal stress on the ruined male phallus; the emphasis on idealized beauty in *The Rose* gives way to an insistence on its opposite and counterpart, physical decrepitude, in the companion volume. The earlier accent on "you" and "youth" is displaced by a corresponding stress on the "I," in whom "age" has produced "rage." The pun emerges as a submerged controlling device that monitors the changing intertextual relations of the poems and volumes as they accrue. *The Winding Stair* is built of verbal echoes of the wind (in "winding") and the air (in "stair"), but the wind/winding of the later volume is a labored ascent, a painful affirmation rather than a Dantesque limbo of insatiable desire (as in *The Wind Among the Reeds*). What Yeats achieves by such precisely tuned transpositions is expansive rather than reductive, because it is shifting and unstable without being incoherent and random; the corpus that results is a richly intercalated tissue of images, emotions, moods, and insights that slowly recomposes the poet, Ireland, and language as constructs that recognize no lasting hierarchy of oppression or dominance.

The images of the Rose, the Rood, and the Rose upon the Rood symbolically weave fragile interconnections among the different poems in the cluster, as well as among the different traditions and contexts that frame the poems. In conjunction with the erotic and eucharistic colors white and red, the Rose serves as a symbolic point of reference that highlights different facets of meaning or association at different moments. The Rose is not only a personification of Ireland as Dark Rosaleen, but it is also the first image of Yeats's poetic method, which aims to produce a whorl of unfolding associations from a passionate and fiery center. The symbolist meanings that emanate from the image of the Rose as the volume unfolds are remarkably various, designed to span the usually unspeakable distance between the sexual and the divine. The Rose is a female muse, the personification of Ireland and of poetry, an idealized vision of a real woman (Maud Gonne, the Virgin Mary), a shadow of Dante's image of God in the *Paradiso*, the sun (fire), the heart, the blood, and a representation of a woman's genitals. As the Rose upon the Rood of time she is Christ on the cross (who also a-*rose*), the Celtic cross, the heart in the body, an image of the violent, even apocalyptic conjunction of male and female principles, both spiritual and sexual (the rose female, the cross male), the Holy Grail, and a Blakean image of eternity in love with the productions of time. The Rose is alternately flushed with passion and white from a brush with the Godhead. The symbol of the Rood, although less prominent than the Rose, evokes meanings antithetical to hers. If the Rose suggests eternity and resurrection, the Rood recalls time and mortality; if the Rose is love, the Rood is suffering; if the Rose is poetry, the Rood is the poet; when the Rose is the heart, the Rood becomes the body that flowers at its heart, where the vertical and horizontal lines meet and where rhythm and life begin. The Rood is also a representation of "The Two Trees," the tree of life and the tree of knowledge. Finally, the two symbols together are both Christian and Rosicrucian in their reinterpretation of the mysteries of the Cabala.

The Rose is most obviously an image of love ("rose" is an anagram of "eros"), embodied as a woman and sometimes taking the synecdochic forms of her (red) lips and her lover's (red) heart.[34] At the most general level, then, the Rose is love, a meaning enhanced by the fact that it is the flower associated with both the Virgin Mary and with Venus. In one of the versions of the myth of Adonis discussed by Sir James Frazer in *The Golden Bough*, the rose is reddened by the blood of Venus when she treads on a white rose bush while hurrying toward the mortally wounded Adonis: as his blood was said to have stained the anemone scarlet, "the cruel thorns tore her tender flesh, and her sacred blood dyed the white roses for ever red" (347).[35] In Irish mythology, Dermot is the equivalent of Adonis, and Grania is a version of Venus.[36]

Yeats's Rose is not only sexual but also mythic in her power to inspire and transform. As an image of femaleness, the Rose is graphically and botanically sexual, a transplanted version of Blake's "The Sick Rose" (which Yeats used as the epigraph for *The Land of Heart's Desire*), its "bed of crimson joy" infected by "the invisible worm that flies in the night," a phallic force that in its new setting is also English in its lethal and invasive power.

> O Rose, thou art sick.
> The invisible worm
> That flies in the night
> In the howling storm
>
> Has found out thy bed
> Of crimson joy,
> And his dark secret love
> Does thy life destroy.

Although Yeats's Ireland is sick, his Rose—unlike Blake's—is not; she is redemptive: sexually, spiritually, and prophetically. It bears repeating that Yeats had an aversion to the physical organs of sexuality only to the extent that he insisted upon idealizing them. Instead of denying or erasing physical sexuality altogether, he aimed through the rose to integrate an idealized image of female sexuality with divinity.[37] As Yeats explains in his 1895 essay "The Moods," the instinct of the artist "teaches him to discover immortal moods in mortal desires, an undecaying hope in our trivial ambitions, a divine love in sexual passion" (*E & I*, 195).

Yeats's way of evoking the sexuality of the Rose in the poems themselves is more delicate, euphemistic; the rose has been displaced upward onto facial lips, as in "The Rose of the World," in which the poet encapsulates the beauty and sorrow of the rose through the synecdoche of "these red lips." The image is more unmistakably apparent in the brilliant 1925 version of "The Sorrow of Love," in which Yeats famously puns on the verb *arose* as a noun, *a rose*. The earlier version, in print from 1892 to 1924, addresses the girl who personifies sorrow directly: "And then you came with those red mournful lips, / And with you came the whole of the world's tears" (*VP*, 120). In the 1925 version, Yeats changes line 5 to pun on "arose," repeating the word at the beginning of line 9:

> A girl arose that had red mournful lips
> And seemed the greatness of the world in tears,
>
> . . . .
> Arose, and on the instant clamorous eaves,
> A climbing moon upon an empty sky,
> And all that lamentation of the leaves,
> Could but compose man's image and his cry.

The arising of the girl who is the *rosa* or *anima mundi*, the counterpart of Helen of Troy, not only brings sorrow to the world but also dissolves the distance between the smallness of man and the brilliance, harmony, and vastness of nature; she humanizes nature, transforming it into a magnified expression of human grief, but she also both resurrects and consoles humanity, which had been "blotted out" by the sights and sounds of nature. After she arose, nature "Could but compose man's image and his cry."

"The Sorrow of Love" suggests that, although emphatically female, the Rose is also a version of Christ, who was traditionally associated with the rose by virtue of the thorns that crowned him before he rose from the dead.[38] The association between the Rose and Christ is supplemented by a parallel and contrast from Greek and Irish myth: the Rose is also Helen of Troy and Deirdre of the Sorrows. What is most arresting about this juxtaposition is Yeats's insistence on balance—not only a balance between religion and myth, but also between male and female catalysts, between Christ's suffering in his own person for others, and the suffering of others for Helen/Deirdre. By juxtaposing Christ and Helen/Deirdre, he equates their significance even while registering their structural oppositions, much as in *The Tower* he will juxtapose the Virgin Mary and Leda (mother of Helen), and as he here puts the Rose on an equal footing with God. If God is the principle of "truth's consuming ecstasy," the Rose is the emblem of the mortal and eternal beauty of the world—"the greatness of the world in tears, / Doomed like Odysseus and the laboring ships / And proud as Priam murdered with his peers." The Rose is not only Christ and the Virgin, she is also God, in the tradition of Dante's vision of heaven as a celestial rose of light.[39] Moreover, in "The Rose of the World," Yeats represents her as the Beauty that is coeval with God. He insists that the first principle is not a single Godhead, but a couple, with the Rose in the role of God's beloved, wandering female consort. Before God created the angels, he lived with the Rose, weary and kind; "He made the world to be a grassy road / Before her wandering feet" (*VP*, 112).

Yeats positions the Rose in relation to religion and myth not only in "The Sorrow of Love" and in "The Rose of the World," but also in the poems that begin and end *The Rose*. The volume opens with "To the Rose upon the Rood of Time," which links the Rose with Christ not only by the allusion to the cross but also by the implied connection between blooming and resurrection. The final poem, "To Ireland in the Coming Times," is, in contrast, a nationalist clarion-call:

> *Know, that I would accounted be*
> *True brother of a company*
> *That sang, to sweeten Ireland's wrong.*

In this poem, the Rose is a fitting consort and complement to God—both are gigantic figures of whom we see or hear only the lowest part—her "*red-rose-bordered hem*," his "*white footfall*." Whereas God is white and grave, the Rose is red and dancing, the muse of Ireland and of poetry.

Like God, and like Yeats's poetry, the Rose doesn't have to *do* anything, she simply *is*; the Rose is not only the collection of poems called *The Rose*, but she is poetry. It is in her guise as poetry that she resembles Walter Pater's famous description of Leonardo Da Vinci's Mona Lisa as a female personification of art:

> She is older than the rocks among which she sits; like the vampire, she has been dead many times, and learned the secrets of the grave; and has trafficked for strange webs with Eastern merchants, and, as Leda, was the mother of Helen of Troy, and, as Saint Anne, the mother of Mary; and all this has

been to her but as the sound of lyres and flutes, and lives only in the delicacy with which it has molded the changing lineaments, and tinged the eyelids and the hands.[40]

The Rose also resembles Petrarch's Laura, another emblem of poetry. Like the Rose, Laura lends herself easily to verbal metamorphosis: she can become a flower (the laurel or *lauro*); a breeze (*l'aura*); or gold (*l'auro*).[41] As Petrarch writes, "If my eyes ever saw white with crimson roses in a vase of gold, just then gathered by virgin hands, they thought they saw the face of her who excels all other wonders."[42] Yeats's reason for singing of love, beauty, and poetry as a personified woman may also resemble Petrarch's. In Poem 131 Petrarch confesses that Laura is a projection of inspirational forces that make up for his own sense of inadequacy: "and I would see the scarlet roses moved by the breeze [*Laura*] amid the snow . . . and all for the sake of which I am not a burden to myself in this short life, but rather glory in keeping for a later season" (268).[43]

Near the end of Yeats's Rose cluster, it becomes increasingly apparent that the Rose is not only the heart from which the tree of life and joy grows ("The Two Trees"), but that which gives heart, or literally "encourages."[44] In *"To Ireland in the Coming Times,"* Yeats argues that her dancing *"made Ireland's heart begin to beat"* (*VP,* 138). She does this with "flying feet" that also, in context, become the metrical feet of Yeats's verse, dancing beneath the *"red-rose-bordered hem"* that *"Trails all about* [his] *written page."*[45] It is in this poem that the nationalist dimension of the Rose most unmistakably emerges, since Yeats uses the poem to declare himself *"True brother of a company / That sang, to sweeten Ireland's wrong,"* a company that includes Thomas Davis, Samuel Ferguson, and James Clarence Mangan (the most influential translator of "Roisin Dubh," whose version—"Dark Rosaleen"—restores the power of the dark rose as an image of Ireland). Yeats concludes the poem, and the volume, with a testimony to his poetic sincerity and his love for Ireland's beauty:[46]

> *I cast my heart into my rhymes,*
> *That you, in the dim coming times,*
> *May know how my heart went with them*
> *After the red-rose-bordered hem.*
> (*VP,* 139)

Yeats's use of the Rose as a symbol of Ireland is a vexed issue, which explains both the defensive tone of *"To Ireland in the Coming Times"* (originally titled, "Apologia addressed to Ireland in the coming days," *VP,* 137) and the footnote in *The Countess Kathleen and Various Legends and Lyrics* in which Yeats denies using the Rose in the same patriotic sense that Mangan used it:

> The Rose is a favourite symbol with the Irish poets. It has given a name to more than one poem, both Gaelic and English, and is used, not merely in love poems, but in addresses to Ireland, as in De Vere's line, "The little black rose shall be red at last," and in Mangan's "Dark Rosaleen." I do not, of course, use it in this latter sense. (*VP,* 798–99)

Yeats dropped the disclaimer in all subsequent editions, since it is as misleading to think that Yeats's project *lacks* a nationalist dimension as it is to *identify* him with the primarily oratorical fervor of Irish nationalism. There are obvious problems with presenting the image of a *red* rose as an emblem of Ireland, when red was the color of Lancaster in the largely fratricidal War of the Roses (Ireland supported the white rose of York, which lost) and when the Rose evokes the Tudor Rose as well. It is clear that other Irish writers instantly understood the problem; Joyce, in *A Portrait of the Artist as a Young Man*, has Stephen represent the white rose of York in a math competition (which he predictably loses), and Stephen thinks, "But you could not have a green rose. But perhaps somewhere in the world you could" (*P,* 12–13). Yeats's rose, like the red hollyberries and the green ivy of the Christmas dinner scene in *A Portrait*, symbolizes among other things the hope of an ultimate reconciliation between England and Ireland, unlike *The Wind Among the Reeds*, which is more exclusively Irish in its associations and allegiances. In a note to *The Wind Among the Reeds*, Yeats made an effort to salvage the Irishness of the rose in retrospect, relating,

> I have read somewhere that a stone engraved with a Celtic god, who holds what looks like a rose in one hand, has been found somewhere in England; but I cannot find the reference, though I certainly made a note of it. If the Rose was really a symbol of Ireland among the Gaelic poets, and if 'Roseen Dubh' is really a political poem, as some think, one may feel pretty certain that the ancient Celts associated the Rose with Eire, or Fotla, or Banba— goddesses who gave their names to Ireland—or with some principal god or goddess, for such symbols are not suddenly adopted or invented, but come out of mythology. (*VP,* 811–12)

Appropriating the Rose as a symbol of Ireland allowed Yeats to speak to the inscription of social conditions that made Ireland what it was, which in turn made him and his poetry. To paraphrase Auden's elegy for Yeats, the Rose allows Yeats to imagine a more ideal version of the "mad Ireland" that hurt him into poetry.

In *The Secret Rose* (1897), which bridges the publication of the Rose cluster in *Poems* (1895) and *The Wind Among the Reeds* in 1899, Yeats delves more deeply into the occult meaning of the Rose. In this collection of stories, the Rose is predominantly an image of fire,[47] suggesting both desire and divine power. The connection between the Rose and fire is important both because it underscores the difference of *The Rose* from *The Wind Among the Reeds*, which concentrates less on the fire of love than on its liquid depths, and because it highlights the similarity between *The Rose* and *The Tower*, which takes another occult symbol of fire, the tower, as its organizing motif. In "Where There is Nothing, There is God," Brother Dove explains that a ruby on the side of a box "is a symbol of the love of God . . . Because it is red, like fire, and fire burns up everything, and where there is nothing, there is God" (*SR,* 27). In "Out of the Rose," the Rose is not only interchangeable with the sun, whom the old knight addresses as "Divine Rose of Intellectual Flame" (*SR,* 54), but it also replaces the burning bush of Moses in order to tell humankind that "the wayward light of the heart" that kept the world alive was dimming. Out of "a great Rose of Fire" the voice of God warns a knight from Palestine that "men would turn from the light of their own hearts, and bow down before external order and outer fixity" (*SR*, 63). When the Palestinian knight tells the story to the Knights of St. John, they seem to see "a crimson Rose spreading itself about him, so that he seemed to speak out of its heart, and the air was filled with fragrance. By this we knew that it was the very Voice of God which spoke to us by the knight" (*SR*, 64). In the stories of *The Secret Rose*, fire in the heart is kindled by otherworldly wisdom, sensual desire, and the desire for justice.

The importance of the fiery Rose is most readily apparent in the symbolism of Rosicrucianism, which not only influenced Villiers de l'Isle-Adam's *Axël* but also shaped the rituals of the Order of the Golden Dawn, which Yeats joined in 1890 shortly after Constance Wilde had left. (Soon after he joined the Order, Madame Blavatsky asked him to resign from the Theosophical Society for, among other things, his experimental attempt to raise the ghost of a flower.)[48] Yeats was initiated into the grade of Adeptus Major in 1893, which is the grade in which Rosicrucian symbolism begins to be elaborated (the initiate is even asked to enter the "tomb" of Father Christian Rosenkreuz).[49] But a fuller account of Rosicrucian history and symbolism—one that is much closer to Yeats's own use of Rosicrucianism in its relation to druidical learning and ancient Celtic history—may be found in a book by Hargrave Jennings, whom Madame Blavatsky irritably alludes to in *The Secret Doctrine*.[50]

Celtic Rosicrucianism

For most readers, the cabalistic aspects of Yeats's treatment of the Rose seem esoteric as well as somewhat dated. However, a reading of less familiar discussions of Rosicrucianism reveals how the emblem of the Rose has served to integrate elemental, sexual, national, and spiritual concerns for hundreds of years with remarkable economy. The Rose serves essentially the same function in Yeats's poetry as it does in Rosicrucian symbolism: it magnetically attracts, constellates, and transforms a host of apparently disparate meanings. In *The Rosicrucians: Their Rites and Mysteries* (1887), Jennings describes Rosicrucianism as a belief in correspondences that is remarkably close to Yeats's view of poetic genius as a unifying force. Jennings stresses that the Rosicrucians are exponents of the mysteries of the Cabala who want to find "the *real tie* which binds all things together" (vii–viii). Moreover, Jennings anticipates Yeats's interest in the rose and the tower as sexual symbols. (Blavatsky, in contrast, reacts strongly against any interpretation of such symbols as sexual, asking, "Shall we, then, regard the evolution of the Universe as simply a prototype, on a gigantic scale, of the act of procreation?" *SD* II, 544.)[51] Occult symbols are not only sexualized, they are also, to some extent, Irish—figuring both in Celtic legend and in druidical magic. It is evident from reading Jennings that the occult must have appealed to Yeats as a way of exploring the relation between psychology and history; symbols act as a gateway not only to the communal unconscious, but also to the buried shards of ethnic experience, particularly Irishness.

Jennings's view of Rosicrucian philosophy emphasizes four essential precepts, all of which have important implications for an understanding of Yeats's poetry. First, he argues that many potent symbols were originally intended to represent or evoke the powers of the four elements, thereby linking the Rosicrucians to the ancient Celts, who also worshipped the elements (or the spirit that animated the elements); Yeats relies heavily on the four elements to structure poems in *The Wind Among the Reeds*.[52] The power of fire was associated with the gods, and Jennings reads several images as attempts to signify the sublime and generative power of fire: the rose (identified with the sun); towers, especially Irish round towers, and later steeples; and the Holy Grail.[53] Second, Jennings describes the role of the alchemist or Rosicrucian much as Yeats would later define the goal of the artist: to lay "the bridge between the world possible and the world impossible." He explains that Rosicrucians claim to be able to enter the other world—the "Twilight" of the Soul—at will, and that when they return they bring back old things "metamorphosed into new things," magic or "fairy" gold (215). Rosicrucians, then, perceive the realm of inspiration as a kind of "Celtic Twilight," a means of communicating between the natural and supernatural worlds. (Yeats would later replace twilight with the swan as an emblem of communication between two worlds.)[54] Third, Jennings insists not only upon seeing opposites as gendered, but also as reversible, which does away with the hierarchical ordering of gender—in the mind, if not in society.[55] Finally, Jennings is firm and unambiguous about what the Rosicrucians trust and value above all, which is also the force that motivated Yeats: the heart or emotions rather than the intellect. Jennings explains, "the apparent and the reasonable . . . *is never true*. Hence we cannot know God through God, or rather through the Intellect; but we must know God through the 'Saviour', or through the heart or affections" (377). This important point bears repetition, and its relevance to Yeats's lifelong obsession with the heart and with the "revolt of the soul against the intellect" is perhaps obvious. Jennings emphatically clarifies the Rosicrucian view of "whether 'Man'—and therefore 'art'—is from the HEAD, or the HEART": "We think entirely the latter, in as far as 'LOVE' is greater than 'WISDOM', and is its ruler. In this great fact lies all the hope of the world. . . . In this emotion from the heart lies all religion, and all that we can know of ourselves of hope" (430).

As interpreted by someone like Jennings, Rosicrucianism is not only related to the lore of the druids of ancient Ireland, but it also attempts to recover the ancient view that the sexual and the divine are interdependent. When discussing *phalloi*, Jennings firmly dissociates his own position from a more reductive modern reading of sexual symbology, asserting that "[t]he coarse sensuality which seems inseparable from modern ideas about the worship of the pillar or upright had no place really in the solemn ancient mind, in which ideas of religion largely and constantly mingled" (233). What Jennings provides is an account of ancient connections between the symbol of the crucified rose and both the tower and the musical harp, an account that informs Yeats's treatment of these symbols as interrelated (the harp lingers in the background of Yeats's image of the wind in the reeds).

Jennings associates the Rose as a "female" life-giving principle with magic, with the sun, with female sexuality, and with the sacred objective of King Arthur's knights—the Holy Grail itself (although King Arthur has become a symbol of England, the legends surrounding him are Celtic). He argues that the English word "rose" is linked to the Irish *Rus*, which he translates as "tree," "knowledge," "science," "magic," and "power."[56] The ingenious if irregular suggestion (which Yeats would also follow) is that the similarities across languages connect the rose with the cross (or tree), unifying them in a way that produces knowledge and magical power, which is certainly how Yeats treats their intersection in "To the Rose upon the Rood of Time."

The fire of the Rose connects its divinity with its power as a symbol of female sexuality, subsuming both in an image of the Rose as sun, source of all life.[57] Jennings argues that the Tudor Rose is the Rosicrucian Red Rose, crucified, with a lily-white "center-point" and surrounded by rays of glory that are either sunbeams or thorns (288). When discussing the rose window or the Catherine wheel, Jennings again describes the pattern as a representation of the sun in the heavens; the opening rose in the glorified center of the window represents the sun or "beginning of all things," and the twelve pillars or radii that issue out from it are the signs of the zodiac (178).

Most surprisingly, Jennings also connects the Rose with the Holy Grail, arguing that King Arthur's Round Table, around which the sentinels of the Holy Grail arranged themselves, displayed the crucified rose in its center. (The Irish identified the Grail with the Cauldron of the Dagda, one of the four treasures brought to Ireland by the Tuatha Dé Danaan).[58] Moreover, Jennings argues that when the alchemical "Philosophers' Stone," "being obtained 'out of the material' by 'supernatural' means," undergoes its magical transfiguration, it blossoms into the blood of Christ. It

> glows (or martyrises) into *flaming red*, or possession, or Glorified Agony. . . .
> From thence it is said to be the 'Blood' of Christ (and the 'Cross' of Christ).
> . . . This is the 'Holy Grail', or 'Sangreal', or 'Sang-Reale' or 'Fire', or
> 'Mighty Redeeming Magic', sought by the Champions, or the Knights, of
> King Arthur's Round Table. (382–83)

Such an argument implies that the "real" blood or fire of crucified divinity that the alchemists and Rosicrucians were seeking is what the true *Cabalistae*, "the Magi, Wise Men, Philosophers, Priests, and Heroes" have always sought; represented by the Rose, this fire, blood, or "sang-reale" Grail is the source of all magic.

Jennings even reads the origin of the Order of the Garter (begun by King Edward III in 1344) as homage to a rose that is also the female sex organ, which is in turn the Rose of the World (see Yeats's poem entitled "The Rose of the World," *VP*, 111–12). The argument runs, "the Order of the Garter is feminine, . . . its origin is an apotheosis of the 'Rose', and of a certain singular physiological fact connected with woman's life" (323). Jennings goes so far as to suggest that the whole order was a revival of King Arthur's Round Table, and that the round table has been concentrated into "the apotheosized female *discus*" (327):

> In the 'tables' . . . of the Order of the Garter . . . the microcosmical, miniature 'King Arthur's Round Table' becomes the individual female *discus*, or organ, waxing and waning, negative or in flower, positive or natural, alternately red and white, as the Rose of the World: *Rosamond, Rosa mundi.* (178)[59]

Yeats's symbol of the Rose draws upon a panoply of resonant meanings ranging from the sexual and local to the divine and universal in a way that is comparable to the Rose venerated by King Edward's Order of the Garter. Yeats's Rose is decidedly female and therefore loosely aligned with Christianity, which, with its emphasis on love, is often designated "feminine" in contrast to a "masculine" Judaic law (Jennings, 251) and also with the Irish (whom Ernest Renan had praised as a "feminine" race). Despite such general associations, the problem with adopting a Rosicrucian approach from a nationalist point of view is obvious: the symbolism here employed is more English than Irish, even with the added references to Roisin Dubh or the dark rose of Ireland. Irish history can be encapsulated as the history of a crucified flower, but the redness of the Rose is too immediately evocative of the red of England, and the Rosicrucians are too closely connected with Protestantism for the Rosicrucian Rose to be an unequivocal symbol of Irish beauty and power. (The Rosicrucians, said to be an offshoot of Freemasonry, were historically at odds with Catholicism, especially the Jesuit order.)

Yeats's early enthusiasm for Rosicrucian symbolism was fanned by his 1894 excursion to Paris with Maud Gonne to see a lengthy production of Villiers's *Axël* in French.[60] *Axël* confirms Jennings's understanding of the Rose and the Tower as similar symbols representing opposite sexes. In *Axël*, the crucified rose is associated with Sara,[61] whereas the Tower, where Axel spends the best years of his life studying occult manuscripts night after night (47), is Axel's symbol. Sara refers to her "mysterious flower" as "the unconsolable rose . . . victorious over Winter, . . . symbol of [her] destiny, a kindred and divine *correspondence*" (161). She describes the Rose as a kind of muse, "a supernatural guide . . . [that] seemed to be begotten of [her] own soul"; it represents her god, her sexuality, her consciousness of history, and the magical source and guiding spirit of her life. She recounts kissing the rose, plucking it, and accidentally placing it upon a hermetic, cruciform dagger, "forged in olden days," that she happened to be holding. When she inadvertently makes the sign of the crucified rose, she experiences a sudden, almost mystical, insight into history, and she views this sign as a magical formula for destroying the power of empires:

> Spirits,—or perhaps . . . genies were surely enclosed in her beauty! . . . For immediately passages in human History, until then veiled in my mind, lit up my memory with august and supernatural significance. Thus I understood, without being able to explain even the interest I took in understanding, why this flower so placed by chance upon the cross of the dagger between my

hands formed the Sign which in former times had dispersed the proudest and mightiest empires like sands in the wind. (162)

The conjunction of a Rose and dagger-cross figures a meeting of opposites, and Yeats saw such a meeting as kindling a divine, sexual, and historical energy, which he would later try to harness in his poetry for national purposes.[62] When Sara and Axel meet, and she entreats him, "Let me veil you in my hair so you may inhale the attar of roses of all time" (155), their meeting reproduces the conjunction of rose and cross with its ecstasy and its destructive power; Sara's love of spring, dawn, and the future intersects with Axel's obsession with the world of night, spirits, and the past, and they experience in the imagination, briefly, "the ideal moment" (170). While listening to a marriage procession outside in the forest, they drink poison, *"their lips exchanging the supreme sigh"* (175). The final stage directions indicate that their mutual self-sacrifice is to have reawakened the sensual and spiritual beauty of life in the world:

> *disturbing the silence of the awesome place where two human beings have just freely dedicated their souls to the exile of Heaven—are distant murmurs of the wind in the forest vastness, vibrations of the awakening of space, the surge of the plain, the hum of life.* (175)

In *Axël*, the intersection of rose and dagger foretells the erotic collision between Sara and Axel, a collision that can topple empires and bring about the recovery of lost national treasures (Sara and Axel rediscover Germany's national treasure in the play). By grouping an early cluster of poems around the Rose, and juxtaposing them with his drama of national salvation, *The Countess Cathleen*, Yeats was attempting to tap the power of the symbol to free the Irish nation through blossoms of blood.[63] Yeats was also hoping to unite the Irish people around a central symbol, much as he made disparate meanings cohere around the Rose. Disappointingly, however, the more subtle connotations of the Rose proved to be inaccessible to most readers, Irish or English, and the Rose is often tossed aside as an overly elaborate cliché.[64]

A Woman's Rose

The elastic capacity of the Rose image is, unexpectedly, still apparent in the work of more recent women writers who have consciously taken up and continued to revise Yeats's poetic vocabulary. Angela Carter, Eavan Boland, Paula Meehan, Nuala ní Dhomhnaill, Sara Berkeley, and Medbh McGuckian are all engaged in the kind of revisionary image-making that was characteristic of the early Yeats; moreover, they react to the ultimate inadequacy of his image of the Rose as woman and nation much as Yeats himself did in his later poetry. These writers, too, are engaged in putting images into dynamic play for serious aesthetic, political, and ethical reasons. What these revisions of the personified Rose from a woman's perspective show is what Yeats also came to discover when he translated the image into new forms: despite the dazzling comprehensiveness of the Rose in theory, and her revolutionary status as a counterpart and equal to God, she—like God—exists primarily in the imaginary and the symbolic registers, but not in the real. Despite being an emblem of the heart, she herself has no feelings, and although she is represented by the lips, she does not speak.

In "The Lady of the House of Love," a vampire version of "Sleeping Beauty," Angela Carter recycles Yeats's rose imagery in order to reinterpret the passivity of the sad woman who incarnates the bloody beauty of a Rose.[65] In Carter's version, the woman's passivity is due not to the weariness of divinity but to the damning legacy of her forebears, who have shaped her, as they shape nations, to suck the blood of men. Unlike the early Yeats, Carter reads the flawless beauty of the Rose-woman as "an abnormality, a deformity, for none of her features exhibit any of those touching imperfections that reconcile us to the imperfection of the human condition. Her beauty is a symptom of her disorder, of her soullessness" (94). Carter highlights the kinship between being worshiped and being damned by depicting the divine Rose as a vampire; moreover, she interprets the interimplication of sex and death not as an inevitable psychological reality but as a function of a social script that allows women neither to live nor die, relegating them instead to a gothic night world—a world of sensuality and humdrum terror—where they must night after night put on the virginal wedding dress of their mothers to drain the life from new husbands-to-be. Her sadness is "the perennial sadness of a girl who is both death and the maiden" (93).

Sleeping Beauty of fairy-tale fame is implicitly a rose by virtue of the thick hedge of thorns that surrounds her. In a thinly veiled sexual allegory, the legend stipulates that her protection must be heroically penetrated if she is to be awakened.[66] Carter's Beauty, in significant contrast, never sleeps. She is not a treasure to be won, but a deadly predator, a bloodthirsty huntress made helpless by her unquestioning obedience to tradition, or what she sees as her destiny. She is a queen of vampires, repeatedly counting out Tarot cards that always fall in the same pattern, as she sits alone "under the eyes of the portraits of her demented and atrocious ancestors, each one of whom, through her, projects a baleful posthumous existence" (93). Like Sleeping Beauty, she is incarcerated in "the castle of her inheritance" by "a huge, spiked wall" of roses; only her roses were planted by her dead mother, and her garden "bears a strong resemblance to a burial ground" (95).

At this point, the story changes direction momentarily, and instead of a heroic prince, in rides a Parsifal figure on a bicycle, a "beautiful two-wheeled symbol of rationality" (99). He is a compassionate, pure, literal-minded man, doomed to die for his nation in World War I, whom Carter has sent to save-and-destroy the queen of the vampires by making her human:

> He has the special quality of virginity, most and least ambiguous of states: ignorance, yet at the same time, power in potentia, and, furthermore, unknowingness, which is not the same as ignorance. He is more than he knows—and has about him, besides, the special glamour of that generation for whom history has already prepared a special, exemplary fate in the trenches of France. This being, rooted in change and time, is about to collide with the timeless Gothic eternity of the vampires. (97)

Like Parsifal, the queen's lover draws his heroism from a "lack of imagination" (104) that allows him to register the intoxicating promise of her roses as excess, a "faintly corrupt sweetness strong enough almost, to fell him":

> Too many roses. Too many roses bloomed on enormous thickets that lined the path, thickets bristling with thorns, and the flowers themselves were almost too luxuriant, their huge congregations of plush petals somehow obscene in their excess, their whorled, tightly budded cores outrageous in their implications. (98)

Like Yeats's Rose, the vampire queen replicates the rose in her lips, "red lips like the obese roses in her garden," but her lips never move, and she speaks with a voice not her own: "she is like a doll, he thought, a ventriloquist's doll" (102). He sees her as "an inbred, highly strung girl child, fatherless, motherless, kept in the dark too long" (104), as she takes him to an inverted marriage bed with "eyes that deny all the erotic promises of her body with their terror, their sadness, their dreadful, balked tenderness" (105).

The queen refrains from destroying her lover because he "mothers" her. When she cuts her thumb he puts his mouth to the wound, "as her mother, had she lived, would have done"; he inadvertently models an alternative to the idea of love as destructive blood-sucking that she had always known. Instead of draining his blood, she disappears, leaving a lace négligé stained with blood "as it might be from a woman's menses," and a rose. She seems to tell him that she was only an invention of darkness, and she leaves behind only the emblem of a deadly, cloying sexuality: "I leave you as a souvenir the dark, fanged rose I plucked from between my thighs, like a flower laid on a grave" (107).

This story implicitly points up a shortcoming in Yeats's "The Rose" that he would only recognize and redress later in his career: his Rose may be woman's lips, but they cannot speak; for all her symbolic power, the Rose has no agency but is a divine puppet, much like "The Magi" of his later poem. What Yeats saw as the romance of the past is as easily construed as a curse, not only on women, but on Ireland as well. Carter calls her grotesque Unsleeping Beauty "a haunted house":

> She does not possess herself; her ancestors sometimes come and peer out of the windows of her eyes and that is very frightening. She has the mysterious solitude of ambiguous states; she hovers in a no-man's land between life and death, sleeping and waking, behind the hedge of spiked flowers, Nosferatu's sanguinary rosebud. The beastly forebears on the walls condemn her to a perpetual repetition of their passions. (103)[67]

If Angela Carter refigures the Rose in order to criticize social, familial, and sexual traditions that define women as psychological bloodsuckers and condemn them as embodiments of a sexuality toward which men are highly ambivalent, several contemporary Irish women poets have chosen to address Yeats's personification of Ireland as a female flower directly. Women such as Nuala Ní Dhomhnaill, Eavan Boland, Anne Hartigan, Deirdre Brennan, Sara Berkeley, Mary E. O'Donnell, Paula Meehan, Eithne Strong, Roz Cowman, and

Medbh McGuckian challenge the symbolic, decorative function of a female Ireland in their poetry. They register and resist what Boland refers to as "the power of nationhood to edit the realities of womanhood."[68] Many of these women, such as Eithne Strong, definitively dissociate themselves from nationalism (Smyth, ed., *Wildish Things*, 113), from the old ideal of political martyrdom, from Yeats's Rose Tree watered in the Christian tradition with human blood, which flowered into the Easter Rising. As Paula Meehan relates in "Don't Speak to Me of Martyrs," listening to a political speech brings her back to the nationalist propaganda of her childhood, when nine- and ten-year-old children recited nationalist verse in school:

> I wind up in the ghost place
> the language rocks me to,
> a cobwebby state, chilled vault
> littered with our totems;
>
> a tattered Plough and Stars,
> a bloodstained Proclamation,
> Connolly strapped wounded to a chair,
> Mayblossom in Inchicore.

In contrast to the Rose, with its twin connotations of sexuality and death, Meehan evokes a different image, of the swollen genitalia of the Sheila-na-Gig in the national museum, her "yoni made luscious in stone," and the peace and touch of her mother. She concludes by rejecting the male fantasy of violent and secret martyrdom:

> Don't speak to me of Stephen the Martyr
> the host snug in his palm
> slipping through the wounded streets
> to keep his secret safe.
> (Smyth, ed., *Wildish Things*, 74–75)

Roz Cowman, too, indicts the Church as well as nationalism for its erasure of women. In "Medea Ireland," she suggests that the snake that St. Patrick drove out of Ireland when he Christianized the country was the power of the mother, who would then no longer mate and breed with him, with his hell-thunderings and madness. In angrier retaliation, Medea-like, she killed her children: "The rime of death on children's bodies still / delays his pursuit of her flight through time."[69] Cowman's image of Ireland as Medea, enraged by St. Patrick's denaturing of her, puts some of the burden of Ireland's violent self-division on St. Patrick and the Church, redrawing Stephen Dedalus's misogynist image of Ireland as "the old sow who eats her farrow."

When women poets begin depicting their own mythology, their own experience, and their own bodies (in relation to the once invisible sexuality of men), the result seems, when generalized, rather predictable: women become more real, more ordinary, more flawed, and threatening in new ways. But the central aim of much contemporary poetry by women is to eschew generalizations about women, to unveil the hidden complexities that the dominant stereotypes had, in the interests of national and personal pride, resolutely disguised.[70] As Eavan Boland argues, "There are certain areas that are degraded because they are silent. They need to be re-experienced and re-examined. Their darker energies need to be looked at" (*Sleeping with Monsters*, 82).

Boland voices the difficulty of being a woman poet "in a nation whose poetry on women consistently simplifies them . . . [through] powerful, simplifying fusions of the feminine and the national" (*Sleeping with Monsters* 86–87). Her goal is to complicate that field of force. She explains,

> Irish poets of the 19th Century, and indeed their heirs in this century, coped with their sense of historical injury by writing of Ireland as an abandoned queen or an old mother. My objections to this are ethical. If you consistently simplify women by making them national icons in poetry or drama you silence a great deal of the actual women in that past, whose sufferings and complexities are part of that past, who intimately depend on us, as writers, not to simplify them in this present. (*Sleeping with Monsters*, 87)

Boland proclaims her position on women and nationalism most movingly in "Mise Eire" ("I am Ireland") (*Sleeping with Monsters*, 89–90):

I won't go back to it—

my nation displaced
into old dactyls,
oaths made
by the animal tallows
of the candle—

land of the Gulf Stream,
the small farm,
the scalded memory,
the songs
that bandage up the history,
the words
that make a rhythm of the crime
where time is time past.
A palsy of regrets.
No. I won't go back.
My roots are brutal:
•　•　•　•　•　•　•
I am the woman
in the gansy-coat
on board the 'Mary Belle',
in the huddling cold,

holding her half-dead baby to her
as the wind shifts East
and North over the dirty
water of the wharf

mingling the immigrant
guttural with the vowels

of homesickness who neither
knows nor cares that

a new language
is a kind of scar
and heals after a while
into a passable imitation
of what went before.

What happens to the Rose, female sexuality, the muse, Cathleen Ní Houlihan and the Shan van Vocht (the "Poor Old Woman" who also personifies Ireland) in these poets' "new language" is that the defining image shatters into many component images, and it also loses its sheen of unreal perfection. The rose is still apparent as an image of female sexuality and poetic inspiration, but it is no longer a prescriptive image—the diversity of femaleness is represented by the many flowers that now figure female sexuality and its potential productivity. For McGuckian, woman is a begonia (Medbh McGuckian, "Collusion");[71] "a garden escape in her unconscious / Solidarity with darkness, clove-scented / As an orchid taking fifteen years to bloom" ("The Flitting," *Sleeping with Monsters,* 7); a fertile sunflower, filled with "decorous seeds" that lie "in wait" ("Death of a Ceiling").[72] Sara Berkeley, in "Seeding," describes woman as a splitting pea-pod awaiting "the tiny explosion / Of ripe, tense seeds . . . The floating time seeds of the dandelion" (*Pillars of the House,* 168). In "Learning to Count" (*Bitter Harvest,* 201–202), she describes the sound in a mother's throat as "the music of blossom"; she portrays the female child, who "sleeps through the shrouded night," as blooming

with such pretty grace, snapping in my hand
Like the daffodil, dusting my fingers with the dry powder of her lust
Curving from earth as she will,
Neither drooping nor withered.

Deirdre Brennan presents herself as an aging flower in a pot, "Compressed in a web of roots / The seasons gone astray / In the damp press of peat" (*Wildish Things,* 81). She asks,

When will I break
My binding pots? . . .
I will suck the rain
That will run dry in me
Until great summer daisies sprout
From the seedbed of my heart.
I will toss out the petals of my hair
In every wind that blows
And in icy winter clay
I will cover resurrection seeds.

Mary E. O'Donnell describes the modern woman poet as a starving reader of fat, yellow, fertile sunflowers, a genderless reincarnation of the Word, which is also Christ (*Wildish Things,* 95):

She reads sunflowers daily,
the spindles of her fingers reach out,
stroke yellow ellipses
as if each petal were a sign.
What really holds her are the seeds,
Tucked tight like critical reviews
within a yellow convention.
They swell and separate while autumn
seems to idle . . .

She is bent on hers,
knows what she creates will have it all—
the Word made genderless.

It is McGuckian, though, who in addition to diversifying female sexuality as a variety of flowers, constructing men as the root (*Sleeping with Monsters*, 3), takes on the image of the rose explicitly, appropriating it for private use, making it an image not of national but of highly personal poetic inspiration. She turns the Rose into Rosalind, the girl who can play the boy at will, in "The Unplayed Rosalind," proclaiming in a kind of dialogue with Yeats, "I have been the poet of women and consequently / Of the young." She explains,

The room which I thought the most beautiful
In the world, and never showed to anyone,
Is a rose-red room, a roseate chamber.
It lacks two windowpanes and has no waterjug.
There is red ink in the inkwell.

Yet this poet in the roseate chamber has a double who accepts a lover; the double prefers to read "the fire-red rip down heaven / As a saucer of iced water where she could / Dip her hands, as in the reciprocal blue / Ashes of his eyes." By so doing "She remove[s] the rose from" the speaker's mouth, betraying the man in her with another.[73]

McGuckian's matter-of-fact assumption that the woman speaker also contains a man in her is replicated in the ways that the various female poets gender their muse. Yeats's muse was female, although at another level both male and female (if we see the muse of "The Rose" as double, encompassing both the Rose and Christ, as in "To the Rose Upon the Rood of Time"). Interestingly, both McGuckian and Ní Dhomhnaill also choose a double muse that is partly or sometimes male. McGuckian writes that she wouldn't have been a poet if she had lived anywhere other than Belfast, that the conflict in the North gave her "a sense of dislocation, a sense of being two people or a divided personality" (*Sleeping with Monsters*, 2). This divided personality is "as much male as female"; she describes her poems as arguments between the male and female sides of experience, and Irishness as "something [she doesn't] understand" (*Sleeping with Monsters*, 4). McGuckian again takes up the issue of the composition of the poetic self and the limitation of being "merely female," an "open rose," in "Open Rose" (*Marconi's Cottage*, 80). She depicts the gradual loss of the man in her as a diminishment, comparing her femaleness to a partly empty house or to the fetal confinement of an open rose, unborn within a womb of nurturing words, a rose that can only say so much:

> His head is there when I work,
> It signs my letters with a question-mark;
> His hands reach for me like rationed air.
> Day by day I let him go
>
> Till I become a woman, or even less,
> An incompletely furnished house
> That came from a different century
> Where I am a guest at my own childhood.
>
> I have grown inside words
> Into a state of unbornness,
> An open rose on all sides
> Has spoken as far as it can.

Ní Dhomhnaill, too, consciously alternates between several muses—one male and black; another a destructive old woman whom she calls the Tooth Mother; and of course Eire herself—the country, "the whole sovereignty of Ireland" (*Sleeping with Monsters*, 153). She argues that male poets have always identified the muse as female, when they were really "talking about their inner woman and projecting it onto us," while "women have had a male muse" who is "ferociously dangerous" because, being a man, he's (1) "inclined to all-or-nothing action," and (2) "allied with society against you, against your deeper levels of femininity" (*Sleeping with Monsters*, 150). She argues that her female muse is, as a rule, much softer, having to do with the joy of being (which is not goal-directed), although she has also felt the *cailleach*, the hag—the female and ugly spirit at the corner of every road. She cherishes the energy of Negative Femininity, too, considering herself lucky to be writing in Irish, which, she argues, "wasn't industrialized or patriarchalized. . . . Irish in the Irish context is the language of the Mothers, because everything that has been done to women has been done to Irish" (*Sleeping with Monsters*, 154). Ní Dhomhnaill is most like Yeats in her sense that the land is "the muse . . . and an echo of an inner landscape" (154), but for her that inner landscape is not only mythical and linguistic, it is also female and subconscious. She describes her goal as a poet as bringing things up from the subconscious, which she likens to the *lios*, or fairy fort, of which there are sixteen hundred in Ireland (149), and as an attempt to reclaim a lost continent, a new psychic land. She writes,

> What women find when they go in there [to the deeper levels of consciousness] is very different from what men have written about. That's the really exciting thing. Lots of women's poetry has so much to reclaim: there's so much psychic land, a whole continent, a whole Atlantis under the water to reclaim. It's like this island . . . in Irish folklore, which surfaces under the water every seven years, and if somebody can go out to it and light a fire, or do something, it will stay up forever." (*Sleeping with Monsters*, 152)

Ní Dhomhnaill is impatient with old idealizations. Compare her version of the Shan van Vocht and Cathleen Ní Houlihan with Yeats's Rose: she dismisses the Shan van Vocht as a cranky, cantankerous, and cancered woman, "locked into self-pity," and says she would do "anything at all / To get this old bitch to shut the fuck up."[74] Cathleen Ní Houlihan is placed, cursing, in a "secret room at the top of the stairs" of the poet's household; she is ignored, the madwoman in the attic who once said her real name was Grace Poole ("Mo Theaghlach," trans. Eiléan Ní Chuilleánain as "Household," *Pharaoh's Daughter,* 153). The wind, unlike Yeats's Eire, is an indifferent, rapacious housewife as she-wolf who "hasn't the slightest interest / In you or your sore throat: / The solar system is all hers / To scrub like a floor if she pleases" ("An Casadh," trans. Medbh McGuckian as "Nine Little Goats," *Pharaoh's Daughter,* 111). What Ní Dhomhnaill evokes instead is a "dark mother, cave of wonders," to whom the race spins on its violent course, whose "kiss is sweeter than Spanish wine, Greek honey, or the golden mead of the Norse" ("An Ras," trans. Derek Mahon as "The Race," *Pharaoh's Daughter,* 97). The land is a terrifying giantess: "O, Mam, I'm scared stiff, / I thought I saw the mountains heaving / like a giantess, with her breasts swaying, / about to loom over, and gobble me up" ("Cailleach," trans. John Montague as "Hag," *Pharaoh's Daughter,* 137).

The Rose has moved inward, and what has replaced her is a mighty mother, a formidable hag, a personified fault, who, as Sara Berkeley writes, someday "will burst her corset of rock / And take the air" ("Valley Poem I," *Wildish Things,* 127). The earth is moving, transforming the old female and national icons into what Anne Hartigan calls "the new political force" (*Sleeping with Monsters,* 206). And this powerful, earthy mother who is not virgin has a new promise for the *daughter* that unto her "was given" ("Mac Airt," trans. Tom Mac Intyre, *Pharaoh's Daughter,* 79), because, as McGuckian writes, "Between every two moments stands a daughter" ("The Horse Fair," *Wildish Things,* 141). That promise is voiced in Ní Dhomhnaill's "Poem for Melissa":

> O white daughter here's your mother's word:
> I will put in your hand the sun and the moon
> I will stand my body between the millstones
> in God's mills so you are not totally ground.
> (*Bitter Harvest,* 169)

Not to be ground—not to be background nor dirt nor wheat totally ground into flour/flower—this is the determination with which contemporary Irish women poets would imbue their daughters, and this is their answer to the early Yeats. They have punningly revised the red rose into ground flour, and they have replaced the roseate chamber with a profusion of wilder blooms. Their response to the early Yeats is to reproduce the discourse of nationalism as an unstable and complex cacophony of desires and, instead of figuring the nation through the image of a beautiful woman, to tell the future of Ireland with a woman's breaking voice.

The Secret Rose

The unexpected fact that the wind among the reeds is a translation of the personified Rose emerges from an analysis of Yeats's treatment of the two images in *The Secret Rose*, stories that Yeats published midway between *Poems* (1895) and *The Wind Among the Reeds*. The rose and the wind do have an occult connection, which is apparent in a ritual of the Golden Dawn that directs the initiate to inhale the perfume of the Rose as a symbol of *air* (Putzel, 21). However, the full imagistic logic of the transition from the rose to the wind, the similarity and tension between these images as versions and antitheses of each other, is best revealed in Yeats's stories.[75] In *The Secret Rose*, not only the wind but also the Rose signal the presence of the *sidhe*. The wind not only represents the *sidhe* themselves but also the poet's desire *for* the *sidhe* (who represent the past with its imagined ghostly perfection). Moreover, the wind is the principle of change, "a power, which was *hysterica passio* or sheer madness," that makes fixed habits and principles dissolve (*SR*, 240); it is the element of what Deleuze and Guattari call rhizomatic movement, which delivers a shock to ingrained "habits of thought and of feeling" (*SR*, 242).

Poets such as Aodh in "The Binding of the Hair," Cumhal in "The Crucifixion of the Outcast," and Hanrahan in the stories of Red Hanrahan are described as passionate and unstable, easily blown about by their own intense and easily fanned emotions; they are "blown hither and thither by love and anger" (*SR*, 2). When a lay brother tells Cumhal, "My soul is decent and orderly, but yours is like the wind among the salley gardens," Cumhal answers, "My soul, friend, . . . is indeed like the wind, and it blows me to and fro, and up and down, and puts many things into my mind and out of my mind" (*SR*, 46). Cumhal's confession reflects Yeats's use of the wind as a traditional symbol of poetic inspiration, "a blowing into." What inspires the poet, however, is not just the Christian God but the many pagan Irish gods that preceded him: the numerous, half-historical and half-fantastical figures of the *sidhe*,[76] who speak with "reedy" voices (*SR*, 194) and who include the Rose among them. As Cumhal recalls,

> I have been the more alone upon the roads and by the sea, because I heard in my heart the rustling of the rose-bordered dress of her who is more subtle than Angus, the Subtle-Hearted, and more full of the beauty of laughter than Conan the Bald, and more full of the wisdom of tears than White-Breasted Deirdre, and more lovely than a bursting dawn to them that are lost in the darkness. (*SR*, 50–51)

Yeats explicitly connects the Rose and the wind, the rood and the reed in the tale "Of Costello the Proud, of Oona the Daughter of Dermott and of the Bitter Tongue." Like Red Hanrahan, Costello abandons the woman he loves out of pride. The narrator predicts that Costello will experience a crucifixion of the heart: he will only "come to the Divine Essence by the bitter tumult, the Garden of Gethsemane, and the desolate Rood ordained for immortal passions in mortal hearts" (*SR*, 112). His crucifixion, however, takes the form of rejection by the Rose and the *sidhe*: when Costello belatedly comes to lie on Oona's grave, she appears as the Rose and the wind, attended by "women of the Shee with crowns of silver and dim floating drapery." Then, in response to Oona's anger, "the whole glimmering company rose up into the air, and, rushing together in the shape of a great silvery rose, faded into the ashen dawn" (*SR*, 123). Costello, devastated by her rejection, swims away until he drowns in a manner that conjoins reeds with a rood of suffering and passion: he is found among reeds "with his arms flung out as though he lay upon a rood" (*SR*, 124).

"Of Costello the Proud" helps to illustrate not only the continuity between the image of the Rose and that of the wind, but also the opposing moods of Yeats's two late *fin-de-siècle* productions, *The Secret Rose* and *The Wind Among the Reeds*, on the one hand, and the Rose poems he wrote earlier in the decade, on the other. *The Rose* is idealistic in every sense; it optimistically cherishes the hope that opposite energies—such as the rood and cross, male and female— can be conjoined, but both *The Secret Rose* and *The Wind Among the Reeds* express a fear bordering on despair that such extremes do not meet in actual life; that the most we can hope for is a brief intimation of connection before the dream is destroyed by impending apocalypse. This movement from hope to fear reverses itself in the sequence of later companion volumes, *The Tower* and *The Winding Stair*; it is *The Tower* that expresses apocalyptic despair at a nightmare that is more historical than mythic, and *The Winding Stair* answers by suggesting the difficult compensations a more internal focus may produce.

The warring forces of mortal and immortal desires are deadlocked in *The Secret Rose* and *The Wind Among the Reeds*; the conflict seems resolvable only through apocalypse—perhaps at the last great battle in the Valley of the Black Pig. As the wise king counsels in "The Wisdom of the King," human order and supernatural wildness are mutually destructive: "law was made by man for the welfare of man, but wisdom the gods have made, and no man shall live by its light, for it and the hail and the rain and the thunder follow a way that is deadly to mortal things" (*SR*, 23). The weary despair of the young Yeats springs from the same source as the witty humor of Wilde: the incompatibility of action and vision, the squalid hypocrisy of daily life and the sublimity of natural and supernatural power, the objective and the subjective. It is this mutual repulsion separating opposite poles that Yeats would eventually address through his theories of the antiself (in "Per Amica Silentia Lunae") and antithetical historical gyres (in *A Vision*). It is only by straining to become one's opposite that one can equally distribute the claims of the ordinary and the sublime by alternating between them; one must come, like the swan, to be equally at home in two different elements—water and air (or earth and fire). The Rose and the wind among the reeds provide an early example of such commensurate opposites.

Yeats's poets and prophets are necessarily exiled from life; it is the condition of their absorption in dream. "The Crucifixion of the Outcast," which Wilde extravagantly praised (see *A*, 191), suggests that the feared poet/prophet will inevitably be immolated because he wakens "forgotten longings in [the] hearts" of his listeners (*SR*, 49); even the social outcasts—beggars—turn against the poet. Like Angus in "The Heart of the Spring," the poet longs for "a life whose abundance would fill centuries" (*SR*, 85), but such a possibility seems to exist only in the imagination, as represented by the shadowy world of the *sidhe*.

The world of *The Secret Rose* and *The Wind Among the Reeds* is hopelessly riven by the incompatible extremes of ideal and real, spirit and flesh, imagination and action, male and female, mythology and history. None of the figures who preside over the two volumes can bridge this divide; in their different ways, Michael Robartes, Owen Aherne, and Red Hanrahan (and, by implication, the men who inspired them)[77] all lose contact with what it means to be human and mortal. Michael Robartes, in "Rosa Alchemica," and Owen Aherne, in "The Tables of the Law," are unable to survive in the outside world. Both forsake the mortal world for the world of the spirit and as a result suffer the fate of the outcast: Michael Robartes is killed by a mob of angry local people, and Owen Aherne, in learning to follow the law of his own being, finds that in spurning the commandments of the Father he has lost the love and redemption of the Son. When the narrator sees him again he is a living ghost, a ghastly reminder that arbitrary laws are necessary to teach the soul the meaning of sin, which alone can kindle the hope of redemption.

The power that Yeats attributes to outcasts is the same capacity for originality and individualism—a potential for revisionary thought—that Wilde associated with criminals. As the youngest magus in "The Adoration of the Magi" explains, "when people are good the world likes them and takes possession of them, and so eternity comes through people who are not good or who have been forgotten" (*VSR*, 170). "The Adoration of the Magi" illustrates the incompatibility of the spiritual and the quotidian worlds by enclosing a magical neonativity within a narrative frame that tries to contain the event by opposing it. A dying woman driven by unquenchable desire gives birth to her opposite, a dancing unicorn, which is "most unlike man of all living things, being cold, hard and virginal" (*VSR*, 168), but the narrator reacts strongly against such a celebration of the alien by returning to orthodoxy, adopting humility, and submersing himself in the common life. He relates, "I no longer live an elaborate and haughty life, but seek to lose myself among the prayers and the sorrows of the multitude. I pray best in poor chapels, where frieze coats brush against me as I kneel, and . . . I pray against the demons" (*VSR*, 171–72).

What Yeats does, by enclosing the imaginative extravagance of this neonativity within the narrative of a humble man who reaffirms the simplicity of the common life, is to balance the two perspectives on the fulcrum of their mutual incompatibility. The extreme the narrator adopts is too narrowly obedient, and the extreme that the Magi have witnessed is too vertiginously lawless and wild. Such a nonresolution, which leaves the reader with two equally unacceptable choices between spiritual wildness and domestic discipline, is the quandary to which *The Secret Rose* is devoted: Yeats claims, in his often-quoted dedicatory letter to AE, that the stories in the collection have but one subject: "the war of spiritual with natural order" (*VSR*, 233), and the two orders are definitely at odds with each other. Moreover, it is the spiritual order that is lawless; it is peopled by thieves, prostitutes, rebels, and outcasts. Yeats believed that this affinity of the supernatural for the reviled is what made the Irish such a spiritual and imaginative people; as he once claimed, "the spiritual history of the world has been the history of conquered races" (*UP*, Vol. 2, 70).

Yeats sees the incompatibility of the spiritual world and the quotidian one as a version of the opposition between mind and body, which is for him a highly gendered opposition. Woman represents the mother goddess—Nature—and the male poet plays the slain god who dies for love of her. Nature/woman is pure body, a dancer, tragically divided from the poet/man who is all head, a singer. Yeats interprets Salomé's dance with the severed head in Wilde's *Salomé* as an illustration of this archetypal conflict, and in the first story of *The Secret Rose* (1897), "The Binding of the Hair," Yeats reframes this seasonal and eternal conflict in specifically Irish terms. The mother goddess of the story is Dectira, who is also an embodiment of the Rose/Lily (Aodh refers to her as "the Rose of my Desire, the Lily of my Peace," *SR*, 4), and the slain poet/god is Aodh, who is killed in battle before he can fulfill his promise to sing his praise of Dectira. Dectira searches for him and finds only his head hung on a bush. In fulfillment of its promise, the head sings "He Gives His Beloved Certain Rhymes" and then rolls to the feet of the queen. The poet-lover, like the prophet John the Baptist, must be sacrificed by a beautiful woman to ensure the continuation of imaginative life: she is all body, he is all foolish head, and their union a dance of living and dead.[78]

The Wind Among the Reeds

When Yeats turns at the very end of the century to *The Wind Among the Reeds*, he again uses many of the symbolist techniques that he used in *The Rose*, although he employs them in more local and specifically Irish ways. In *The Wind Among the Reeds*, as in "The Rose," the magnetizing central image is once again a symbol of the heart (a usage anticipated at the end of "The Lake Isle of Innisfree").[79] Like the Rose, the image of the wind among reeds gathers around it a rich array of associations. Again, the muse of the volume is a female figure animated by puns: the wind is the *sidhe* (the fairies), but it is also a *she* (in English), and this she is *Eire* (air), a slant English/Irish pun reinforced by the pun on Gael/gale. (Gaelic, as Yeats was quick to apprehend, is the language of Eire or air, where the fairies are felt in the wind.) Eire is also, of course, the woman from Irish mythology after whom Ireland was named; Yeats evokes her explicitly in "Into the Twilight," in which he reminds the worn-out heart that "Your mother Eire is always young."

Like the Rose, who is a poetic muse as well as a national one, the image of wind among reeds also evokes a musical "reeding": the production of music and an awareness of reading as musical (since poetry is also musical). If the Rose's dancing produces a combined image of poetic feet and a beating heart, and if her association with the mouth or lips accents her role as muse, the wind among reeds transforms these associations into a related set of allusions to the actual production of speech, music, and poetry. The movement of wind through reeds calls up not only the pastoral associations of a shepherd's pipe and other reed instruments, but also figures the physical basis of speech, the wind passing through the vocal chords, the literal meaning of inspiration. (As Yeats writes in "He Thinks of Those Who Have Spoken Evil of His Beloved," he made his song "out of a mouthful of air.") Yeats's evocation of reed instruments also suggests the plaintiveness of unrequited love through its allusion to the story of Pan and the wood nymph Syrinx. When Pan fell in love with Syrinx, he pursued her until she prayed for release. To help her escape him, her sisters the water nymphs transformed her body into a handful of marsh reeds. As Pan stood gazing and "sighing, the wind blew through the reeds, and produced a thin plaintive sound," which enchanted him. Pan vowed that he and Syrinx would always produce the sweet music together, so he fastened together reeds of different length and made his famous pipe out of her body.[80]

In *The Wind Among the Reeds*, breath is divine as well as musical and passionate. If the Rose is Christ, divine beauty crucified on the cross of time, the wind is the Holy Spirit of the Christian trinity ("blessedness goes where the wind goes"), as well as the pagan people of the *sidhe*. The wind echoes the eucharistic emphases of "The Rose" by its association with the Host in the opening poem, "The Hosting of the Sidhe," and in "The Unappeaseable Host." Again like the rose, the wind is sexual as well as divine—it is the wind of unending desire in which the spirits of Paolo and Francesca perpetually blow in Dante's *Inferno*. Finally, Eire is literally the land: a lake edge or shore in Sligo (*sidhe* literally means "hillside") personified as a "she." Like the Rose, Eire is implicitly a supernatural woman whose breast is the surface of the lake or sea that encloses the depths of her heart. Eire's hair is reeds (as is clearly apparent in "The Host of the Air"), and what blows through her is not only the animating wind of desire, inspiration, music, poetry, myth, and nation, but also the wailing of the banshee, harbinger of destruction. The woman's heart and the poet's heart sometimes change places, so that the lake or ocean becomes an image of the *poet's* heart, which his beloved inhabits in the form of a fish, one of the shapes typically assumed by the *sidhe* (see "The Fish" and "The Song of Wandering Aengus"). As Yeats represents her, Eire, like the Rose, is complex and powerful, a brilliant riposte to the degradation of Ireland's image by the English, but, despite her kinship to an idealized Maud Gonne, who presents herself in *A Servant of the Queen* as the "woman of the Sidhe," Eire is ultimately no more real or individual than the Rose. Although she represents the conditions of speech, she is always spoken through.

At the core of *The Wind Among the Reeds* is a simple and powerful personal memory. Yeats recalls a "perfect" moment from a night "long ago, when I heard the wind blowing in a bed of reeds by the border of a little lake" (*UP* I, 324). Yeats was not alone in the intensity of his feeling about the sound of wind among reeds; Ella Young, a literary figure associated with both Yeats and Maud Gonne, treats it as a figure of mystery: "Who could make known, to one ignorant of it, the wind's path among reeds?"[81] According to P. W. Joyce, appreciation of the rustling of the wind is commonplace among the ancient Irish. He writes,

They loved the music of the wind and the waves. The sound of the breeze rustling through the foliage so struck the imagination of those spiritual people, that in Cormac's Glossary the word *omna*, one of the Irish names for the oak- tree, is derived from *fuamna*, "sounding": "because"—in the words of the Glossary—"great is the sound of the wind blowing against it." (*Social History* 2, 503)

When Yeats returned to the lakes of Sligo for an aural as well as a visual and literary symbol for his volume of poems, he was recording his love of the land, and, as Maud Gonne recalled, "We were both held by the mysterious power of the land."[82] Gonne and Yeats treat the land—the actual dirt, rocks, and bog of Ireland, replete with invisible inhabitants—as the source and pattern for the nation. Gonne recounts that both she and Yeats believed the land of Ireland to be "powerfully alive and invisibly peopled," relating that "whenever we grew despondent over the weakness of the national movement, we went to it for comfort. If only we could make contact with the hidden forces of the land it would give us strength for the freeing of Ireland" (Gwynn, *Scattering Branches*, 22). The fairy tradition grounds the imaginative history of the nation in its topography, and Yeats, whose room in Bedford Place had a map of Sligo painted on the ceiling, believed that by exhuming the ancient gods "buried" in the landscape, Ireland could reconstitute the unity of the Irish race. In *Four Years*, he asks, "Have not all races had their first unity from a mythology [polytheism] that marries them to rock and hill?"[83]

The Wind Among the Reeds commemorates not only the power of the land in Ireland but also the importance of the people, especially the peasants. In a long footnote to the 1899 edition, Yeats is careful to explain that the powerful and wealthy refer to the ancient gods as the Tuatha Dé Danaan, or the tribes of the goddess Danu, "but the poor called them, and still sometimes call them, the Sidhe" (*TWAR*, 65):

> Sidhe is also Gaelic for wind, and certainly the Sidhe have much to do with the wind. They journey in whirling winds. . . . When the country people see the leaves whirling on the road they bless themselves, because they believe the Sidhe to be passing by. They are almost always said to wear no covering upon their heads, and to let their hair stream out; and the great among them, for they have great and simple, go much upon horseback. (1899 *Wind Among the Reeds*, 65–66)[84]

Yeats's note announces that *The Wind Among the Reeds* will not follow the aristocratic and cultured precedents of "The Rose," but will concern itself with the land and its people—both the *sidhe* who haunted it and the peasants who tended it.

In *The Wind Among the Reeds*, the human body is a frail instrument—for Yeats a mere reed[85]—through which the divine wind passes to produce music. The reeds are also, however, *hair* blown by the wind, and by extension the strings of an Irish harp (both the aeolian harp and that of Aengus, strung with the hair of his beloved). According to a Rosicrucian account that forms part of the occult background of *The Wind Among the Reeds*, when the female deity of Ireland is, like the Rose, crucified, her hair becomes a harp that produces music, speech, and the rainbow. As a personification of the supernatural, this deity's color is green, "the spirit-colour, a magic colour, the colour of the 'fairies'":

> In Ireland, green is universally regarded with distrust; but with veneration, in the spiritual sense. It is the national colour; for the Patroness of Ireland is the female deity, the Mother of Nature, known in the classic mythology as Venus—equally Venus the graceful and Venus the terrible, as the Goddess of Life and Death. . . . [This] presiding deity . . . is the mythic 'Woman,' born out of the fecundity of nature, or out of the 'Great Deep.' This is the genius . . . who is 'impaled' or 'crucified'—in its real, hidden meaning—upon the stock, or 'Tree of Life', indicated by the Irish Harp. Her hair, in the moment of agony, streams Daphne-like, as 'when about to be transformed into the tree,' behind her in the wind, and twines, in the mortal, mythical stress, into the *seven* strings of the magic Irish Harp, whose music is the music of the spheres, or of the Rosicrucian, assumed penitential, visible world. (Jennings, 202–203)

The seven strings stand for the seven vowels, "by means of which came speech to man," the seven pure tones in music, and the seven prismatic colors of the rainbow. The smell of flowery air that dominated *The Rose* has made way for appeals to other senses, especially hearing and sight, via music and the colors of the air.

This Rosicrucian tale about the crucifixion of an Irish, female nature god whose hair becomes a harp producing all music, speech, and color, helps to explain not only Yeats's connection of Eire and wind with music and poetry, but also his treatment of hair as eerily alive, like the wind itself (in English, the link between "hair" and "air" is also reinforced verbally). When the boy sees the women of the *sidhe* in "The Heart of the Spring," they are crowning themselves with roses and lilies and "shaking about their living hair, which moves . . . with the motion of their thoughts, now spreading out and now gathering close to their heads" (*SR*, 83).

In the poems, harpstrings, hair, and reeds are all imagistically akin, and all are seen as magical and erotic means of seduction and containment. As Yeats writes in "He wishes his Beloved were Dead" ["Aodh to Dectora," "Aedh wishes his Beloved were Dead"], "Were you but lying cold and dead, / . . . You would come hither, and bend your head":

> Nor would you rise and hasten away,
> Though you have the will of the wild birds,
> But know your hair was bound and wound
> About the stars and moon and sun.
> (*VP*, 176)

The association between music, frustrated love, and confinement seems to spring from Yeats's interest in the story of Edain and Aengus, to which he devotes the prologue to the poetic version of *The Shadowy Waters*.[86] While Aengus and Edain were together, she "*wove seven strings, / Sweet with all music, out of his long hair, / Because her hands had been made wild by love*" (*VP*, 219). Then later, when Edain had been changed into a fly, Aengus made a harp in turn in order to communicate with her as she flew through the winds, "[*t*]*hat she among her winds might know he wept*" (*VP*, 220). The love of Aengus and Edain, frustrated by Edain's consignment to the winds, stays in the background of *The Wind Among the Reeds* (the queen in the first version of "The Cap and Bells" was named "Edane");[87] the harp of hair is both a symbol of eternal love among the *sidhe* and a traditional symbol of Ireland. Moreover, harp music is a figure of the harmony and dissonance between the human body and the divine/natural spirits, a harmony and dissonance we experience as the play of emotion. In the Rosicrucian view, "Music is . . . master of the man's emotions, and therefore of the man" (Jennings, 222); it is "produced in the ceaseless operations of material nature, because nature itself is penitential and but the painful (and musical) expression between two dissonant points. . . . Music is life and life is music. Both are pain, although made delightful" (Jennings, 221). Music unites the divine, natural, and human worlds; the Rosicrucians saw it both as the enchantment that pervades all nature and as "the wail, or plaint, of the instinctive soul on its 'wounded', or 'sacrificed', or *Ruined Side*" (Jennings, 386).

The atmosphere of the 1899 *Wind Among the Reeds* is dominated by Dantesque torment and a driving desire for rest—either sleep, forgetfulness, or the end of time—a torment intensified by the lover's intermittent conviction that "his head / May not lie on the breast nor his lips on the hair / Of the woman that he loves, until he dies" ("He [Mongan] thinks of his Past Greatness when a Part of the Constellations of Heaven," *VP*, 177). In "He [Aedh] hears the Cry of the Sedge," the despair is wilder, and the wind cries to him that "*Your breast will not lie by the breast / Of your beloved in sleep*"

> *Until the axle break*
> *That keeps the stars in their round,*
> *And hands hurl in the deep*
> *The banners of East and West,*
> *And the girdle of light is unbound.*
> (*VP*, 165)

The yearning for "the sleep / Men have named beauty" ("The Secret Rose") or violent apocalypse also drives such poems as "The Everlasting Voices," "He [Mongan] mourns for the Change that has come upon him and his Beloved, and longs for the End of the World," "He [Michael Robartes] bids his Beloved be at Peace," and "The Valley of the Black Pig." The most memorable image of the end of time is Mongan's wish that a wild, gigantic, and bestial pig would uproot the heavens:

> I would that the Boar without bristles had come from the West
> And had rooted the sun and moon and stars out of the sky
> And lay in the darkness, grunting, and turning to his rest.
> (*VP*, 153)

In "He Wishes for the Cloths of Heaven," Mongan's wish is more gently echoed by Aedh, who also wants to bring the heavens low, but as an act of homage rather than a victory of darkness:

> Had I the heavens' embroidered cloths,
> Enwrought with golden and silver light,
> The blue and the dim and the dark cloths
> Of night and light and the half-light,
> I would spread the cloths under your feet.
> (*VP,* 176)

Even the seductive call of the *sidhe* promises release from the heart's "*mortal dream,*" a release that the world regards as impotence and that constitutes another form of loss. In "The Hosting of the Sidhe," Niamh warns, "*if any gaze on our rushing band, / We come between him and the deed of his hand, / We come between him and the hope of his heart.*" (*VP,* 141) Finally, Yeats sees his excess of love in terms of Christ's passion. In "The Travail of Passion," the speaker explains that

> When an immortal passion breathes in mortal clay;
> Our hearts endure the scourge, the plaited thorns, the way
> Crowded with bitter faces, the wounds in palm and side . . . (*VP,* 172)

The poet longs for the destruction of nature and song, but these are also his consolations; he sees his heart as a lake, his beloved's hair as the reeds that shelter it, and the wind that blows through the reeds as the poetry and song that shake the heart and express its desire, a desire that can escalate into a passionate tempest of ecstasy and death, or that can recede into simple merriment, as in the poem that concludes the volume, "The Fiddler of Dooney." "The Host of the Air" best illustrates the relation between heart and lake, hair and reeds, air and emptiness. It follows "The Lover [Aedh] tells of the Rose in his Heart," where the poet alludes to the "deeps" of his heart, thereby introducing his heart as a body of water. "The Host of the Air" begins with O'Driscoll, who "drove with a song / The wild duck and the drake / From the tall and tufted reeds / Of the drear Hart Lake." In earlier versions Yeats made the pun more explicit by writing "*Heart* Lake" (Holdsworth, ed., *WATR,* 29, 43). As he watches the darkening of the reeds, they remind him of "the long dim hair / Of Bridget his bride." He loses his bride to the *sidhe,* and then high up in the air he hears music, a piping both sad and gay. The poem that follows is called "The Fish," and the fish is the beloved, uncapturable denizen of the liquid depths of the heart. This motif is picked up again in "The Song of Wandering Aengus," in which the trout caught by Aengus becomes a "glimmering girl" whom he never ceases to pursue. That these "fish" are also the Rose is clear from a poem that precedes both in the volume, "The Lover [Aedh] tells of the Rose in his Heart," in which the lover's heart has depths like a lake, and the image of the beloved's beauty blossoms perpetually (and impossibly) in those watery depths: the point of reference for all his perceptions is "your image that blossoms a rose in the deeps of my heart."[88]

In *The Wind Among the Reeds*, as in *The Rose*, the governing images might seem to suggest completeness in their attempts to map the complex relations among divinity, sexuality, material reality, mythology-geography, intellect, and emotion, but that impression of completeness is deceptive. Yeats's images, far from being complete or totalizing, are simply concrete, and what confesses their incompleteness is their heterogeneity and their dynamism, their propensity for constant transformation. The dynamism of Yeats's images is partly propelled by wordplay; in his early explorations of the heart, he at first emphasizes the "art" buried in the word (*The Rose*), and next he lays stress on the "ear" buried within it, remaining sensitive all the while to the suggestive proximity of "heart" with "hearth." If "rose" as a verb intimates transcendence and growth, "wind" as a verb introduces a more serpentine, demonic motion that allows Yeats to explore a darker range of emotions (punctuated by occasional lightness of heart, as in "The Fiddler of Dooney"). The poet of *The Wind Among the Reeds* is like Cumhal in "The Crucifixion of the Outcast"; his soul "is like the wind among the salley gardens": "it blows me to and fro, and up and down, and puts many things into my mind and out of my mind" (*SR*, 46). The wind becomes a vehicle for the moods, which Yeats saw personified in the *sidhe*: as the wise king teaches in "The Wisdom of the King," "the great Moods are alone immortal, and the creators of mortal things," and they wear the shape of the children of Dana (*SR*, 21). After *The Wind Among the Reeds*, Yeats dresses moods in different shapes, but they continue to be the spirits that animate his poetry and his landscapes.

The apparent comprehensiveness of each of Yeats's touchstone images is exposed as illusory by the mysteriousness that is also characteristic of each. Yeats's images work like the old knight in "Out of the Rose"; their function is "to bind the hearts of men as within a leash of mystery" (*SR*, 53), and it is the mystery that drives the poet to a constant articulation and retranslation of images. Yeats's early poetry intertwines emotional extremes with great skill; he, like Hanrahan in "The Twisting of the Rope," makes his audience know "a joy that was kneaded up with melancholy" (*SR*, 146). Also like Hanrahan, the early poetry and stories are haunted by the ghost of a more full-blooded life that seems to have eluded them; the question that hovers over Yeats's work of the 1890s is whether, like Axel, "in our strange hearts we have destroyed the love of life" (*Axël*, 169). All Yeats's subsequent images represent renewed attempts to capture, not just the feeling of life as expressed by a poet's severed head, but *individual embodiments* of that life, with all the harmonies and dissonances that connect them.

In 1932, Yeats asked, after reading the first volume of his collected lyric poetry, "what man is this who . . . says the same thing in so many different ways?" (Wade, ed., *L*, 798). In the volumes of poetry that follow *The Rose* and *The Wind Among the Reeds*, these images undergo many transformations; the wind among the reeds intensifies into the "big wind of nineteen hundred and three" that blew down many trees in the seven woods of Lady Gregory's estate, Coole Park (*VP*, 814), suggesting the governing image of *In the Seven Woods*. The seven hairs of the harp correspond to the seven woods of the estate and to the string of the bow of "that Great Archer, / Who . . . hangs / A cloudy quiver over Pairc-na-lee" ("In the Seven Woods"), and the reeds have hardened into trees and arrows that move through the wind (instead of vice versa). (The correspondence between trees and bows is strengthened by Yeats's emphasis on "boughs" in such poems as "The Withering of the Boughs.")

The Lily—muted counterpart to the Rose in *The Rose*—mutates into the swan of *The Wild Swans at Coole* and later poems, who resemble a blank page, its "stormy white"

> So arrogantly pure, a child might think
> It can be murdered with a spot of ink.
> ("Coole Park and Ballylee, 1931," *VP*, 491)

Yet the swan is also a reembodied image of the Celtic Twilight, with its symbolic meaning as an intermediary between two worlds. The swan who rapes Leda exemplifies such doubleness in its powerful conflation of the divine and the bestial. In addition, the swan serves as an image of old age, a state that mediates between life and the afterlife, in poems like "The Tower," in which Yeats imagines himself singing a swan song while floating on the stream toward death.

The Rose of sacrifice undergoes manifold permutations, as well. In "Easter, 1916" Yeats ponders the possibility that the heart he once saw as a crucified rose is actually a stone: "Too long a sacrifice / Can make a stone of the heart." "The Rose Tree," too, reflects Yeats's slightly horrified awareness that the self-sacrifice he once saw as divine compassion has a gruesomely practical side to it. The Rose Tree of Ireland was withered by "a breath of politic words" or a bitter wind, and it needs watering. Padraic Pearse's pragmatic solution is "There's nothing but our own red blood / Can make a right Rose Tree." At the same time, as Donald R. Pearce convincingly argues, the Rose metamorphoses into the "antithetical" phases of the moon in *A Vision*.[89] The logic of such a transformation was laid as early as *The Secret Rose*, in which the moon is described as glimmering "in the dimness like a great white rose hung on the lattice of some boundless and phantasmal world" (*SR*, 118).

The tension between Yeats's Wildean self-portrait as a severed head and his depiction of woman as pure dancing body reemerges in *Michael Robartes and the Dancer*, in which Michael Robartes's occult preoccupations place him in haunted opposition to the dancer, so that they become an unsolved antimony.[90] The incompatibility of Michael Robartes and the dancer becomes the basis for Yeats's theory of necessary antiselves that fulfill and complete each other; the story allowed him a way to purge himself of judgmental rejections of otherness.

The fire of the Rose gives way to a temporary preoccupation with coolness, perhaps under the influence of "Coole" Park, and from a sensuous love of veils (especially veilings of hair), he adopts the opposite image of the eagle staring at the sun with lidless eyes. The many-faceted changes of symbolic images ultimately culminate in two volumes that reverse and antiphonally "answer" the emphases of *The Rose* and *The Wind Among the Reeds*: *The Tower* and *The Winding Stair*.

The Tower and The Winding Stair

Despite the fact that "tower" rhymes with "power," and that the poems in *The Tower* are committed to exploring abuses of power and instances of oppression, *The Tower* (1928) is not the celebration of male power that it is sometimes taken to be. The tower is certainly a phallic image—in ancient symbolic dialogue with the female rose—but it is also, like the Irish nation, "half dead at the top" ("Blood and the Moon," *VP*, 480). The tower evokes not only a decrepit social structure, a monument to a disintegrating and nightmarish male sexual power, but also the head, severed from its body and in unreal exile from the world, the towers Yeats remembers Shelley identifying as "thought's crowned powers" ("Blood and the Moon"). *The Tower* is a relentless, agonized interrogation of the social implications of male control, as well as a probing self-examination of Yeats's own imprisonment in and complicity with the male structures that both provoke conflict and insulate men against a more nuanced and chaotic reality.

Yeats began his program of self-questioning as early as "The Dolls," where the dolls shriek that the noise and filth of a real baby is an insult and a disgrace to them, and the dollmaker's wife apologizes to him for having introduced the disorder of life into the controlled world of art: "My dear, my dear, O dear, / It was an accident." "The Magi" similarly comments on the ease of favoring art over the terrifying unpredictability of life by contrasting the stiff, ancient, painted kings who appear and disappear against the sky with the lowly and divine revelation they long to see again: "The uncontrollable mystery on the bestial floor." What makes Yeats turn against his early poetry is not its "femininity," but its evasion of disorder and ugliness (an evasion that also characterized Wilde's earlier work); *The Tower* suggests that such preferences for fantasy are in fact products of the dreaming male head, severed from the world. Moreover, a diet of fantasy and a life of isolation produces brutality: "We had fed the heart on fantasies, / The heart's grown brutal from the fare" ("Meditations in Time of Civil War," *VP*, 425). In "Nineteen Hundred and Nineteen" Yeats confesses he has learned in his old age "that we were crack-pated when we dreamed," and he looks out on a half-ruined, violent world in which the night sweats with terror and

> days are dragon-ridden, the nightmare
> Rides upon sleep: a drunken soldiery
> Can leave the mother, murdered at her door,
> To crawl in her own blood, and go scot-free.
> ("Nineteen Hundred and Nineteen," *VP*, 428)

He tries to comfort himself for being able to "read the signs" without sinking "unmanned / Into the half-deceit of some intoxicant," and he tries to rationalize that "triumph would / But break upon his ghostly solitude," but his defense crumbles:

> But is there any comfort to be found?
> Man is in love and loves what vanishes,
> What more is there to say? (*VP*, 429–31)

The Tower articulates not only the terror of destruction in the midst of civil war, but also, more unexpectedly, the horror of creation—artistic creation, motherhood ("Two Songs from a Play," "Among School Children," "The Mother of God"), and even birth:

> Never to have lived is best, ancient writers say;
> Never to have drawn the breath of life, never to have looked
> 　into the eye of day.
> ("A Man Young and Old," XI, *VP*, 459).

At the beginning of "Blood and the Moon" in *The Winding Stair*, Yeats makes it emphatically clear that his celebration of the tower is in part a mockery of the privileges of gender and class that produced the nightmare of his time:

> Blessed be this place,
> More blessed still this tower;
> A bloody, arrogant power
> Rose out of the race
> Uttering, mastering it,
> Rose like these walls from these
> Storm-beaten cottages—
> In mockery I have set
> A powerful emblem up,
> And sing it rhyme upon rhyme
> In mockery of a time
> Half dead at the top.
> (*VP*, 480)

The tower is a structure "[e]mblematical of the night" ("A Dialogue of Self and Soul"), storm, and the darkness of the soul.[91] In Irish mythology, the tower is associated with shadowy decay through the battle of Moytura, which, as Yeats explains in the notes to *The Wind Among the Reeds*, means "the Towery Plain." The battle of Moytura was the battle between the tribes of Danu, "powers of light, and warmth, and fruitfulness, and goodness, and the Fomor, the powers of darkness, and cold and barrenness, and badness" (1899 *TWAR*, 100–101). In *The Tower*, the Fomorians have come again in the shape of the Black and Tans of 1919, and the battle of Moytura is bleakly restaged in the darkness of Ireland's civil war. The events which lie behind *The Tower* are among the worst in Ireland's long and bloody history, as Yeats observes and meditates upon them in *his* protective but crumbling tower home, Thoor Ballylee.

Like the Rose, the Tower becomes a symbol of Yeats's poetry that accents his aging body as well as the esoteric isolation of his thought. It also, as he wrote Sturge Moore, stresses his actual contact with the earth: "As you know all my art theories depend upon just this—rooting of mythology in the earth."[92] Moreover, the Tower produces its own opposite both nearby and within it; on its "acre of stony ground . . . the symbolic rose can break in flower" ("Meditations in Time of Civil War"), and inside its rigid, ancient walls is a laborious winding stair, a spiral famous for its "steep ascent" ("A Dialogue of Self and Soul," *VP*, 477).

In *The Tower*, Yeats reaches back to the Rose to retrieve the emblem of his yearning heart and presents that heart as it was in the 1920s: sharply wrenched and despairing, or flaming with rage and embittered idealism. In the famous poem that introduces the volume, "Sailing to Byzantium," the aged speaker's central plea is for the sages standing in God's holy fire to "Consume my heart away; sick with desire / And fastened to a dying animal / It knows not what it is" (*VP*, 408). The next poem, "The Tower," asks the same "troubled heart" what to do with the "Decrepit age that has been tied to me / As to a dog's tail" (*VP*, 409). In "Meditations in Time of Civil War," Yeats confesses that "only an aching heart / Conceives a changeless work of art" (*VP*, 421), implying that his heartache lies behind his desire to create an unchanging "monument" in his *Tower* poems, even though he knows, as he proclaims in "Nineteen Hundred and Nineteen," that "no work can stand, . . . / No honor leave its mighty monument" (*VP*, 429). At the end of "Meditations," he calms his "ambitious" heart, which wanted him to prove his worth "In something that all others understand or share," with the reassurance that he would not have been satisfied by such an endeavor (*VP*, 427). Yeats again questions the value of his labor-intensive poetic art when, in "Nineteen Hundred and Nineteen," he proposes, "Come let us mock at the great / That had such burdens on the mind / And toiled so hard and late / To leave some monument behind, / Nor thought of the levelling wind" (*VP*, 432).

The poems in the center of *The Tower* turn to mythology to dramatize the strangeness and violence to which great hearts are subject. In "Two Songs from a Play," Yeats pictures a staring virgin tearing the heart out of Dionysus's side (Yeats implies that when the heart is eaten, the god will be reborn from another "fierce virgin," Mary, and will issue "thence / In Galilean turbulence" (*VP*, 437). The poem concludes with an assertion that the heart fuels *all* achievement, whether creative or destructive: "Whatever flames upon the night / Man's own resinous heart has fed." When Leda is raped by Zeus in "Leda and the Swan," the poet asks if "body, laid in that white rush," can "feel the strange heart beating where it lies?" (*VP*, 441). In "Among School Children," Yeats returns to his own heart, which is "driven wild" when he sees a young girl who reminds him of the "Ledaean body" he once loved (*VP*, 444); in the end, Yeats chides religious icons and dreams of human perfection alike, because they, being unattainable, "break hearts."

The experience of heartbreak dominates the concluding poems of *The Tower*. In "Owen Aherne and his Dancers," a personified "Heart" goes mad when it realizes that it "Should find no burden but itself and yet should be worn out" (*VP*, 449), and "A Man Young and Old" turns lunatic when he finds that the woman he loves bears not "A heart of flesh and blood," but "a heart of stone" (*VP*, 451). The man, "like a bit of stone," lies under a broken tree and explains,

I could recover if I shrieked
My heart's agony
To passing bird, but I am dumb
From human dignity.
(*VP*, 452)

The lover's "heart is wrung" in recollection of the lost "wildness" of the woman he once pursued, and he fears that if he were to have any of the satisfaction for which he thirsts, "his beating heart would burst" (*VP*, 453–54).

The Tower is battered by winds that are no longer those of "Sleep, Hope, Dream, endless Desire" as in *The Wind Among the Reeds* ("He bids his Beloved be at Peace"), but instead they are tempestuous and violent—winds of storm and war. Yeats prophesies that these winds will destroy him and level his achievements; his role is implicitly that of John the Baptist, about to be beheaded once again by Salome (Herodias' daughter), or that of the poet Aodh, who lost his head in war ('The Binding of the Hair," *The Secret Rose*). "Nineteen Hundred and Nineteen" ends with shrieking winds, which are now peopled not by the women of the *sidhe* but by Salome and her sisters, who have returned again, amorous, angry, and blind, to dance furiously in the gales:

> Herodias' daughters have returned again,
> A sudden blast of dusty wind and after
> Thunder of feet, tumult of images,
> Their purpose in the labyrinth of the wind.
> (*VP*, 433).

Out of the physical, emotional, and historical destruction that Yeats records in *The Tower* comes an important revelation, the realization that came to Wilde in prison: the desire for perfection and purity paradoxically *produces* its opposite, a ruinous admixture of hope and despair. As Yeats writes in "From 'Oedipus at Colonus,'" the last section of "A Man Young and Old,"

> Even from that delight memory treasures so,
> Death, despair, division of families, all entanglements of mankind grow,
> As that old wandering beggar and these God-hated children know.
> (*VP*, 459)

What the mythical Greek Oedipus had learned from his travails once he was old, blind, and outcast, the famous figures of recent history always knew. In the next poem, "The Three Monuments," Yeats describes a public political meeting in Dublin under the statues of Horatio Nelson, Daniel O'Connell, and Charles Stewart Parnell. The popular statesmen are saying "That purity built up the state / And after kept it from decay," and they admonish the crowd to abstain from base ambition, intellect, and pride because such attributes will "bring in impurity." The response of the three statues, "The three old rascals," is to "laugh aloud" (*VP*, 460). Yeats suggests that although he too has engaged in it, the worship of purity is itself corrupt. Life is more labyrinthine than a "pure" vision would allow, as the "heroes" of myth and history, with their aching hearts, know only too well. As Yeats makes clear in "A Prayer for My Son," even Christ had to experience "All of that worst ignominy / Of flesh and bone" (*VP*, 436).

At the beginning of *The Tower*, in the poem by the same name, Yeats accuses himself of having committed the "crime" of preferring a simpler, nostalgic, imaginative vision over the greater and more frightening challenge of plunging "Into the labyrinth of another's being" (*VP*, 413). Like Wilde, Yeats indulged artistic tendencies that, although formally brilliant and complex, were motivated by feelings that were both escapist and narcissistic. Yeats asks these difficult questions of himself by calling up his old creation and alter-ego, Red Hanrahan, whom he had driven "drunk or sober through the dawn" over twenty years earlier. Yeats recalls that Hanrahan "stumbled, tumbled, fumbled to and fro / And had but broken knees for hire / And horrible splendour of desire" (*VP*, 411), but Yeats asks Hanrahan to stay after he dismisses the other ghosts he summoned, "For I need all his mighty memories." The question that he asks this "Old lecher with a love on every wind" is this:

> Does the imagination dwell the most
> Upon a woman won or woman lost?
> If on the lost, admit you turned aside
> From a great labyrinth out of pride,
> Cowardice, some silly over-subtle thought
> Or anything called conscience once;
> And that if memory recur, the sun's
> Under eclipse and the day blotted out.
> (*VP*, 413–14)

Yeats is tentatively admitting that he (and his youthful alterego, Hanrahan) privileged his own imagination over the greater and more frightening mystery of another's reality. By posing this immensely disturbing question to himself, Yeats remakes himself anew as someone willing to face uncertainties he had once shunned.

The Tower as Yeats conceived it not only represents the impossibility of wisdom and the triumph of power among the living, but it is also, as he indicates in his note to "Blood and the Moon," a watch tower and a *pharos* or lighthouse that sends a beacon of warning to those navigating in darkness and storm. (*VP*, 830 and Clark, xxiv). As Yeats began work on *The Winding Stair* he began to suspect that *The Tower* "was exaggerated in certain directions" (*The Winding Stair*, xxii), and he began to concentrate not only on the dark night of history and the soul, but on the flashes of illumination that stand out more sharply in such darkness. The famous moments of hard-won affirmation in *The Winding Stair* are products of Yeats's gritty realism—his refusal to take refuge from sorrow and horror in dreams or love of beauty—in *The Tower*. So, in "A Dialogue of Self and Soul" the self can will a repetition of not just the beauty or triumph but the toil and ignominy of life:

> I am content to live it all again
> And yet again, if it be life to pitch
> Into the frog-spawn of a blind man's ditch . . .
> I am content to follow to its source
> Every event in action or in thought;
> Measure the lot; forgive myself the lot!
> (*VP*, 479)

Like the speaker in Auden's "Lullaby," Yeats summons the laborious discipline to "find this mortal world enough," and he is rewarded by moments of intense illumination such as the one recorded in a crowded London bookshop in "Vacillation":

> While on the shop and street I gazed
> My body of a sudden blazed;
> And twenty minutes more or less
> It seemed, so great my happiness,
> That I was blessèd and could bless.
> (*VP,* 501)

Such light moments exist in close proximity to the heaviness of responsibility and remorse, a remorse that weighs on him for the same reason that it briefly and periodically makes way for ecstasy—because he has with much effort and suffering relinquished the consolations of imaginative denial.

The Winding Stair, culminating in *Words for Music Perhaps* (a volume published the previous year that Yeats incorporated into *The Winding Stair*), is first of all an antiphonal response to *The Tower,* containing poems that expressed the resurgence of life Yeats experienced in the spring of 1929, with its "impression of the uncontrollable energy and daring of the great creators" (*VP,* 831). The volume's dialogue with *The Tower* is varied and complex; if *The Tower* rejects nostalgia and criticizes purity and innocence as containing the seeds of their own corruption, *The Winding Stair* relives the seduction of innocence and beauty all over again (especially in the first poem, "In Memory of Eva Gore-Booth and Con Markievicz," in the reminiscent Coole Park poems, and in "The Results of Thought"). Whereas *The Tower* exposes art as a consoling artifice, *The Winding Stair* replies that art can nevertheless help to contain or order ("break") the bitter "complexities of mire or blood," as the mosaic dancing floor at the end of "Byzantium" shows (*VP,* 498). If Yeats criticizes the "images" worshiped by nuns and mothers in *The Tower* ("Among School Children"), he takes another, equally true perspective in the companion volume, celebrating the "superhuman" power of "Those images that yet / Fresh images beget" ("Byzantium," *VP,* 498). *The Winding Stair* is infused with a resurgence of quixotic determination, peppered with references to the "savage indignation" that lacerated the heart of Jonathan Swift in Ireland, producing "The strength that gives our blood and state magnanimity of its own desire" (*VP,* 481), a strength incompatible with "Whiggery," "A levelling, rancorous, rational sort of mind / That never looked out of the eye of a saint / Or out of drunkard's eye" (*VP,* 486). Finally, if *The Tower* is concerned primarily with male power and its effects on the world, *The Winding Stair* focuses on the power of women (such as Con Markievicz, Lady Gregory, Maud Gonne, the Virgin Mary at the moment of conception, Crazy Jane, and "A Woman Young and Old"). Although Yeats loves their beauty (the "yellow hair" of "For Anne Gregory," *VP,* 492), he also pays homage to the inner resources women govern, which their beauty represents. As the young man's heart asserts with "noble rage" in "Young Man's Song," "She would as bravely show / Did all the fabric fade; / No withered crone I saw / Before the world was made" (*VP,* 516).

The Winding Stair replies not only to *The Tower,* however, but also to *The Wind*

Among the Reeds. The wind has become "winding," the air a "stair," the expectation of apocalypse only the movement of a gyre or whorl, which Yeats associates with the winding stair (*VP,* 850). The preoccupation with reed music in the
earlier volume is transposed into the lyrics of "Words for Music Perhaps." "Your
mother Eire" of *The Wind Among the Reeds* is no longer "always young" (*VP,*
148), however; Ireland is still a mother, but her womb is small, and her children
are full of rage: "Out of Ireland have we come. / Great hatred, little room, /
Maimed us at the start" (*VP,* 506). The heart of the poet is a "fanatic" one, in
love with sword *and* silk, men and women ("Symbols," *VP,* 484). Most important, though, Yeats is still affirming the contradictory complexity of his heart,
an emotional contradiction and volatility that complements Wilde's insistence
on the intellectual validity of paradox. The heart is the blood-watered soil out
of which the great contradiction of night and day emerges: "From man's blood-
sodden heart are sprung / Those branches of the night and day / Where the
gaudy moon is hung" (*VP,* 502). In a sense, Yeats is still affirming the principle
of balance he once represented through a Celtic twilight, but without the misti-
ness and softening of the contrast that twilight also connotes. In "Stream and
Sun at Glendalough," he portrays the dynamic contradiction that enlivens him
not as twilight, but as dappled sunlight and moving water. He chides himself for
fancying that he could "Better conduct myself or have more / Sense than a
common man," and once he has confessed his common humanity, he is free to
feel the exhilaration that the intricate motions of sun and water also inspire:

> What motion of the sun or stream
> Or eyelid shot the gleam
> That pierced my body through?
> What made me live like these that seem
> Self-born, born anew?
> (*VP,* 507)

Finally, as *The Wind Among the Reeds* was more erotic than *The Rose,* more suf-
fused with the restlessness of physical desire, *The Winding Stair* affirms the vi-
brancy of age, a strength of will and emotion that is undiminished by physical
decay.

In *The Tower,* Yeats raged against his own aging body because it provided no
refuge, no thoughtless alternative that he might turn to in his greater rage
against the illusions of intellect and imagination. Like Michael Robartes, as he
studiously searched in an isolated tower for "thought's crowned powers," Yeats
conceived a love for his own opposite, the dancing body (as in "Ego Dominus
Tuus" from *The Wild Swans at Coole*). In the 1920 poem "Michael Robartes and
the Dancer," Robartes tries to convince the dancer of the vitality of sinew, but
she quite naturally disputes with him, since she is pursuing the knowledge of
conceptual power that *she,* in her bodily youth and grace, still lacks. Michael
Robartes nonetheless argues that "blest souls are not composite," expressing
his new conviction that physicality and thoughtlessness offer an "uncomposite
blessedness" that he has never known.

In "Words for Music Perhaps" and especially in "A Woman Young and Old" and the Crazy Jane poems, Yeats continues to complicate and develop this affirmation of the physical by speaking not to a woman, but as one, and by taking physicality as an aged condition that encompasses ugliness and pain as well as youth and beauty. In a draft of "A Dialogue of Self and Soul," he had written of the indignities of rage and desire, thought and imagination, telling himself that

> Rage that is thoughts [sic] creator, desire that is
> creator of all temporal images
> Have made your intellect impure.
> (*The Winding Stair,* 39)

The desire for purity may be—as it always was—a misguided one, but what it drives Yeats toward in this late phase of his career is what was missing from his idealized rose—a recognition of the vital power of the minimal. From an airy everything, the woman of his dreams has shrunk and grown into a particular vibrant vagabond, a social outcast, a broken lover whose mind is cracked but whose faith and will are stronger than that of the bishop who reviles her. Crazy Jane is Yeats's most realistic and courageous anti-self; she makes concrete the abtract promise of *The Winding Stair* to provide a serpentine, laborious means of ascent, which is also a model of assent to life as it is lived, not as it is dreamed. In her simplicity and assertive physicality, Jane becomes the spokesperson for love as that which accepts everything, without judgment or denial: "'Love is all / Unsatisfied / That cannot take the whole / Body and soul'; / *And that is what Jane said*" ("Crazy Jane on the Day of Judgment," *VP,* 510). Jane is in love with the journey of life, its adventure, personified in her dead lover, Jack the Journeyman, who is diametrically opposed to the safety-loving bishop. Like Jack, Jane has pledged her troth to an uncertainty the bishop cannot abide; she knows that "The more I leave the door unlatched / The sooner love is gone," but she also knows that her very separation from Jack binds her to him with a greater and surer connection, one that will survive even death. She proclaims that she would leave her tomb to follow Jack's ghost:

> But were I left to lie alone
> In an empty bed,
> The skein so bound us ghost to ghost
> When he turned his head
> Passing on the road that night,
> Mine must walk when dead.
> ("Crazy Jane and Jack the Journeyman," *VP,* 511)

In "Crazy Jane on God," Jane accepts the unpredictability of life—"Men come, men go"—and her body does not moan but sings of its state of being "like a road / That men pass over." Her faith is that the battle of life gives way to unexpected illumination, that fighting men-at-arms will finally see a house "That from childhood stood / Uninhabited, ruinous, / Suddenly lit up / From door to top: / *All things remain in God*" (*VP,* 512).

What Jane tells the Bishop is what the young Yeats never conceded, that "Fair and foul are near of kin, / And fair needs foul." What she learned is also what Yeats only learned in old age, in the fissure between "bodily lowness" and "the heart's pride," that "Love has pitched his mansion in / The place of excrement" (*VP*, 513). Jane's last poem in *The Winding Stair* series is a thinly disguised lament for the loss of Yeats's own dancing days, punctuated by a refrain that insists on the interdependence of fulfillment and violence. When Jane looks at the dancers she asks God's indulgence for the times when she "cared not a thraneen" whether the dancers lived or died, "so that I had the limbs to try / Such a dance as there was danced—*Love is like the lion's tooth*" (*VP*, 515).

Yeats, then, came full circle from the air and fire and depths of his early imaginative work to—at the end—the earth. Although he began by privileging imagination over action, near the end of his life he adopted the opposite point of view, an assertive appreciation of "embodied truth" and all its marbled contradictions. The early work that he had deprecated for its unmanliness was in fact conceived from a stereotypically male—but not macho—perspective that idealized and objectified the female; it is only in *The Tower*, Yeats's ostensibly "phallic" volume, that he begins to explore how women themselves might experience their femaleness, and how such an exploration might provide a much-needed balance to the violent chaos of patriarchal power. Yeats came to appreciate the nomadic values of change, acceptance, and flexibility over such absolutes as beauty, and he eloquently showed that male fantasies are responsible for much brutality—a brutality frequently enacted against women. In the posthumously published poem "Crazy Jane on the Mountain," Crazy Jane, "tired of cursing the Bishop," instead mourns for the waste caused by the differences in power that divide, paralyze, and even kill men and women:

> A King had some beautiful cousins,
> But where are they gone?
> Battered to death in a cellar,
> And he stuck to his throne.
> (*VP*, 628)

In contrast to the immobility and powerlessness of the king to protect his beautiful cousins, Jane envisions "Great-bladdered Emer" and "Her violent man / Cuchulain," both independent, powerful, and earthy, but gone from Ireland. At the memory, Jane "kissed a stone":

> I lay stretched out in the dirt
> And I cried tears down.

Ironically, while in his poetry Yeats was learning to celebrate the wildness and freedom of a common woman, he was becoming more ominously antidemocratic in his politics. As early as 1924, at a gala event hosted by the Irish Free State, Yeats disturbed his audience with a speech in which he proclaimed that war is not going away, that the world is not getting better and better, and that our collective duty is therefore to "trample on the decomposing body of the goddess of liberty." Yeats's sense of the world as a place where "there is so much that is obscure and terrible" prompted him to champion a fascistic bundling of social institutions, a building up of discipline to replace the euphoric promise of liberty. He argued,

> The world can never be the same. The stream has turned backwards, and generations to come will have for their task, not the widening of liberty, but recovery from its errors—the building up of authority, the restoration of discipline, the discovery of a life sufficiently heroic to live without the opium dream. (Hone, 390)

Yeats's biographer Joseph Hone recalls spending a morning in Rome "searching the book-shops with Mrs. Yeats for works dealing with the spiritual antecedents of the Fascist revolution" (Hone, 393).[93] It is important to stress that Yeats's later political conservatism sprang from the same root as his avant-garde appreciation for the wild, free realism embodied by Crazy Jane. Yeats's growing despair about the state of the world pushed him in two antithetical directions— toward advocating a fascistic tightening of social authority and toward resisting such authority insofar as it is represented by the bishop.

What integrates the dramatically different experimental impulses that drove Yeats's long and varied career is a quality reflected in his name: he had an abundance of Will. It is strength of will that drove him to interrogate himself, and also to cease interrogation, to write and rewrite his poems until the cadences were exactly right, to work tirelessly to create a national theatre for Ireland, and to bring about almost singlehandedly an Irish literary renaissance. Finally, it was an act of will to sustain and rekindle the strength and vitality of his love again and again— love for Maud Gonne, for poetry, for his children, for youth, and for Ireland. This love never lessened, even when he was crippled by age and infirmity and had seen his homeland ravaged by the Black and Tans and by a bloody civil war. He registered such atrocities as clearly as he did the moments of exaltation, but neither extreme tempted him to soften or annihilate the other. Yeats's feelings of excitement about the things he loved would resurge unexpectedly in the most unpropitious places or moments. What Stephen McKenna once said about Yeats's feeling for Ireland is representative of his capacity to experience the rekindled excitement of desire anywhere, anytime. McKenna said, "If W. B. were in the desert of Gobi and someone mentioned Ireland, he would be all aquiver."

Four

Joyful Desire

Giacomo Joyce *and* Finnegans Wake

Both Wilde and Yeats, in different ways, idealized art and beauty in their youth. Only gradually and under pressure did they come to see the beauty of art differently, not as an alternative to life, but as an expression of life's contradictory, contingent, and volatile nature. Moreover, the aesthetic idealism of both Wilde and Yeats was importantly connected with their love of Ireland, which both constructed as a "lost" world of imagination and art, an alternative to the materialistic and urban values they associated with England. Wilde, with his love of green, and Yeats, with his adoration of flowers, paid homage to their common homeland by abstracting it into a pastoral Utopia to which they could secretly, imaginatively return in their art. Fortunately, the art of both was governed by laws so flexible and precise that it gave them a model for a revised view of life, in which life and art overlapped, differing primarily in their capacity to be replayed.

James Joyce, who was deeply influenced by both Wilde and Yeats, understood that the lives of these men were not deeply informed by the insights that shaped their art. Like Shakespeare, as Stephen Dedalus describes him in the "Scylla and Charybdis" episode of *Ulysses,* they moved through much of their lives "untaught by the wisdom [they had] written or by the laws [they had] revealed" (*U,* 9.477–8). When Joyce developed the semi-autobiographical character of Stephen Dedalus, he presented Stephen as someone whose artistic values were importantly shaped by Wilde and Yeats, but he also emphasized Stephen's discomfort with those influences. At the end of *A Portrait of the Artist as a Young Man,* Stephen is less like Wilde than he is like Dorian Gray recalling *Hamlet:* "'Like the painting of a sorrow, / A face without a heart'" (*DG,* 163). Like Dorian, and to a lesser extent like the young Wilde and Yeats, Stephen can commit excesses without ever taking a genuine risk, because he accepts no responsibility for the consequences of his actions or emotions. But Stephen not only resembles but also differs from Yeats, in that he does not share idealizing nostalgia for a distant past. In his diary entry for April 6, Stephen recalls Yeats's poem, "Michael Robartes Remembers Forgotten Beauty" (from *The Wind Among the Reeds*), and he protests the sentiment that drives it:

Michael Robartes remembers forgotten beauty and, when his arms wrap her round, he presses in his arms the loveliness which has long faded from the world. Not this. Not at all. I desire to press in my arms the loveliness which has not yet come into the world. (*P,* 251)

Even when Stephen is at his most impressionable, he rejects Yeats's orientation toward the past, voicing his determination to look toward the future instead.

Unlike Wilde and Yeats, Joyce published only one early work in praise of youth and beauty, *Chamber Music,* which was composed very much under the influence of Yeats's *The Wind Among the Reeds* (see chapter 3, note 88). In everything that he actually published after *Chamber Music,* his characters' idealistic tendencies are carefully framed with irony. Moreover, Joyce's work becomes increasingly denser and more opaque, a development that goes hand in hand with his growing suspicion of the abuses that fantasies—whether erotic or national—tend to produce and mask. Having learned his craft from Wilde and Yeats, the young Joyce quickly became well versed in the Wildean virtuosity of an intellectual play of ideas, and in the equally agile play of images and emotions characteristic of Yeats's poetry. Where Joyce most strongly differed from his fellow countrymen was in his growing concern with the rhetorical effects of "aquacities of thought and language" on his readers, with the politics of style.

Each of Joyce's works reflects an increasingly sharper awareness that an appreciation of otherness—the appreciation that Yeats won with such labor near the end of his career—is only enhanced through encounters with the unfamiliar, and language and narrative as they were conventionally employed were too familiar to resist easy appropriation by readers as reflections of their own desires. Most books were, like women or the poor, too frangible, too easily penetrable, their difference too readily assimilable into the hegemony of the known. In the 1930s, as the Third Reich was gaining power and as the world moved toward the most widespread elimination of difference it had ever known, Joyce—like Yeats—was laboriously rearranging individual words and letters in a doomed attempt to resist such invasiveness at the most microscopic level. Joyce once implied that people would do better to read *Finnegans Wake* than to invade Poland.[1] Although the comment itself seems self-evident, Joyce did believe that horrifying abuses of human rights are the logical, macroscopic extensions of apparently "innocent" practices we engage in every day. The practice he was trying to inoculate his readers against was that of thoughtlessly appropriating what they read, of mistaking the complex and delicate strands of linguistic and material reality for invitations to penetrate those strands with blunt human energy, for its brief consolation.

Although Wilde, Yeats, and Joyce all practiced contradiction in their art and came to recognize how subtly and deceptively such contradictions inform life as well, Joyce worked in *Finnegans Wake* to fashion contradictions so concentrated that the reader had to experience the discomfiting tension between incompatible extremes at every moment—or not at all. In the process, Joyce produced an understanding of Irishness not as a pure category, but as an admixture of heterogenous elements that the reader had to encounter again and again, so that we could only appreciate the fissures that underpin national identity as a "micronational" confluence of foreign words and meanings, replayed over and over in the successive neologisms of his most experimental book of Irish "History," *Finnegans Wake.*

Joyce read his Irishness as a condition that promoted respect for foreignness—both because the British had historically lacked such respect in their treatment of Ireland, and because modern Ireland is the product of successive waves of foreign invasion and influence. But one incident in particular served as a watershed in Joyce's lifelong engagement with an ever-denser and more impenetrable otherness: a brief, erotic fantasy about one of his Jewish pupils in Trieste that would proleptically figure the atrocities of the 1930s and 40s in Nazi Germany and fascist Italy. For Joyce, Amalia Popper played a role in his imagination that approximates the role played by greenness for Wilde and the Rose for Yeats; she was the idealized and insubstantial other from whom he eventually gained a fuller, less sanitized, and more complex appreciation of human, sexual, and social difference.

Unlike Yeats, who critically reevaluated his beliefs and allegiances every time he began a new volume of poems, or Wilde, who accused himself of one-sidedness only after he had been formally indicted and convicted of wrongdoing in a court of law, Joyce seems to have realized his own unintentional arrogance twice, relatively early in his writing career. These major epiphanies were both retrospective and prospective, in that they allowed Joyce to finish one book with added complexity and to plan the ones that followed with greater precision. Joyce's first major self-indictment occurred in 1907, after an illness that inspired him to compose "The Dead" as the conclusion to *Dubliners* and to revise *Stephen Hero* into *A Portrait of the Artist as a Young Man.* The sensation of being close to death made him see things differently, and he invented the character of Gabriel Conroy to expose his own propensity toward intellectual arrogance and condescension, and thereby to puncture it. "The Dead" dramatizes Gabriel's numerous strategies for not hearing the poignant calls of those whom life has, like the lass of Aughrim, left out in the cold. In particular, Gabriel has inoculated himself against the feelings of women,[2] and the story gradually unveils the price he has paid for such inoculation: he has deprived himself of any meaningful experience of life or love.

In the same year that he conceived of Gabriel as a self-portrait that exposed and exaggerated his own narcissistic tendencies, Joyce saw that the autobiographical figure of Stephen as a hero had to be reconceptualized along less self-congratulatory lines, and the subtle ironies of *A Portrait of the Artist as a Young Man* were born. After 1907, Stephen reemerges as a younger version of Gabriel Conroy, sensitive, verbally gifted, but constantly battling against an instinctive disgust for the real. In particular, Stephen hates not only difference but also any respect for difference, which is why when he realizes that Cranly understood a mother's love, and felt "the sufferings of women . . . and would shield them" (245), he decides that "it is time to go." Like Gabriel (and even Mr. Duffy in "A Painful Case"), Stephen in his self-absorption lacks compassion, which is to say that he lacks meaningful connection with others.

Sometime between 1911 and 1914, as he was working on the conclusion to *A Portrait of the Artist*, Joyce had another self-excoriating insight comparable to the one that had revolutionized his writing in 1907. Once again, this realization concerned his imperviousness to the desires and histories of women, only this time the woman against whom he inoculated himself, with self-defensive scorn, was also Jewish. In *Giacomo Joyce*, a notebook that he was keeping around the time that he was finishing *A Portrait of the Artist*, Joyce recorded his lust for a young, Jewish woman to whom he was teaching English, a lust that when thwarted gave way to imaginative reprisal against her for her apparent indifference to him. Joyce's Gabriel-like experience of frustrated attraction kindled in him a sudden and unexpected vindictiveness that he vented against women and Jews in general near the end of the notebook. When Joyce realized the implications of his knee-jerk impulse to, in the words of Oscar Wilde, "kill the thing he loved," he promptly made the hero of his next book a Jew and set himself the difficult therapeutic task of loving (without idealizing) an unfaithful, "impure" woman—Molly Bloom. *Ulysses* grew out of Joyce's determination to conquer his own squeamishness about ugliness, poverty, unfaithfulness, wandering—the seamy yet exuberant side of life that both Gabriel Conroy and Stephen Dedalus fastidiously hoped to transcend. In this sense, *Ulysses* is akin to Yeats's Crazy Jane poems and to Wilde's *De Profundis*; it grows out of Joyce's conviction that the greatest moral challenge individuals face is the challenge to see things as they really are, to appreciate the beauty of imperfection, loss, and change, and finally to "find this mortal world enough."

Joyce's interest in engaging difference—without idealizing or degrading its unfamiliar otherness—unexpectedly grew even more insistent after he completed *Ulysses*. During the next seventeen years, he worked to design a new way of using language that forced readers to recognize the power of the unknown in virtually every word. In the "Work in Progress" that became *Finnegans Wake*, Joyce drew upon over sixty-two different languages to forge a more comprehensive and elusive "language" that balanced the alien with the familiar more realistically. The pun, as a linguistic crossroads where different meanings meet and diverge, became the structural unit of composition, and the metaphor that guided the "narrative" was not the light of rationality but the obscurity of dream. This is a book that accents the interdependence of death and life (Finnegan is a dead giant who dies and comes to life many times), and that insists upon the buried magic of what we usually regard as shameful, repulsive, difficult, or corrupt. It is Joyce's greatest and most prolonged effort to challenge established "states of desire" with the uncannily productive possibilities of experiment, and it is virtually unread. As a widespread "revolution of the word," Joyce's experiment failed, but as a storehouse of alternative strategies of thinking, writing, and desiring, it is incomparably rich and strange.

In the pages that follow, I trace the major crisis that took as its text the small, posthumously published notebook called *Giacomo Joyce*, moving back and forth in time to show how much social history is attached to what seems at first glance to be a minor and slightly embarrassing incident. I show how *Giacomo Joyce* was seen through the eyes of a post-World War II German artist, illustrating how that view deepens when framed with fuller biographical knowledge of its subject's life. I turn to *Finnegans Wake* as Joyce's last and densest commentary on the issues that were raised by *Giacomo Joyce*—issues of sexism, racism, and a transparency of meaning that fosters both. *Finnegans Wake*, written under the global political pressure exerted by the rise of the Third Reich, resurrects buried differences with an energy born of mingled hope and despair. It is Joyce's most desperate and sustained effort to illustrate what is at stake in practicing more experimentally daring modes of expression, and it is the most detailed example in the history of literature of the vertiginous slippages and frustrating exhilarations of punning and rhizomatic thought.

Joyce's War on Status

In the years between 1908 and 1914, while he was living in Trieste, Joyce began a probing investigation of the privilege of status, and whether a concern with status is compatible with a desire for communication. The word "status" derives from the Latin root *stare*, to stand, which literally designates an individual or a work's *standing* in the eyes of the world. The strength and limitation of the current concept of "status"—remembering always the metaphor from which it grew—is that it refers to a single human position among many possible ones: it measures only the capacity to stand erect in the eyes of others. In short, it gauges potency (erectness), which makes it a significant if somewhat phallic indicator. Even more significant, however, is what "status," as we have defined it for our time, can*not* represent—the full range of human activity, which includes sitting, lying, prevaricating, and erring as well as the erectness of standing. Joyce's desire for and vengeful impulse to revenge himself against the Jewish student who had rejected him in Trieste—as recorded in *Giacomo Joyce*—was revisited by a contemporary German graphic artist, Paul Wunderlich, in such a way as to raise the following questions: what are the political implications of privileging status as a measure of cultural, social, or ethical achievement? If, as the etymology of "status" seems to suggest, privileging status is a mechanism for dissimulating and invalidating a wider range of human possibilities, then it would seem to be akin to other exclusionary habits of mind, such as prejudice. If this is true, what does the similarity between status and prejudice imply about the politics of according special status to works of art, and artists? In what specific ways can works of art undermine their own status, and authors call into question their authority? Such questions are particularly vital wherever the political climate is extreme—whether in countries subject to another country's authority, such as Ireland when Joyce was writing, or countries, such as Nazi Germany, whose power has raged unchecked to exclude and even exterminate others. It is precisely such unsettling correspondences—between Ireland and Germany, oppressed and oppressors, and even artists and their subjects—that give urgency to Wunderlich's visual commentary on Joyce. Both artists present intensely motivated explorations of the politics of representation.

Status, I would argue, presents itself as *static* ("stasis," like "status," derives from a word for "standing," although its parentage is Greek rather than Latin), although a resistant interpreter would argue that status is always only meaningful in relation to the fuller context from which it has been plucked. When status is accorded, however, the vexed circumstances that prompted the achievement—troubling our admiration of it—tend to fall away. As a result, the value of something that has been accorded status may be transferred to a subsequent generation more or less intact, despite the fact that the historical and cultural contexts that made such standing meaningful have changed. What happens when we pass down—to our readers, our students, our children—only our judgments about the relative status of individual achievements, paring away the injustices and inequities that alone make such judgments significant? What happens when values—even the value of reading a work like Joyce's *Ulysses*—are divorced from the historical and political situations that produced them and outlasted their production? What happens when the stasis of appreciation is defended on aesthetic grounds that are presented as inviolate and self-justifying? These are questions which not only Joyce, but also Yeats, asked in times of intense social turmoil, urging us not simply to accept our cultural legacies but to "*Test* every work of intellect or faith" ("Vacillation," *VP*, 501). As we have seen, Yeats's late poems derive their urgency from his relentless inquisition into the "fallout" of his poetic power; in "The Man and the Echo," for example, he relates that

> All that I have said and done,
> Now that I am old and ill,
> Turns into a question till
> I lie awake night after night
> And never get the answers right.
> Did that play of mine send out
> Certain men the English shot?
> Did words of mine put too great strain
> On that woman's reeling brain?
> Could my spoken words have checked
> That whereby a house lay wrecked?
> (*VP*, 632)

But it is earlier, in "Meditations in Time of Civil War," that Yeats poses the question of art's legacy in more general (and less personal) terms, when he contemplates the dark and empty beauty of the ancestral houses that we inherit, houses that represent and perpetuate the status of past accomplishment. Yeats describes the idealistic sweep of artistic production as an intense counterplay to the manifold disillusionments of real circumstances, proposing bitter and violent men as producers of architectural sweetness and calm:

> Some violent bitter man, some powerful man
> Called architect and artist in, that they,
> Bitter and violent men, might rear in stone
> The sweetness that all longed for night and day,

The gentleness none there had ever known;
But when the master's buried mice can play,
And maybe the great-grandson of that house,
for all its bronze and marble, 's but a mouse.
(*VP*, 418)

By suggesting that bitterness engenders its opposite, sweetness, and that violence produces gentleness, Yeats implies that the value of this artistic enterprise
lay in the relationship between the violent makers and the stone sweetness they
reared, not in the stone alone.[3] Once the master is gone (if we choose to pause
in our reading after "master's buried," so that "mice can play" becomes a
"then" clause), the building becomes a shell, big becomes small; the master
of the house declines, over three generations, to a mouse; monument becomes
toy. Yeats concludes this section of "Meditations" by asking whether such
monuments—once they have outlasted the conflicts that produced them—
may actually *sap* the energies even as they soothe the distress of subsequent
generations:

What if the glory of escutcheoned doors,
And buildings that a haughtier age designed,
The pacing to and fro on polished floors
Amid great chambers and long galleries, lined
With famous portraits of our ancestors;
What if those things the greatest of mankind
Consider most to magnify, or to bless,
But take our greatness with our bitterness?
(*VP*, 418)

Yeats is moving toward an indictment of all the museum pieces of a bygone culture; the love of the beautiful, the desire for perfection, the need to represent
and symbolically realize transcendence are all emotions that should be *reen-
acted* by future generations—they should not be passed down via monumental
legacies. This is why criticism is an essential discipline; its function is to demystify and humanize as well as to preserve the monuments of the past. Yeats is focusing on the legacies of the rich—social, economic, and artistic status—but by
doing so in a poem addressed to subsequent generations of readers he is calling
into question the status of his own verbal artifacts as well. Yeats prompts his
readers not to admire his poem or play with it, but to relive it in relation to what
inspired it, the terror of the Irish civil war. The price of isolating Yeats' status as
a poet from the complexities of his experience is the pointless repetition of that
experience; respect for status perpetuates stasis, re-engendering the nightmares
of history that also haunted Stephen Dedalus.

In *The Tower*, Yeats's personal desire for status in "Sailing to Byzantium"—
for the young to appreciate "monuments of unageing intellect"—gradually re-
cedes before a larger appreciation of the importance and beauty of change. Art,
like life, is most joyous when not calcified by homage, but when seen as a par-
ticipatory process in which painful or even culpable representations coexist
with generative ones, training us not only to admire, but to revise, with a flexi-

ble independence of mind that can continue to change in response to changing circumstances. Distrust of status and a view of writing as a continuing, complex *process* of interpretation and response can prompt us not only to revise and expand the canon of works that we analyze and teach, but also to demystify the legacy of works that have attained a certain ponderous status, such as *Ulysses*. When an admirer asked Joyce if he could kiss the hand that wrote *Ulysses*, Joyce said, "No. It's done a lot of other things too." *Ulysses* may be an encyclopedia of writing strategies designed to resist and draw attention to the reader's desire to appropriate and sub*ject* the book's subject, but it also relentlessly exposes Joyce's blindnesses through its representation of the misogynistic and intermittently anti-Semitic characters of Stephen and Bloom.[4] In view of Joyce's immense status, we need an account of the "other things" that Joyce did with the hand that wrote *Ulysses* that do not call for us to kiss it. We need to see, for example, how Joyce's understanding of sexism and racism grew out of his own inadvertent complicity in both, how his controversial and complex treatments of women and Jews in *Ulysses* grew out of precise and relentless self-observation. Such an investigation reminds that racism and sexism not only take the threatening form of policies or campaigns, but they are also reflexes to which everyone is subject under certain (often predictable) conditions.

An autobiographical record of Joyce lashing out against a woman and Jew who he believed had rejected him has been preserved in the manuscript of *Giacomo Joyce*, which Richard Ellmann discovered when he was working on his biography of Joyce in the late fifties, and which he published with much fanfare in 1968. Interestingly, *Giacomo Joyce* was so extravagantly recommended to the reading public only on the basis of its status as a Joycean artifact,[5] with no mention and little recognition of the fact that it shows Joyce, in the guise of a lover ("Giacomo" is Casanova's first name as well as the Italian translation of "James"), defending himself against the pain of rejection by adopting conventionally sexist and anti-Semitic attitudes. *Giacomo Joyce* reflects not Joyce's standing, but his capacity for adopting a variety of other less upright positions, which contribute to the complexity of Joyce's treatment of prejudice and the compromised "heroism" of his protagonists in *Ulysses*. It details some of Joyce's less attractive postures, thereby underscoring the presence of these postures— among many others—in *Ulysses*.

Giacomo Joyce, a sixteen-page series of jottings, is generally thought to be interesting primarily for biographical reasons; it is a disjointed fantasy of erotic gratification that Joyce devised in response to a fairly desperate domestic situation. In the years from 1909 to 1914, when he was 27–32 years old and an expatriate in Trieste, Joyce was impoverished, virtually unpublished, suffering from iritis, and responsible for supporting two illegitimate children and their mother, which he did by teaching English with all the ingenuity of a courtly desperado. He supplemented his meager income from classroom teaching by giving private lessons, and one of his pupils, Amalia Popper, gradually began to absorb more and more of his imagination, frustration, and desire. She is the subject of *Giacomo Joyce*, where she appears as an icon of everything Joyce was not—wealthy, beautiful, socially and politically correct, but also Jewish and female. It is the Jewishness and the femaleness that Joyce targets as areas of vulnerability.

Giacomo Joyce: Joyce and Wunderlich

The "plot" of *Giacomo Joyce*, obliquely unfolding through a series of images, seems to trace the waxing and waning of Joyce's desire for his wealthy, attractive Jewish student, a waning precipitated by the appearance of a rival. In its emphasis on visual images, voyeurism, and the eroticism associated with such furtive observation, it anticipates the "Nausicaa" episode of *Ulysses*. Unlike "Nausicaa," however, *Giacomo Joyce* allows only one perspective—that of the observer—and its climax is sharp and bitter rather than comic. Unlike "Nausicaa," which spends itself in an overblown image of sexual release set against the heavens—Bloom's "fireworks"—*Giacomo Joyce* ends when the object of the artist's gaze announces her preference for another man, for someone Joyce offensively calls "Barabbas" (who is probably Popper's fiancé Michele Risolo), melodramatically casting himself as Christ. Joyce's stung reaction to his pupil's indifference to him is not only anti-Semitic, since he equates her rejection of him with the refusal of the Jewish people to liberate Christ when given the opportunity, it is also sexist and authoritarian.

The impetus behind *Giacomo Joyce*, the cause of Joyce's attraction to and bitterness toward Amalia Popper, is the inequality of their status. Joyce ironically emphasizes his social and economic inferiority throughout. He refers to his pupil as "your ladyship" and describes her as "a young person of quality" (*GJ*, 1); he lingers over the richness of her attire and closes in on the bows of her slim bronze shoes, which he deprecates as "spurs of a pampered fowl" (*GJ*, 8). Joyce's lack of economic power underscores his powerlessness as a man, and his response is to enter an arena in which his power outweighs hers—the male-dominated realm of art. He takes what is in this case a truly phallic revenge with his pen, describing his writing and her reading as a "sex" scene in which "her eyes have drunk [his] thoughts: and into the moist warm yielding welcoming darkness of her womanhood [his] soul, itself dissolving, has streamed and poured and flooded a liquid and abundant seed. . . . Take her now who will!" (*GJ*, 14). He also insinuates his own superiority to her Jewishness by casting himself as God and Christ; she is like Abraham being called to God (*GJ*, 14) and a "daughter of Jerusalem" weeping for and then reviling him in the role of Christ (*GJ*, 10, 15). Giacomo sees himself and Amalia as locked in a struggle for hegemony, although she is represented as unaware of the conflict, which makes her more vulnerable. Their situation is precarious because her half-conscious exercises of power make his claims to power seem ambivalent and even suspect in his own eyes. Joyce acknowledges his motive in writing as a reaction to her power when he writes, "It will never be. You know that well. What then? Write it, damn you, write it! What else are you good for?" (*GJ*, 16)

The problem with *Giacomo Joyce* is that between its covers the artist's control is too absolute; his character is utterly at the mercy of Joyce's representations of her. She is powerless even when depicted as threatening, since the independent perspective that alone gives her a measure of autonomy and independence has been stripped away. As Joyce says in one sketch, she is "clothed with . . . shadows" (*GJ*, 10). The relationship between Joyce and Popper in *Giacomo Joyce* has nothing to do with love, and everything to do with regard; their struggle for regard is represented in the text as a contest of eyes. Her "black basilisk eyes" have the power to poison him (*GJ*, 15), and his have the power to undress and expose her, but since we see her, first and last, through Joyce's eyes and never see him from hers, his is the ultimate privilege. He makes the finality of his view triumphantly apparent by metaphorically "burying" his subject at the conclusion of *Giacomo Joyce*, derisively arranging her red-flowered hat and umbrella into a heraldic and pointedly literary epitaph: the roundness of the hat, flanked on the right by a vertical line formed by a furled umbrella, resemble a lowercase "a," which signifies both her name, Amalia, and her shame as the bearer of a scarlet letter. Joyce's double gesture of homage and defamation epitomizes the ambivalence of his regard for her: "A long black piano: coffin of music. Poised on its edge a woman's hat, red-flowered, and umbrella, furled. Her arms: a casque, gules, and blunt spear on a field, sable" (*GJ*, 16).

Giacomo Joyce focuses on the antagonism of mutual regard in a world where privilege is precariously uneven. Regarded sympathetically, the piece seems to represent Joyce's desire to reverse the power flow in an unequal relationship by asserting his prerogative as a writer. Regarded against the background of World War II, though, *Giacomo Joyce* illustrates the axiom that inequalities of privilege create and prolong not only desire but also its double, hatred, as the sensual desire to unveil shades gradually into the desire to expose and finally to exterminate and bury unnegotiable differences of cultural and sexual privilege. If desire and hatred both move towards a stripping of the seductive and threatening subject, then art might seem to promise a necessary redress. But art, as Joyce would later see more sharply, is too often a simple strategy for reversing the flow of power, allowing the victim and aggressor to change places, and this is precisely what happens in *Giacomo Joyce*. The *story* of *Giacomo Joyce* presents Joyce as Popper's suffering victim, but its *mode of presentation* makes her utterly subject to his representation of her. In short, *Giacomo Joyce* has sexist and anti-Semitic overtones that are essential to an understanding of the operations of prejudice and the power of art; in it, Joyce found himself to be inconsequential and undesirable in the eyes of an attractive Jewish woman and responded by instinctively and shamefully defending himself by appealing to the traditional privilege of a man, a Gentile and a writer to help him contain her power. Clearly Joyce used *Giacomo Joyce* as a way of testing his own conditioned defenses against differences of race, sex, and class, and he found his initial defense to be a strong counteroffense, waged in an arena where he had greater skill and authority. Total respect for the autonomy of another person may not be possible, but a recognition that there are different levels of vulnerability dictated by differences in social, political, and even biological status is imperative. What must be respected is the ease with which certain kinds of power can be eradicated in a social and historical context which values some of its members more highly than others.

Interestingly, although *Giacomo Joyce* was published twenty-two years ago, it has never been regarded as either sexist or anti-Semitic by literary critics.[6] It took a German graphic artist who had learned about the ease of inadvertent complicity firsthand, and who therefore lacked the idealizing impulse born of a naive desire for cultural and professional "regard," to appreciate the significance of *Giacomo Joyce* and to illustrate its significance in relation to the lessons of World War II. Paul Wunderlich, who became a professional artist after the war (in which he had briefly served on the German side), shows an acute and personal awareness of the complex interdependence of desire and horror, art and politics. In 1976, eight years after the publication of *Giacomo Joyce*, he issued a limited edition (125 copies) of the drawings for ten multicolored heliographs that constitute a highly politicized illustration of Joyce's text.[7] As the son of a career officer and someone who had himself served in the German army from 1943 to 45, becoming a prisoner of war in 1945 at the age of seventeen,[8] Wunderlich could not have begun his career with many illusions of personal or cultural innocence. After the Third Reich suppressed modern art, artistic innovation had come to a temporary standstill in Germany, its artists apparently paralyzed by the difficulty of coming to terms with what had happened during the war. Edouard Roditi wrote in 1965 that

> until very recently most German art of the past couple of decades has somehow failed to convey to us a clear notion of the specific problems that a creative artist might have to face or solve in a nation that has just emerged from the terrors of a political dictatorship and a disastrous defeat. . . . Suddenly, in the past two years, we have at last begun to discover in the work of a few German artists some willingness to face these haunting memories of the immediate German past. One of the outstanding examples is Paul Wunderlich.[9]

Wunderlich's reputation began with a political series of lithographs ("20 July 1944") that controversially focused on the von Stauffenberg attempt against Hitler's life. But nowhere is Wunderlich's sense of the relationship between politics—sexual, racial, and national—and art more clearly apparent than in his illustrations for *Giacomo Joyce*, which he reads as deeply disturbing intimations of the Holocaust, for which he, Joyce in the guise of "Giacomo," and all comfortable "onlookers" (including ourselves, as we look at these pictures) bear a shared responsibility.[10]

Wunderlich's sketchbook begins with a drawing (Fig. 4.1) that raises the first question of *Giacomo Joyce*—"Who?" "A pale face surrounded by heavy odorous furs. Her movements are shy and nervous. She uses quizzing-glasses" (*GJ*, 1). Wunderlich shows the swathed upper body of a woman, her wraps drawing the eye down to a suggestive V, her mystery provoking the (male) spectator's curiosity and desire. Significantly, though, Wunderlich portrays her two eyes differently—one is seeing (with the help of a monocle, or quizzing-glass) and the other seen, although through a shadow, which figures a mutuality of

FIGURE 4.1. *Giacomo Joyce* I (courtesy of Paul Wunderlich)

regard that is conspicuously missing from Joyce's text. Wunderlich is depicting the difficulty of mutual regard as well as its possibility, though, since the eye through which *she* sees appears blank to the spectator (although it also has the capacity to reflect the spectator's own image), and the eye that we can see is only barely discernible through a patch of darkness. The overall effect is that of a suggestive and elusive pastiche of identity and difference, an imagistic equivalent of Joyce's question, "Who?" Her answer, "Yes," is almost imperceptibly traced in block letters (the Y resembling a V) in the lower right quadrant of the drawing. This image of Amalia's upper body is followed by a drawing of Wunderlich talking to Joyce (Fig. 4.2), presumably about *Giacomo Joyce*. Wunderlich is gesturing, his lips slightly parted, and Joyce attends with his forehead creased, his glasses dark and blank. We can therefore see in Joyce's eyes only a blank, a possible reflection of ourselves, although we can see one of Wunderlich's eyes focused on Joyce.

The third sketch shows what the two artists have in common (Fig. 4.3): on the lower right side the heads of Joyce and Wunderlich reappear, Joyce now hatless and the eyes behind the glasses mere points. Above them is a double exposure of a Jewish woman: the upper figure is partially clothed and adorned with a star of David, her shorn head chillingly caressed by a hand in uniform; the lower figure is nude, suggestively reclined with her knees spread, her dark hair unshorn and luxurious, her pubic area shaved and clearly drawn. Falling from her hand, which points downward in both sketches, is a lorgnette and an open book, its spine fiery red in the heliograph; the handwritten exclamation "Jamesy" from *Giacomo Joyce* appears above the book. What presumably narrows Joyce's eyes to points is his realization of the identity of these two female images, which figure both desire and desire's destructive capacity to unveil and expose woman and Jew—to pluck the heart out of her mystery. The seductive authority of Joyce's book mirrors the authority of the uniformed hand caressing the stubbly scalp of the inmate above.

A comfortably seated Joyce speaks to the observer in the next drawing (Fig. 4.4), while the eyes and erogenous zones of a drawn and composed woman materialize on the table behind and above him. The image on the writing table illustrates Joyce's selection of her features for presentation to the reader, and we can see that his picture is both seductive and reductive: she is drawn as a shapeless "hill" marked only by dark eyes, breasts, a navel, and pubic hair. In the heliograph Joyce's hat is tinged with Irish green, but his vest is the red of English rule: in his head he supports independence, but his heart is the heart of a British imperialist, and the "country" he has colonized is a woman's body.

In *Giacomo Joyce V* the veiled woman comes back (Fig. 4.5), but she is now double, split into a woman and someone who may be either a man or a wilder and bespectacled version of herself. Like the first sketch, the fifth contains a figure with asymmetrical eyes: one eye of the "man" gazes with heavy-lidded patience from behind its eyeglass, whereas the other eye is rubbed out. The hair on this figure is wild and disheveled, its overall look androgynous, and a third of the figure is cut off by a vertical line to his left. On the right of this tall figure is the veiled woman of *Giacomo Joyce I* with her lorgnette falling away and her left

FIGURE 4.2. *Giacomo Joyce* II (courtesy of Paul Wunderlich)

FIGURE 4.3. *Giacomo Joyce* III (courtesy of Paul Wunderlich)

FIGURE 4.4. *Giacomo Joyce* IV (courtesy of Paul Wunderlich)

hand peeking out from behind the line that cuts off part of her companion's body. In the lower right-hand corner is a pile of spectacles, which, as Hermann Lenz, who wrote the commentary in the Manus Press edition, observes, recalls the heaps of eyeglasses found in the concentration camps after World War II.[11] Both figures have the "dark languor-flooded eyes" that Joyce attributed to Amalia Popper in *Giacomo Joyce* (*GJ*, 13), eyes replaced by two pairs of skull eye-holes in the next sketch.

Giacomo Joyce VI reinterprets an early passage from Joyce's manuscript (Fig. 4.6): "High heels clack hollow on the resonant stone stairs . . . Tapping clacking heels, a high and hollow noise. There is one below would speak with your ladyship" (*GJ*, 1). In *Giacomo Joyce*, Joyce focuses on his pupil's high heels to pinpoint her privilege and superiority as she descends to meet him, but Wunderlich draws the high-heeled boots to resemble skulls with the laces bound together (the skulls are whitened in the heliograph); fragments of the handwritten text of *Giacomo Joyce* are faintly visible in the foreground. Lenz explains that the knotted laces recall the way shoes were collected in concentration camps, and the shoes with skull eyeholes endow Joyce's strange vision of corpses in *Giacomo Joyce* with an uncanny prescience: "Corpses of Jews lie about me rotting in the mould of their holy field. Here is the tomb of her people, black stone, silence without hope" (*GJ*, 6). The juxtaposition of Joyce's perspective against Wunderlich's again highlights the disturbing kinship between privilege and degradation, status and victimization.

Giacomo Joyce VII complicates any impulse to condemn Joyce too readily for his voyeuristic desires by illustrating not his power over his victim, but his identity with her, as well as the probable narcissism of his regard for her (Fig. 4.7). Here the figure of Joyce is superimposed onto that of Amalia Popper—her hat is also his hat, her glasses his glasses, one hand is bare and the other cuffed, and only half of the star of David, accented by a glob of yellow paint (making it a "gelbe stern," a yellow star),[12] is apparent. The palms of both uplifted hands bear the stigmata of a weeping eye, serving to remind us of one of Joyce's favorite ironies—that, as Bloom tells the Citizen in *Ulysses*, "Your God was a jew. Christ was a jew like me." Christian and Jew, man and woman meld horrifyingly together in the memory and expectation of massacre, and the wounds in the hands offer a vision that bleeds tears. Here it is apparent that "the other" is always an antithetical aspect of the self; the psychological underpinning of oppression emerges as self-hatred, and war against another race—in the light of such identity of self and other—is always civil war. The cause of conflict also enfolds its solution: to recognize and represent the common humanity of man and woman, Gentile and Jew, oppressor and victim; to balance identity and difference.

The eighth drawing in Wunderlich's series details the detached power of the male artist (here Joyce) over his nude, wounded, and desired female subject (Fig. 4.8). The passage being illustrated is the one in which Giacomo learns that Amalia has had an emergency operation, and he accuses God—who has wanted to wound her so "cruelly"—of libidinousness: "Operated. The surgeon's knife has probed in her entrails and withdrawn, leaving the raw jagged gash of

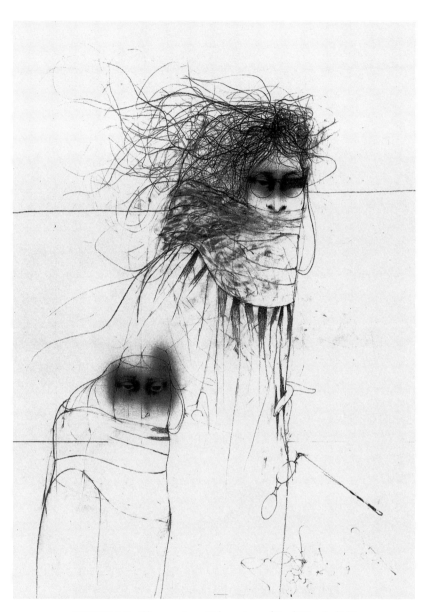

FIGURE 4.5. *Giacomo Joyce* V (courtesy of Paul Wunderlich)

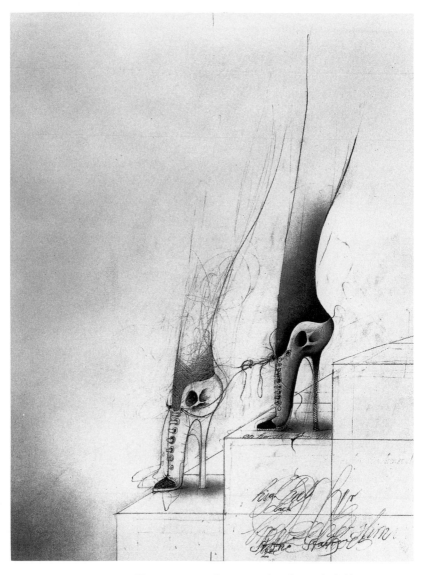

FIGURE 4.6. *Giacomo Joyce* VI (courtesy of Paul Wunderlich)

FIGURE 4.7. *Giacomo Joyce* VII (courtesy of Paul Wunderlich)

its passage on her belly. I see her full dark suffering eyes, beautiful as the eyes of an antelope. O cruel wound! Libidinous God!" (*GJ*, 11). In Wunderlich's treatment, significantly, the operating table on which the decollated, nude, and wounded body lies is both the artist's drafting table and the writer's desk, and Joyce sits at the table composing both her desirability and her pain.[13] Joyce's responsibility for desiring and wounding her clearly mirrors that of the surgeon-God he accuses, as Wunderlich emphasizes through the word "operated" written over and around her thigh. The pencil lines that swirl over her lower body and over the table/desk remind us that Wunderlich is implicated, too, in the very victimization he exposes, an artistic "privilege" that implicitly licenses the libidinous hatred that allowed the Nazis to experiment so freely with the human body.

The next drawing (Fig. 4.9) illustrates a sledding scene from *Giacomo Joyce*, in which Joyce salaciously enjoys a view of "Papa and the girls sliding downhill, astride of a toboggan: the Grand Turk and his harem" (*GJ*, 4). Joyce catches a glimpse of Amalia's white underclothing, recording his exhilaration at the sight of "the short skirt taut from the round knobs of the knees. A white flash: a flake, a snowflake: *"And when she next doth ride abroad / May I be there to see!"* Wunderlich's version realizes an implication of Joyce's elated voyeurism that Joyce fails to consider in *Giacomo Joyce*. He shows father and daughter standing on a toboggan, but they are heading towards a long stretch of wall and a roof with a smoking chimney, which Lenz identifies as the gate of Auschwitz. Amalia is dressed in a transparent gown, which emphasizes the relationship between her erotic desirability and her vulnerability as woman and Jew, and she is riding Pegasus. Art, or poetic inspiration, as represented by Pegasus, is literally drawing her into the furnace. Two versions of her father stand behind her, the first holding out an eye-marked palm, the second whitened into a figure of a patriarch, Noah or Moses, with the "long white whiskers" Joyce attributed to Amalia's father (*GJ*, 5) and the rainbow of God's covenant—colored in the heliograph—ironically rising behind him. Riding from Exodus back into bondage in Auschwitz, the figures of father and daughter are surrounded by faint drawings of animals—wild dogs and boars—all of whom are crying. The beasts suggest that yet another threat "the other" poses is that it represents the wild animality of the body and therefore must be domesticated and leashed. The signs of vision and visionary knowledge are again prominent—not only in the eye in the middle of the father's left hand, but in the proliferation of eyeglasses and the multiplication of images. In the lower right corner, a bespectacled Amalia faces and accuses Wunderlich, who is taken aback by her accusatory stare.[14]

The final sketch (Fig. 4.10) evokes a complicated reaction by representing the sorrow of the comfortable, well-dressed artist in the same frame as the nakedness and vulnerability of the woman. Amalia's figure is dark and hatched over with pen scratches, her hands crippled and the eyes behind her glasses weary and sad. Partly formed faces peer from the background around her, showing that her pain is not hers alone; some of the faces are animalistic. Wunderlich himself sits in the foreground, mouth open, eyes closed, comfortably

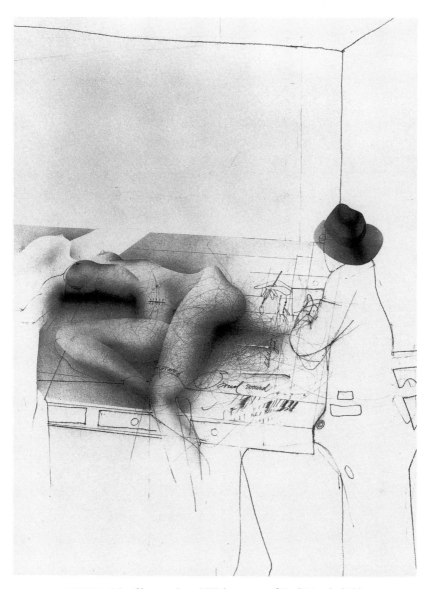

FIGURE 4.8. *Giacomo Joyce* VIII (courtesy of Paul Wunderlich)

FIGURE 4.9. *Giacomo Joyce* IX (courtesy of Paul Wunderlich)

FIGURE 4.10. *Giacomo Joyce* X (courtesy of Paul Wunderlich)

dressed, with a tear squeezing out from under the eyelid, his hands on his thighs. Lenz calls this Wunderlich's lament for the dead.[15] Wunderlich's decision to include a lightly drawn self-portrait of the grieving but otherwise well-off artist inside the frame of his work raises an interesting question: isn't this a facile, inappropriately sentimental portrayal of sorrow by a German? The answer is clearly yes; Wunderlich's tears are almost insultingly inadequate, as he is sure to have known. What is interesting about his self-representation is that it invites such criticism; by putting himself inside the frame he forgoes the privilege of the artist to make himself invisible, and this is his most important response to art's commodification of human life—he gives up his exemption from representation; like Joyce before him, he subjects himself as well as others to the workings of his pencil, thereby complicating the relation between subject and object in his work.

What Wunderlich has done by supplementing Joyce's verbal prewar manuscript with his own postwar sketchbook is to multiply the available perspectives on the complicated interdependence of artist and subject, sexism and racism, hatred and desire. In the process, he illustrates specific strategies that writers and artists can use to reduce their power over their subject/victims, thereby attacking the unjust univocality of social and political authority by exposing and diffusing artistic authority. The first technique is to introduce equal and competing perspectives; Wunderlich does this by supplementing the dominant perspective—that of Joyce himself—with that of the Jewish woman after the Jews' most horrifying victimization, and with his own, that of a German man and artist determined to arraign himself and his medium for their complicity in what was done. In short, he equalizes the status of everyone involved by positioning himself, his interlocutor, and their mutual victim in relation to the nightmare of the Holocaust. Wunderlich further diminishes the speculative power of the artist and of the observer by multiplying the eyes of the subjects so that they stare back at us accusingly from unexpected locations; the picture so conceived becomes less like a window and more like a mirror that forces us to determine our own relationship to both artist and victim. Wunderlich has challenged and disrupted the logic of identity, as Joyce had done before him through the multiple structures of *Ulysses*: Popper is never just herself—she is Joyce, Wunderlich, all women, and all Jews, a subject that both suffers and resists subjection. Finally, neither Wunderlich nor Joyce allows himself to escape the frame of representation—to stand "behind or beyond or above his handiwork, invisible, refined out of existence, indifferent, paring his fingernails" (*P,* 215); like Yeats when he begins to question himself directly in *The Tower*, they give up their privilege of being exempted from the representations they promulgate, with the result that history and politics refuse to be divorced from aesthetics and eroticism. Wunderlich's illustrations help to turn *Giacomo Joyce* from an ugly but realistic attempt to even the score with a Jewish woman into a series of dialogues—of Wunderlich with Joyce, Popper with both, and the artist with the reader/observer. Wunderlich's drawings historicize *Giacomo Joyce* by projecting onto it, and almost implicating it in, what was to come: the massacre of the Jews.

Wunderlich's *Giacomo Joyce* accuses everyone—including the artist and spectator—of participating in some system of relationships—whether sexual, racial, artistic, or political—that works through imbalances of power. He makes it clear that prejudice is called forth by the need to protect our status, by the fear that the prevailing balance of power will be reversed, a fear intensified, paradoxically, by the ability of the less privileged group to win admiration or to provoke desire. Prejudice is a knee-jerk response to the feelings of powerlessness to which the powerful are especially vulnerable because of their investment in stasis, which is why no one may be free from it, even the traditionally exempted artist/spectator and author/reader. What differentiates the privileged from the less privileged is not a freedom from prejudice or fear, but the power to act on that prejudice, and even in extreme cases to exterminate the other. Wunderlich emphasizes what Joyce himself eventually came to see, that the unexpected enemy is unrequited desire; as Stanley Kubrick dramatized more recently in *Full Metal Jacket*, the enemy of the present male establishment is also, in other contexts, represented as hidden booty; if she can be found and unveiled, she will always be foreign, resistant, and female. *Giacomo Joyce* marks the point where Joyce learned to bury the hatchet against woman, encouraging her to break into, disrupt, question, and conclude all of his subsequent fictional discourses. Like Wunderlich, Joyce strove to respect the autonomous status of his female and Jewish subjects, but he records his failures along with his successes. Wunderlich's commentary on Joyce leaves us with a complex image of not one but two artists who have learned to reject the simplicity of privileged status in favor of double vision in a darkening world, frankly avowing their differences and their similarities, subsuming their competitive concern for their status in a larger concern for the welfare of an immensely complex and besieged humanity. Wunderlich, like the later Joyce and other avant-garde artists of the twentieth century, has had the courage to change enemies; instead of exposing people, he exposes the hidden premises of art, how they work to the advantage of the artist and the critic, and to the dehumanization of those subjected to mass representation. As he told Frank Whitford, "I like thoroughly comfortable bathrooms on every floor. I have nothing against big country houses and nothing against fast and luxurious cars, nothing against money and nothing against security, but a great deal against pictures, my own included."[16]

Fascism and Silence: The Coded History of Amalia Popper

One question about *Giacomo Joyce* that neither Joyce nor Wunderlich answers with precise historical specificity is the question that opens the notebook: "Who?" The subject of the study is almost certainly Amalia Popper, as Ellmann suggested as early as 1959, and there is ample evidence to suggest that she is in fact the Italian model for Molly Bloom.[17] However, what had been published about her lacked biographical or historical depth: there was no context I could use to offset Joyce's representations of her, no way to reconstruct the meaning of his desire—with its inevitable distortions of reality—at that particular time and place. As a result, I have tried to recover as much as possible about who Popper really was; what it must have meant to be a woman in Trieste in 1908; to be a Jew; to be a scholar and teacher; to have achieved minor notoriety through association with an Irish writer celebrated for what the popular press believed was obscenity. To address these questions I consulted a variety of sources: the Ellmann Papers at the McFarlin Library, the University of Tulsa; histories of Trieste and the rise of fascism; articles from Triestine newspapers; the writings of Popper's husband, Michele Risolo, who became a prominent official in the fascist government; a 1991 reprint of Popper's *Araby*, with a note by Stelio Crise; and Popper's daughter, Silvia Risolo, with whom I corresponded.[18]

I had hoped to find in Popper not only an intellectual woman, but a strong, courageous, and vocal one. If, as Joseph Valente argues in his powerful treatment of *Giacomo Joyce*, the book is an exercise in objectification that is significant primarily because it fails;[19] if the turning point in *Giacomo Joyce* is also the turning point in Joyce's career, a moment when a woman's voice breaks through the varied constructions of her and speaks, with decisive resistance (*"Non hunc sed Barabbam!" GJ*, 16), I had hoped it was because Joyce's words were turned back on him by the power of this young woman's assurance and self-possession. And when she was young, Popper *was* extraordinary in several ways, most notably in her love of languages and her determination to receive a university education. With her marriage, however, she lost the voice that Giacomo had painfully schooled himself to hear; at least concerning her relationship with Joyce, she never again spoke directly or unconstrainedly. Instead, in the brief biography and translation of *Dubliners* she did in 1930–35, Joyce and possibly Stanislaus spoke through her; thereafter, her husband spoke for her. In a strange way, the story of what happened to her potential as a professional woman writer is a micropolitical version of what happened to nationalism in Italy at roughly the same time, as it moved from proud self-assertion into the fascism that co-opted it.

Amalia Popper was the daughter of Leopoldo Popper, a Jew from Bohemia who ran a shipping company in Trieste, and Letizia Luzzatto, a Venetian painter. Leopoldo Popper's first language was probably German (like Franz Kafka, who was from Prague and spoke German), but he spoke such fluent Italian that it marked him as an irredentist in Trieste, where the language one spoke was taken as a sign of one's political sympathies. His pro-Italian bent was further marked by the fact that although Trieste had two sets of institutions, Italian and German, he chose to send his children to Italian schools. According to Richard Ellmann, the large Jewish community in Trieste supported the unification of Italy because, although Austria-Hungary had shown signs of anti-Semitism, Italy at that time had not (Ellmann, *JJ* II, 196). Popper's husband, Michele Risolo, testifies that Leopoldo Popper "had a great liking for Joyce."[20] Bruno Cherslica relates that Leopoldo "loved his family, music, his job. . . . He lived in England and had a great respect for the British culture. Therefore, he decided to have his daughter Amalia tutored in English."[21]

Popper's mother, Letizia Luzzato, was "a painter and a very good one," according to her granddaughter Silvia Risolo. "She belonged to a well-known

Venetian school of painters, who used to exchange paintings and often didn't sign them." Like Molly Bloom's mother, "She and her family were Jews originally from Spain and I was told much later in life that Spanish Jews were a different streak, not the same kind as those in Central Europe.[22] She and my aunt, my mother's sister, produced so many paintings that a vast number of them had to be stacked away in trunks; during the war, the Germans stole them and carried them off to Germany" (letter from S. Risolo to Mahaffey, 11 January 1993).

Amalia Popper was born in Trieste in August 1891 and died in Florence of cancer on February 19, 1967. According to her husband, Joyce began to tutor her during her last year of high school at the Liceo Femminile, which would have been 1908–9.[23] The next year she spent five months auditing courses at the University of Vienna, hoping to enroll in a program in history. Risolo reports that because "she felt Italian like her mother," she moved to Florence in 1910, hoping to attend the university there. She was told she could not enroll without proficiency in Latin and Greek, which were not taught in the lyceum for women she had attended (they had taught Italian, German, and two other modern languages). Upon the advice of Giuseppe Picciola, and with the support of a senator, Guido Mazzoni, she asked the minister of education for permission to take proficiency exams in Greek and Latin and her request was granted. She began auditing classes while studying Greek and Latin from scratch.

According to Risolo in his response to "Casanova without qualities," one of her teachers was Medea Norsa, assistant of Gabinetto Vitelli of the papyrology department (after her teacher's death, Norsa became head of the department, an extraordinary position for a woman at that time). "In ten months, she was able to master perfectly both Latin and Greek and also could read all the classics so she could enroll at the university" (M. Risolo to Ellmann, 24 November 1967). She joined the Italian literature department with a concentration in classical philology. According to her husband, the two of them met on November 5, 1911, in a classroom where Italian, Latin, and Greek were taught.[24] They studied together, and he visited her family twice in Trieste in 1912. They got engaged over the Easter holidays of 1913.[25] In July 1914 World War I began, and they decided to marry quickly for fear that a war between Italy and Austria would cause them to be separated. This was the beginning of their fourth and last year of college; on December 22, 1914, they were married at the city hall in Florence. Their first child was a son, Leopoldo Angelo, born in 1915. He became a physician in Trieste and died in 1977. His wife, Albertina, is still living, and they have a daughter, Antonietta, who published the reprint of Amalia Popper's *Araby* in 1991. A daughter, Silvia Lucia Letizia, was born in 1920, and a second son, Fausto, (now an architect living in Rome) was born four years later (letter from S. Risolo to Mahaffey, 11 January 1993).

In the spring of 1915, when Italy entered the war, the Popper family went to Zurich, where they met the Joyces. Later, Popper's mother, sister, and brother moved to Florence, but Leopoldo remained in Zurich (where he had very good friends, such as Rudolf Goldschmidt and Ottocaro Weiss) until the end of the war (letter from M. Risolo to Ellmann, 21 April 1968, and letter from Weiss to Ellmann, 6 August 1967). Joyce seems to have seen a lot of Leopoldo Popper during the war, while he was writing the first half of *Ulysses*.

Michele Risolo, Amalia's husband, who was not Jewish, was born in Lecce in 1889 and died in Florence in 1975. He moved to Trieste in 1918, at the end of the war, and taught for a few years, later joining the newspaper staff of *Il Piccolo*. Two years after his marriage, in 1916, he published a reprint of the 1868 version of Arrigo Boito's opera, *Mefistofele*, based on Goethe's *Faust*.[26] In 1923, pursuing an apparent interest in the satanic, Risolo published a monograph on the nineteenth-century French writer and critic Jules Amedee Barbey d'Aurevilly, best known for his dislike of naturalism and for his hallucinatory stories *Les Diaboliques* (1874). Risolo's *Carducci e d'Annunzio nella storia della poesia italiana*, an account of how the poetry of Giosuè Carducci (1835–1907) and Gabriele D'Annunzio (1863–1938) has influenced the history of Italian poetry, appeared in 1928, and in 1931 Risolo published his study of "Fascism in Venezia Giulia." By 1935 he was the director of the organ of the National Fascist Party, *Il Popolo di Trieste*. However, because he was married to a Jew he had to leave *Il Piccolo* in 1938; he moved to Florence, where he worked at *La Nazione* and, according to Roberto Curci, "devoted himself to minimizing the meaning of the relationship between his wife and Joyce."[27] Stelio Crise describes him as a shy and introverted "Pugliese" with a complex about being too short (Crise, note to *Araby*, 1991, 99). Risolo's daughter, Silvia, relates,

> My father was not a writer. He was a journalist, but not at the time when he met my mother at the University in Florence and married her; in those days he was aiming at a University career.
>
> After the First World War, he joined the newly born fascist movement and although he was never a "squadrista," gangs of fascists who went about beating people up and forcing them to drink castor oil, he took part in 1922 in the so-called March on Rome, which marks the official beginning of fascist dictatorship, rule and government, in Italy. Fascism in those days had nothing whatsoever to do with racism; there were no coloured people living in Italy and, as for Jews, no one knew they existed. That was Hitler's invention, later on, and as a matter of fact, Hitler and Mussolini were enemies for several years. My father's fascism was purely interested in getting rid of the Communists (who had just emerged in Russia and assassinated the Royal Family there), because they caused endless havoc all over Italy, so that a stronger hand was needed to govern the country.
>
> In 1924(?), '25(?), '26(?) my father was offered the editorship of *Il Popolo di Trieste*, one of the three Italian newspapers actually belonging to the Party (the Government, I mean); a bomb had been planted in the building and had killed the editor. That night, as a little girl, I was woken up by the telephone and an endless argument between my parents and that was when my father accepted the offer and became editor of the paper. Under him, the paper flourished but in 1938, when as a result of the alliance between Hitler and Mussolini the Jewish laws were imported into Italy, he was sacked because he had written and published in his newspaper disapproval of the anti-Jewish laws.

However, in 1943, during the war, that is, when Italy collapsed and was in-vaded by the Germans and when Mussolini reappeared on the scene, my fa-ther joined the new fascist party, in the belief that by so doing he would be able to save his half-Jewish children as well as my Jewish grandfather. He soon regretted it: I can still see him dashing around the house and shouting "Sono capaci di tutto! di tutto!" "They are capable of anything, anything at all, any atrocity."(letter from S. Risolo to Mahaffey, 11 January 1993).

Despite her education and her facility with languages, Popper, as her daugh-ter testifies, "was not a writer. Besides the 'Doubliners' [sic], I believe she only wrote—much later in her life—reviews of German (and English?) books, novels mostly, for newspapers and she also translated (and published?) some poems by the contemporary German poet, Rilke" (letter of 11 January 1993).[28] In 1929, Stanislaus asked her to contribute an article on Samuel Butler's *Erewhon*. He also encouraged her to write about the popular Jewish writer Israel Zangwill, but she decided to do a translation of *Dubliners* instead.[29] Risolo told Helen Barolini that "[s]he translated the whole volume, encouraged by Stanislaus, from whom she was taking lessons in English literature to prepare her for the teaching exams."[30] Risolo told Ellmann that it was he who urged his wife "to translate a group of stories and to secure from Joyce the basic biographical facts for a quick but dependable sketch of his character."[31] As a preface to the vol-ume, she wrote what she called an "Essential Biography" of Joyce, often re-ferred to as his first Italian biography, but if her husband can be believed, she herself contributed almost nothing to it: "she simply compiled the data fur-nished by James Joyce and his brother."[32] Risolo argues that Joyce sent the notes for the biography through Stanislaus in order "to clarify in his own way some aspects of his work and of his art."[33] Risolo insists that the only work by Joyce that his wife knew was *Dubliners* (whereas the "Essential Biography" dis-cusses both *Ulysses* and "Work in Progress"). According to Risolo, Joyce not only supplied the biographical facts but also meticulously checked the six-page manuscript, either personally or through a proxy.[34] Risolo wrote to Ellmann to explain that his wife had actually "translated more than five" stories (Risolo calls them "letters," writing this sentence in English).[35] He gives two different accounts of how it came about that only five of the stories were published, first telling Barolini that it was difficult to find a publisher and that therefore Stanis-laus, after consulting James, chose the five stories to be published under the title *Araby*[36] and then telling Ellmann a slightly different version:

> After a while Joyce got tired of reading and correcting (maybe he did not have time for it any more) and sent back the translations *marking* the ones he would love to see published. We followed his indications in spite of our regret at leaving some of the stories unpublished that he had already corrected, touched up, and approved.

In this letter, Risolo refers specifically to some of the changes he remembers Joyce making on the printed proofs, commenting, "He was so scrupulous." He particularly recalls that Joyce modified some sentences in "Eveline" and revised the last paragraphs of *The Dead* from the words "pochi battiti" to the end: "This editing was obviously only stylistic, as far as I can remember, not substantial: he cared about preserving a certain rhythm at the end of the short story."[37]

Whether knowledgeably compiled by Popper with the disapproval of her husband or ghostwritten by Joyce or Stanislaus, it is notable that this "first Italian biography"[38] unaccountably fails to emphasize Joyce's years in Trieste. Barolini writes,

> This slight *Biografia essenziale* is significant for the document it provides of how Joyce wanted to appear publically [*sic*], so to speak. And, I should think, precious information for a biographer. Joyce patently wanted to be presented as a serious, correct, regularly married, highly thought of, first-of-the-class genius—nor does Signora Risolo relieve the cut and dried tone with any attempt at personal recollection of the punning, merry, bizarre, singing Irishman she knew in Trieste. It's as if she never knew Joyce. (*New York Review of Books,* 20 November 1969)

The "essential biography" presents Joyce as precocious, spiritual—"the religious experiences of his childhood years left indelible traces on his spirit"—and musically talented (it mentions that he had considered taking up singing as a profession).[39] It presents Joyce's literary credentials, repeating endorsements by William Butler Yeats and by the prominent critic and translator of Ibsen, William Archer. The biography defends Joyce's rejection of the Irish nationalist literary movement (described as "the most important movement in contemporary English literature"), by focusing on Joyce's early essay, "The Day of the Rabblement," in which Joyce proposed using models from abroad for the new Irish Literary theater. According to this biographer, the Irish theater would not present foreign plays due to their fear of the nationalistic hoodlums ("teppa"). What is fascinating about this argument is that it is implicitly a socialist one— in its internationalism, in its opposition to nationalist fervor, and in its characterization of the nationalists as rabble—that places Joyce in sharp contrast to Risolo, who was then a prominent fascist (and nationalist).

The biography goes on to discuss the contrasting elements of mysticism and realism in Joyce's lectures on William Blake and Daniel Defoe, and the metamorphosis of the delicate poet of *Chamber Music* into the bitter and satirical author of *Dubliners*. It characterizes *A Portrait of the Artist* as a depiction of a "psychological crisis," which traces the "transfer of the conscience from . . . the impending sense of sin to an almost painful sensitivity to the magic of words." Finally, it offers a defense of *Ulysses,* arguing against a view of this book, on which Joyce's fame will probably rest, as sinister, pessimistic realism, emphasizing instead its symbolism and lyricism. It says of the repeated "yes" at the end of Molly Bloom's scandalous monologue that it stimulates in the reader "a growing excitement, a throb of genuine lyricism. . . . Since Joyce is such a meticulous writer that he doesn't include or omit even a comma without intention, this 'yes' is the 'everlasting yea' of Carlyle, the statement of the goodness of life, not by a romantic who lives in a world of his own, but by a realist who lives in the world as it is, and who can look ugliness in the face, without letting his heart be turned to stone."

The emphasis on the lyrical, even spiritual dimension of Joyce's work sounds more like James than Stanislaus, although the short paragraph on "Work in Progress" bears the imprint of Stanislaus's skepticism: it comments that in these works Joyce invents words instead of using "the ready-made words which the language offers him in endless abundance," which makes the "Work in Progress" very difficult to read. Stanislaus is famous for his critical dismissal of what would become *Finnegans Wake*; Risolo mentions that he was influenced by Stanislaus's disparagement of *Finnegans Wake*, which Risolo also extends to *Ulysses*.[40] As intermediary between the author and translator of the biography, Stanislaus clearly had some input. When Joyce died, six years after *Araby* was published, Stanislaus used several of the same details emphasized in the "Essential Biography" in his two-part reminiscence, "Ricordi di James Joyce."[41]

Picture, then, the peculiarity of this situation: it is the late 1920s in Trieste. Risolo is soon to be named director of *Il Popolo di Trieste*, an organ of the National Fascist Party, and is working on a history of fascism in the region (*Il Facismo nella Venezia Giulia Dalle Origini alla Marcia su Roma* would be published in 1932–33). Risolo's history describes, among other things, the instability of the spring of 1920 in Trieste (before the Joyces unexpectedly left for Paris in July, never to return). Every day there are strikes and uproar; "uneasiness, restlessness, and uncertainty dominate all aspects of life in Trieste in the Guilian region." Risolo decries what he refers to as the "defamatory hate of our Socialists against Italy," their "friendship with the foreigner" that he describes as "miserably sad and disgraceful." At the same time that he is writing against the socialists, his wife is translating stories by a man who, according to Stelio Crise, didn't bother to hide his liking for Triestine socialists such as Giuseppe Bertelli, a writer for the socialist paper *Il Lavatore*,[42] and who clearly identified himself as both pacifist and internationalist to the point that he had separated himself from nationalist Ireland (also under imperial control). Joyce made it clear that he liked Trieste under the rule of Austria-Hungary; he later told Mary Colum that he had never been happier than when under the permissive regime of Austria-Hungary in Trieste: "They called it a ramshackle empire. . . . I wish to God there were more such empires."[43] He also frequently expressed skepticism about Italian patriotism: "I don't like Italian literature because the mentality of the degenerate Italian writers is dominated entirely by these four elementary themes: beggared orphans and hungry people (will these Italians never stop being hungry?), battlefields, cattle, and patriotism."[44]

Popper's decision to promote in Italy the works of a man whose views were diametrically opposed to those of her husband is a startling one. Moreover, her husband argues, rather improbably, that his wife did this at his own suggestion. Even if Joyce's politics had been congenial to him, would Risolo have encouraged his wife to translate the work of a man who had written what he considered to be an indecent book? Silvia Risolo recalls one of her holidays in Italy around 1958, when she brought *Ulysses* with her and was trying to read it. "This brought about a terrific quarrel between my parents and I heard my father angrily calling Joyce obscene and filthy" (letter of 11 January 1993).

Of course, Risolo's book on fascism and his wife's concomitant translation of

Dubliners were done long before Ellmann publicly identified Amalia as the subject of *Giacomo Joyce* and a model for Molly Bloom. The crucial figure who brought Ellmann into the picture was Ottocaro Weiss, whose sisters had gone to high school with Popper[45] and who married Ettore Schmitz's (Italo Svevo's) niece, Ortensia in 1923 (Ellmann, *JJ* II 272n). The Weisses had been in Zurich with the Poppers and the Joyces during the First World War; Ira Nadel writes that, in 1918, Weiss's brother, Edoardo, who had been a pupil of Freud's as early as 1908, introduced psychoanalysis into Italy with the publication of his Italian translation of Freud's *Introduction to Psychoanalysis* (Nadel, 203). Edoardo Weiss practiced in Trieste until 1931, then moved to Rome where he lived until 1939, when with his brother Ottocaro, he left Italy to avoid the racial laws. As Crise relates, Ottocaro Weiss went to New York, where he was the U.S. representative of Assicurazioni Generali, a Triestine insurance company. In New York, he was sought out by and became friends with Ellmann, the young professor who shared his strong interest in Joyce. In 1953, Weiss brought Ellmann to Trieste to visit Stanislaus, who had lived there since his release from semi-internment in Florence in 1945. This is how Ellmann discovered that Stanislaus had all of Joyce's Trieste library and papers, minus only a box of books and the notes for *Ulysses* that Joyce had wanted sent to him when he abruptly left Trieste for Paris in July of 1920. Ellmann gathered an enormous number of anecdotes and amount of documentation during his stay. On his second visit, in 1954, according to Crise, Stanislaus mentioned a love story between Jim and one of his pupils in Trieste, whom Nellie and Stannie identified as Popper.[46] When Stanislaus died on June 19, 1955, his widow received no pension, so Weiss helped her sell off the Trieste library, in return for which she gave him *Giacomo Joyce*.[47] Crise asserts that Weiss remembered Leopoldo Popper and found out that his daughter, then living in Florence with her husband, was not in good health. Crise claims that Weiss refused to allow *Giacomo Joyce* to be published in order to spare her the gossip that its publication would provoke. After her death in February of 1967, Weiss reluctantly allowed Ellmann to do a critical edition. According to Crise, after *Giacomo Joyce* was published, "Everybody [went] bananas trying to find out some saucy biographical details. Everybody ignore[d] the angry anguish of professor Michele Risolo who insistently [fought] to deny any suspicion and insinuation against his Amalia" (Crise, "Una Nota," *Araby*, 98–99).

Crise seems to have taken over Risolo's role as protector of Popper's reputation; in the 1991 article by Curci, he is reported to have offered another candidate for the subject of *Giacomo Joyce*, Annie Schleimer. However, Crise was not always so determined to deny Popper's association with *Giacomo Joyce*, and Ellmann himself never succeeded in talking with her. In 1953, he got her address from Stanislaus and wrote to her but received no answer. His friend Jean Hagstrum tried to see her when he was in Florence in 1953–54, but he "was diverted by Mr. Risolo, who said that instead he would himself write Mr. Hagstrum on this subject. Mr. Hagstrum felt that some effort was being made to head him off; when Mr. Risolo's letter arrived, he sent it to [Ellmann] on 20 May 1954 with a note saying, 'He has confirmed my suspicions that he doesn't want people to be in direct contact with Mrs. R. Why I don't know. I shall try to find out'" (Ellmann, *New York Review of Books*, 2). Ellmann spent a year in Italy and met Crise, who knew the Risolos. Ellmann told him he was uncertain of his identification of Popper, and Crise responded that "he had brought up the matter with Mr. Risolo, who, on hearing what [the] biography said, had commented, 'The professor has been indiscreet'" (Ellmann, *New York Review of Books*). Crise urged Ellmann to try again to see Popper, and he telephoned her in February 1961. She answered the phone, saying she was ill and could not see him. He asked her if she did not want to see him, and she answered that she *could* not ("Non posso"). A few days later he received a letter of apology from Risolo, who said his wife was ill and exhausted from teaching (Ellmann, *New York Review of Books*).

Ellmann's papers contain letters that show he continued to worry about his identification of Popper with the woman in *Giacomo Joyce*, probably because of her husband's vehement protests; however, Weiss claimed he was "certain" that Popper was the one referred to in the manuscript.[48] Neither Stanislaus nor Weiss had any doubts, and Crise has made it clear that what he calls "vain gossip" was hurtful to Popper's family. However, the fact that Popper was never allowed to tell her own story makes the situation more complicated, and Risolo is certainly vulnerable to the charge that he protested too much. Moreover, although Ellmann tried to soften his identification of Popper with the woman of *Giacomo Joyce* in the second edition of his biography, he still says that "the seductiveness of Molly came, it seems, from Signorina Popper" (*JJ* II, 376), a statement that would hardly have allayed her husband's anxieties, had he still been alive. To have had one's wife publicly identified as a model for an adulterous woman character in a book once banned for obscenity in the English-speaking world must have occasioned some embarrassment, and Ellmann's uncritical replication of Joyce's own insistence (in *Giacomo Joyce*) on Popper's sexual allure at the expense of her intellectual curiosity and facility with language made things worse.[49]

Whatever did or did not happen between James Joyce and Amalia Popper is hardly relevant, any more than the point of *Exiles* is whether or not Bertha betrayed Richard with Robert. (Interestingly, the situation between Joyce and his pupil, represented by Richard and Beatrice in *Exiles*, mirrored the situation of Robert and Bertha more closely than Joyce chose to dramatize in the play: we will never know what, if anything, happened between them.) Instead, the focus (as in *Exiles*) is on Popper's impossible position between two well-intentioned men, one of whom (the author) tries to get her to speak, ventriloquizing through her, and the other (the husband) to prevent her from speaking. Like Bertha, who is suspended between Richard's prescribed "emancipation" and Robert's urge for possession, Popper's real needs and desires have been airbrushed out of history. *Exiles* suggests that compulsory emancipation (dictated by Richard) is only marginally better than being possessed, if only because its operations are less secretive. But *Exiles* shows that Richard's insistence on emancipating his partner at the expense of the trust and intimacy between them still constitutes a privileging of his desire over hers, which is sexist in effect if not in intention. Joyce recognized that his practice of speaking for women, although preferable to the sexually motivated practice of objectifying them, is nonetheless fraught with presumption. The problem, however, is inherent in the logic of representation itself.

The histories of fascism and Nazism testify to the vital importance of preserving and attending to the voice of the other. Risolo was caught in the crossfire; the problem with nationalist politics is that they are implicitly xenophobic, intolerant of difference. Although his careful monitoring of his wife's statements suggests that he may have been fearful of sexual difference or female autonomy, he had no difficulty with racial difference and accepted his wife's Jewish family and friends wholeheartedly (letter from S. Risolo, 30 July 1991). When he rejoined the Fascist Party in 1943 in a desperate attempt to protect his Jewish relations, privately expressing his despair at being unable to do so, his situation was tragically ironic. Furthermore, his prediction about the Nazis proved correct: Popper's sister Lisetta (most probably the classmate who speaks "boneless Viennese Italian" in *Giacomo Joyce*, 1) and her husband were killed at Risiera di San Sabba (the only concentration camp in Italy) during the Nazi occupation of Trieste.

Joyce may not have censored Popper's voice, but his construction of her is differently distorted; he attributes to her more agency than she actually had. He is exploring her *potential*, without attending sufficiently to the social realities that circumscribed her: her desire for a formal education and accreditation, the limitations imposed by her social position, her youth, her gender, and later her marriage. This is odd, because it seems it was precisely the constraints of his own position—his responsibility for Nora and their children, his poverty and failing vision—that produced the compensatory fantasy of *Giacomo Joyce* in the first place.

Popper's daughter writes that her mother was "a marvellous scholar but a terrible woman" and that her father, "in a different way, was a terrible man" (letter, 30 July 1991). She recounts that her mother "made scenes" and "was very difficult to live with," although "she could be very charming too" (letter, 17 January 1993). Although, as Silvia Risolo comments, her parents are both dead and "cannot answer" (30 July 1991), it is tempting to interpret what Popper might have been saying to Joyce, in code, by holding the mirror of his own words up to him via a translation of *Dubliners*.[50] Her oeuvre is a truncated echo of his, and it tells him, in Italian this time, about the anguish of naive admiration ("Araby"), about dreams of literary accomplishment aborted by the responsibilities of marriage and child-rearing ("A Little Cloud"), and about men driven to brutality by their political, economic, and even physical subordination to a government with values that they do not share ("Counterparts"). She repeats back to him the story of "Eveline" (presented not as an early story, as in *Dubliners*, but as the penultimate story in the volume), which describes a woman who is finally unable to leave her homeland for the appeal of an unknown frankness, who grows dumb and sightless with terror at the barrier, and who is left behind. Finally, in "The Dead," she tells him the plangent tale of a woman haunted by a first love presented as both dead and immortal (in Italian, the verbal proximity of death and immortality is better represented by the similarity of "I Morti" and "immortalità"): "The Dead." Popper's coded message to Joyce recalls him to an awareness of the power of social, sexual, economic, and cultural limitations; her title serves as a gentle reminder that the exotic goal of desire—"Araby"—is never what we imagine it to be. By writing only through repetition (translation of his own work), she tells him what Virginia Woolf thought to tell the women of the London/National Society for Women's Service at approximately the same time (1931): that women, even more than men, "will find it extremely difficult to say what [they] think." Woolf pictures the censorship and abuse to which women would be subject if they aspired to the openness of Joyce or Proust, "their determination to say everything," which she strongly supports: "litera-ture which is always pulling down blinds is not literature. All that we have ought to be expressed—mind and body—a process of incredible difficulty and danger."[51] In a dream set in Paris and later interpolated into the text of *Giacomo Joyce*, Popper says something similar about the importance of openness and frankness to Joyce—"I am not convinced that such activities of the mind or body can be called unhealthy" (*GJ*, 15)—and he is terrified. As beset as Joyce was because of the frankness of his books, a woman writer's vulnerability is even greater.

Amalia Popper's life testifies to the importance of voice, which must at least equal that of vision and appearance. What remains of her is primarily images, not words; her power was in her eyes, not her voice. As Silvia Risolo writes, Pop-per had "extraordinary eyes . . . , such as in all my life I have never seen in anyone else, except a cinema actress of long ago, large and dreamy, and of a brown-greenish colour" (letter, 30 November 1992). It may be that Popper only found her voice in the next generation, in an expatriate (not a nationalist) who never married. Her daughter, Silvia, teaches classics in London, where she has been living since World War II. She has written a book of short stories, *Il bigliettaio di Leicester Square* (1953), and a novel, *L'ammirevole e fortunatissima Letizia Lloyd* (1965), both about London. In addition to serving as London cor-respondent for *Il Mondo* of Pannunzio, she has also authored *È tardi ormai, Madeleine* (Firenze, 1957) and *"Cargo" a sud* (Bologna, 1959).

From Italy to Ireland: The Ambivalence of Men toward Men

What did Joyce learn from his impassioned, escapist fantasy about Popper? He was certainly prompted to ask himself the question Yeats posed in *The Winding Stair:* "But what am I that dare / Fancy that I can / Better conduct myself or have more / Sense than a common man?" (*VP*, 507) More importantly, like Yeats before him and Wunderlich after him, Joyce resolved to translate his expe-rience into something that a reader would also be forced to confront, not ab-stractly, but in the actual experience of reading; for as Wilde had proclaimed in the preface to *The Picture of Dorian Gray*, "It is the spectator, and not life, that art really mirrors" (*DG*, 3). Joyce fashioned his prose so that it might reflect the slip-page between the reader's unconscious desires and her conscious intentions, which are most often shaped by social norms and expectations. It is because he, like his Irish models, crafted his work to expose this incongruity, writing not from a position of superiority but from one of humility, that Joyce has Stephen describe Irish art as "the cracked lookingglass of a servant" (*U*, 1.146).

In both *Dubliners* and *A Portrait of the Artist as a Young Man*, Joyce "cracks" or splits the reader's reaction to the people of Dublin and to Stephen Dedalus, respectively, pulling the reader between sympathy and ironic detachment. In *Ulysses*, Joyce broadens his canvas, painting his characters against a background of social norms and values that would normally discourage readers from sympathizing with them. He chooses as heroes a drunken, over-educated coward, a peace-loving, wandering Jew, and an adulterous woman, portraying them as society would see them, as incompatible with any familiar models of heroism, and as they see themselves, representing their desires and disappointments through interior monologues. Although initially, Joyce complicates the reader's desire to "take sides" at the level of character, as the novel progresses he multiplies the reader's angles of vision by antically adopting many styles and by repositioning his "heroes" at different points in literary history, especially ancient Greece and Renaissance England. Throughout *Ulysses*, Joyce is careful to show that different laws apply to women and to Jews than to young men, and in "Cyclops" and "Penelope," he provokes the reader—especially the Irish reader, who has experienced the disadvantage of a colonial double standard for hundreds of years—to question any assumption of sexual or racial superiority.

The problem with *Ulysses*, as Joyce saw from watching its controversial reception, is that readers were still able to take sides, although they did so more stridently and with greater discomfort and even defensiveness. Most readers reviled Molly, and many saw Bloom primarily as a cuckold whose weakness was underscored by his Jewish ancestry. Joyce designed *Finnegans Wake* so that it would be impossible for a reader to take sides for or against a character or a position with any assurance. A reader cannot encounter a single word without confronting and struggling with the reality of adulteration, and perhaps even questioning the comforting illusion of purity and simplicity that ordinary language so easily promotes. Joyce suggests that we see ourselves in every word, and in *Finnegans Wake* the words he holds up as mirrors to the reader are saturated with historical and linguistic difference, inconsistent, and unstable, yet rife with creative possiblities, like individual identity itself.

Joyce's discoveries about *Giacomo Joyce* led to the obscurities of *Finnegans Wake* partly through an understanding of sexual difference, which is not only gender difference but also difference from heterosexual norms. In Joyce's work, respect for sexual difference brings with it an appreciation of racial and national differences; in *Finnegans Wake*, Joyce treats misogyny and homophobia as akin to xenophobia, while treating desire for the "other" as original "sin," a temptation that Judeo-Christians are instructed to resist. Respect for difference demands a sharper, more detailed or local focus, because that is the level at which the minor variations that produce difference are most apparent. At the verbal level, the pun expresses a respect for difference and an acceptance of contradiction in highly concentrated form, an expression that becomes denser in macaronic puns, which draw on more than one language for their meanings. Joyce compares such densely layered language to the thickness of porter, or stout: it is both spiritual (insofar as it is an alcoholic "spirit") and sinful; a potential *port*al and a letter in a closed bottle, "screwed and corked" (*FW,* 624.1); a burden (via the French word *porter,* to carry) and a shipping port, where many different cultures meet and make profitable exchanges. Such language attempts to bring us closer to our origins (in this respect it is the Genesis/Guiness of Scripture), but it also makes us realize how far we have strayed from that first garden of meaning by describing its fake etymology as "falsemeaning adamelegy" (*FW,* 77.26).

On the one hand, Joyce sees the pun as more perfectly balancing the perceptions of the eye with those of the ear, which makes it a "sound sense sympol" (*FW,* 612.29, a symbol reminding us that we hear is also both sensible and simple), but on the other hand he knows that people who prefer to think of languages, nations, and genders as "pure" will "Shun the Punman" (*FW,* 93.13) as the "seeker of the nest of evil in the bosom of a good word" (*FW,* 189.28–9). Shem's etymological artistry will be seen as rude, and he may even be excommunicated "for his root language" (*FW,* 424.17), a sinfully adulterated refuseheap of letters "that is nat language at any sinse of the world" (*FW,* 83.12). Shem's—and Joyce's—language will be condemned as neurotic and promiscuous in its exploration of difference; readers will pronounce, "[t]o the hardily curiosing entomophilust then it has shown a very sexmosaic of nymphosis" (*FW,* 107.12–13). But Joyce responds that his is a *realistic* treatment of language as it changes over time, with its "variously inflected, differently pronounced, otherwise spelled, changeably meaning vocable scriptsigns" (*FW,* 118.26–8). Moreover, Joyce treats the long and obscure "letter" to the reader that is *Finnegans Wake,* based as it is on over sixty languages, as emphatically Irish. By so doing, he implies that Irishness is not the insular, defensive category that it is sometimes thought to be, but a richly adulterated history of many cultures, a compilation of their legacies. Ireland is rendered as "errorland" (*FW,* 62.25), a specific locus riddled with changes that the book itself reflects and consolidates. Joyce depicts Ireland (and the book that performs its contradictions) as a "bottlefilled" (*FW,* 310.26): it is a battlefield littered with drink bottles, a country torn by spiritual yearnings (peopled by "romance catholeens," romantic Cathleens and Roman Catholics, *FW,* 239.21) and by centuries of war. Joyce highlights the irony of Ireland's propensity for war, in view of the fact that the Greek word *eirene,* which contains the word "eire," means "peace"; "how paisably eirenical" it is that this country (French "pays") of Greek peace is so warlike (*FW,* 14.30). Locked in conflict with what Joyce refers to as the "benighted queendom" (*FW,* 241.22), Ireland overlooks the power of a "punsil shapner" (pencil sharpener, pun as shrapnel, *shap,* meaning *cunt* in M.E., *FW,* 98.30), in which we may sharpen the world (wood) through a war of words: "The war is in words and the wood is the world. Maply me, willowy we, hickory he and yew yourselves" (*FW,* 98.34–6). And, "You is feeling like you was lost in the bush, boy? It is a puling sample jungle of woods. Bethicket me for a stump of a beech if I have the poultriest notions what the farest he all means" (*FW*, 112.3–6).

In *Finnegans Wake*, Joyce takes the view of language as local color to its logical extreme, using present-day Ireland as a prism through which to refract history and the world. This is experimental language at its most precise and almost unbearable, developed over seventeen years not to "dizzledazzle" its readers "with a graith uncouthrement of postmantuam glasseries from the lapins and the grigs" (Latins and Greeks, *FW*, 113.1–2), but to remind readers of the vital "automutativeness" of language, which resembles that of the potentially productive female body (*FW*, 112.12). By learning to think in an automutative way (instead of aiming primarily to acquire and possess knowledge), we can create alternatives to the "jolting series of prearranged disappointments" we experience as "our social something bowls along bumpily" (*FW*, 107.32–4); we can avoid being "envenomoloped in piggotry" (enveloped/envenomed by/in bigotry/forgery, *FW*, 99.19).

Finnegans Wake is about desire, focusing on the place where "the dart of desire has gored the heart of secret waters" (*FW*, 599.25–6), the sea and sky of Ireland. Using what he had learned from *Giacomo Joyce* about how instinctively he had tried to insulate himself against the threat of sexual, racial, national, and linguistic difference, Joyce invested enormous effort in an attempt to embrace and employ such differences, and in so doing to approximate the libidinal and spiritual energy of the unconscious mind. His experiment was also intended as a response and a tribute to the life and writings of Yeats and Wilde, the most influential Irish writers of the last two generations.

The debts to Yeats and Wilde throughout *Finnegans Wake* are many and varied. At the most general level, Joyce's decision to name his Odyssean figure "Bloom" in *Ulysses* and to call his female protagonist in *Finnegans Wake* Anna Livia Plurabelle ("plur" means "flower" in Irish, and, as a river, ALP's flow makes her a flow-er) is in part a tribute to Yeats's comprehensive treatment of the Rose in his early poetry. When Joyce puns on the Irish as "Airish" and calls Eire "Aira" (*FW*, 192.26, 353.32), he is continuing the tradition established by Yeats in *The Wind Among the Reeds*. Moreover, Joyce's decision to base the male protagonist, HCE, on the legendary figure of Finn MacCool is partly a reaction to Yeats's lifelong fascination with Cuchulain and the stories of the Red Branch kings of Ulster. Irish heroic literature falls into two main cycles, the Ulster Cycle, centered on Cuchulain, and the Fenian or Ossianic Cycle, which revolves around Finn MacCool. Yeats was entranced by the Ulster Cycle, which celebrates the lone champion, the individual hero, magnificent in his superiority to and difference from his people. In sharp contrast, Joyce's HCE, the Hero as Everyman, is based on the Fenian Cycle, which focuses on the *fiana*, "a band of roving men whose principal occupations were hunting and war."[52] In *Celtic Heritage*, Alwyn and Brinley Rees note that the word "fian" is sometimes used in board games to denote pieces of inferior status; they use this fact to argue that the Fenian tales are more popular than heroic, and focus more on camaraderie and community than on individual feats of heroism. Furthermore, the Reeses argue that, unlike the Ulster stories, which feature willpower, "the distinctive quality of the Fenian tales is 'human warmth of feeling'" (Rees, 69). By constructing his last book against the background of ancient Irish literature, Joyce is at once following Yeats and marking an important difference between his work and Yeats's; instead of focusing on the heroic and embattled individual, Joyce evokes instead the communal fellow-feeling and cooperative ethos of the *fiana*, which underscores the deeply democratic vision behind the book.

If Yeats's influence was basic to the design of *Finnegans Wake*, Wilde's life is, in large part, what the book is about: the relation between sexual and linguistic errancy. As a major prototype for HCE, or Here Comes Everybody, Wilde is not only a writer who let "punplays pass to ernest" (in *The Importance of Being Earnest*, *FW*, 233.19–20), but he also provides a precedent for HCE's humpty-dumpty-like fall from the wall of the law ("law" is "wall" spelled backward) for "licentious" behavior. Wilde is the "Wildemanns" (*FW*, 358.23) who, like the Russian general, is found guilty of sodomy, which Joyce significantly redefines as making free with the "sod" of the old country (the Irish Buckley shoots the Russian general when he sees him wipe his ass with a sod of turf). The sin for which HCE is prosecuted under subsection 32, section 11, of the 1885 Criminal Law Amendment Act (the law under which Wilde was prosecuted, which Joyce refers to, *FW*, 61.9–10) is exposure: he has exposed his naked posterior to younger boys, first as the Irish Duke of Wellington (to the Napoleon boys), then as the Russian general (to the Irish boys, Butt and Taff, who together make up Buckley). In both cases, the boys respond to the sight of the older man's bared backside by shooting him in the arse, which in the Wellington episode doubles as Wellington's big white "harse," named Copenhagen (*FW*, 10.10–22). In the Buckley episode, Butt (with a gesture reminiscent of Wilde, the great white caterpillar with sunflowered buttonhole at the Old Bailey Court, *FW*, 350.10–11), shoves his thumb and four fingers up the Russian General's ass (*"shouts his thump and feeh fauh foul finngures up the heighhos of their ahs,"* *FW*, 352.28–29). Finally, in the Ricorso, the pagan High King Leary (who is also the Irish idealist philosopher Berkeley and a version of Buckley), in a moment of anger against the light of Christianity, surprised a praying St. Patrick by sticking "his thumping fore features apt the hoyhop of his Ards" ("High," and "arse," *FW*, 612.32–35). Joyce further connects the Wellington episode, the Buckley episode, and Oscar Wilde's experience when he introduces Wilde as "Oliver White," together with "his speak quite hoarse" (big white horse/ass, *FW*, 334.15–16).

The three incidents in which HCE (as Wellington, the Russian general, and St. Patrick) exposes himself to boys are also scenes of confrontation between different nationalities (Irish and French, Russian and Irish, Irish and British). Joyce describes the encounters as "pedarrests" (*FW*, 349.34) in which children are arresting their "pederastic" elders for revealing vulnerability. The younger generation's response to their elders' "indecency" is to break their father's arse, which is also his heart and art. (In the *Scribbledehobble* notebook, Joyce writes that "OW [Oscar Wilde] died of a broken arse").[53] The chastened father, in turn, reacts by writing, from an exile like that of "foull subustioned mullmud" (Sebastian Melmoth, as Wilde called himself in France after his release from prison), "his farced epistol to the hibruws" (forced, first; letter, pistol; Hebrews, highbrows; *FW,* 228.33–34). Joyce turns the back of HCE's britches into the ruin of London Bridge, which no verbal virtuosity can fix: "Lonedom's breach lay foulend up uncouth not be broched by punns and reedles" (pins and needles, puns and riddles; *FW,* 239.34–6).

Interestingly, in the Buckley episode Wilde is not only the Russian general, but is also—with Yeats and Joyce himself—associated with his antagonist Butt, whose very name underscores his similarity to the arse he will assassinate (together, Butt and his Irish associate, Taff, signify a fat ass since Taff is "fat"—or "ffat"—spelled backwards). When Butt is first called forth, he is described as wearing a Borsalino hat of the kind Joyce used to wear (*FW,* 337.33), and he is associated with Yeats through his pseudonym of Barnabas Ulick Dunne (George Moore's name for the figure he based on Yeats in his novel *Evelyn Innes*). A little later, Butt's "*face glows green, his hair greys white, his bleyes bcome broon to suite his cultic twalette*" (*FW,* 344.11–12); he has become the fashionable Yeats of the Celtic Twilight "cult." Finally, he resembles a blackmailed Oscar Wilde telling the court at the Old Bailey that "*the whyfe of his bothem was the very lad's thing to elter his mehind*" (*FW,* 350.14–15; the wife of his bosom was the last thing to enter his mind, and the white/wipe of his bottom was the lad's thing to enter or alter his behind). In nationalist terms, the "gentlemen's seats" that antagonists shoot at are always, on some level, the viceroy's residence in Phoenix Park, and the shooting itself a replay of the Phoenix Park murders, with a forged letter in their wake. Piggott's attempt to implicate Parnell in the murders is discussed in chapter 2; also see *FW,* 564.6–17 for a description of the Park as a man's "beauhind.")[54] Joyce is depicting nationalist *ass*assinations in terms that are indistinguishable from male homosexual love, thereby exposing the love-hate relationship that underlies all the encounters between males in the book.

The account of how the Russian general is shot for having shat illustrates not only the instability of the roles of shooter and shitter, nationalist and imperialist, son and father, but it also shows how sexual currents subtend all war. The forged letter that would implicate a man in the assassination of another is also a disavowed love letter; homophobia is driven by a repressed homophilia. As he did in his critique of *Giacomo Joyce,* Joyce exposes all conflict as a product of what he calls "pridejealice" (*FW,* 344.32–33); from one angle, it looks like prejudice (homophobia, racism, misogyny), but all prejudice is ultimately traceable to the tension between pride and jealousy. Trouble over sexual orientation and national difference, like gender trouble and religious difference, stems from an intolerance of ambivalence, an insistence on recasting a love/hate relationship into one of pure hatred, or prejudice, in a spasm of pride and jealousy.[55] But the attacks spurred on by prejudice are tantamount to shooting oneself in the ass; the "arse" at which the Irish aim is also "erse" ("airse," *FW,* 489.9), or Irish; the Irishman is "iris maimed" (*FW,* 489.31), maimed by his nationality and visually impaired.

Female Desire and Power in *Finnegans Wake*

Joyce's writing followed a trajectory that was the inverse of Yeats's: it became more and more veiled, more deliberately impenetrable, as he grew more aware of the hostility that those who advocate full and impartial comprehension provoke (in his schema for "Scylla and Charybdis," he mentions Socrates and Jesus as examples of historical figures who were martyred for seeing both sides of every opposition). Like the Yeats of *The Winding Stair*, he turned away from rage as "thought's creator" and turned instead to a determined acceptance of waste, a condition of *not* being mad in a land defined by "ire," but instead being a nomad (and as Shaun points out, "There's no sabbath for nomads," *FW,* 410.32). Like Wilde and Yeats before him, Joyce tried to invent new ways of thinking, desiring, and writing that would be propelled not by unconscious anger but by *joy,* a project supported by the "joy" lodged with his name (which was echoed in the name of "Freud"). He devised an alternative to the English language that was at the same time an alternative to German, a speaking through joy or "Djoytsch" (*Deutsch; FW,* 485.13) that operated entirely through macaronic puns and partook of the energy and obscurity of unconscious desire. His puns begin as a revolution of the word, and they end as an undoing of Ireland, human history, consciousness, and the world; *Finnegans Wake* is both the apogee of a freedom for the reader that is paradoxically shaped and made concrete by its difficulties, and a book that has been dismissed as unreadable and utterly opaque. In its impenetrability and its immense—if unrealized—promise, it represents the most complex "assemblage" that a reader was ever called upon to learn to play. And it must be played; it is not susceptible to the kind of automatic self-appropriations that are most often referred to under the rubric of reading. Its decoding involves great labor, but the point of labor is to learn to perform rather than absorb or devour the intricate possibilities locked in language, in subconscious thought, in sexual and national difference, and in history.

Finnegans Wake is history, presented to its readers as a collection of "presents" (present moments that double as Christmas presents). Into the present moment, figured as a personal letter and a collection of written characters, is packed not only the past, "Then's now with now's then in tense continuant" (*FW,* 598.28–9), but also the potential of the future (like tea, "the brew with the foochoor in it," *FW,* 608.21). In addition, Joyce is exceptionally attentive to the "story" in "history"; his history is both a record and a self-conscious, beneficent fiction: "For nought that is has bane" (been; poison; *FW,* 614.7–8). It is also *his* story, a story dominated by the actions of men, as Joyce makes clear via the puns on history as "hissheory" (his/she; his theory, *FW,* 163.25), and "histry" [his try; 52.05 and 161.22].[56] More thoroughly than the "Ithaca" episode of *Ulysses, Finnegans Wake* is the result of collapsing the macroscopic and the microscopic, objective with subjective experience, the global with the local: a violent and dynamic conjunction of the infinite with a grain of sand. This is a book in which turning pages is equivalent to "tearing ages" (*FW,* 582.02), and the justification for raiding/reading the past hinges on the certainty of death and a vision of time as something that both passes and returns: according to *Finnegans Wake*, we have "Scant hope" to escape "life's high carnage of semperidentity" (eternal identity, serendipity; *FW*, 582.14–5). If identity is multiple as well as individual, eternal as well as mortal, driven by the unconscious as well as by reason, then eternity is always already a return:

> Bloody certainly have we got to see to it ere smellful demise surprends us on this concrete that down the gullies of the eras we may catch ourselves looking forward to what will in no time be staring you larrikins on the postface in that multimirror megaron [Gk. bedchamber] of returningties, whirled without end to end. (*FW*, 582.16–21)

For Joyce, history is an abstraction that is interwoven into the phenomenal (and the literal) at every point. As the geography of the ancient Mediterranean world was mapped onto the city of Dublin in *Ulysses*, in *Finnegans Wake* the history of humankind gets told through glimpses of six thousand years of Irish history set against the background of the animate hill and river, sea and sky of "Howth Castle and Environs" (*FW*, 3.3). If the design of *Ulysses* packs ten years of Homeric wandering into a single day, the even more ambitious design of *Finnegans Wake* is to force "now" into a powerful union with "forever," and to multiply these presents into "a long, very long, a dark, very dark, an allburt unend, scarce endurable, and we could add mostly quite various and somenwhat stumbletumbling night" (*FW*, 598.6–9).

In Joyce's "book of the dates" (a construction that again conflates the temporal with the eternal, evoking the "dates" of past times and the Egyptian Book of the Dead, or guide to the afterlife, *FW*, 580.16), history is figured as that which we with labor unbury, re-member, and freshly construe: it is a lost letter buried in a midden, scratched up by a "gnarlybird" (gnarled earlybird?) who is also a hen; it is the legendary Irish "god" Finn MacCool (MacCumhail, from *finn cumhal*, or "white cap") being perpetually waked (mourned and awakened). The history of Ireland is so richly storied and ancient, so heavily inflected with folklore, that it should perhaps be rechristened "mythstory" (a lisping enunciation of "mystery"), in which myth and history are hopelessly intertwined. Despite its archeological determination to disinter the past, *Finnegans Wake* does not recount events in chronological order ("Only is order othered," *FW*, 613.13–4), nor does it disregard the discoveries of Einstein by detaching the temporal from the spatial: absorbing the successive waves of foreign invasions and registering the shocks that precipitated massive emigrations, the history of Ireland becomes the geography of the world. Norwegian and Danish Vikings, Jutes, Milesians, the Tuatha Dé Danaan, Normans, Firbolgs, Celts arriving via Spain, and of course the British provide precedent for a geographic and linguistic extrapolation that is as extensive and precise as Joyce in seventeen years could make it.

History in *Finnegans Wake* is not only the residue of action and event, a joyous parody of the Irish *Annals of the Four Masters*, it is also, most notoriously, a dream, a model of an individual and communal unconscious (or "sobsconcious," *FW*, 377.28) in which the passing of time becomes conflated with loss, grief, repression, burial, and eventual resurrection. The conflation of history with the psyche is reinforced by the story of the ancient Irish gods, the Tuatha Dé Danaan, who when defeated by the Milesians (the alleged ancestors of the Gaels) were driven underground, inside the hills, to become the "little people": the *sidhe*, or fairies. The great sun god Lugh, for example, after whom so many cities were named (including London, Lyons, and Leiden), was eventually demoted to a tiny craftsman, Lugh-chromain, or "little stooping Lugh," which was Anglicized as Leprechaun.[57] Yeats, in his introduction to Lady Gregory's *Gods and Fighting Men*, describes the world of Finn and the Fianna as "one of the oldest worlds that man has imagined";[58] we have moved, according to both Yeats and Lady Gregory, out of actual history into the realm of "fantastic history,"[59] or childlike wish fulfillment, where wonder is heaped upon wonder and where whatever the Fianna do they do for joy: "The Fianna and their like are themselves so full of power, and they are set in a world so fluctuating and dream-like, that nothing can hold them from being all that the heart desires."[60] When driven underground, such gods lose some of their majestic glory and instead grow mischievous, posing as a seductive but serious threat to mortal aims and ambitions. The most specific way in which Irish history melts into the world of the unconscious in *Finnegans Wake* is represented by the fate of the gods, driven underground as early humans were once driven into caves at the sound of thunder (evoking that which is "under" as well as a rumbling sound associated with the voice of divinity),[61] and as layers of Irish civilization are literally preserved beneath the surface of Dublin.[62] The rule that unites the fate of the gods with the movement of history and the "rationalization" of the mind is the rule of burial/repression, conjoined with the inevitability that the buried will resurface, in fragments, to form combinations that are at once new and old.

In addition to being a mass of verbiage through which unconscious, multilingual, and ancient energies move and strain, Wakean history is governed on the macro-level by a grand scheme, Giambattista Vico's theory of history as a cylical progression. In *The New Science*, Vico outlined the cycle of successive periods in history—from divine to heroic to a human era, followed by a ricorso or return—that repeats itself, but with a difference. Joyce not only uses this pattern to structure the four books of the *Wake*, but he also applies the Viconian scheme to the main movements of Irish history as Lady Gregory characterizes them, superimposing both onto the cyclical/mutating rhythms of generational succession in an individual family.[63]

Vico's overall aim was to derive "the principles of the ideal eternal history traversed in time by every nation in its rise, development, maturity, decline, and fall" (*NS*, 37). Of the three stages, culminating in ricorso, that he identifies, the first, like Irish history, begins in "mythstory": "the first history must have been poetic" (*NS*, 257). Vico argues that this "divine" stage is governed by providence and is marked by a fear of nature, which was seen as "a great animated body" (*NS*, xxvi): these "theological poets" "attributed senses and passions . . . to bodies . . . as vast as sky, sea, and earth" (*NS*, 86). The poetic logic of such thinking is apparent through etymology, which Vico claims was defined as "*veriloquium*" (true speech; *NS*, 87): the words *nature* and *nation*, he argues, both derive from roots that mean "being born";[64] moreover, "among the Greeks and Latins 'name' and 'nature' meant the same thing" (*NS*, 123). Names, nature, and nations are all, by implication, smaller or larger animate counterparts of the human; they are all "born" out of the ineluctable materiality of the real.

Vico's characterization of an initial poetic stage in the tripartite ideal history of all nations influenced the conception of *Finnegans Wake* in at least two important ways: first of all, Vico lauds the imaginative potential unleashed by *not* knowing, by ignorance, a potential that has been disregarded in a philosophical tradition founded on reason:

> So that, as rational metaphysics teaches that man becomes all things by understanding them (*homo intelligendo fit omnia*), this imaginative metaphysics shows that man becomes all things by *not* understanding them (*homo non intelligendo fit omnia*); and perhaps the latter proposition is truer than the former, for when man understands he extends his mind and takes in the things, but when he does not understand he makes the things out of himself and becomes them by transforming himself into them. (*NS*, 88)

Finnegans Wake, which Joyce designed as a book that both teases forth and resists rational apprehension, can only be experienced poetically; the reader is blocked from appropriating the book and is instead invited to become it through the act of performance.[65]

Secondly, Vico's account of the three stages of history is based on an essentially inductive model, so that language, customs, nations all are firmly rooted in the phenomenal world that Vico refers to as poetic, and they grow into abstraction, reason, prose, and equality through time, until the process begins all over again. Joyce's "history" demands an inductive approach to reading in exactly Vico's sense (see Vico's endorsement of the inductive method in *NS*, 125), which prompts the reader ideally to undergo the three stages of history microcosmically while reading: we must begin by starkly encountering the material dimension of language, its letters, its etymologies, its webs of multilingual association. We learn in frustration to try an unfamiliar word backward as well as forward,[66] to register the first letters of words to see if they form acrostics, to count words in a series to see if their "meaning" is numerical, to think about letters individually as well as in combination, to investigate the national origin of words and their multivalent referents.

Vico's three-stage outline of the ideal history of all nations, like Yeats's later vision of history as interlocking gyres, is a way of explaining how a given tendency grows into its opposite via a kind of "marriage" and "war" of extremes and ricochets back again. Vico uses his model to show how a mute embodiment of nature gives way to heroic verse and finally prose; how the first language of the gods, which he says was hieroglyphic, is supplemented by a second language of heroes, which is symbolic, and a third language, which is epistolary, "for men at a distance to communicate to each other the current needs of their lives" (*NS*, 98); how religion (which Vico derives from the action of "binding") is displaced by aristocracy and finally popular liberty; how human wisdom begins with sense and culminates in intellect before the cycle begins anew (*NS*,

241); how reverence for omnipotent divinity eventually produces its opposite, reason, after an intervening period ruled by the "heroic" law of force.

Vico's ideas about the history of language and letters are equally important for *Finnegans Wake*. Vico insists that "the first nations thought in poetic characters, spoke in fables, and wrote in hieroglyphs" (*NS*, 97). He is adamant in his opposition to philologians who hold that "in the vulgar languages meanings were fixed by convention," arguing instead that "because of their natural origins, they [meanings] must have had natural significations" (*NS*, 104). Vico uses Latin to support his contention that at its inception, language was heavily referential and concrete, as etymological research shows; he argues that "Latin . . . has formed almost all its words by metaphors drawn from natural objects according to their natural properties or sensible effects" (*NS*, 104). Etymology, for Vico as for Joyce, becomes a thread through the labyrinth of human history that intertwines the experiences of many different nations; vulgar language is a vast field in which a nascent poetry has been buried. Vico concludes that the most beautiful language is dense and bears witness to the "many different points of view" represented by languages of diverse nations: "languages are more beautiful in proportion as they are richer in these condensed heroic expressions; that they are more beautiful because they are more expressive; and that because they are more expressive they are truer and more faithful" (*NS*, 105–106).

One of the most striking attributes of Wakean history, which is also a feature of Viconian history, is its dynamism, its unstable tracing of a "progression" that climaxes in fragmentation and recombination. Like Vico, Joyce used language to replay not only the flows and eddies characteristic of time in the mind, but also to conjoin movement in time with movement through space by packing references to different national origins into a single word or phrase, thereby cleansing what Vico calls "the other eye of poetic history, namely poetic geography" (*NS*, 234). Poetic geography maps the traces of historical movement—emigrations and invasions—in such a way as to adulterate the authority or superiority or "purity" of any one nation's identity and achievements. Poetic geography, like poetic history, is radically internationalist, dynamic, and potentially overwhelming in its vibrant particularity; it exemplifies the operations of mind that Deleuze and Guattari in *A Thousand Plateaus* would later call rhizomatic, micropolitical, schizoanalytical, and nomadic, an exhilarating and joyful process of "becoming-intense" and "becoming-imperceptible."[67] Deleuze and Guattari present their "nomadology" as diametrically opposed to what is typically meant by "history," a static encapsulation of events by those in power. They argue that "[h]istory is always written from the sedentary point of view and in the name of a unitary State apparatus, at least a possible one, even when the topic is nomads. What is lacking is a Nomadology, the opposite of a history" (*TP*, 23).

Deleuze and Guattari's project could be described as an alternative way of "going between" Vico's first and last ages—the divine/poetic age and the egalitarian/rational age—that avoids the desire for acquisition and dominance characteristic of Vico's second, heroic/aristocratic age. The play of thinking and writing throughout *A Thousand Plateaus* resembles that of *Finnegans Wake* in its energetic shifting of metaphors and paradigms, if not in its attention to the word. In theory, Deleuze and Guattari celebrate "close-range vision" as an essential feature of what they call "nomad art" (*TP,* 492), but in practice Joyce's microscopic scrutiny of language is far closer than theirs. Joyce is much more consistent in his "'atomization' of the motif, 'a subdivision into infinitely small units'" (*TP,* 308), but it is Deleuze and Guattari who help to clarify the political implications of such a technique.

In *Finnegans Wake,* Joyce designs an elaborate group of narrative set-pieces to rewrite not only Irish and world history, but also the history of sexual relations, according to what Deleuze and Guattari would define as a nomadic model. One of the best instances of Joyce's use of a nomadic historical model is his characterization of the Prankquean in book 1, chapter 1.

Like Yeats before him, Joyce here explores mythological and historical personifications of Ireland as a woman. In *Cathleen ní Houlihan, The Rose,* and *The Wind Among the Reeds,* Yeats preferred to embody Ireland poetically in the sorrowful figure of Dark Rosaleen, or the aged figure of Cathleen ní Houlihan being rejuvenated by the blood of Irish heroes, or even Eire, the Dé Danaan goddess who asked the Milesians to name the country after her.[68] Joyce, in sharp contrast, turns Cathleen ní Houlihan into Kate the Slop, the older version of ALP, and evokes a very different poetic personification of Ireland: the historically identifiable sixteenth-century pirate, Grace O'Malley, or Granuaile (c. 1530–1603), who is comparable to Yeats's Crazy Jane in her sexual assurance and independence.

O'Malley is a compelling figure for many reasons: unlike most female representatives of Ireland, she is active rather than primarily reactive, and she is equally adept at crossing gender boundaries and national boundaries. Moreover, O'Malley is not a nationalist in the usual sense of the term; although she was an enemy of the British for several years and her father was one of the few Irish chiefs never to have acknowledged the English crown, she was able to form an alliance with either side when it was advantageous to do so.[69] Most interestingly, though, O'Malley was completely omitted from the *Annals* and neglected by historians; her story was preserved instead by the poets, who celebrated her as a symbolic figure of "fiery patriotism" comparable to Roisin Dubh and Cathleen ní Houlihan (Chambers, 177). Anne Chambers relates that

> While the Elizabethan State Papers and manuscripts contain numerous accounts of her deeds, her unusual life-style and her involvement not only in the affairs of Connaught but also of the country, the Irish historians and the annalists totally excluded her from their records. This is quite extraordinary as they record other quite trivial accounts of places, events and people of the time. Given that Grace successfully pursued a career so contrary to the mores of the time, there is reason to believe that the annalists of the sixteenth and seventeenth centuries, rather than acknowledge that a woman could dominate in such an unfeminine way, excluded her completely. (Chambers, 88)

By associating ALP with Grace O'Malley so early in the book, Joyce accomplishes a number of things: he underscores the extent to which *both* his main characters (male *and* female) are formidable boundary-crossers, whose power and ingenuity are fully comparable. If HCE is a Viking invader (or "pirate"), a Norwegian captain, in addition to his many other roles (Norman invader, Russian general, etc.), ALP in the guise of Grace O'Malley is a pirate whose success in both plundering and placating her enemies is nothing short of remarkable. By constructing his male and female protagonists/agonists as marauders, Joyce brings into play a vision of history not as a "State apparatus," a history written to illustrate the glory of the nation, but history as a creative transgression and subversion of the law (*nomos*) for purposes of survival—a true nomadology that is akin in its operation to that of providence, or *Grace*.

The different versions and spellings of Grace O'Malley's name are one economical index of her transgressive power. Not only does the name suggest a possible connection between her Odyssean opportunism and providence (*grace* derives from *gratia* or "thanks"), but Grace is sometimes (given the vagaries of Elizabethan spelling) referred to as "Granny" ("*E'en Tho' I Granny a-be He would Fain Me Cuddle,*" *FW,* 105.03) and also Grania, the legendary figure who long delayed marriage with the aged Finn MacCool by running away with one of his younger and more attractive followers, Dermot: "our own little Graunya of the chilired cheeks" (*FW,* 68.10). Grania is the Guinevere-figure of Irish mythology, and in the Prankquean episode Grace and Grania are conflated to emphasize not only the decisive independence of their sexual preferences, but also their propensity to abduct younger men (the Prankquean, like Grace O'Malley in history, abducts the Earl of Howth's heir).[70] The Irish version of Grace's name, Granuaile, is probably a corruption of the Irish *Grainne Ui (Ni) Mhaille* (Umhall or O'Malley), but the legendary explanation of the name is that it refers to the Irish word for "bald"—she is Grainne *Mhaol* (Chambers, 55). The story that explains the name's origin stresses Grace's determination to do everything men could do: "According to the legend, as a young child, she begged to be taken on one of her father's ships which was leaving for Spain. She was reminded . . . that a seaman's lot was no life for a young lady and . . . she departed and returned later with her long locks cut as a boy's" (Chambers, 55). The legend is that Grainne's father then relented and took her with him, teaching her the seamanship for which she later became infamous.

Grace's last name, too, reflects her extraordinary propensity to cross boundaries. She was sometimes referred to as "Granny Nye *Male,*" which clearly reflects her appropriation of the prerogatives of maleness, as well as "Granny Imallye" (Chambers, 55), a name that breaks down as "I'm all ye"—anticipating the inclusiveness of Here Comes Everybody and Anna Livia Plurabelle. Joyce elsewhere transforms "O'Malley" to contain the name of the sea between Ireland and Scotland, "moyle," which emphasizes her Viking-like power as a sea captain; he makes reference to "the O'Moyly gracies and the O'Briny rossies . . . playing him pranks" (*FW,* 95.03).

Even Grania's nicknames make their way into the *Wake*: her first husband was called Donal-an-Cullagh, "the Cock," for his courage in defending a castle called Hen's Castle on Lough Corrib against the Joyces. Legend has it that the Joyces killed Donal for seizing this castle from them, and subsequently Grace defended the castle so skillfully and heroically that they gave her the nickname "the Hen" (Chambers, 70). The hen and the cock appear as versions of ALP and HCE in the *Wake*, resurrected by another, later Joyce. Grace's name is also associated with another castle, Castleleaffy near Westport, a name that of course recalls "Liffey," like that of ALP ("I am leafy speafing," *FW*, 619.20; Chambers, 173).

In addition to playing on her given name, Joyce also designates his "ribber-robber" (*FW*, 21.8; robber who also "ribs," or jokes—a re-reading of what it means to draw woman from the "rib" of man) a "prank quean," or queen of pranks.[71] The Prankquean tricks the Jarl van Hoother as Saint Patrick ("sen peatrick's," *FW*, 361.3–4) once tricked the druid, which also makes her a "Clopatrick" (*FW*, 508.23): Cleopatra is both a cloacal "Peequeen" or "peahen" (508.26) and also Clio, muse of history, + *patra*, nation, which suggests that the history of the nation is a woman. After subjecting him to a "pea trick" by urinating, she ap*pea*ses him ("pea" is etymologically related to "appease," *OED*) and makes peace. She both moans—Joyce calls her granne*wail* (22.12) and a "Pranksome Quain" (508.28) (to "quain" is to lament, bewail)—and pranks, (to prank is "to prance, to dress or deck in a gay, bright, or showy manner, . . . to brighten or set out with colors," *OED*); Joyce calls her a "prancess" (312.22), as well as a "queen of prancess [princes]." The narrator directs, "Pet her, pink him, play pranks with them. . . . they are as piractical jukersmen" (piratical/practical jokers, *FW*, 337.22).

The historical Grace O'Malley seems to have been heartily disliked by most of the Englishmen with whom she had to deal, though Sir Henry Sidney speaks of her with grudging respect in a letter to Sir Francis Walsingham, the Queen's secretary, in 1577:

> There came to me also a most famous feminine sea captain called Grany Imallye, and offered her services unto me, wheresoever I would command her, with three galleys and 200 fighting men, either in Scotland or Ireland; she brought with her her husband for she was as well by sea as by land well more than Mrs. Mate with him; . . . This was a notorious woman in all the coasts of Ireland. (Chambers, 85)

Lord Justice Drury spoke of her more harshly in March 1578 after she had been captured and imprisoned in Limerick jail by the Earl of Desmond for plundering his land. Drury writes:

> Grany O'Mayle, a woman that hath impudently passed the part of womanhood and been a great spoiler, and chief commander and director of thieves and murderers at sea to spoille this province, having been apprehended by the Earle of Desmond this last year, his Lordship hath now sent her to Lymrick where she remains in safe keeping. (Chambers, 93)

Sir Richard Bingham was perhaps O'Malley's greatest enemy; he described her in 1593 as "a notable traitoress and nurse to all rebellions in the Province for 40 years" (Chambers, 126).

Queen Elizabeth, in sharp contrast to Bingham and against his advice, conferred a royal pardon on Grace and her family at Grace's request in May of 1588, and, in 1593, Queen Elizabeth took seriously O'Malley's petition for "free liberty," in which O'Malley rather unexpectedly described herself as Elizabeth's "loyal and faithful subject" (Chambers, 131). The queen sent eighteen articles of interrogatory to O'Malley, which O'Malley obligingly answered,[72] but when O'Malley's son was arrested, Grace decided to travel to London to meet with the queen personally, which she did in September 1593, becoming "the only Gaelic woman ever to appear in court" (Chambers, 145). One heroic poem (translated from the Irish) attempts to imagine Grace's stance at this famous meeting:

> Before the English Queen she dauntless stood,
> And none her bearing there could scorn as rude;
> She seemed well used to power—as one that hath
> Dominion over men of savage mood,
> And dared the tempest in its midnight wrath,
> And thro' opposing billows cleft her fearless path.
>
> And courteous greeting Elizabeth then pays,
> And bids her welcome to her English land
> And humble hall. Each looked with curious gaze
> Upon the other's face, and felt they stand
> Before a spirit like their own.
> (Quoted by Chambers, 181–82. From J. O'Hart Vol. II., *Irish Pedigrees*, 675).

Grace's mission succeeded, and Elizabeth granted all her requests (Chambers, 150).

According to tradition, it was on O'Malley's return from England to meet with Elizabeth "as an equal" that she stopped at Howth, where the incident on which the Prankquean episode is based occurred. Legend has it that she landed at Howth to seek hospitality in accordance with Gaelic custom, but the gates of Howth Castle were locked, and the lord of the castle refused her admittance because he was at dinner:

> Furious with this disregard, . . . she stormed from the castle and on returning to her ship came upon and seized the young heir of Howth and sailed for Clew bay. The Lord of Howth, on learning of the abduction, repaired immediately to Cannaught and pleaded with Grace for the safe return of his son at any price. Grace, scorning the offer of ransom, demanded that in return for his son, the gates of Howth castle would never again be closed against anyone who requested hospitality and that an extra plate would always be laid at his table. (Chambers, 87)

The lord agreed and gave Grace a ring as pledge on the agreement (Chambers, 91). Anne Chambers argues that the episode at Howth must have taken place not on Grace's return from England in 1593, but in 1576, when the Lord of

Howth was Christopher St. Lawrence, and the heir that she seized was his grandson, who was also named Christopher (Chambers, 91). (He becomes Tristopher/Hilary in *FW* after Bruno's insistence that "in tristitia hilaris hilaritate tristis," or hilarity is in sadness and vice versa. Extremes exchange places; the prankqueen makes tristopher a luderman and hilary a tristian.)

Joyce rewrites this history as a kind of knock-knock joke in which the Prankquean, or Grace, knocks three times at the castle of a man described not as the Earl of Howth, but as the Jarl van "Hoo-ther" (Howth, but also "who's there"). She comes and makes her wit (intelligence, water) against the door, the window, and the archway, asking a slightly altered version of a riddle each time: "why do I am alook alike a poss of porterpease?" The riddle is first of all a request for hospitality (history is here depicted as "hostery," 378.32); she is asking the "everybully" (21.7) to open his door, to give her access to his toilet (see Benstock, 27–73), and to give her some porter (*leann dubh* in Irish, the opposite of *Dubh linn*, Dublin, or *lionn dubh*, melancholy). She suggests that she looks as like something or someone as two peas in a pod. (She *is* the earl's niece-in-law; perhaps she resembles the dummy, or girl-child, since "dummy" is also a term for "pirate.") Perhaps she is telling him that she resembles *him*; that she is his counterpart in every way.

By making water she is raining, or making a flood (recalling Noah through the punning reference to a reign of forty years and through the appearance of a rainbow at the end of the episode), reigning (she is a queen), and u*rain*at[ing], which is what excites HCE in women throughout the book. She, in other words, pees (Joyce elsewhere calls her the "Peequeen," 508.26), evoking several associations with p's and q's (*prankquean*, mind your pints and quarts in a pub, don't mix up *p*'s and *q*'s when writing, and remember the p–q split in Gaelic, which differentiated Brythonic from Goidelic Gaelic, the British Celts from their Irish counterparts[73]).

The Prankquean's openness contrasts with the earl's insistence on closing all apertures against her, and her association with urination is balanced by the earl's Russian-general-like association with defecation and anality. The door and window answer her grace with "shut!" (also "shit"), whereupon she becomes "grace o'malice" (21.20–21) and kidnaps first Tristopher and then Hilary, raining for forty years each time in "Woeman's Land" (22.8).[74] The third time she knocks, van Hoother comes *out*, a terrifying hybrid of Brian Boru (who defeated the Danish Vikings at Clontarf) and one of the Viking invaders. He orders (ordured) her to "shut up" shop; she does (thunderword)—and "they all drank free." In a story as layered as the city of Dublin itself, at least three different things are happening at once here: he is a proprietor of a pub who decides to close it up and offer drinks on the house; he is a man whose propensity to ordure/give orders is in part a response to her urination/reign; and he is also ordering her to start the ritual of social reconciliation: Polly put the kettle on and we'll all have tea. The rhythm of sociability, though, coincides with the language of mutual animosity. The narrator relates that "the duppy shot the shutter clup" (shot or shut up the shitter) as well as put up the shutter and they all drank free. She defeats him (by shooting him), he defeats her (by shutting her up—both silencing and confining her), and the tale ends in a highly traditional and comic truce: a marriage and conflict in which the two make *three* (which is how Joyce interprets the significance of the ring given Grace by the Lord of Howth).

The Prankquean episode shows ALP as an equally powerful and duplicitous match for HCE. Moreover, both play both sides of the conflict: HCE is a Viking *and* the Irish destroyer of Vikings; he is a Norman (like both the first lord of Howth and Strongbow) *and* the city of Dublin (he emerges from the "three shuttoned castles" on the Dublin coat of arms, 22.34). He is not just green and orange, he is a rainbow, "a rudd yellan [rude, yelling; red, yellow] gruebleen [bluegreen, grumbling] orangeman in his violet indigonation [indigo and a version of "Ire-land," land of ire or indignation]" (23.1–2); he is the product of many nations, a human rainbow signaling the end of Woeman's flood. The prankquean, like her historical counterpart and like HCE, here plays the role of both native and invader, aggressor and victim, man and woman: she both threatens to give the earl a child—"why do I look like a pint of stout"—i.e., why am I pregnant—and takes his children away from him, bringing them back under her pinafore or apron. Her trickiness and facility at changing sides recalls the duplicity of Grace O'Malley, who "[t]hroughout most of her chequered career . . . managed to combine effectively with the power of the day, English or Irish, to enlarge and strengthen her own position" (Chambers, 101).

Joyce portrays his characters as turncoats not only to emphasize the easy reversibility of domination and oppression, a recognition and acceptance of which would uncover a fundamental if currently buried sexual equality. He also uses the multiple, often conflicting allegiances of his characters to represent a non-partisan view of nationhood as dynamically inclusive, thereby anticipating the nomadic antihistories endorsed by Deleuze and Guattari. Joyce's redefinition of *nation* as an entity dependent upon a history of adulteration also highlights one of the most significant associations of the word *finn*—the name the Irish called the Vikings, *Finn Gall*, or white strangers. White light is of course made up of a spectrum of colors, like a nation with many cultural roots, and the tenth century "saw the rise and fall of" an Ireland known as *Fingal*, land of the foreigners (Somerville-Large, *Dublin*, 18, 23; see also *FW*, 22.10, where the Jarl van Hoother calls after the prankquean with a loud "finegale"). For Joyce, a nation is always, paradoxically, a land of foreigners, a locality that contains all localities, at present moments that both rob us of and return to us the "gift" of human history.

Marriage as "Marrage"

In addition to disinterring history as a living collection of presents, *Finnegans Wake* also challenges the oppression licensed by gender, particularly the institution of marriage, which is presented in the book as deceptive and destructive, a mirage that mars. The problem with marriage is that it encourages identification between partners, and that identification diminishes the very otherness—

the principle of erotic attraction—that brought it about in the first place. In *Dialogues*, Deleuze and Claire Parnet argue that the world lays two traps for us—the trap of distance and the trap of identification—both of which, they stress, "one must resist." The way to resist is not to "marry" oneself to what one sees, but to exercise the imagination's negative capability: if you see an Eskimo,

> you do not need to mistake yourself for him. But you may perhaps put yourself in his shoes, you have something to assemble with him, an Eskimo-becoming which does not consist in playing the Eskimo, in imitating or identifying yourself with him or taking the Eskimo upon yourself, but in assembling something between you and him, for you can only become Eskimo if the Eskimo himself becomes something else. (*Dialogues*, 53)

The challenge of "assembling something between" two people without identification or alienation is a revisionary definition of utopian (as opposed to historical) marriage; moreover, the implied imperative is to multiply such "marriages" among many different kinds of people. One could argue, then, that the antioedipal marriage that resists identification is figuratively adulterous in the conventional sense; conversely, one could argue that the antioedipal is produced through a slippage in the oedipal, that the two are continuous and implicit in one another.

One concrete way to trace the slippage between the oedipal and the antioedipal, thereby analyzing the "micro-politics of desire," is by examining the contradictory attitudes towards marriage in *Finnegans Wake*. Marriage, historically, has been the basis of an oedipal triangle; moreover its stasis and its hierarchical structure have been protected by law. Despite the fixity of the legal and economic structure that circumscribed it, marriage has nevertheless provoked the ambivalent, contradictory responses characteristic of an antioedipal assemblage. The main difference between the two models is that the contradictions in an "oedipal" schema are inadvertent, dictated by the laws of balance; the surfacing of each extreme necessitates the repression of the other, which produces a repetitive "seesaw" of opposite responses such as idealization and contempt, obedience and rebellion. In an antioedipal framework, by contrast, contradictions are stressed as deliberate, mutually determined, and circumscribed by temporal and geographical determinants that will necessarily change. Most important, the only form of marriage Joyce advocates in the *Wake* is free of idealization and the disappointment that attends on it; the other is neither better nor worse, but simply elusive, incapable of being fully possessed or known.

To marry in *Finnegans Wake* is to produce at once a merrymaking and a marring, an inspiration to couple and a drive toward uncoupling. In its merrymaking aspect, marriage is a momentary union, a union not just of two people, but of all the multiple aspects of the self—in other words, it is a dance, a "coincidance of . . . contraries reamalgamerg[ing]," a brief assemblage of "the centuple celves of [the] egourge" (*FW*, 49.36, 33–34). When the Nowedding/Norwegian captain marries the tailor's daughter, the narrator exults that there was "lease on mirth" (peace on earth) (*FW*, 329.19), while "[t]he soul of everyelsesbody rolled into its olesoleself," and "Dub did glow that night" (*FW*, 329.18–19, 14).

The characters of *Finnegans Wake* sometimes idealize marriage, yearning for the pastoral bliss of its lost beginning, as when HCE as hill is lying peacefully next to ALP's stream: "Before he fell hill he filled heaven: a stream, alplapping streamlet, coyly coiled um, cool of her curls" (*FW*, 57.10–12). The joys of marriage are displaced not only onto the past, they are also projected into the future, so that "tomarry" becomes synonymous with "tomorrow," as in the weather forecast in II.3. The broadcaster announces that "the outlook for tomarry . . . beamed brider, his ability good" (*FW*, 324.33–34). But then he asks, "What hopends to they?" (*FW*, 324.35), which is at once "what happens today," "what happens *to them*," and "what *hope ends* today." And the hope that ends today is the fall that brings with it an uncoupling: "Giant crash in Aden. Birdflights confirm abbroaching nubtials" (*FW*, 324.36–325.1). The nuptials are broken off even as they approach; Eden cannot last.

Another ebullient transformation is to represent the wedding as a *wetting*, which is partly a sexual image, partly an environmental one in which the Liffey wets and thereby greens the landscape, and partly a social image represented by making tea (or *wetting* the tea, a locution which Joyce plays on throughout as the mechanism whereby two make three). Earwicker's name even takes the form of "Eri*wedding*" in the Norwegian captain episode, in which ALP plays the role of fire as well as water. As in the prankquean episode, ALP is described as "our fiery quean" (here she is Spenser's Fairy Queen, Queen Elizabeth, *FW*, 328.31), a "roaryboaryellas [that] would set an Eriweddyng on fire, let aloon an old Humpopolamos with the boomarpoorter on his brain" (*FW*, 327.32–34). Similarly, when the prankquean "lit up . . . fireland was ablaze" (*FW*, 21.16–17); she can turn Ireland into fireland.

Playing against the rhythm of the wedding vows, Joyce rehearses the hackneyed hope that marriage will bring both sex and friendship, a lap and a pal as well as ALP, a ditch for the plow: "Him her first lap, her his fast pal, for ditcher for plower, till deltas twoport. While this glowworld's lump is gloaming off and han in hende will grow" (*FW*, 318.12–14). Not only does this last phrase suggest "hand in hand we'll go," evoking the end of *Paradise Lost* ("They, hand in hand, with wandering steps and slow, / Through Eden took their solitary way"), it also means in Norwegian that *he in her* will grow. Now, however, she says that things are different between them—this is the winter of their discontent: "Now eats the vintner over these contents" (*FW*, 318.20). Marriage is referred to as a "gentlemeants agreement"—a gent's lament, or a gentleman's agreement that was gently meant—and a "womensch plodge": a woman's pledge that means woe to men (*FW*, 318.26–27).

The celebratory and destructive phases of marriage are sometimes arranged as a seasonal cycle, ending in the winter of our discontents, and at other times they are presented as simultaneous and mutually dependent. Against the rhythm of the nursery rhyme, "Needles and pins, needles and pins, when a man marries his sorrow begins," Joyce pits a reference to marriage as merriment and music which revolves around the image of the lute as a Chinese symbol of matrimony: "Mastabatoom, mastabadtomm, when a mon merries his lute is all long" (*FW*, 6.10–11). A long lute would not be so bad in itself, but "all long" also calls up the echo of "all wrong." Marriage is both right and wrong, fight and song.

This brings me to the destructive side of marriage, which is the side which has the most interesting colonial overtones: marriage as fight, as a struggle for power and domination. Comically, the narrative shows that even the attempt to gain control is a method of preserving chaos; as Joyce says in II.3, "How they [HCE and ALP] succeeded by courting daylight in saving darkness he who loves will see" (*FW*, 321.18–19). When we court daylight, or enlightenment, in *Finnegans Wake* we too see that we have succeeded in saving darkness, but the pleasure of the process is as much in the uncoupling of words as in their recombination. As Joyce suggests at the end of I.3, we are often waiting until our sleeping stops: "Humph is in his doge. Words weigh no more to him than raindrips to Rethfernhim. Which we all like. Rain. When we sleep. Drops. But wait until our sleeping. Drain. Sdops." (*FW*, 74.16–19). The punchline here is "sdops," spelled with a "d," thereby evoking the Italian verb *sdoppiare*, to uncouple, open out. In the sleep induced by overstimulation, we are waiting till the condensed quality of dream unfolds.

It is no revelation to say that marriage, in one of its aspects, is war to the death. It mars the individual by limiting her or him to another person; it is a bond that binds. Joyce alters the marriage vows to emphasize this: "For mine qvinne [queen, "kvinde" (Danish for "woman")] I thee giftake and bind my hosenband [husband, German for "belt"] I thee halter" (*FW*, 62.10–11). The restrictions imposed by marriage cause both partners to chafe; of the 111 abusive names HCE is called in I.3, several are antimarriage: *"Luck before Wedlock," "I Divorce Thee Husband,"* and *"Wants a Wife and Forty of Them"* (*FW*, 71.27–28, 72.7–8). The problem with marriage is that to the extent that the two partners are seen as opposite and interlocking, their needs are also mutually exclusive— marriage is a kind of seesaw; when one is up the other is down. This is also, of course, how the relationship between colonizer and colonized is frequently constructed; what is good for the one is harmful to the other, but to a different degree. In the case of England and Ireland, England has the edge for as long as it maintains its sovereignty; in the case of man and wife, it is the man whose dominance is reinforced by law. Joyce reflects this by associating HCE with England and ALP with Ireland, although he also explores ways in which the so-called victim is empowered over the so-called oppressor, when he reverses the association. The song about London Bridge, for example, is used as background music for the fall of HCE's breeches; his is the fall of London Bridge, whereas ALP emerges as both granny spreading the board and as the Irish Grania, spreading abroad (and spreading her brood): "Longtong's breach is fallen down but Graunya's spreed's abroad" (*FW*, 58.10–11).

The clearest example of how the conflicting interests of man and wife represent those of colonizer and colonized, though, is in I.3, when ALP in the guise of a female reporter is interviewing a chef about the fall of HCE. Eiskaffier (Escoffier, the famous chef; Eiskaffee [iced coffee]) says: *"Mon foie* [ma foi (my liver)], you wish to ave some homelette, yes, lady! . . . your hegg he must break himself. See, I crack, so, he sit in the poele [frying pan], unbedimbt! [and be damned, unbedimmed, and German "undoubtedly"]" (FW, 59.30–32). If the woman wants a home (here *omelet*), HEC or he-egg must be broken. What this means in terms of the war between the sexes is that if she wants a home she must break the man's masculinity, since the word for "egg" in german—*eier*—also means testicles. The necessity of this is underscored by the proverb that you can't make an omelette without breaking eggs; to achieve any desirable objective you must pay a price.

Egg, then, becomes an important image for conflating or at least relating male and female sexuality, since it is associated both with testicles (*eier*) and with ovaries (ovo=egg). In casting ALP as the original hen (FW, 110.22) and HCE as egg, Joyce is playing against the question of which comes first, the chicken or the egg. The answer can of course never be determined, and neither can we be sure that the opposition is even stable. There are times when she is the egg—*"It Was Me Egged Him on to the Stork Exchange"* (FW, 106.17–18); conversely, he is identifed as *"Hatches Cocks' Eggs"* (FW, 71.27)—a hen.

The same sort of crossover occurs in the association of eggs with England and Ireland. In *Through the Looking-Glass*, Alice and Humpty Dumpty discuss the possibility of his falling from the wall in a way that highlights its political implications. He says to her, "If I *did* fall, . . . the King has promised me— . . . with his very own mouth—to—to—" and Alice finishes the sentence for him: "[t]o send all his horses and all his men." He is furious and accuses her of eavesdropping to find that out, whereupon she explains gently, "It's in a book." He is appeased, and replies, "Ah, well! They may write such things in a *book*. . . . That's what you call a History of England, that is."[75] Humpty Dumpty has unlimited faith in the king to put him together again if he falls, conveniently forgetting that the king's men were *unable* to put him together again. It is such misplaced faith in the benevolence or competence of the state to help the individual that, Carroll implies, characterizes English history.

In her foreword to *A Servant to the Queen*, published in 1938, Maud Gonne MacBride uses the same image of breaking eggs to illustrate what the British Empire is doing to Ireland, here represented as the eggs that must be broken to make the imperial omelette. She writes,

> Every logical mind will assent to the proposition that omelettes cannot be manufactured without a continual breaking of eggs. No more can the British Empire stand or go without famine in Ireland, opium in China, torture in India, pauperism in England, disturbance and disorder in Europe and robbery everywhere.[76]

She concludes that it is not worth the price, and goes on to introduce the autobiography that follows as a record of how she reached this conclusion.

The reversibility of male and female, oppressor and victim, takes me, by a commodius vicus of recirculation, to a point about the micropolitics of marriage, a point about hierarchies of power, and a point about writing. That point is expressed not only by Yeats in "Who Goes with Fergus" but also by Deleuze in

Dialogues: "What a depressing idea of love, to make it a relation between two people."[77] What Deleuze implies is that it is a mistake to define people—and desire—in terms of their limits, what they are *not*, which is exactly what a gender construction helps us to do. It is equally self-defeating to reduce people to objects that may be possessed, or to interpret (i.e., overcode, classify, categorize) people *or* books. Deleuze urges that we "[b]ecome capable of loving without remembering, without phantasm and without interpretation, without taking stock. Let there just be fluxes, which sometimes dry up, freeze or overflow, which sometimes combine or diverge. A man and a woman are fluxes. . . . [There are] n sexes in a single one, or in two, which have nothing to do with castration. . . . Experiment, never interpret" (*Dialogues*, 47–48).

Joyce, too, urges us to forget, not remember, to experience flux, not to classify or overcode it. "Begin to forget it. It will remember itself from every sides, with all gestures, in each our word" (*FW*, 614.20–21). Similarly, gender in *Finnegans Wake* is always unsettlingly and exhilaratingly fluid, as any reader will have noticed. All the characters change gender repeatedly, just as their sexual orientations range from the homosexual to the heterosexual. Not even a national hero such as Daniel O'Connell is exempt: he mutates into "Mrs Dana O'Connell," whose statue is "prostituent behind the Trinity College" (*FW*, 386.22–23).

What are the implications of such a view of love for an understanding of *Finnegans Wake*? Deleuze writes that "all writing is a love letter" (*Dialogues*, 51), which is certainly a view that Joyce anticipated. It is written by a writer complexus (*FW*, 114.33) out of love for an impossibly heterogenous assemblage of readers. This love is not expressed through representation; as Deleuze explains, it is not love to speak *for* or *in place of* another. "One must, on the contrary, speak *with*, write *with*" (*Dialogues*, 52). In practical terms, we can do this by inviting readers to participate in the flux of desire by creating their own assemblages of meaning in connection with our own. To subvert the hegemonic potential of language one can only attend more and more finely to its many corruptions and variations, to the minor meanings within the major ones. When one becomes a foreigner in one's own language, one regains access to what Deleuze calls real-desire, which is the exhilarating activity of *producing* the unconscious (*Dialogues*, 59, 78).

"Male and Female Unmask We Hem"

As Judith Butler influentially proposed in *Gender Trouble: Feminism and the Subversion of Identity*,[78] gender is not something we are but something we perform. Butler argues, brilliantly, that gender and identity are categories similarly constructed and reified *through prohibition and exclusion*; moreover, these restricted definitions are produced by what she calls the "regime of presumptive heterosexuality" to perpetuate itself and the asymmetrical relationship between opposites upon which it is structured. As an alternative to seeing identity as "natural" or inevitable, Butler suggests regarding identity—the so-called "coherence" and "continuity" of the person—as "a normative ideal rather than a descriptive feature of experience," a "socially instituted and maintained [norm] of intelligibility (16–17)." The illusion of stable identity allows the culture to "read" its otherwise unreadable members in relation to a program of sexual asymmetry designed for the satisfaction of a male, heterosexual subject, who is also a fiction, a social construct. One problem with "compulsory heterosexuality"—in addition to the fact that it produces an asymmetrical relation between the sexes—is that the unnatural stabilization or freezing of identity produces anxieties about insufficiency. The perception of inadequacy, then, I would argue, is always only meaningful in relation to a constructed, normative ideal of gendered personhood. Castration anxiety is not a function of embodiment; it is instead produced by the differential between socially prescribed fictions of sexual relation and the undifferentiated, multiple, productive possibilities relegated to the unconscious, possibilities figured by the body's many protrusions and orifices (and not simply those of male and female genitalia). To me, this is the meaning of Lacan's famous assertion that "there is no sexual relation"; sexual relation, like sexual identity, is a socially constructed fiction.

How, then, assuming that it is naive to hope that we can escape such social constructions, can we practice—in language and in deed—a sexuality that does not uncritically confirm the reductive, oppressive, heterosexual matrix of desire? Butler's suggestions all involve resisting the restriction and definitiveness of categories. She suggests that we promote the proliferation of categories of sex, that we "expand the boundaries of what is . . . culturally intelligible" (29), that we define terms such as "woman" as "an ongoing discursive practice," "a term in process, a becoming, a constructing that cannot rightfully be said to originate or to end" (33). As common sense might dictate, we can practice variable constructions of identity and explore not the stereotypical and value-laden but the complex and associative meanings of "heterosexuality," "homosexuality," and "bisexuality," the "subversive sites of their convergence and resignification" (32).

I would argue that *Finnegans Wake* is precisely the kind of subversive practice Butler prescribes. First of all, identity is always "in process," and male heroism is presented as the flip side of male criminality, both of which are socially constructed (and reductive) fictions (unless, of course, the hero is punningly redefined as someone who "hears," *FW*, 398.29). At the end of III.4, Luke writes of HCE, "They know him, the covenanter, by rote at least, for a chameleon at last, in his true falseheaven colours from ultraviolent to subred tissues" (590.7–9). HCE (Humphrey Chimpden Earwicker or Here Comes Everybody) illustrates— in the world of the unconscious that is *Finnegans Wake*—the proliferation of identities Butler endorses: he is "king of the yeast" (578.4). The pun on "yeast" here collapses the normative perception of him as hero of the solar system, the sun, king of the East, who rises daily and around whom the system revolves, into the unconscious truth that his power, like that of woman, is actually proliferation, fermentation, intoxication: the yeasting productivity of the unconscious, which is not socially regulated. Daytime identity is not only a pose (HCE's true colors are also false), it is a bore: "Others are as tired of themselves as you are. Let each one learn to bore himself" (585.35–36). Joyce not only yawns over the predictableness of daily identity; he also indicts the product of (heterosexual) union as invariably lop-sided, and therefore hypocritical in its claims to intersubjective equality. He takes as his example the 1801 act of union between England and Ireland that so notoriously worked to Ireland's disadvantage, proclaiming, "who so shall separate fetters to new desire, repeals an act of union to unite in bonds of schismacy. O yes! O yes! Withdraw your member!" (585.24–26). This is a good description of Joyce's own project in *Finnegans Wake*, to separate the fetters of men and women, thereby producing a novel experience of desire, to repeal the act of union only to reunite in "bonds of schismacy." Joyce does not suggest for a moment that his alternative model of desire will be free of bonds, of the law, but the bonds will be different, accepting of schism, and we will bear them more equally. If *Finnegans Wake* promotes a dynamic view of identity and a more clear-eyed critique of the fairness of union, it is also a labor-intensive attempt to "expand the boundaries of cultural intelligibility." It presents significations not as unreadable, but as unstable, elusive, not easily appropriated. The term woman is rendered as "Whoam"; woman is, on one level, unrepresentable. *Finnegans Wake* is a writing that "fears all masters" (587.36), eluding even the mastery of readers whose understanding is subtly conditioned by the cultural norms that make people seem intelligible to one another.

Book III, section four of *Finnegans Wake* best illustrates Joyce's radical critique and rewriting of the otherwise prescriptive plot of heterosexuality and gender. The episode presents a primal scene, narrated by the synoptic gospellers, Matthew, Mark, and Luke. What they see, through their common optic, or glass, is what the children might call "Sin" (this is what makes their view synoptic): sexual intercourse between husband and wife that is interrupted by the cry of one of their children upstairs. Issy (the daughter) sees her father's drawn weapon when the parents go upstairs, and laughs at the spectacle of the condom on the end of his penis, and the twin boys (here Kevin and Jerry) are presented with their father's rear end as he turns. Those recording the event for posterity are the historians who wrote the Irish *Annals of the Four Masters* as well as Matthew, Mark, Luke, and John (the four annalists are anal analysts who write annals and record scripture). A brief prologue describes the sleeping household, in which only Kate the Slop and the father are awake. She hears a knock on the downstairs door and a creak on the staircase and falls to her knees, which were knocking together, only to see HCE "in his honeymoon trim" with the "clookey" in his fistball telling her to be quiet (*FW*, 557.3–12). This admits of at least two readings: the publican is locking up, with the key in his hand, or he is naked, ready for honeymoon activity, his penis in hand. Next, the father's sin is rehearsed, and the prologue makes clear that the punishment for his sin is castration: his "contravention of common and statute legislation" requires corporal amputation (558.12–14). Then the play—a dumbshow or silent moving picture—begins, its setting announced as "Chamber scene. Boxed. Ordinary bedroom set" (559.1–2). The first part of the scene is narrated by Matt, from the "[s]ide point of view," with the man "fore" and the woman "hind," in the "First position of harmony," "[m]ale partly masking female"

(559.20–22). Matt describes the Porters—"very nice people" (560.23)—as they hear a cry offstage—the man's rage, the woman's fear—and likens their moves to those in a game of chess as they go upstairs to check the children. He describes Issy as the pussycat in bedroom number one, and Jerry and Kevin as the two birds in bedroom number two. Jerry is crying in his sleep and has wet the bed.

Mark takes another view, "a second position of discordance," from the rear this time: "the male entail partially eclipses the femecovert" (564.1–3). Mark's narration entails much about rears, gentlemen's seats, and homosexual encounters. He puts his hand upon one of his colleague's knees to emphasize what he is saying and the man trembles, "like a verry jerry" (565.10). The analogy suggests that Jerry, too, is trembling at a dream of sexual threat from a man—here his father. The mother reassures him, "You were dreamend, dear. The pawdrag? The fawthrig? Shoe! Hear are no phanthares in the room at all, avikkeen. No bad bold faathern, dear one. . . . Sonly all in your imagination, dim. Poor little brittle magic nation, dim of mind!" (565.18–30).

It is also in Mark's section that the infant Isabella sees her father's weapon, "blade drawn to the full," which she calls "a stark pointing pole" (566.22, 34–35). Even the laughter in this section is gendered; first it is "he, he, he!" then it is "She, she, she!," although the second time the speaker protests to be "highly sheshe sherious" (567.4–5, 570.24). Finally, there is a long section about Honuphrius, a Roman version of HCE/Mr. Porter, who puts his wife Anita (Anna) on trial for debt to him. Luke's section, the last of the synoptic perspectives, is presented as the "third position of concord," a view from the front, "female imperfectly masking male," and begins with the exclamation that "woman's the prey!" (*FW*, 582.29–32) The Porters have now returned to their bedroom and he is riding her like a horse in a race: "The galleonman jovial on his bucky brown nightmare" (583.8–9). The lamp casts their shadows on the blind, so that "The man in the street can see the coming event" (583.15). Their activity is also described in terms of a cricket match, and it ends when his cock crows, "cocorico," signaling comically, blasphemously, as it does in the New Testament, the Peter's betrayal (*FW*, 584.27). Luke ceremoniously thanks the lamp, the mattress, and the condom for their role in this play (in an interesting reinterpretation of who the players are and in a gospel celebration of a thwarted nativity), and the scene is over. The last, shortest view is Johnny's: "Fourth position of solution . . . Finest view from horizon (*FW*, 590.22–23)." Whereas Matthew, Mark, and Luke all see man and woman, parents and children as discrete, and partly masking one another, John sees a creative synthesis. He recommends an unmasking of the apparent opposition of gender in a reversal of *Genesis*: "Two me see. Male and female unmask we hem" (590.24).

How, then, could III.4 be said to depict gender? Homosexuality? Heterosexuality? First of all, it presents sexual acts as multiply framed: within a bed frame, within a window frame (when the policeman outside sees shadows of coitus on the blind), within a chamber and a court (defined as a four-sided structure), and by the successive views of the four old historians who witness and recount it: Matthew, Mark, Luke, and John. The framing of sexuality and transgression is also represented through the mechanisms of trial: the mock-trial of Christ is set against the trial of Oscar Wilde. In both cases the guilt of the defendants is presupposed by the normative matrix against which they are judged, and within which they are framed. Woman, too, is put on trial, here, as Anita, for owing her husband her sexual favors (and withholding them.) Heterosexuality is also presented as performance—a play or "moving picture"—and a sport; ranging from the more private, rule-bound game of chess to the spectator sports of racing (reproducing the human race, or pretending to) and cricket. Joyce quite definitively presents heterosexual congress as a performance for an implied audience. It is not a private affair, but a primal "scene," played for a large audience with "tiers, tiers, and tiers" of seats, greeted by "rounds" of applause (FW, 590.30). In heterosexual performance, the costume is never removed, and the rules of conduct are strict. After Mr. Porter's cock has crowed and intercourse is over, Luke stresses the masked nature of the performance by abjuring men, paradoxically, to "disrobe *clothed* in the strictest secrecy which privacy can afford" (FW, 586.4). He warns them not to urinate before the grate or out the window, and never to remove their condom in bed, to which the male member is by implication wed: "never divorce in the bedding the glove that will give you away" (586.5–6).

What does the masquerade of gender in a heterosexual play mask? For Lacan, the mask disguises a lack—the lack of potency or efficacy—although men and women experience their lack differently, both personally and politically. Joyce, however, in the three "synoptic" versions of the primal scene, presents the male and female genders as masking *each other*, if unevenly: men mask women twice as often as women mask men. It is only the gospel of John, who does not share the same view as the first three (his is not one of the synoptic gospels), that proposes a more radical unmasking/unmaking of men and women. John represents men and women collectively as "them," a novel recombination of "her" plus "him."

The view that men and women experience a lack in abiding by a social contract that is also implicitly an economic contract underlies the scene when Anita is put on trial by Honuphrius for debt. The relations between Honuphrius and the other Romans are complicated and even incestuous; the sexual charge is clearly not limited to Honuphrius and his wife, Anita. Sulla, the orthodox savage, wants Anita to yield to him and deceive Honuphrius by continuing to have marital relations with him; she would, except that she fears it would cause her sons, Eugenius and Jeremias, to act reprehensibly with each other. So Honuphrius *pretends* to possess Anita (this is the illusion of male control). The narrator asks, "Has he hegemony and shall she submit? . . . This, lay readers and gentlemen, is perhaps the commonest of all cases arising out of umbrella history . . . in our courts of litigation" (573.32–574.1). Honuphrius then accuses Anita of owing him tithes; she responds in turn that payment had been made. He is described as the "trusthee"—he who is trusted and who holds value for her "in trust"—and she as the "bethrust" (574.24). He betrays that trust. He is impotent, though cunning: "whenever he has rendered himself impotent [he manages] to consummate by subdolence" (It. cunning, 573.22–23).

Women are sold, as Joyce emphasizes again and again through the pun on Isolde's name: I sold. She sings sadly, "sell me, my soul dear," and her Tristan responds by punning on his own name: "it is triste to death" (in Elizabethan England, "debt" was pronounced the same as "death"; 571.13–14). Sexual intercourse is therefore represented as a potentially lethal IOU, as Joyce indicates by mixing the refrain of the crowing cock—Cocorico—with the refrain of debt between "you" and "I": "O I you O you me" (584.34). Anita/Anna is sometimes moved to rejoin in "pardonership" with him, as the one who "seemed to proffer the steadiest interest towards her" (575.28–31) but the judge rules this out, finding that she was "born into contractual incapacity" (576.2–3). She is not really a free agent. Joyce describes women elsewhere as "maidbrides," punning on maid and "made" (566.16). This is how the case ends: there can be no contract when the woman is not free and the man is not alive, "as no property in law can exist in a corpse" (576.5), but this is how the genders are socially and performatively constructed. The "little green courtinghousie" (575.26) is at once a court of law, a countinghouse where an economic transaction is going on in the name of sexuality, a courtinghouse where men and women court and marry (there's a courthouse on Green Street in Dublin), and a prison (Little Green is the site of Newgate Prison). The same pattern of asymmetrical indebtedness (and lack) applies to the relation between parents and child as to the relation between man and woman: our first parents are really our "forced payrents" (576.27), those to whom we are involuntarily indebted and in relation to whom we are defined as lacking. Finally, Joyce plays on the sense of "rents" as tears, slit-like openings, "portals" (monitored by "Porters") in the body. If your rent is open to be foreclosed you are female; if it is back in arrears you are a male homosexual, and the voice of society warns, "Every ditcher's dastard in Dupling will let us know about it if you have paid the mulctman by whether your rent is open to be foreclosed or aback in your arrears. This is seriously meant. Here is a homelet not a hothel" (Home, Hamlet; hotel; brothel, Othello, 586.15–18). The point is that we all pay our rent—to our parents and our lovers. Does it matter with which bodily rent—front or back—we pay?

Joyce suggests through different perspectives on his heterosexual couple that in our current gender system, homosexuality is always *behind* heterosexuality, partly masked by it, as constructions of feminity mask the males who desire and produce them in. The heterosexual in III.4 is almost always male; lesbianism is downplayed—restricted to Issy—perhaps because the focus is really on the hidden homosocial subtext of heterosexual desire. Joyce defines the "right renownsable patriarch" as "hemale man all unbracing to omniwomen" (581.5, 581.18). On one level, this formulation seems to confirm the stereotypically heterosexual opposition between the sexes: men are hemales who embrace all women. But on another level the hemale man unbraces to "hommes né" women (men who were born women and born *of* women), and read yet another way hemales are female men and omniwomen are "hommes women." Mark describes heterosexuality as a hunt (Luke adds that "Woman's the prey!"), and in the hunt "ommes will grin . . . when each riders other's ass" (567.26–27); in other words, the pleasure of the hunt is homosocial. But social and religious mores direct us never to look behind at the ass that always follows us: "Do not show ever retrorsehim; crookodeyled, till that you become quite crimstone in the face" (570.33–34); like Lot's wife, if we look back to see Sodom(y), we are told we will turn to salt: "I am anxious in regard you should everthrown your sillarsalt" (570.35–36). When two men love one woman, it is really "boyplay" (569.34); Mark comments appreciatively, grotesquely, "what tyronte power" (tyrant power, Tyrone Power, 569.35).

Finally, in III.4 and elsewhere in *Finnegans Wake* Joyce presents the body not as evidence of a differential between (male) potency and (female) lack, but as an authorized site of multiple sexualities that far exceed genital oppositions. It is men who would be "genitalmen" in service of a unified truth: Joyce alludes to "two genitalmen of Veruno [one truth]" (569.31). Joyce does provide images of female and male genitalia, but he also traces their mutation in language, showing how the words for sexual difference collapse into one another and are transposed onto other bodily sites and organs, effectively decentering the genitalia—displacing them from center stage. The chapter begins with the man and woman "in their bed of trial, on the bolster of hardship, by the glimmer of memory, under coverlets of cowardice, Albatrus Nyanzer with Victa Nyanza, his mace of might mortified, her beautifell hung up on a nail" (558.26–29). The mortified "mace of might" is of course his penis, her "beautifell" is her gown hung up on a nail (the implication being that her sexuality is a covering, a veil). But "beautifell" is also "beautiful"—"belle" (and belle of course rhymes with "fell"). Bells, also an image of female sexuality, are an important attribute of Anna Livia Plura*belle*, who started out as only one bell (Is a bell/Isabelle) but multiplied as she matured. Anna Livia now has many bells: riding a cock horse to Banbury Cross, "with *rings* on her fingers and bells on her toes, she shall have music wherever she goes." It is of course the cuplike shape of the bell that makes it an image of female sexuality, combined with the fact that it is made to ring by a blow from a clapper or tongue inside of it (or by a blow from a hammer outside of it). The clapper or tongue in turn recalls the male's "mace of might"; the penis is a cricket bat, a crowing cock that pees (otherwise known as a peacock), the cock on a barrel of porter, a swaystick (swastika, 569.19), a key, a penisill (pencil or ill penis, 566.9), a hand-in-glove (the glove being the condom, giving "true glover's greeting"), a burning lampwick, and a bow for playing stringed instruments. Primarily, though, it is a stick, defined as a tree-stone (a pun on the name Tristan). The vagina or bell is forbidden fruit, specifically an apple (from the Latin *abella*), the lamp that encloses his wick, a teakettle brought to boil. In Anna Livia Plurabelle's role as Issy she is described as a bell-shaped flower, "Buttercup," a child-doll—Bambolina—and a pussycat. Finally, female sexuality is strongly associated with fluid—rain, urination, pee (and peas), number one—whereas the harder male sexuality is associated with defecation, shooting, and shitting, number two. What is interesting, however, is how Joyce traces the transformation of one extreme into its so-called opposite, thereby unsettling the oppositions themselves. Everyone urinates and defecates and finally the bell and clapper are shown to be two parts of the instrument of the body, inscribed differently in different places. A bell is an image of the mouth as well as of female genitalia: the etymology of "bell" is probably to make a loud noise (as in "bellow," *OED*). Ring is an image of the enclosure of marriage as well as an allusion to the sound of ringing wedding bells (and later the wringing of hands and clothes). Men are ringed into marriage as well as women; HCE is once described as "the slave of the ring" (580.26). ALP's body is described as a "bodikin" (578.16), a needle, belying her apparent lack of phallic power; he in turn is described as a "bow," which in French becomes "beau," beautiful: his opposite has turned into hers. He is a wick, she a wicket in cricket. Moreover, HCE is described throughout as having a wig in his ear—he is hard of hearing—and the ear is another bell that works through vibration. In this case, the wick in his ear parallels the wick he puts in his wife's lamp; the difference between ALP and HCE again disappears if the priority given to the genitals disappears. "Bell" is also the root of the Latin word for war as well as beauty—*bellum*, so, as Greek mythology long ago suggested, beauty and conflict (like Venus and Mars) are siblings as well as spouses. And as the Italian tale of Pinocchio suggests, HCE is "finocchio" (It. homosexual) as well as Lampwick, the fire within the female lamp. The hemale and the female are virtually identical, although performatively different: the "position of solution" is to unmask this identity, their common lack and their equal potential, to decreate them and in the process to produce a new social Genesis: "Male and female unmask we hem."

Waking Desire

The desire that animates *Finnegans Wake* is the desire to remain open to unexpected, chance affinities and incompatibilities, open to foreignness and to change. As Joyce suggests near the end of the book, "In that european end meets Ind" (In that open ear the end meets the beginning; in Europe west meets east, 598.15–16). Like Wilde, for whom nothing was unthinkable, and Yeats, for whom nothing was incredible, Joyce saw nothing as inexpressible, not even the movement of the mind in sleep or the darkness of world history. He wrote as if the individual mind could compass the rich strangeness of global and historical differences—not consciously, but through the senses, by registering the tensions between what we see, hear, hope and remember. He believed that the imaginative capacity of individuals may be measured by what they have perceived, not by what they understand, but human perception is subject to a set of provisional rules that we often misread as universal rather than culturally and historically specific. These constraints range from gender and nationality to vocabulary and grammar: categories that make the world seem legible and controllable.

What price do humans pay for the illusion that they control their thoughts and their lives? Joyce suggests that the price can be estimated by holding the fabric of history against the richer texture of myth and dream. For most of us, history is little more than what it is for the children Stephen teaches at Deasy's school in *Ulysses*: "For them too history was a tale like any other too often heard, their land a pawnshop" (*U*, 2.45–7). *Finnegans Wake* implies that history recycles a few simple narratives: it is about individuals climbing up and falling down, about youthful camaraderie and growing isolation, about breaking conglomerates apart and gathering them together, about alienated desire and potential reconstructions of meaning; but it harps throughout on the widespread lust for possession, repeatedly reminding its readers that no possession is permanent. "This ourth of years" (*FW*, 18.4) is not only "this earth of ours" and "these hours and years," but also this "ours" of "yours," and the business of "ours" and "yours" "is not [naught] save brickdust and being humus." The certainty of death renders the desire for possession void; we are "rich in death anticipated" (*FW*, 78.6). The desire to "have" is not only temporary, it also, paradoxically, impoverishing, urging us to "halve" our experience (see 309.17).

History is also the story of the human race, a race that is between "I" and "you," and the story of a debt (I.O.U.). "I" and "you" are, in theory, "equals of opposites, evolved by a onesame power of nature or of spirit, *iste*, as the sole condition and means of its himundher manifestation and polarised for reunion by the symphysis of their antipathies" (*FW*, 92.8–11). In practice, however, one party is typically constrained by sociohistorical circumstances to be indebted to the other, which upsets the essential equality between them. "I" and "you" are sometimes "Mutt" and "Jute," or native and invader (*FW*, 15.29–18.16); they are often black and white ("two races, swete [white] and brack [black]," 17.24): brunette and blond, female and male ("dunkledames . . . with the hellish [Ger. light] fellows," 15.17–18); old and young; homosexual and heterosexual; gentile and Jew (see the rendering of "I" and "you" as "goy" and "jew," 273.14). Of couse, "I" and "you" are also the two parties linked by a letter, or book; they are the writer and the addressee, joined and divided by attraction and "pridejealice" (prejudice, pride, jealousy; 344.32–33).

Joyce sums up human history by explaining, "There are two signs to turn to, the yest and the ist, the wright side and the wronged side, feeling aslip and wauking up, so an, so farth . . . Why? Such me" (*FW*, 597.10–22). The reason for injustice cannot be found in the superiority or inferiority of the other, "pridejealice," because the other is always a reversed reflection of the self. What is it, then that makes two equals feel at odds? Joyce's answer—in the wake of Wilde and Yeats—is first, idealism (of the self or of the other), which springs out of the desire to have or halve experience and to discard the darker half, and second, an oversimplified understanding of the relation between perception and language. The commandment to love our neighbor like ourselves has been trumped by another one, the determination to "love my label like myself" (*FW*, 579.18). As Wilde discovered, too late to avoid ruin, love of life has been displaced by a love of labels, and sentencing has come to be synonymous with punishment. In *Finnegans Wake*, Shem's first riddle of the universe is "when is a man not a man?" (170.5) His answer is when he is a "sham" (170.24). "Sham" is a play on Shem's name, which means "name" in Hebrew; a man is a sham when he is too closely identified with a name, a label.

Those who see language primarily as a repository of easily legible labels are driven by the desire to organize and categorize the chaotic vitality of human experience. As both the book of Genesis and the fairy tale of "Rumplestiltskin" differently show, we gain sovereignty over things by naming them, as Adam named the animals and as the queen vanquished Rumplestiltskin by learning his name. The twin desires to tame and name are inspired by a fear of wildness, but Joyce, like Wilde, Yeats, and Freud, valued a strategic fearlessness instead. His last book, like Freud's first, explores "the intrepidation of our dreams" (*FW*, 338.29–30). Joyce appreciates the secret power of dreaming, of desire, of raving (which is a version of the French "rêve," or dream), as a creative resource that is lost with the light of morning and chilled by "bleakfrost," or breakfast: he laments the loss of the "intrepidation of dreams which we foregot at wiking when the morn hath razed our limpalove and the bleakfrost chilled our ravery" (*FW*, 338.29–31).

We might ask, with the narrator of *Finnegans Wake*, "what matter what all his freudzay" (*FW*, 337.6–7): what does it matter what "friends" say or what Freud says? "Freudzay," however, is also "hearsay"—Freud was a man who could *hear* what people say, including the frightening meaningfulness of their errors. As Shaun protests in III, 1, "You never made a more freudful mistake" (*FW*, 411.35–6; "freudful mistakes" are not unlike the "clerical horrors" out of which *Finnegans Wake* itself is composed, 419.35). One answer to the question of what Freud says and why it matters for an understanding of *Finnegans Wake* may be found in the second chapter of *The Interpretation of Dreams*, where Freud first discusses the process of preparing the patient to make him or her a productive partner in dream interpretation. The two most important changes that Freud wants a patient to make are (1) to increase "the attention he pays to his own psychical perceptions," and (2) to eliminate "the criticism by which he normally sifts the thoughts that occur to him." Freud stresses that "it is precisely his critical attitude which is responsible for his being unable, in the ordinary course of things, to achieve the desired unravelling of his dream" (133).

Freud's prescription for a patient who wants to understand his dream and thereby unravel his symptoms is exactly the same as Joyce's prescription for someone who wants to read *Finnegans Wake* in order to undo conventional habits of mind: the reader must increase her or his attention to sensory imput and delay using "the critical function" (135). One of the foundational insights of psychoanalysis was the insight that fantasy (defined as an unchecked yeasting of involuntary ideas that turn into visual and acoustic images, 134) has the potential to unlock the chains of introjected ideals, whether those ideals have been projected by society or by a powerful individual, usually a family member. When we internalize demands from the outside world, those demands harden into a kind of interpretive "program" that limit our capacity to assimilate details. As a result, Freud argues that it is essential for us to make our readings more specific, local, and precise; he argues that his method of decoding employs "interpretation *en detail* and not *en masse*" (136).

Freud actually traces his own reading practice to Friedrich Schiller, who in a letter written in 1788 emphasized the danger of allowing reason to constrain the imagination too tightly. Schiller writes,

> It seems a bad thing and detrimental to the creative work of the mind if Reason makes too close an examination of the ideas as they come pouring in—at the very gateway, as it were. Looked at in isolation, a thought may seem very trivial or very fantastic; but it may be made important by another thought that comes after it, and, in conjunction with other thoughts that may seem equally absurd, it may turn out to form a most effective link. Reason cannot form any opinion upon all this unless it retains the thought long enough to look at it in connection with the others. On the other hand, where there is a creative mind, Reason—so it seems to me—relaxes its watch upon the gates, and the ideas rush in pell-mell, and only then does it look them through and examine them in a mass.—You critics, or whatever else you may call yourselves, are ashamed or frightened of the momentary and transient extravagances which are to be found in all truly creative minds and whose longer or shorter duration distinguishes the thinking artist from the dreamer. You complain of your unfruitfulness because you reject too soon and discriminate too severely. (135)

Joyce's late works, *Ulysses* and *Finnegans Wake*, are designed to shortcircuit the reader's tendency to label and analyze too soon. Joyce's propensity to postpone answering a reader's most pressing questions until the reader has been pummelled with apparently chaotic ideas and sense impressions is an attempt to disconnect reason temporarily in order to nurture fantasy and desire, with their apparently spontaneous generation of highly specific associations. Joyce saw that fantastic desire, in its most specific and associative forms, has been largely exiled to the nighttime, and that paradoxically, our desire for control serves to *make us more controllable.* In order to read rationally, a reader must resist specificity and novelty, because they defy categorization. The rational reader must fight the volatility of life and letters in order to support the illusion of personal mastery, a fight that makes the reader more passive; he does not generate creative possibilities, but expends energy resisting them, so that reading becomes a kind of prophylaxis against thought or the play of mind. *Finnegans Wake* will not lend itself to this kind of reading.

Instead of helping readers reduce reality to a collection of manipulable categories, *Finnegans Wake* refuses to treat language as a collection of labels. On the contrary, it attempts to revive the spiritual dimension of scripture by using the waywardness of letters as a model and inspiration for apprehending the movements of an expansive desire. The *Wake* approaches all names as if they were the name of God, which the Hebrew Bible warns should not be spoken or written because naming implies ownership or control or understanding. God could only be signified by four mysterious Hebrew letters, the tetragrammaton, sometimes interpreted as "Yahweh" or "Jehovah," although the letters were not to be confused with a comprehensible name. By focusing attention more onto constituent individual letters rather than names and categories, Joyce tried to restore to language its joyous vitality, its pleasurable power to stimulate new insight, or "jehovial oyeglances" (*FW*, 405.20). He designed not a tetragrammaton but a "tetradomational gazebocroticon" that he associates with the novel gaze of Matthew, Mark, Luke, and John ("the 'Mamma Lujah' known to every schoolboy scandaller," 614.27–29). His "jehovial" language strives to restore equality to the different pairs of human beings made in God's image (black and white, male and female, young and old, Gentile and Jew), and to remind his readers of the irreducible mystery of physical and verbal creation.

Five

Conclusion

Antioedipal reading, like antioedipal loving, is predicated on an emphatic refusal to shun "mistakes," or deviations, and on an acute appreciation of volitional errors as portals of discovery. What Wilde, Yeats, Joyce, Deleuze, and Guattari all valorize is less the accumulation of prestige than the generation of energy via rapidly shifting mechanisms for verbal and physical connection and uncoupling. Instead of striving to purge the foreignness of matter within (and outside) ourselves, or within (or in the exchange of) words, these Irish writers, like Deleuze and Guattari, suggest that we multiply it, and they differently demonstrate the vitality of the fortuitous and yet rigorous recombinations that result. Similarly, for the "love letter" that is literary criticism, what matters is not the critic's dominance over the text, but her ability to *use* it, to extend it, to allow the variousness of the unconscious to unfold itself across the tracings of the known. As Deleuze concludes,

> This is the good way to read: all mistranslations are good—always provided that they do not consist in interpretations, but relate to the use of the book, that they multiply its use, that they create yet another language inside its language. [As Proust says,] 'Great literature is written in a sort of foreign language.' That is the definition of style. (*Dialogues*, 5)

I have argued throughout *States of Desire* that sexual and national identities are too often defined through rigid oppositions, rather than as dynamic states that are richest and most productive when they hold complex contradictions in momentary suspension. This is to say that self-definition is optimally more than a purely rational process; it is also a way of integrating currents of conflicting emotion that in ancient times were seen as the signature of the supernatural, and more recently as a sign of the powerful energies of the unconscious. What Deleuze and Guattari call the process of "becoming minoritarian" (becoming-woman, becoming-animal), a localization of focus that remains alive to the possibility of multidirectional movement, is engendered by envisioning a zone of conflict or flux that defies stable regulation by rational categories. This zone is sometimes described as a "sacred state between being and nonbeing"; Alwyn and Brinley Rees remind us that "[t]he individual who dares to enter it in defiance of the spirit of reason places himself within reach of salvation, but he also exposes himself to the dangers of annihilation" (Rees, 346). Wilde entered that zone through a play of wit and through sexual daring (although his personal life was almost conventional in its idealization of youth). Yeats accessed the "sacred state" by meditating on multidimensional and metamorphosing symbols and by exploring the "otherworlds" of Rosicrucian magic and the *sidhe*. Joyce tried to recreate the world of dream itself, not only by excavating ancient Irish myth and by disinterring buried histories, but also by charging each of his words with the greatest possible meaning, by writing in a language of puns.

In *Celtic Heritage*, the Rees argue that the concentrated, "sacred" power of enigmatic situations, characters, and deeds "is bound up with coincidences which are essentially the same as those found in puns" (347); that puns and riddles are verbal "abnormalities which demonstrate the ultimate inadequacy of logical categories" (348). Puns, they suggest, are the most local and concentrated examples of how art, myth, and even religion work to remind us of "the inexhaustible analogical riches of the universe" (351). We tend to think of such reminders as detached from the real world of action and politics, but in fact they are essential to the reimagining of human communities that is the aim of love, politics, and nationalism.

Ireland, whether it is the "green world" responsible for Wilde's productivity and untimely fall, the celtic twilight of Yeats, or the night world of Joyce, has proven itself particularly susceptible to imaginative transformation. In the hands of these three writers, Ireland is both less and more than a nation; it is sometimes a country village and sometimes the world. At its most powerful, Ireland—like the gendered individual—is reduced and expanded to what we see when we close our eyes: everything and nothing. This is what it becomes to Celia (whose name is derived from the Latin word for the sky or heavens) at the end of Samuel Beckett's *Murphy*. She looks at the sky and sees not only herself reflected there, but also Ireland: "Moving away a little, Celia also looked at the sky, . . . simply to have that unction of soft sunless light on her eyes that was all she remembered of Ireland."[1]

Notes

Preface

1. *Reauthorizing Joyce* (Cambridge: Cambridge University Press, 1988; paperback ed. University of Florida Press, 1995).

2. Samuel Beckett, *Endgame* (New York: Grove Press, 1958), 62–63. Hereafter cited parenthetically in the text.

3. Samuel Beckett, *Waiting for Godot: A Tragicomedy in Two Acts* (New York: Grove Press, 1954), 58. Hereafter cited parenthetically in the text.

4. See W. B. Yeats, *Letters to the New Island*, ed. George Bornstein and Hugh Witemeyer (New York: Macmillan, 1989), 12: "Cosmopolitan literature is, at best, but a poor bubble, though a big one. Creative work has always a fatherland." Almost a year later, Yeats returned to the subject in his articles for the Boston *Pilot;* speaking of the traps laid for the Irish writer, he asserts, "Cosmopolitanism is one of the worst. We are not content to dig our own potato patch in peace. We peer over the wall at our neighbor's instead of making our own garden green and beautiful" (*LNI,* 32). Hereafter cited parenthetically in the text as *LNI.*

5. "The Soul of Man under Socialism," in *The Artist as Critic: Critical Writings of Oscar Wilde,* ed. Richard Ellmann (Chicago: University of Chicago Press, 1969), 266. Hereafter cited parenthetically in the text as *A as C.*

6. James Stephens, *In the Land of Youth* (New York: Macmillan, 1924), 36.

7. Nuala Ní Dhomhnaill, "Why I Choose to Write in Irish, The Corpse That Sits Up and Talks Back," *The New York Times Book Review* (January 8, 1995), 28.

8. Mary Daly, especially in *Gyn-Ecology,* appropriates punning as a language for women; punning has always been an important part of children's literature; and psychoanalysis and deconstruction have both appreciated the pun as a symptom of the possibilities denied and buried by the conscious mind and by intentionality.

1 Introduction

1. Richard LeBow identifies the stereotype (or closed image) as the linguistic basis of prejudice, arguing that stereotypes serve a double function for those who rely upon them: they express hostility and aggression while simultaneously functioning as a "perceptual blinder, protecting the personality from information likely to produce internal stress," and furnishing "the basis for the development and maintenance of solidarity among the prejudiced." *White Britain and Black Ireland: The Influence of Stereotypes on Colonial Policy* (Philadelphia: Institute for the Study of Human Issues, 1976), 22.

2. In his preface to Roland Barthes's *S/Z*, Richard Howard cites reading as a strangely unindicted solitary vice: "For reading is still the principal thing we do by ourselves in culture, and it has too long been granted—as when Valery Larbaud calls it the one unpunished vice—the amnesty of our society." Howard celebrates Barthes's criticism as a meditation on reading that affords "a convinced, euphoric, even a militant critique of what it is we do when we read . . . [and an explanation of] [w]hy we read in this repressed and repressive way." "A Note on *S/Z*," in Roland Barthes, *S/Z*, trans. Richard Miller (New York: Hill and Wang, 1974), x–xi.

3. For a discussion of the relation between "representative" language and consolidating or "territorializing" movements of the State see Gilles Deleuze and Félix Guattari, *Kafka: Toward a Minor Literature*, trans. Dana Polan (Minneapolis: University of Minnesota Press, 1986), 20–27, and Gilles Deleuze and Claire Parnet, *Dialogues*, trans. Hugh Tomlinson and Barbara Habberjam (New York: Columbia University Press, 1987), 46–51, especialy the emphasis on how language begins to resist interpretation *by* its users, and instead interprets both them and itself, like the despot.

4. For Freud's first discussion of the Oedipus complex, see *The Interpretation of Dreams* (Avon reprint; London: Hogarth Press, 1953), 294–300.

5. Both "experience" and "experiment" come from the same root, *experiri*, to try, although "experience" has come to take on a retrospective cast, so that it denotes an accumulation of trials: "What has been experienced; the events that have taken place within the knowledge of an individual, a community" (*OED* sb.6).

6. An "assemblage" is the term Deleuze and Guattari use to designate a multiplicity. The renaming of units such as words, ideas, and books as assemblages highlights a view that we have personalized such units, along with seemingly individual emotions and attitudes, instead of seeing them as a machinelike construct, a mechanical intersection of different social and historical forces. See "What Is an Assemblage?" in *Kafka: Toward a Minor Literature*, 81–88; Deleuze and Parnet, *Dialogues*, 51–54 and 69–74; and *A Thousand Plateaus: Capitalism and Schizophrenia*, trans. Brian Massumi (Minneapolis: University of Minnesota Press, 1987).

7. See Foucault's preface to Deleuze and Guattari's *Anti-Oedipus: Capitalism and Schizophrenia*, trans. Robert Hurley, Mark Seem, and Helen R. Lane (Minneapolis: University of Minnesota Press, 1983), xi–xiv; Fredric Jameson, *The Political Unconscious: Narrative as a Socially Symbolic Act* (Ithaca: Cornell University Press, 1981), 53, in which Jameson emphasizes Deleuze and Guattari's resistance to "totalizations," and Felix Guattari, "Everybody Wants to Be a Fascist," *Semiotext(e)*, 2, no. 3 (1977), trans. Suzanne Fletcher.

8. Alice Jardine, "Woman in Limbo: Deleuze and His Br(others)," *SubStance* 44/45 (1984):47.

9. See P. W. Joyce, *An Illustrated History of Ireland* (Dublin: Educational Co. of Ireland, 1923), 382–93. The most active penal legislation was enacted in 1695, and more laws against Catholics were passed in the years that followed (in clear violation of the terms of the Treaty of Limerick, 1691, which guaranteed religious liberty to Irish Roman Catholics). These laws were not repealed until the Catholic Emancipation Act of 1829, although in some parts of the country some of the statutes fell into disuse by the late eighteenth century. Roy Foster cites a particularly chilling example of anti-Catholic sentiment as expressed by a preacher in England, who warned that his parishoners' wives could be

prostituted to the lust of every savage bog-trotter, your daughters ravished by goatish monks, your smaller children tossed upon pikes, and torn limb from limb whilst you have your own bowels ripped up . . . or else murdered with some other exquisite torture and holy candles made of your grease (which was done within our memory in Ireland).

Quoted in R. F. Foster, *Modern Ireland: 1600–1972* (New York: Penguin, 1988), 120.

10. Giovanni Costigan, *A History of Modern Ireland, with a Sketch of Earlier Times* (New York: Pegasus, 1969), 127.

11. See Brian Friel's *Translations* (1981) for another example of a work that relies upon a comparison between the British and the Romans. In *Translations*, the Irish are comparable to the Greeks whose civilization was pillaged by the Romans; many of the Irish characters are actually learning Greek in the hedgeschools as the play begins.

12. Karl Bottigheimer, *Ireland and the Irish: A Short History* (New York: Columbia University Press, 1982), 4.

13. Oliver MacDonagh, *States of Mind: Two Centuries of Anglo-Irish Conflict, 1780–1980* (London: Pimlico, 1983), 15–33. For an account of how the Irish landscape was used to advantage by rebels and hated by the English in Elizabethan times, see Foster, *Modern Ireland*, 5–7.

14. Quoted in James Bonwick, *Irish Druids and Old Irish Religions* (1894; reprint Dorset Press, 1986), 311. P. W. Joyce, in *A Social History of Ancient Ireland* (London: Longmans, 1920), vol. 1, adds that *"feada,"* the collective name for the letters, means "woods," and that "the order of the letters is totally different from that of the Latin or any other alphabet" (398).

15. The tree/stone (or Tristan) motif in Joyce's *Finnegans Wake* is in part a reference to the history of the book in Ireland, and a specific reference to the inscription of the ancient language of Ogham on trees and stones.

16. Nigel Pennick, *Celtic Sacred Landscapes* (New York: Thames and Hudson, 1996), 59. See also the section on "Sacred Trees" (21–38).

17. Brian Friel, *Translations* (1981), in *Modern Irish Drama*, ed. John P. Harrington (New York: Norton, 1991), 350–51.

18. In lenition, the initial consonant changes when a proper noun (in the genitive) follows another noun (to give just one example). In eclipsis, the initial consonant of a singular noun is said to be "eclipsed" by another consonant that is added when the noun follows a preposition; for example, *cloch* becomes *ar an gcloch* (the "c" is eclipsed), and *fear* becomes *leis an bhfear* (the slender "f" takes on the sound of "v" after being eclipsed). See Mícheál Ó Siadhail, *Learning Irish: An Introductory Self-Tutor* (New Haven: Yale University Press, 1988), 15, 23.

19. *Complete Works of Oscar Wilde*, with an introduction by Vyvyan Holland (New York: Harper and Row, 1966), 326. Hereafter cited in the text as *CW*.

20. If, as Christopher Craft has persuasively argued, the name "Ernest" also puns on "urning," a code term for the pursuit of homosexual or Uranian love, then the desire for the moral authority of fatherhood is never more than a cover-up for more covert pleasurable activity. See "Alias Bunbury: Desire and Termination in *The Importance of Being Earnest*," *Representations* 31 (Summer 1990):19–46.

21. In "Ars Est Caelare Artem," Frederick Ahl argues that the ancients were much less resistant to the latent, pluralizing, humorous implications of words than

the moderns, adducing as one prominent example the argument of Plato's *Cratylus*. Ahl gives numerous instances of playful etymologies, puns, and anagrams (visual puns) in the work of Greek and Latin writers, asserting that they "were more sensitive to the possibilities—including what they took to be the scientific, even divine possibilities—of wordplay than we are." *On Puns: The Foundation of Letters*, ed. Jonathan Culler (Oxford: Basil Blackwell, 1988), 43.

22. I am indebted to Jean-Michel Rabaté for pointing out the pun on *j'ouïe sens*. The fact that the ear (unlike the eye) is always open has prompted several critics to trope the subversions heard by the ear as democratic and gynocentric, especially in contrast to the dominance of the male gaze. Joyce goes even further in *Finnegans Wake* by associating the power of sound not only with the "babble" of women-as-rivers, but also with divinity. Following Giambattista Vico's theory in *The New Science*, Joyce interprets thunder both as the voice of God and as "th(undertones)" that make humans afraid. He designs *Finnegans Wake* as a book that you can only "read" by attending to these undertones: "if you are looking for the bilder [builder; Ger. pictures] deep your ear on the movietone!" (*FW*, 62.8–9).

23. Hayden White, *The Content of the Form: Narrative Discourse and Historical Representation* (Baltimore: Johns Hopkins University Press, 1987), 11, 21. Although White's main interest is in *historical* narrative, his insights are equally applicable to fictional narrative, which, like historical discourse, both depends upon and works to construct an illusion of the real.

24. See Socrates' suggestion in Plato's *Cratylus* that truth, *aletheia*, may be an anagram for "divine wandering" (*theia . . . ale*) (421B). Cited by Ahl, *On Puns*, 28.

25. Luce Irigaray defines maleness in terms of the unity of erotic intensity, contrasting it to femaleness, which she associates with multiplicity:

> [Woman] experiences pleasure almost everywhere. Even without speaking of the hysterization of her entire body, one can say that the geography of her pleasure is much more diversified, more multiple in its differences, more complex, more subtle, than is imagined—in an imaginary centered a bit too much on one and the same.

"This Sex Which Is Not One," in *New French Feminisms: An Anthology*, ed. Elaine Marks and Isabelle de Courtivron (New York: Schocken Books, 1980), 103.

26. For an account of how colonial difference and gender difference inform and support each other, see Joseph Valente, *James Joyce and the Problem of Justice: Negotiating Sexual and Colonial Difference* (Cambridge: Cambridge University Press, 1995).

27. Maud Gonne MacBride, *A Servant of the Queen: Reminiscences* (1938; Great Britain, Boydell Press, 1983), 90.

28. Richard Ellmann argues that another event in Joyce's life contributed to his decision to give Bloom the middle name of Paula. In *James Joyce*, he asserts that Joyce's name (James Augustine) was incorrectly registered at his birth as "James Augusta." *James Joyce* (1959; rev. ed. New York: Oxford University Press, 1982), 21.

29. Lacan, "A Love Letter," *Feminine Sexuality: Jacques Lacan and the école freudienne*, ed. Juliet Mitchell and Jacqueline Rose (New York: Norton, 1982), 157.

30. Such a conjunction of ethical judgment and the flexibility characteristic of play is also one of the definitions Freud quotes for *der Witz* in *Jokes and their Relation to the Unconscious*, trans. and ed. James Strachey (New York: Norton, 1960), 10: "A joke is a *playful* judgement."

31. Jacques Lacan, *Television; A Challenge to the Psychoanalytic Establishment*, ed. Joan Copjec, trans. Denis Hollier, Rosalind Krauss, and Annette Michelson (*Televi-*

sion); trans. Jeffrey Mehlman (*A Challenge to the Psychoanalytic Establishment*) (New York and London: Norton, 1990) 10. See also the introduction to the Names of the Father Seminar, 81–95.

32. William Faulkner, *As I Lay Dying* (1930; New York: Random-Vintage, 1964), 34.

33. Although Deleuze and Guattari are diametrically opposed to Anse in their appreciation of dynamic, experimental innovation ("travelling") and in their repudiation of "rootedness," they resemble him in their assumption that a model consciousness is male. Anse's insistence that a "man," in his erectness, was never intended to move doesn't extend to women, who—especially when dying or dead—typically serve as instigators of movement. If men dehumanize themselves through "arborification," men reduce women to mere causes or agents of momentary and fleeting connection. They are condemned to *represent* the desires that men pursue and disavow, and, as stimuli, they are always only the *cause* of movement; they may never realize such movement themselves. For Faulkner, the role of women as catalysts is emphasized by his decision to design his novel around a dead woman at the center, nailed upside-down in a coffin in her wedding dress, a rotting corpse dragged with indignity through flood and fire, and also a voice who speaks from beyond the grave with a passion that has never been recognized, let alone satisfied.

34. Félix Guattari, "Everybody Wants to Be a Fascist," *Anti-Oedipus* issue, *Semiotext(e)* 2 (1977): 87–98.

35. This is of course a reference to the famous textual crux in Hamlet's suicide soliloquy in I.ii.: "O that this too too sullied [solid] flesh would melt, / Thaw, and resolve itself into a dew." Hamlet is here referring to his own flesh; however, it is Gertrude who acts as the personification of agonizingly sullied flesh in the play. Her too solid flesh stands in sharp contrast to the phantasmal authority of her former husband.

36. As Deleuze and Guattari write in *Anti-Oedipus*, "In a word, the opposition of the forces of attraction and repulsion produces an open series of intensive elements, all of them positive, that are never an expression of the final equilibrium of a system, but consist, rather, of an unlimited number of stationary, metastable states through which a subject passes" (19).

37. *Hamlet*, ed. Willard Farnham (Baltimore, Md.: Penguin, 1957; rev. 1970), V.ii.77–78. All further references will be to this edition.

38. In *Kafka*, Deleuze and Guattari argue that the idea of transcendent law depends upon an a priori assumption of guilt, so that the first step in dismantling the illusion of transcendent law is to eliminate "any idea of guilt from the start": "culpability is never anything but the superficial movement whereby judges and even lawyers confine you in order to prevent you from engaging in a real movement—that is, from taking care of your own affairs" (45).

39. Hamlet puns on "heir" as "air" in his famous "To be or not to be" soliloquy:

> To die, to sleep—
No more—and by a sleep to say we end
The heartache, and the thousand natural shocks
That flesh is heir to.
III.i.63

40. Ernest Jones, *Hamlet and Oedipus* (New York: Norton, 1949), 24, n. 1; 77–78, n. 2; Vining's theory is also mentioned in *Ulysses*. See also Claudius' reproach to Hamlet, "'Tis unmanly grief" (I.ii.94).

41. See Mahaffey, "*Ulysses* and the End of Gender," in *A Companion to James Joyce's Ulysses*, ed. Margot Norris (New York: Bedford Books, 1998), 151–68.

42. Deleuze and Guattari caution in *Kafka*, "One would be quite wrong to understand desire here as a desire *for* power, a desire to repress or be repressed, a sadistic desire and a masochistic desire. . . . There isn't a desire for power; it is power itself that is desire" (56). A little later, they once again stress the needlessness of constructing power as a transcendent "other," repeating that "[t]here is no longer a revolutionary desire that would be opposed to power" (57).

43. Or, if the subject is a woman, one could argue that she has only been deterritorialized through her massive reterritorialization within the home.

44. The kind of reading and writing that Deleuze and Guattari endorse is "determined not by theoretical analyses implying universals but by a pragmatics composing multiplicities or aggregates of intensities" (*TP*, 15).

45. Jacques Mercanton, "The Hours of James Joyce," in *Portraits of the Artist in Exile: Recollections of James Joyce by Europeans*, ed. Willard Potts (Seattle: University of Washington Press, 1979), 249.

46. It is interesting to compare Joyce's belief that one's mode of reading or interpretation preconditions his or her actions with Stanley Milgrim's charge that "so-called 'intellectual resistance' in occupied Europe—in which persons by a twist of thought felt that they had defied the invader—was merely indulgence in a consoling psychological mechanism." *Obedience to Authority: An Experimental View* (New York: Harper and Row, 1974), 10. Milgrim is undoubtedly right in asserting that "between thoughts, words, and the critical step of disobeying a malevolent authority lies another ingredient, the capacity for transforming beliefs and values into action." What I am suggesting here is the possibility that the way we interpret signs importantly influences "the capacity for transforming beliefs and values into action." A more responsible way of reading corresponds with a sense of greater personal responsibility for one's actions. (Milgrim shows that the experimental subjects who were best able to defy inhumane authority were also those who refused to assign responsibility for their actions to either the experimenter or the victim; see pp. 51–62.) Reading is an action; it is simply a mental action, and its consequences are real but indirect.

2 Wilde's Desire

1. Frank Harris, *Oscar Wilde* (East Lansing: Michigan State University Press, 1959), 271. See also Lord Henry's deprecation of women in *The Picture of Dorian Gray*: "I am afraid that women appreciate cruelty, downright cruelty, more than anything else. They have wonderfully primitive instincts. We have emancipated them, but they remain slaves looking for their masters, all the same. They love being dominated." In *The Complete Works of Oscar Wilde*, with an introduction by Vyvyan Holland (New York: Harper & Row, 1966), 86. Lord Illingworth takes much the same stance in *A Woman of No Importance*, asserting that "Women are pictures. Men are problems. If you want to know what a woman really means—which, by the way, is always a dangerous thing to do—look at her, don't listen to her . . . women represent the triumph of matter over mind" (*CW*, 460).

In sharp contrast, both Mrs. Allonby and Hester Worsley in *A Woman of No Importance* speak wittily and sometimes eloquently against sexist assumptions. Hester passionately exclaims,

If a man and woman have sinned, let them both go forth into the desert to love or loathe each other there. Let them both be branded. Set a mark, if you wish, on each, but don't punish the one and let the other go free. Don't have one law for men and another for women. You are unjust to women in England. And till you count what is a shame in a woman to be infamy in a man, you will always be unjust. (*CW*, 450)

2. Frank Harris, *Oscar Wilde*, 284–85. Wilde's defense of the aesthetic superiority of sexual immaturity is most fully developed in his appreciation of Willie Hughes, boy actor, in *The Portrait of Mr. W. H.*

3. The Narcissus myth runs throughout *Dorian Gray*, of course, with the portrait serving as the reflection Dorian learns to love, and Sibyl Vane playing the role of Echo, with her powerless sorrow. It is precisely because the portrait acts as a mirror, a supposedly objective reflection of the real, that it gains the power to inculcate narcissism and idolatry. At the end of chapter 8, Dorian explicitly evokes the parallel between himself and Narcissus, recalling that "Once, in boyish mockery of Narcissus, he had kissed, or feigned to kiss, those painted lips that now smiled so cruelly at him," and he draws out the analogy by referring to the portrait as "the most magical of mirrors" (*CW*, 88). Sibyl Vane's kinship with Echo is underscored when, after Dorian's fatal rejection of her, Dorian remembers her as pure voice, a voice at odds with Harry's more polished satanic one:

And her voice—I never heard such a voice. It was very low at first, with deep, mellow notes, that seemed to fall singly upon one's ear. Then it became a little louder, and sounded like a flute or a distant hautbois. In the garden scene it had all the tremulous ecstasy that one hears just before dawn when nightingales are singing. There were moments, later on, when it had the wild passion of violets. You know how a voice can stir one. Your voice and the voice of Sibyl Vane are two things that I shall never forget. When I close my eyes, I hear them, and each of them says something different. I don't know which to follow. (*CW*, 51)

Wilde hammers home the ugly consequences of Dorian's narcissism not only via the changing portrait, but also through Dorian's own complaint to Lord Henry: "'I wish I could love,' cried Dorian Gray, with a deep note of pathos in his voice. 'But I seem to have lost the passion, and forgotten the desire. I am too much concentrated on myself.'" (*CW*, 154)

4. When Wilde uses the term "sorrow" to encompass all the myriad instances of pain and injustice in the lives of others that he confesses to have taken too lightly, it should be understood that he sees sorrow as the emotional equivalent of ugliness. Interestingly, the worship of beauty is linguistically related to gaiety, since most scholars believe that the word "gay" derives from an Old High German word meaning "pretty" (*OED*). Wilde is implicitly indicting himself for an overattention to physical beauty and for an overindulgence in the gaiety and slackness beauty inspires.

5. Written by Harry Adams and composed by E. Jonghmans. Quoted in H. Montgomery Hyde, ed., *The Annotated Oscar Wilde: Poems, Fiction, Plays, Lectures, Essays, and Letters* (New York: Clarkson N. Potter, 1982), 372. Hereafter cited as *AOW*. Wilde's name was also transformed in a way that played on his obscurity and his exile; in *Punch* he was portrayed as "Oscuro Wildgoose." Cited by Frank Harris, 58. Also included along with other parodies of Wilde in Walter Hamilton, *Parodies of the Works of English and American Authors*, vol. 6 (London: Reeves and Turner, 1889), 82.

6. See also the cartoon of Wilde in *Punch,* 25 June 1881, with the following verse caption:

Aesthete of aesthetes,
    What's in a name?
The poet is Wilde
    But his poetry's tame.

Vyvyan Holland, Wilde's son, quotes an article in the *Tribune* that described Wilde's American lecture tour and the way Wilde's image was picked up for advertising purposes in the West. It describes a typical newspaper ad by a clothing dealer, which once again suggests that Wilde is a "tame" beast (here an ass) and a figure of fun, while evoking homosexual overtones: "Wild Oscar, the Ass-thete, buys his clothes of our establishment." Holland, *Oscar Wilde* (London: Thames and Hudson, 1960; rev. ed. 1966), 36.

7. Wilde was initially arrested on 5 April 1895, formally indicted on 25 April, and found guilty on 25 May of seven counts of gross indecency with other male persons, under section 11 of the Criminal Law Amendment Act (which had only been in force for ten years). See Cohen, *Talk on the Wilde Side,* 91–92, 175–76. James Joyce, whose character of Humphrey Chimpden Earwicker in *Finnegans Wake* is partly based on Wilde, plays on the rather arbitrary appeal to such an act as punishment for an "indecency" that Joyce depicts as universal in I, iii. Sylvia Silence, lisping girl detective, tells a reporter, "Have you evew thought, wepowtew, that sheew gweatness was his twadgedy? Nevewtheless accowding to my considewed attitudes fow this act he should pay the full penalty, pending puwsuance, as pew Subsec. 32, section 11, of the C.L.A. act 1885, anything in this act to the contwawy notwithstanding" (*FW,* 61.6–11).

8. Interestingly, Wilde has been variously associated with both Bunthorne, the fleshly poet, and Grosvenor, the idyllic poet, which provides a capsule illustration of the difficulty of dissociating the idyllic and the sensual in the aesthetic movement. Walter Hamilton, in *The Aesthetic Movement in England* (1882), identifies Bunthorne with Swinburne and Grosvenor with Wilde, although Bunthorne has been more generally associated with Wilde (along with Rossetti and Whistler) since that time. See Walter W. Nelson's discussion of the parodies of Oscar Wilde in *Oscar Wilde from Ravenna to Salomé: A Survey of Contemporary English Criticism* (Dublin: Dublin University Press, 1987), chapter 1.

9. Wilde's American lecture tour, under the auspices of Richard D'Oyly Carte (the producer of *Patience*), took place in 1882, whereas his meeting with Robert Ross, who according to Hyde "initiated Wilde into homosexuality," was 1886 (*Oscar Wilde,* 120). Ed Cohen argues that effeminacy was not associated with homosexuality at the time when *Patience* was presented, but that the association resulted from newspaper accounts of Wilde's trial (136).

10. Wilde's determination to invert the habitual hierarchy of values is also apparent in his description of the philosophy of *The Importance of Being Earnest* in an interview for the *St. James Gazette:* "That we should treat all the trivial things of life very seriously, and all the serious things of life with sincere and studied triviality" (quoted in Hyde, *Oscar Wilde: A Biography,* 177).

11. See, for example, the argument against journalism advanced in "The Soul of Man under Socialism," which suggests that by giving the public information about the private life of a great statesman, journalists invite the public to judge the morality of his behavior, to exercise an inappropriate authority in the matter. (It is likely

that this particular example was prompted by the case of Parnell, which was being debated at the time the essay was written.) Implicitly, journalism encourages the public to conflate the personal with the professional, individual conduct with the capacity to design creative and effective policy (*A as C*, 276–77).

12. This point is emphatically underscored at the end of *Lady Windermere's Fan*, when Lord Windermere calls his wife an innocent child and she vehemently protests his presupposition that people exist in "pure" categories: "Don't say that, Arthur. There is the same world for all of us, and good and evil, sin and innocence, go through it hand in hand. To shut one's eyes to half of life that one may live securely is as though one blinded oneself that one might walk with more safety in a land of pit and precipice" (*CW*, 429). Although Wilde is careful to stress the mingling of good and evil within every individual, I am arguing that he fails to take equal account of the structural inequities of the social system, inequities that cannot be explained in terms of good and evil, but which nevertheless limit one's capacity for associating with others on a free and equal basis.

13. Wilde's emphasis on the distinction between (free) thought and (limited) action helps to explain his insistence that the sphere of art is irreconcilably different from the sphere of ethics; he sees the former as an extension of thought, the latter as pertaining to action. In his first letter to the editor of the *St. James Gazette* in defense of *Dorian Gray* (25 June 1890), he makes this clear by arguing that the figure of Mrs. Grundy, arbiter of middle-class values, grew out of the popular confusion between art and ethics (thought and action) (*A as C*, 237–38). See also "The Critic as Artist," II, in which Gilbert asserts the difference between art and ethics in terms of the incompatibility of thought and action: "all the arts are immoral, except those baser forms of sensual or didactic art that seek to excite to action of evil or of good. For action of every kind belongs to the sphere of ethics. The aim of art is simply to create a mood" (*A as C*, 385). Gilbert goes on to extol the importance and rarity of "anything approaching the free play of the mind" later in the dialogue (*A as C*, 406), and in *A Woman of No Importance*, Lord Illingworth affirms that "All thought is immoral" (*CW*, 464).

14. Jules Laforgue, in his ironic retelling of the story of Salomé in *Moralités Legendaires* (composed in 1887), which Wilde knew, presents Salomé as an enemy of the individual, exhorting her audience of princes and court-officers, "O Sectarians of consciousness, why label yourselves individuals—indivisible, that is to say?" *Moral Tales*, trans. William Jay Smith (1956; New York: New Directions, 1985), 105. Salomé's disdain for the view that we are indivisible/individual implicitly authorizes her request for Iokanaan's head.

15. Oscar Wilde, *Salomé*, ed. Pascal Aquien, illus. Aubrey Beardsley; with English version by Lord Alfred Douglas (Paris: Flammarion, 1993), 56. All further citations will be noted parenthetically in the text.

16. See Ed Cohen's related argument in *Talk on the Wilde Side* that in the newspaper accounts of Wilde's trial, Wilde's use of paradoxical, playful language became one of the signs of his "immorality" (136–37).

17. Interestingly, the man who introduced Wilde to Lord Alfred Douglas (and Yeats to Olivia Shakespear) was also a Pigot: Lionel Pigot Johnson.

18. Joyce highlights the ironic contrast between the public's attitudes toward Edward VII and Parnell in "Ivy Day in the Committee Room." See also the comment by Wilde's friend Frank Harris that "sexual perversion is a 'Jacob's Ladder' to most forms of success in our time in London"; Harris points out that most successful men in Wilde's situation were allowed to escape to France (64).

19. Robert Sherard, *Oscar Wilde: The Story of an Unhappy Friendship* (1905; New York: Haskell House, 1970), 156. Sherard also relates that when Wilde was released from prison on bail and staggered to his brother's house, his brother described him as having come "like a hunted stag" (155).

20. Published in part in 1905; complete version (which includes a highly personal indictment of Douglas's behavior toward Wilde), published in 1960.

21. This sacral dimension comes out in the comparison of both men to Christ, as the prototype of a "savior" who is denied by *both* Jews and Romans. Wilde's mother, Lady Wilde, was one of many who regarded Parnell as the predestined savior of Ireland (Harris, *OW*, 49); Joyce, too, portrayed him as a Christ figure undersold to the enemy by his disciples. Joyce's "Ivy Day in the Committee Room" ends with a poem by Hynes depicting Parnell as a slain Christ, and the tag attributed to Parnell that runs throughout *Finnegans Wake*—"When you sell, get my price"—expresses Parnell's fear not only that his countrymen will betray him for money, but that they will sell him cheap. To some extent Wilde preempts comparisons of himself with Christ by making the comparison himself in *De Profundis*, but others do take up the strain. Harris compares Sir John Bridge, the magistrate who refused bail for Wilde, to Pilate (249), and he casts Wilde's lifelong interest in the Man of Sorrows as uncannily prophetic (146, 79–81).

22. Edward Carson was not only Irish, but he was also a Unionist who was later known for his formidable opposition to home rule and his determination to exclude Ulster from inclusion in any home rule bill. See R. F. Foster, *Modern Ireland 1600–1972* (New York: Penguin, 1988), 465.

23. See Joseph Valente's comparison of the downfall of Mrs. Kearney in Joyce's "A Mother" with that of Parnell for a relevant complication of the dynamics of Parnell's "crime." In chapter 2 of *James Joyce and the Problem of Justice: Negotiating Sexual and Colonial Difference* (Cambridge: Cambridge University Press, 1995), Valente argues that Parnell violated the separation of public and private spheres, and in so doing allowed the "male" sphere of political negotiation to be marked by the "female" world of private intrigue. Parnell's followers perceived this as a betrayal, and responded by feminizing him, which had the effect of discrediting his leadership.

24. See Wilde's "Pen, Pencil and Poison: A Study in Green" in *Intentions*, a wry appreciation of the forger and poisoner Thomas Griffiths Wainewright, and *Finnegans Wake*, in which the figure of the writer, Shem the Penman, is vilified as a forger.

25. Quoted in Charles Norman, *The Genteel Murderer* (New York: Macmillan, 1956), 44.

26. Gedeon Spilett, *Gil Blas*, 22 November 1897, quoted by Gary Schmidgall, *The Stranger Wilde: Interpreting Oscar* (New York: Dutton, 1994), 40.

27. For a more detailed, biographical account of Wilde's experience of and attitudes toward Ireland, see Davis Coakley, *Oscar Wilde: The Importance of Being Irish* (Dublin: Town House, 1994).

28. The Young Ireland group was an offshoot of Daniel O'Connell's movement to repeal the Act of Union (effective 1801) between England and Ireland that had abolished the Irish parliament. Increasingly critical of O'Connell for avoiding open confrontation with England, the Young Irelanders disseminated a strong nationalist rhetoric, promoting the romance of revolution and of violent resistance. The beginning of the famine in 1846 added fuel to the separatist feeling. The unrest culminated in William Smith O'Brien's failed uprising in Tipperary in July 1848, for

which he was sentenced to death (the sentence was later commuted to transportation). It is notable that, in his San Francisco lecture on "The Irish Poets of '48," Wilde identifies Smith O'Brien as "[t]he earliest hero of my childhood" (Hyde, *AOW*, 374). See Foster, *Modern Ireland*, 310–17.

29. Quoted in Terence de Vere White, *The Parents of Oscar Wilde* (London: Hodder and Stoughton, 1967), 87.

30. Terence de Vere White disputes the heroism of her demeanor, suggesting that she tried to speak during the trial, but was silenced by the police (108–109). Interestingly, it was Isaac Butt who defended Duffy; Butt would later represent Mary Travers in her libel suit against Lady Wilde, who had accused Travers of alleging that she had been taken advantage of by Sir William Wilde.

31. Quoted by Hyde, 74. It is interesting to note that Wilde's oversimplified view of the South's position in the Civil War as that of an oppressed colony, which prompted him to associate the South with Ireland, takes no account of the issue of slavery, which he would unequivocally condemn in "The Soul of Man under Socialism": "Human slavery is wrong, insecure, and demoralizing" (*A as C*, 269).

32. Wilde's love of "ignorance" and "irrationality" is apparent both in *De Profundis* and in his essays. In all his criticism, Wilde represents the conscious life as unnaturally restricted, which makes it both inadequate and unreal; as a corrective to the hegemony of reason, he proposes art as the main vehicle through which the secrets of the unconscious may be dimly apprehended. In "The Portrait of Mr. W. H.," he argues, "It was we who were unreal, and our conscious life was the least important part of our development. The soul, the secret soul, was the only reality" (*A as C*, 211) and "[i]t is Art, and Art only, that reveals us to ourselves" (*A as C*, 209).

33. According to Robert Sherard, the affectation of feminine attributes was a characteristic of Wilde's early aesthetic phase. He claims in *Oscar Wilde: The Story of an Unhappy Friendship* (1905; New York: Haskell House Publishers, 1970), that by the time Wilde was twenty-eight, "His affectation of effeminacy, the keynote of his first period, had been thrown aside" (21).

34. Wilde's dandyish dress began, literally, as a costume, which he wore when he went to a fancy-dress ball as Prince Rupert during his last term at Oxford (Hyde, *OW*, 46).

Vsevelod Meyerhold played up the importance of sexual ambiguity in Wilde by casting a woman, Varvara Yanova, as Dorian in his 1915 film of *Dorian Gray* (he played Lord Henry himself). See Hyde, *Annotated OW*, 178.

35. The "Comtesse" de Brémont was, at least for a time, a member of the Order of the Golden Dawn and would invite Yeats to her flat for coffee. Her advances apparently became more obvious; see R. F. Foster, *Yeats: A Life*, I: *The Apprentice Mage, 1865–1914* (New York: Oxford University Press, 1997), 105.

36. Robert Hitchens seized on this detail for the title of a thinly disguised novel about Wilde and Lord Alfred Douglas, *The Green Carnation* (published anonymously in 1894).

37. As Rupert Hart-Davis notes in his edition of the *Selected Letters of Oscar Wilde* (New York: Oxford University Press, 1979), Wilde insisted on the nobility and purity of homosexual love, which he refers to as Uranian love. Hart-Davis explains, "The word was apparently first used in this sense by the Austrian writer Karl Heinrich Ulrichs (1825–1895). It was derived from the Greek Uranos (Heaven) in the belief that such love was of a higher order than ordinary love, and referred to Plato's *Symposium* (181 C)" (327, n. 2). I am grateful to Chaim Potok for providing me with this reference.

38. If Frank Harris is to be believed, when he and Wilde were summering together in the south of France after Wilde's release from prison, Wilde told him that girls had once impressed him in much the same way as boys, and for the same reason (youth's combination of sexual ambiguity with sexual immaturity).

See also the "The Burden of Itys," with its reference to Salmacis,

Who is not boy nor girl and yet is both,
   Fed by two fires and unsatisfied
Through their excess, each passion being loth
   For love's own sake to leave the other's side
Yet killing love by staying . . .
(CW, 739)

39. Lord Goring formulates the same idea more humorously when he explains his appreciation for stupidity: "There is more to be said for stupidity than people imagine. Personally, I have a great admiration for stupidity. It is a sort of fellow-feeling, I suppose" (CW, 505).

40. An Ideal Husband dramatically stages the Triumph of Love, the theme of the French tapestry that hangs on the staircase wall, while exposing the falsity of ideals, especially the idealized views that the Chilterns have of each other. In Lady Windermere's Fan, it is not idealization but judgmental contempt that is revealed as a self-serving, artificial construction, as Lady Windermere is forced to reevaluate her disdain for Mrs. Erlynne when she comes to the brink of duplicating Mrs. Erlynne's error and discovers Mrs. Erlynne's readiness to sacrifice her reputation again to save her daughter's. In A Woman of No Importance, it is Hester who learns to be more flexible and charitable in her judgments of "fallen" women.

41. In "The Star-Child," too, the beautiful eponymous hero (like the young king) must learn to accept rather than deny his kinship with the poor and the ugly, at great cost to himself.

42. Teleny, the anonymous erotic novel published in 1893 (the same year that Salomé was published) that has been attributed to Wilde among others, although never definitively, was published by Leonard Smithers (who later published The Ballad of Reading Gaol). Charles Hirsch, owner of a London bookshop (who published a French translation of Teleny in 1934), claims that Wilde brought him the manuscript, wrapped and sealed, to deliver to a friend. After the manuscript had gone back and forth several times, poorly sealed, Hirsch opened it and read it. Noting the different handwritings, he concluded, "It was evident to me that several writers of unequal merit had collaborated on this anonymous but profoundly interesting work." John McRae, ed., Introduction, Teleny (London: GMP, 1986), 9.

I have chosen to discuss the novel, despite the uncertain attribution, on the grounds that it provides rare insight into the attitudes of Wilde's homosexual circle; moreover, with the exception of the sexual explicitness, many elements of Teleny harmonize with the rest of Wilde's corpus, especially The Picture of Dorian Gray and "The Harlot's House." It is interesting, too, that Des Grieux receives a card threatening to brand him as a sodomite two years before Wilde would receive Queensberry's card, and Des Grieux is both prostrated and sickened by "the horrible, infamous, anonymous threat, in all its crude harshness. . . . What was I to do? To be proclaimed a sodomite in the face of the world, or to give up the man who was dearer to me than my life itself? No, death was preferable to either" (T, 132–33).

43. That Wilde was familiar with the use of "fan" to mean a winnowing basket is clear from his admiration for Baudelaire's poem "La Charogne," in which the poet

compares the sound made by the maggots in a carcass to "le grain qu'un vanneur d'un mouvement rhythmique / Agité et tourné dans son van" ("the rattle of chaff the winnower / loosens in his fan"). Charles Baudelaire, *Les Fleurs du Mal*, trans. Richard Howard (Boston: David R. Godine, 1982), 213 and 36. Sherard identifies "La Charogne" as one of Wilde's favorite poems from *Les Fleurs du Mal*; see Sherard, *OW*, 46–47.

44. Critical self-awareness is crucial to the process of constantly translating and transforming language. As Wilde shows in "The Remarkable Rocket" (*The Happy Prince and Other Tales*), verbal cleverness can be as self-serving as any other form of interpretation. The remarkable rocket uses his cleverness to hide from reality; he boasts, "I have imagination, for I never think of things as they really are" (*AOW*, 120). When he has fizzled out and is dismissed as a bad rocket and an old stick, he molds the plasticity of language to his own advantage, transforming these epithets into "grand rocket" and "gold stick." With impressive articulateness and ludicrous hauteur, the rocket goes out in full denial of his own insignificance: "I knew I should create a great sensation."

45. Stephen delivers a similar charge to Buck Mulligan in *Ulysses*, when he sends him a telegram defining a sentimentalist: "The sentimentalist is he who would enjoy without incurring the immense debtorship for a thing done." Both Wilde and Joyce are echoing Meredith's *Ordeal of Richard Feverel*.

46. I am grateful to Jean-Michel Rabaté for pointing this out.

47. That in Wilde's view true individualism is not possible without social change is apparent from *The Picture of Dorian Gray*. Lord Henry preaches to Dorian the doctrine of individualism:

'There is no such thing as a good influence, Mr. Gray. All influence is immoral—immoral from the scientific point of view.'
'Why?'
'Because to influence a person is to give him one's own soul. He does not think his natural thoughts or burn with his natural passions. His virtues are not real to him. His sins, if there are such things as sins, are borrowed. He becomes an echo of someone else's music, an actor of a part that has not been written for him. The aim of life is self-development.' (*CW*, 28–29)

In the current social system, Dorian's heedless pursuit of self-realization is monstrous.

48. In view of what happened to Wilde, it is important to consider the counterargument that some degree of nonstereotyped representation is essential, especially when a given activity is dismissed as "unspeakable." Sodomy is a good example of a "sin" designated as unrepresentable except through identification with a people or place (Sodom). Because a precise definition of sodomy was forbidden, it had to be defined through its representatives. This is what happened to Wilde in the course of his trials; his name became a cipher for undescribable sexual practices and, at the same time, for the danger attending them. In short, his name and case were used, quite literally, to "characterize" secret sins and their consequences.

49. When the actor-manager Herbert Beerbohm Tree complimented Wilde on the plot of *A Woman of No Importance*, Wilde replied, "Plots are tedious. Anyone can invent them. Life is full of them. Indeed one has to elbow one's way through them as they crowd across one's path" (Hyde, *OW*, 146).

50. Vyvyan Holland recounts an incident when Wilde made a similar assertion. At a dinner in Paris, Emile Zola, who had assumed that Wilde could not reply to him

in French, announced: "Unfortunately, Mr. Wilde will be obliged to reply in his own barbarous language." Wilde responded in French, "I am Irish by birth and English by adoption so that I am condemned, as Monsieur Zola says, to speak in the language of Shakespeare" (Holland, *OW*, 43).

51. It is interesting to note that the term "buggery," for example, originally denoted not a specific practice but the name of a foreign people (as "sodomy" did), so that the condemnation of buggery is at the same time a form of xenophobia. According to the *OED*, "buggery" is a corruption of *Bulgarus*, a Bulgarian, and refers to a sect of heretics from Bulgaria "to whom abominable practices were ascribed"; it also refers to usurers. Therefore, any practice, whether economic, sexual, or religious, that differed from the socially dominant ones could be stigmatized as "buggery." The association of buggery with foreignness is also apparent in a famous jurist's commentary on it: Sir Edward Coke's *Third Part of the Institutes of the Laws of England* (written during the first two decades of the seventeenth century). Coke emphasizes that *bugeria* is an Italian word and *paederastes* a Greek one, accusing "the Lumbards" [sic] of having "brought into the realm the shamefull sin of sodomy, that is not to be named, as there it is said." Cited by Cohen, *Talk on the Wilde Side*, 106. See also Cohen's fascinatingly detailed account of the changing consequences of sodomy, as its punishment moved slowly out of the ecclesiastical domain into the "moral" one policed by law, in chapter 4, "Legislating the Norm: From 'Sodomy' to 'Gross Indecency.'"

52. Like his constructions of criticism and nationality, Wilde's aesthetics were also predicated on the beauty and truth of adulteration, in this case the adulteration of different arts. When Wilde landed in New York in January 1882, he defined aesthetics to a reporter by saying, "Aestheticism is a sort of correlation of all the arts" (Hyde, *OW*, 51). The idea that aesthetics involves a cross-fertilization—or hybridization—of diverse art forms is repeated in "Pen, Pencil and Poison," where Wilde writes that "In a very ugly and sensible age, the arts borrow, not from life, but from each other" (*A as C*, 330).

53. Wilde's resistant view of conventional dressing, his insistence that it is affected rather than "natural," is articulated in "The Soul of Man Under Socialism," where he argues,

> A man is called affected, now-a-days, if he dresses as he likes to dress. But in doing that he is acting in a perfectly natural manner. Affectation, in such matters, consists in dressing according to the views of one's neighbour. . . . Unselfishness recognises infinite variety of type as a delightful thing, accepts it, acquiesces in it, enjoys it. It is not selfish to think for oneself. A man who does not think for himself does not think at all. It is grossly selfish to require of one's neighbour that he should think in the same way, and hold the same opinions. (*A as C*, 285)

54. Wilde's shunning of sorrow may also reflect a reaction against Celtic myth and legend, "where the loveliness of the world is shown through a mist of tears" (*De Profundis, CW*, 924), especially his mother's version of Celtic myth. In a review of Yeats's *Fairy and Folk Tales* in *Woman's World* (February 1889), he quotes Yeats's appreciation of the sorrowful quality of Lady Wilde's treatment of the Celt: "The humour has all given way to pathos and tenderness. We have here the innermost heart of the Celt in the moments he has grown to love through years of persecution, when, cushioning himself about with dreams, and hearing fairy songs in the twi-

light, he ponders on the soul and on the dead. Here is the Celt, only it is the Celt dreaming" (*A as C*, 131).

55. One of the main problems Wilde encountered in trying to restore a Greek ethics of sexual conduct was with the definition of sexuality itself: to what extent is it expressive and personal, and thereby resistant to control, and to what extent does it constitute action, subject to restriction? Wilde, like the courts, seems to have determined that sexuality becomes subject to regulation when it hurts others. In *Teleny*, Des Grieux's interlocutor asks if Des Grieux considered sodomy a crime, and Des Grieux answers, "No; had I done society any harm by it?" (*T*, 133). The determination of whether one has harmed others hinges on the issue of consent, and on the capacity of the partner to understand the full implications of consent. Wilde's own sexuality was deemed criminal precisely because his partners were not considered his equals, either in class, age, or intelligence; as the *Evening Standard* reported on 4 April, "in not one of these cases were the parties upon an equality with Wilde in any way" (quoted in Cohen, 166). Unequal advantages signified to the court insufficient agency, and Wilde was therefore castigated for having corrupted and contaminated a group of people who had no defense against his "superiority."

The counterargument to this view is that it is inexcusably condescending to the working classes; such an argument unquestionably accepts the superiority of wealth, education, and experience, constructing them as irresistible to a group of people who may in fact hold different values. Wilde's position throughout was that he did not assume his own superiority relative to his partners, that he felt he could learn from them, that he found their perceptions less mediated by tradition and convention. Although the differences in class and education are relatively easy to account for, the most troubling category of difference is the difference in age. It is harder to determine, especially after the intervention of a hundred years, the extent to which Wilde's preference for boys may have constituted abuse, and to what extent youths were considered autonomous agents (who were often responsible for earning their own living at an early age). It is also unclear to what extent Wilde appreciated and respected differences in age, class, and education, and to what extent he may have fetishized them.

56. It is intriguing to note that in this early play, only patriarchal authority is reviled; the authority of the mother is, in contrast, associated with the abused land. Vera apostrophizes Liberty as a crucified mother: "O mighty mother of eternal time, thy robe is purple with the blood of those who have died for thee! Thy throne is the Calvary of the people, thy crown the crown of thorns. O crucified mother, the despot has driven a nail through thy right hand, and the tyrant through thy left! Thy feet are pierced with their iron" (*CW*, 681). By the time Wilde writes *The Picture of Dorian Gray*, he has become much more suspicious of maternal authority, the power of which he associates not with crucifixion, but with idolatry.

57. Stanislaus claims that he suggested the title, and that it was inspired by his reading of Henry James's *The Portrait of a Lady*, but the odd disposition of articles in Joyce's phrase—*a* portrait of *the* artist—intimates that although Stanislaus may have suggested the metaphor of portraiture, the actual title subtly recalls another portrait, this one by a fellow Irishman, the picture of Dorian Gray. In *The Picture of Dorian Gray*, Wilde uses the same locution that Joyce would later adopt, although here the disposition of the articles reads more naturally. The painter Basil Hallward, explaining to Lord Henry Wotton why he is reluctant to exhibit his picture of Dorian Gray publicly, avers that "every portrait that is painted with feeling is a portrait of

the artist, not of the sitter. The sitter is merely the accident, the occasion. It is not he who is revealed by the painter; it is rather the painter who, on the colored canvas, reveals himself." In the preface to *Dorian Gray*, however, Wilde offers a view of art that trumps Basil's; he proclaims that "It is the spectator, and not life, that art really mirrors." By alluding to *Dorian Gray* in his title, Joyce suggests both that his novel is autobiographical (a portrait of the artist), and that it isn't; that it is, on the surface, a self-portrait, but that below the surface it is a mirror (which is also what Dorian's portrait is for Basil). And as Wilde warns in his preface, "Those who go beneath the surface do so at their peril."

58. Seminar of 21 January 1975, from the third issue of *Ornicar?* In *Feminine Sexuality: Jacques Lacan and the école freudienne*, ed. Juliet Mitchell and Jacqueline Rose, trans. Jacqueline Rose (New York: Norton, 1982), 167. Lacan here is speaking of perversion as a tendency apparent in "normal" fathers, not as a clinical category. My understanding of Lacan has been immeasurably enriched by lively and contentious discussions with the members of our Lacan study group: Deborah Luepnitz, Patricia Gherovici, Nick Miller, and Jean-Michel Rabaté, as well as by more spontaneous discussions with Joseph Valente. Of course, responsibility for errors and idiosyncrasies is mine alone.

59. See "God and the *Jouissance* of the Woman," chapter 6 of Seminar XX, *Encore* (Lacan, 1972–73), in *Feminine Sexuality*, Mitchell and Rose, 138–48, in which Lacan argues that to make up for the fact that there is no sexual relation, we introduce a third party into the love affair, an ideal woman who doesn't exist, whose function as an ideal, an all, makes her a vicereine for God.

60. Lacan makes a similar point more obliquely when he writes the French equivalent of "one loves" (*on aime*) as "*on âme*" (one soul[s]). He insists that "there is no sex in the affair. Sex does not count." This primarily male ethic is "outside sex" (*hors-sexe*). See "A Love Letter" (*"Une Lettre d'Âmour"*) in *Feminine Sexuality*, 155.

61. I do not mean to suggest either that *women* inevitably suffocate their children or that *men* abandon them. There is no necessary relation between women, mothers, and immersion, on the one hand, and men, fathers, and perversion on the other; what I am describing is not a natural or biological tendency, but one that is rooted in society's polarization of the social roles of father and mother.

62. Eve Kosofsky Sedgwick, *Between Men: English Literature and Male Homosocial Desire* (New York: Columbia University Press, 1985), 5.

63. Sedgwick's analysis is supported, from another angle, by Suzanne Pharr's emphasis on the "interconnectedness of all oppressions": "It is virtually impossible to view one oppression, such as sexism or homophobia, in isolation because they are all connected: sexism, racism, homophobia, classism, ableism, anti-Semitism, ageism. They are linked by a common origin—economic power and control—and by common methods of limiting, controlling and destroying lives." One of the elements common to all oppressions is "a *defined norm*, a standard of rightness and often righteousness wherein all others are judged in relation to it. This norm must be backed up with institutional power, economic power, and both institutional and individual violence." See *Homophobia: A Weapon of Sexism* (Inverness, Calif.: Chardon Press, 1988), xii, 53.

64. *The Seminar of Jacques Lacan, Book I: Freud's Papers on Technique 1953–1954*, ed. Jacques-Alain Miller, trans. John Forrester (1975; New York: Norton, 1988), 222. All subsequent references will be made parenthetically in the text as Seminar I.

65. See Suzanne Pharr's contention that "in a world without homophobia, there will be no gender roles," *Homophobia: A Weapon of Sexism*, 7.

66. The sexual overtones of the verb "to peach" are apparent again in *Finnegans Wake*, where the two sexually enticing "jinnies" are also referred to as "peaches"; see *FW*, 57.4, 65.26. 113.17, 251.24.

67. The implications of this argument should not be read as an endorsement of sexual conduct between mothers and children (or between fathers and children). Wilde insists that it is imperative "to recognize the essential difference between art and life," about which, Wilde points out, many readers are "in a perfectly hopeless confusion" (*A as C*, 243). Wilde's position is curiously close to that of St. Stephen, the first Christian martyr, after whom Joyce named Stephen Dedalus. St. Stephen was stoned to death for accusing his hearers of being "uncircumcised in heart and mind, like your fathers before you." Both Wilde and Joyce write in the tradition of St. Stephen, urging their readers to remove the "foreskin" of habit that covers their hearts and minds, but not to do away with appropriate restraints on action.

68. *The Picture of Dorian Gray: Authoritative Texts, Backgrounds, Reviews and Reactions, Criticism*, ed. Donald L. Lawler (New York: Norton, 1988), 176. Hereafter cited parenthetically in the text as *DG*.

69. On another level, Wilde suggests that as Dorian—translated into art—has the capacity to mirror Basil, exposing the corruption that shadows his desire for perfection, so Wilde's book (another artistic mediation) has the capacity to mirror the reader. In a famous letter to the editor of the *Scots Observer* (9 July 1890), Wilde claims that "Each man sees his own sin in Dorian Gray. What Dorian Gray's sins are no one knows. He who finds them has brought them" (*A as C*, 248). Wilde's claim supports his assertion in the preface that "It is the spectator, not life, that art really mirrors."

70. What Dorian says to Basil anticipates what Wilde's blackmailer, a man named Clyburn who worked with Allen, will later say to him after Clyburn has given him back the compromising letter that he had written to Lord Alfred Douglas. Wilde gave Clyburn half a sovereign and Wilde said, "I am afraid you are leading a wonderfully wicked life." Clyburn replied, "There is good and bad in every one of us." Wilde told him he was a born philosopher. From a newspaper account of the first trial, London *Times*, 5 April 1895, quoted in Cohen, *Talk on the Wilde Side*, 157.

3   "Horrible Splendour of Desire"

1. Yeats also believed that Wilde wielded these weapons incomparably well; in an 1891 review in the Boston *Pilot*, Yeats refers to Wilde as "the wittiest Irishman of our day" (*Collected Works of W. B. Yeats*, vii, *LNI*, 48).

2. His review appeared in the *United Ireland*, 26 Sept. 1891; *Uncollected Prose of W. B. Yeats*, ed. John P. Frayne, vol. 1: First Reviews and Articles 1886–1896 (New York: Columbia University Press, 1970), 202–205. Hereafter cited parenthetically in the text as *UP*.

3. In *The Autobiography of W. B. Yeats* (cited parenthetically in text as *A*) (1916; New York: Collier Macmillan, 1965), Yeats repeatedly refers to Wilde as "a man of action" (93, 189), and in his *Memoirs*, ed. Denis Donoghue (cited hereafter as *Mem*) (New York: Macmillan, 1972), he confesses that he never cared "greatly for anything in his writings but the wit—it was the man I admired, who was to show so much courage and who was so loyal to the intellect" (22).

4. See also Yeats's 1933 preface to *Letters to the New Island*, ed. Bornstein and Witemeyer: "Gradually I overcame my shyness a little, though I am still struggling

with it and cannot free myself from the belief that it comes from lack of courage, that the problem is not artistic but moral" (5).

5. See the *Autobiography* (*The Trembling of the Veil*), where Yeats asserts that Wilde's father was "a friend or acquaintance of my father's father" (*A*, 92). Yeats discusses the stories that grew up around Wilde's parents, who were "famous people"—dirty, untidy, daring, but also imaginative and learned—and he focuses on Lady Wilde's longing, "certainly amid much self-mockery, for some impossible splendour of character and circumstance" (*A*, 92). Yeats's play, *The Hour-Glass* (1914; prose version 1903), was based on a story recorded by Lady Wilde in *Ancient Legends of Ireland* (*Variorum Plays*, 640). Hereafter cited as *VPL*.

6. See the *Autobiography* (*The Tragic Generation*), 188–93, for an account of the actual difficulty Yeats had in believing the charges against Wilde might be true. He records his inability to discern in Wilde the "voluminous tenderness" of the sensualist, pointing instead to Wilde's "hard brilliance" and "dominating self-possession" (189).

7. In *The Tragic Generation*, Yeats comments upon the almost universal tendency not to take Wilde seriously: "one took all his words for play—had he not called insincerity 'a mere multiplication of the personality' or some such words?" (189). One of the best illustrations of the dynamic complexity of Yeats's use of symbols within and (by implication) across volumes is John Unterecker's *A Reader's Guide to William Butler Yeats*, although it is now almost forty years old.

8. Yeats also tried to reclaim one of his favorite English poets, William Blake, for the Irish: "William Blake, as we call him, was, before all things, an O'Neil. . . . The very manner of Blake's writing has an Irish flavour, a lofty extravagance of invention and epithet, recalling the *Tain Bo Cuilane* and other old Irish epics, and his mythology brings often to mind the tumultuous vastness of the ancient tales of god and demon that have come to us from the dawn of mystic tradition in what may fairly be called his fatherland." See Yeats and Edwin John Ellis, eds., *The Works of William Blake: Poetic, Symbolic, and Critical* (London, 1893; reprint. AMS Press, 1973), 2–4, 142.

9. An example of the comprehensiveness of Yeats's poetic vision may be found in "To the Rose upon the Rood of Time," with its careful balancing of suffering and joy, mortality and eternity, the small and the great. The juxtaposition of the two poems that follow, "Fergus and the Druid" and "Cuchullain Fights with the Sea," counterpoints the futility of achieving knowledge and imagination, in the first poem, with the curse of successful heroic action, in the second.

10. In the first version of "The Book of the Great Dhoul and Hanrahan the Red" (from *The Secret Rose*), published as "The Devil's Book" in *The National Observer* on 26 November 1892, Yeats gives the name of the Hanrahan character as O'Sullivan the Red. Yeats notes that "O'Sullivan the Red was really a noted peasant-poet of the last century. His character was much as I have described it. The Gaelic poets were often thought to have a Lianaan Shee or Fairy-mistress. Cleona of Ton Cleona is the Queen of the Munster Fairies" (*VSR*, 197). Owen Hanrahan the Red is one of the three imaginative personae who dominate the stories in *The Secret Rose* (1897), along with Aedh and Michael Robartes. Yeats takes these characters and uses them along with Mongan "as principles of the mind" in the 1899 edition of *The Wind Among the Reeds*, in which they represent states of the imagination (see note to 1899 *WATR*, 73; he eliminates the characters from subsequent editions of the volume). Then, in 1905, he rewrites "The Stories of Red Hanrahan" with the help of Lady Gregory in an attempt to bring the style closer to folk idiom. He also replaces

the first story of the Hanrahan series in *The Secret Rose*, "The Book of the Great Dhoul and Hanrahan the Red," with a new story, "Red Hanrahan," and separates the Hanrahan stories from *The Secret Rose*.

11. Contrast Yeats's note in the 1899 *The Wind Among the Reeds*, where he interprets Hanrahan as representing "the simplicity of an imagination too changeable to gather permanent impressions" (73). This chameleon-like instability prevents real learning, and Hanrahan's imagination remains imprisoned by the vision that haunts and inspires it.

For a well-informed account of how Hanrahan fits into the tradition of Irish poetry and patriotism, see Elizabeth Butler Cullingford, *Gender and History in Yeats's Love Poetry*, especially "Thinking of Her as Ireland" (Cambridge: Cambridge University Press, 1993), 62–67. Cullingford persuasively reads Hanrahan's passivity before his vision of Echtge as his refusal of a sexual encounter that would bring him pleasure, power, courage and knowledge (the four treasures of ancient Ireland) (62–63).

12. See his 1904 letter to George Russell, in which he writes,

In my *Land of Heart's Desire*, and in some of my lyric verse of that time, there is an exaggeration of sentiment and sentimental beauty which I have come to think unmanly. . . . I have been fighting the prevailing decadence for years, and have just got it under foot in my own heart—it is sentiment and sentimental sadness, a womanish introspection.

The Letters of W. B. Yeats, ed. Allan Wade (New York: Farrar, Straus & Giroux, 1980), 434.

13. Daniel Corkery, *The Hidden Ireland: A Study of Gaelic Munster in the Eighteenth Century* (Dublin: M. H. Gill and Son, 1925), 128–29. See also Steven Putzel, *Reconstructing Yeats:* The Secret Rose *and* The Wind Among the Reeds (Dublin: Gill and Macmillan, 1986), 73–97, and Richard Finneran, "'Old Lecher with a Love on Every Wind': A Study of Yeats' *Stories of Red Hanrahan*," *Texas Studies in Language and Literature* 14 (1972): 347–58. The indebtedness of Hanrahan to Eoghan Ruadh Ó Súilleabháin was earlier pointed out by Thomas R. Whitaker, *Swan and Shadow: Yeats's Dialogue with History* (Chapel Hill: University of North Carolina Press, 1964), 165.

14. This may be partly because by the time O'Sullivan wrote, the Stuart hopes had been dashed. As Alan Harrison explains, in "Literature in Irish, 1600–1900," *The Field Day Anthology of Irish Writing*, vol.1, the poems of Eoghan Rua Ó Súilleabháin "are technically and verbally exquisite, but still express a forlorn hope in the Stuart rescuer who never came and who, by that time, never would come" (276).

15. See Corkery's account of Keating's elegy on John Fitzgerald, which centers around a vision of Cliodhna, 129. According to P. W. Joyce in *A Social History of Ancient Ireland*, vol. 1 (3d ed.; Dublin: M. H. Gill, 1920), tradition has it that Clidna "was a foreigner from Fairy-land, who, coming to Ireland, was drowned while sleeping on the strand at the harbour of Glandore in South Cork, in the absence of her husband" (263). The sea at this spot occasionally gives a melancholy roar that was formerly believed to foretell the death of a king in the South of Ireland; it has been called *Tonn-Cleena*, Cleena's wave.

16. See Ó Súilleabháin's poem and Thomas Kinsella's English translation of it in *The Field Day Anthology of Irish Writing*, ed. Seamus Deane with Andrew Carpenter and Jonathan Williams (Derry: Field Day Publications, 1991), vol. 1, 295–97. See also "Owen Roe O'Sullivan's Drinking Song" in vol. 2, 41–42. Steven Putzel sug-

gests that "The Curse of Hanrahan the Red" may have been inspired by another Ó Súilleabháin poem, "*An t-Arrachtach Sean*" ("The Aged Monster"); see *Reconstructing Yeats*: The Secret Rose *and* The Wind Among the Reeds (Dublin: Gill and Macmillan, 1986), 88.

17. Putzel, quoting Proinsias MacCana, *Celtic Mythology* (New York: Hamlyn, 1975), 120, suggests that Cleena is here the hag that is rejuvenated, a vision of the sovereignty of Ireland (Putzel, 97); Cullingford also reads Whinny as the Cailleac Beare (66). Although the overtones of a nationalist transformation are surely present, to see this scene as a purely triumphant one is to obscure Yeats's later awareness of the irony of Hanrahan's "success" in becoming pure spirit at the expense of a vibrant and connected life in the world.

18. Yeats's use of the Grail myth in these stories (which is here explicitly Celtic) anticipates Eliot's reliance on a similar quest-motif in *The Waste Land*.

19. *Blake* I, xii–xiii; Yeats repeats this claim in *E & I*, 137.

20. See, for example, his pairing of "Fergus and the Druid" with "Cuchullain's Fight with the Sea" in *The Rose* as poems that highlight the futility of living a life of pure imagination or a life of pure action, respectively.

21. In his introduction to *A Book of Irish Verse* (1896; rev. ed. London: Methuen, 1900), Yeats indicates that his preference for the lonely inner world runs counter to that of his countrymen. He writes, "The Irish Celt is sociable, as may be known from his proverb, 'Strife is better than loneliness'" (xvii). Yeats here clearly distinguishes between the orator who influences "men's acts" and the poet who shapes their emotions, and between writing of practical and political importance and that which has literary significance (xxi, xxiii). Finally, he explicitly differentiates between the inner man and the "outer man," suggesting that their relation to one another is antithetical: "the unearthly happiness which clouds the outer man with sorrow . . . is the fountain of impassioned art" (xxii). Finally, Yeats reveals that the main reason for his preference of imagination over action is one that was also expressed by Wilde: he sees the actor as "the slave of life," whereas the poet can be its master though his ability to "mould the world" (xxii, xxiii). Compare Wilde's contempt for the thoughtless and automatic conformity of those who live in the world versus those who dare individuality.

22. Compare Wilde's assertion that "[i]t is proper that limitations should be placed on action. It is not proper that limitations be placed on art" (*A as C*, 243). Art, like the world of the imagination, is predicated on spiritual, intellectual, and emotional freedom (although the mode of expression must be disciplined by style), whereas the world of action (or life) is ruled by law and bound by necessity.

23. William H. O'Donnell, "Newly Identified Chapters for *The Speckled Bird*, 1897–98 Version: 'The Lilies of the Lord,'" *Yeats Annual* No. 7, ed. Warwick Gould (London: Macmillan, 1990), 163.

24. Yeats writes in *The Tragic Generation*,

I had read *Axel* to myself or was still reading it, so slowly, and with so much difficulty, that certain passages had an exaggerated importance, while all remained so obscure that I could without much effort imagine that here at last was the Sacred Book I longed for. An Irish friend of mine lives in a house where beside a little old tower rises a great new Gothic hall and stair, and I have sometimes got him to extinguish all light but a little Roman lamp, and in that faint light and among great vague shadows, . . . have imagined myself partaking in some incredible romance. (*A*, 213–14)

25. He says, "We need not fear that it [the play] will affect the statistics of suicide, for the personages of great art are for the most part too vast, too remote, too splendid, for imitation. They are merely metaphors in that divine argument . . . about the ultimate truths of existence" (*UP*, 325).

26. Yeats, "The Happiest of the Poets," *Ideas of Good and Evil*, in *Essays and Introductions* (New York: Macmillan, 1961), 64.

27. Compare *John Sherman*, in which the conflict between responsibility and dream takes a slightly different, less fantastic form. In this tale of "very ordinary persons & events" (*CL1*, 268), John's "dream" world is the natural landscape of Sligo ("Ballah" in the story) where the woman he loves awaits him, in favorable contrast to the world of adult responsibility, which is here the urban (and English) world of work. In John's eyes, Ballah bade "him who loved [to] stay still and dream, and gave flying feet to him who imagined" (*JS*, 10). When John becomes a clerk at a firm of ship-builders in London and contemplates marriage with a money-conscious woman, he thinks, "He would have to give up the universe for a garden and three gardeners. How sad it was to make substantial even the best of his dreams. How hard it was to submit to that decree which compels every step we take in life to be a death in the imagination" (*JS*, 31).

28. In Yeats's note to "Baile and Aillinn" (1903), he tells how Etain, wife of a king of the *sidhe*, "when driven away by a jealous woman, took refuge once upon a time with Aengus in a house of glass, and there I have imagined her weaving harp-strings out of Aengus' hair. I have brought the harp-strings into 'The Shadowy Waters,' where I interpret the myth in my own way" (*VPL*, 188).

29. That Yeats connected the "calls" of nationalism, religion, and love—defining them all as the promise of immortality through self-sacrifice—is clear from a letter he sent to *The United Irishman* (5 May 1902) about *Cathleen ni Houlihan*: "My play, 'The Land of Heart's Desire,' was, in a sense, the call of the heart, the heart seeking its own dream; this play is the call of country, and I have a plan of following it up with a little play about the call of religion, and printing the three plays together some day" (*VPL*, 235).

30. Like Oscar Wilde, who in "The Ballad of Reading Gaol" proclaims the universality of the desire to kill the beloved object: "all men kill the thing they love, / By all let this be heard" (*CW*, 860).

31. The poem is spoken by Owen Hanrahan in "The Twisting of the Rope" (*The Secret Rose*, 1897, 145), but there Hanrahan mourns, "I never have seen Maid Quiet." In the 1899 version of *The Wind Among the Reeds*, the poem is titled "Hanrahan Laments Because of His Wanderings."

32. Yeats's desire to experience life's plenitude and to share the secret of the natural/supernatural world resembles that of the old man Angus in "The Heart of the Spring." Angus explains, "I longed for a life whose abundance would fill centuries, I scorned the life of fourscore winters. I would be—nay, I *will* be!—like the Ancient Gods of the land" (*SR*, 85).

Interestingly, Yeats seemed to believe that Maud Gonne was also, like himself, ascetic in her personal life, reserving her passion for her (nationalist) ideals. Knowing how Yeats viewed Gonne amplifies our sense of how catastrophic it must have been for him when Gonne told him in 1898 about her affair with Millevoye and her two illegitimate children. See Deirdre Toomey, "Labyrinths: Yeats and Maud Gonne," *Yeats Annual*, 9 (London: Macmillan, 1992), 95–131.

33. Yeats discusses his decision to group a section of poems under the heading "The Rose," dedicated to Lionel Johnson, in his preface to *Poems* (1895): "for in

them he has found, he believes, the only pathway whereon he can hope to see with his own eyes the Eternal Rose of Beauty and of Peace."

34. In "Symbolism and Painting" (1898), Yeats insists on the important difference between symbol and allegory, telling a German symbolist painter who avoided putting roses, lilies, or poppies into a picture because he thought these emblems allegorical, that

> the rose, the lily, and the poppy were . . . married, by their colour and their odour and their use, to love and purity and sleep, or to other symbols of love and purity and sleep, and had been so long a part of the imagination of the world, that a symbolist might use them to help out his meaning without becoming an allegorist. (*E & I*, 147)

35. Compare Wilde's version of this phenomenon in "The Nightingale and the Rose."

36. Patrick Weston Joyce argues in *A Social History of Ancient Ireland*, vol. 1, that many of the Irish tales "correspond with tales in the ancient Romantic Literature of Greece and the East," citing as his main example the similarity between Adonis and Dermot O'Dyna (of Dermot and Grania), both "being distinguished for beauty, and both being killed by a boar. Even their names O'Dyna (Irish *O'Duibne*) and *Adonis* look as if they had come from the same original" (532). He argues that such corresponding tales must have originated centuries before the Christian era, before the separation of the races.

37. It is the idealization of the female sexual organs that sometimes makes them unrecognizable as such. Peter Alderson Smith, in *W. B. Yeats and the Tribes of Danu: Three Views of Ireland's Fairies* (Gerrards Cross: Colin Smythe, 1987), objects strongly: "To say that the Rose symbolises 'the female generative organs' is surely to betray the limitations of Freudian criticism" (176).

38. Charles Singleton, in his commentary on Dante's *Paradiso*, cites some of the instances in which Christ was identified with the rose, including Albertus Magnus, *De laud. b. Mariae Virginis*: "'Et nota, quod Christus rosa, Maria rosa, Ecclesia rosa, fidelis anima rosa.' ['And note that Christ is a rose, Mary is a rose, the Church is a rose, the faithful soul is a rose.']" Dante's *Divine Comedy*, trans. Charles S. Singleton, *Paradiso* (Princeton: Princeton University Press, Bollingen Series, 1975), 511.

39. See Cantos XXX–XXXIII of the *Paradiso*, in which Beatrice leads Dante into the yellow of the eternal rose ["Nel giallo de la rosa sempiterna"] before taking her own place in the roseate city of God. Dante is then shown "the saintly host" in the form of "a pure white rose . . . which with His own blood Christ made His bride" (Canto XXXI, ll. 1–3); Dante, too, draws on the tradition that the white rose is stained red by the blood of a dying god, here Christ. According to John Unterecker, in *A Reader's Guide to William Butler Yeats* (New York: Noonday Press, 1959), "as a young man [Yeats] deliberately extended the symbol [of the Rose] still further by frequently quoting Count Goblet D'Alviella's identification of rose and sun and *later* was pleased to discover Dante's image of Heaven as a white rose with a sun-like yellow center" (76).

40. Walter Pater, *The Renaissance*, 1873. Yeats significantly chose this passage, typeset as poetry, as the first entry in his *Oxford Book of Modern Verse, 1892–1935* (Oxford: Clarendon, 1936). He also echoes this passage in the description of John Sherman's "love . . . of the imagination" for Miss Leland in *John Sherman*:

continually there came through her wild words the sound of the mysterious flutes and viols of that unconscious nature which dwells so much nearer to woman than to man. How often do we not endow the beautiful and candid with depth and mystery not their own? We do not know that we but hear in their voices those flutes and viols playing to us of the alluring secret of the world. (*CWY*, XII, 30)

41. Introduction, *Petrarch's Lyric Poems: The* Rime sparse *and Other Lyrics*, trans. and ed. Robert M. Durling (Cambridge: Harvard University Press, 1976), 27.

42. Se mai candide rose con vermiglie
in vasel d'oro vider gli occhi miei
allor allor da vergine man colte,
veder pensaro il viso di colei
ch'avanza tutte l'altre meraviglie.
(*Rime sparse*, poem 127, 252–53)

43. et le rose vermiglie infra la neve
mover da *l'ora*,

. . . .

e tutto quel per che nel viver breve
non rincresco a me stesso, anzi mi glorio
d'esser servato a la stagion più tarda.
(269, my emphasis)

44. In his 1902 essay "The Happiest of the Poets," Yeats indicates that the emotion expressed by the blooming of the cross is one of reconciliation, forgiveness, the integration of extremes. Speaking of William Morris, he calls him "one of the greatest of those who prepare the last reconciliation when the Cross shall blossom with roses" (*E & I*, 64).

45. In "Poetry and Tradition" (1907), Yeats uses the crucified rose more openly as a symbol of art, arguing that "the nobleness of the arts is in the mingling of contraries, the extremity of sorrow, the extremity of joy, perfection of personality, the perfection of its surrender, overflowing turbulent energy, and marmorean stillness; and its red rose opens at the meeting of the two beams of the cross, and at the trysting place of mortal and immortal, time and eternity" (*E & I*, 255).

Moreover, in "Where There Is Nothing, There is God," Yeats describes the more pagan aspects of the Rose of artistic inspiration. The poet Cumhal confesses that the loneliness of his wanderings has been increased "because I heard in my heart the rustling of the rose-bordered dress of her who is more subtle than Angus, the Subtle-Hearted, and more full of the beauty of laughter than Conan the Bald, and more full of the wisdom of tears than White-Breasted Deirdre, and more lovely than a bursting dawn to them that are lost in the darkness" (*SR*, 50–51).

46. The beauty of Ireland is also celebrated in Yeats's superb revision of the ending of *"The Dedication to a Book of Stories Selected from the Irish Novelists"* in 1925:

Gay bells or sad, they bring you memories
Of half-forgotten innocent old places:
We and our bitterness have left no traces
On Munster grass and Connemara skies.
(*VP*, 130)

47. Yeats points out the relation of the Rose to the sun in a footnote to *The Wind Among the Reeds* (*VP*, 811).

48. Ellmann, *Yeats: The Man and the Masks*, 67. Given this history, it is easy to imagine Yeats's delight when, in his painful and laborious reading of the French *Axël*, he came to the part in which Sara tells Axel, "How happy I am to see that . . . the phantom of a dying flower interests you" (163). Yeats had also gone to see a five-hour production of *Axël* with Maud Gonne in Paris in 1894. See Foster's account in *W. B. Yeats: A Life*, 139–40.

49. Anna Seward, *The Symbolic Rose*, 100, gives the date of the initiation as 1893, as does Ellmann in *Yeats: The Man and the Masks* (New York: Macmillan, 1948), 93. The ritual is recorded in Israel Regardie, *The Golden Dawn*, vol. 2 (Chicago: The Aries Press, 1937), 198–244. See also Ellmann's chapter on "Michael Robartes and the Golden Dawn" in *The Man and the Masks*, especially the account of how Yeats was asked to meditate upon the Rose. Ellmann remarks that "the exact meaning of [the Rose] was hard to determine, though it signified mainly the flower of love that blossoms from the cross of sacrifice" (94).

50. H. P. Blavatsky, *The Secret Doctrine: The Synthesis of Science, Religion, and Philosophy*, 2 vols. (London: Theosophical Publishing Company, 1888): vol. 1, 358, 472; vol. 2, 467, 544. Blavatsky's references to Jennings are not, as a rule, approving ones; she describes his book *Phallicism* as "evilly inspired" (2, 544). See Hargrave Jennings, *The Rosicrucians: Their Rites and Mysteries* (London: Routledge, 3d ed., 1887).

51. If Jennings's bias is Celtic and sexual, Blavatsky's is eastern and metaphysical. Such differences in emphasis help to explain where Rosicrucians and theosophists diverge at the end of the nineteenth century.

52. See P. W. Joyce, *A Social History of Ancient Ireland*, 1, 288–93, for the elemental worship common among the Celts in the ninth and tenth centuries.

The Rosicrucian philosophy received a blast of publicity with the publication of Alexander Pope's *The Rape of the Lock*, which used Rosicrucian spirits proper to the four elements as part of its mock-epic machinery: sylphs, salamanders, gnomes, and daemons. Pope refers readers who wish to learn more about the Rosicrucians to a pamphlet supposedly published by the Abbot de Villars in 1670 called *The Count de Gabalis: Being a Diverting History of the Rosicrucian Society of Spirits, viz. Sylphs, Salamanders, Gnomes, and Daemons: Shewing their Various Influence upon Human Bodies*; the English edition is said to be occasioned by *The Rape of the Lock* and is dedicated to Pope (1670; London: Lintott and E. Curll, 1714).

53. See P. W. Joyce, *Social History*, 1, 289–92 on Irish fire worship.

54. See the analysis of the swan image in the ancient Irish heroic tales by Alwyn and Brinley Rees in *Celtic Heritage: Ancient Tradition in Ireland and Wales* (London: Thames and Hudson, 1961), 236: "the form of a swan—perhaps because it is that of a creature of land, water and air, a creature whose milieu has no boundaries—is appropriate for communication *between* two worlds." They relate that Irish poets had cloaks of bird feathers (like shamans in Siberia and North America), presumably for excursions to the world beyond.

55. The reversibility of opposites is emphasized in Yeats's esoteric motto, "Demon Est Deus Inversus" (Foster, *WBY*, 104). Jennings, when discussing the apparent opposition of natural and supernatural, light and darkness, argues that they are "mistaken by man for opposites, although they are the same": "[One] is only the reversed side of the other." Moreover, we cannot be certain which side is which, because of the deceptiveness of our perceptions: we may think we are living in a world

of light, but in fact be living in darkness, and what we take for darkness may well be a state of light (221).

56. In modern Irish, according to *Foclóir Póca*, *rúsc* means "bark," such as the bark of a tree.

57. That Yeats was aware of this symbolism is apparent from his long footnote about the symbolism of the Rose in the 1899 edition of *The Wind Among the Reeds*, 74–78. With reference to "Aedh Pleads with the Elemental Powers," "Mongan Thinks of his Past Greatness," and "Aedh Hears the Cry of the Sedge," the note explains the Rose as an ancient sun symbol; it stresses its traditional association with the Virgin Mary, its relation to the constellations, and its history as a mythological and patriotic symbol of Ireland.

58. T. W. Rolleston, in *Celtic Myths and Legends* (1911, rev. ed. 1917; reprint New York: Dover, 1990), explains the connection between the Grail (with its "talismanic power" to promote "increase, wealth, and rejuvenation") and the cauldron of the Dagda, also a "talisman of abundance and rejuvenation in Celtic myth." He argues that the cauldron more remotely represents the sun, "a golden vessel which pours forth light and heat and fertility," and traces its transformation into the cup of the Eucharist (409–412).

In *Scattering Branches: Tributes to the Memory of W. B. Yeats*, ed. Stephen Gwynn (New York: Macmillan, 1940), Maud Gonne recalls the dream she shared with Yeats of building a Castle of the Heroes, "decorated only with the Four Jewels of the Tuatha Dé Danaan": "The Four Jewels, as Willie explained, are universal symbols appearing in debased form on the Tarot, the divining cards of the Egyptians and even on our own playing cards, and foreshadowed the Christian symbolism of the Saint Grail, whose legends Willie loved to trace to Ireland" (23).

Gonne goes on to relate that according to Yeats, the Lia Fail (the Stone of Destiny) corresponded to the altar, which even when made of wood should have a stone embedded in it; the cauldron with the chalice or Grail cup; the golden spear of Lugh the sun god with the lance that pierced the side of Christ; the Sword of Light with the cross-handled sword of the Crusaders (knights of the Grail) (24).

Jennings argues that the grail is a vase that is green, because it is made of emerald (420–21). This would support Yeats's sense that the grail legends are rooted in Ireland.

59. Jennings also proposes a reading of the *motto* of the Order, *Honi soit qui mal y pense!* as 'YONI' *soit qui mal y pense!* (178), and he argues that the Latin words from which "garter" is derived "mean *not* a 'garter' but breeches, drawers, or trousers'" (326).

60. In addition to Yeats's review of the production in *UP* I, 320–25, see Arthur Symons's discussion of Villiers in *The Symbolist Movement in Literature*, dedicated to Yeats (1899; rev. ed. New York: Dutton, 1919), 21–32.

61. It is interesting to compare Sara's rapturous paean to the roses of Spain (one in her sequence of dream-mirages near the end of *Axël*) with the end of Molly Bloom's soliloquy in Joyce's *Ulysses*. Sara's monologue shifts direction: "Or suppose we visited the red Spains! Oh! it must be sad and marvelous at the palaces of Granada, the Generalife, the rose-laurel groves of the Cadiz of Andalusia, the woods of Pamplona where there are so many lemon trees that the stars seen through their foliage seem like flowers of gold! . . . The sea, O my beloved, I want the limitless sea!" (163–64, 166). Molly, in much the same tone of ecstatic and despairing longing, exclaims, "I love flowers Id love to have the whole place swimming in roses" (*U*, 18.1557–58), and after skipping through countries with the same imaginative

agility as Sara, returns to the waters and flowers of Spain, "O and the sea the sea crimson sometimes like fire and the glorious sunsets and the figtrees in the Alameda gardens yes and all the queer little streets and the pink and blue and yellow houses and the rosegardens and the jessamine and geraniums and cactuses and Gibraltar as a girl where I was a Flower of the mountain yes when I put the rose in my hair like the Andalusian girls used . . ." (U, 18.1598–1603)

62. Yeats does not always see himself as successful in conjoining the Rose and the Cross, however. In a poem called "A Song of the Rosy Cross" that he chose not to include in his cluster of Rose poems, he writes:

> . . . he who measures gain and loss
> When he gave to thee the Rose
> Gave to me alone the Cross.

Quoted in "'To a Sister of the Cross & the Rose': An Unpublished Early Poem," George Bornstein and Warwick Gould, in *Yeats Studies Annual 7* (London: Macmillan, 1990), 181.

63. Yeats returns to the image of the crucified rose in the context of nationalist sacrifice in "The Rose Tree," where the cross has become a tree watered by the blood of Irish martyrs, especially Padraic Pearse and James Connolly (*VP*, 396). Perhaps the overtly Christian symbolism of the Easter Rising legitimated a return to the image of blood and cross, which the martyrdoms of Pearse, Connolly, and the other rebels had unambiguously reclaimed for nationalism.

64. Despite Yeats's vaunted disdain for "cosmopolitan" as opposed to national literature, "The Rose" *is* cosmopolitan; although the Irish surface of the image is highly glossed, the roots are medieval Italian (Dante), German (Rosicrucian), and French (Guillaume de Lorris and Jean de Meun's *Romance of the Rose*), and Romantic (Blake and Shelley). On Yeats's use of Shelley's concept of intellectual beauty, see George Bornstein, *Yeats and Shelley*, Chicago: Chicago University Press, 1970), 49–54.

A reviewer of *The Secret Rose* faults Yeats not only for his arcane sources, but also for his fashionable imitation of archaic subjects, comparing his overindulgence in introspection to that of Dante Rossetti, Tennyson in "Idylls of the King," and Arnold in his Hellenic mode. Moreover, the anonymous reviewer faults Yeats for what he calls an absence of "the right local coloring." He argues that although "[w]e have abundant local feeling in his names . . . and properly unintelligible Celticisms . . . for all that we can seldom identify in his pictures the marks either of place or time." Unsigned review, "The Illusion of Mystery," *The Athenaeum*, 22 May 1897; in *W. B. Yeats: The Critical Heritage*, ed. A. Norman Jeffares (London: Routledge, 1977), 96–97.

65. Angela Carter, *The Bloody Chamber* (New York: Penguin, 1979), 93–108. In *Nights at the Circus*, Carter addresses the misogyny of Rosicrucianism directly, by having the figure of Rosenkreutz try to stage a sacrifice of the feminine, which he sees as trying to drag his "winged penis" downward to a female abyss. Carter's engagement with the legacy of Yeats is also apparent in her early novel, *The Magic Toyshop*, in which a wicked puppetmaker forces the female protagonist to play the role of Leda in his restaging of Leda's rape by the swan.

66. In some versions of Sleeping Beauty, such as Basile Pentamerone's "Sun, Moon, and Talia" and an Irish version called "The Queen of Tubber Tintye," Sleeping Beauty is impregnated while she sleeps. In Pentamerone's version, Talia is only awakened when one of her children sucks on her finger, accidentally removing the

splinter that caused her to sleep, and in the Irish version the Queen wakes up to find herself with a six-year-old son.

67. Carter again depicts the rose as deadly in her retelling of "Snow White" as "The Snow Child" in *The Bloody Chamber*. The Snow Child materializes in the snow as the child of the Count's desire—stark naked—and he gradually and magically clothes her with the Countess's own furs and boots as the Countess tries to get rid of her. In a last, desperate effort to destroy the Snow Child who is inadvertently stealing her privileges, her defenses, and her husband's love, the Countess asks the child to pick a rose for her. The rose pricks the child, she dies, and the Count deflowers the dead girl. All that is left of her is the rose and a bloodstain on the snow. The Count offers the rose to the Countess and she lets it fall, explaining, "It bites." That rose is not only beauty but also female sexuality—the sexuality that the Count both does and does not desire (his aversion to female sexuality is exposed by the fact that his desire is not for a woman but for a child).

68. *Wildish Things: An Anthology of New Irish Women's Writing*, ed. Ailbhe Smyth (Dublin: Attic Press, 1989), 8.

69. *Pillars of the House: An Anthology of Verse by Irish Women from 1690 to the Present*, ed. A. A. Kelly (Dublin: Wolfhound Press, 1987), 134.

70. The strength of the imperative to maintain an idealized vision of Irish womanhood is apparent in the otherwise bizarre controversy over Yeats's play *The Countess Cathleen* and later in the riots that erupted over the use of the word "shifts" in Synge's drama *The Playboy of the Western World*.

71. *Bitter Harvest: An Anthology of Contemporary Irish Verse*, ed. John Montague (New York: Charles Scribner's Sons, 1989), 145.

72. Medbh McGuckian, *On Ballycastle Beach* (Winston-Salem, N. C.: Wake Forest University Press, 1988), 26.

73. Medbh McGuckian, *Marconi's Cottage* (Winston-Salem, N.C.: Wake Forest University Press, 1991), 59–61.

74. In the translation, "The Shan Van Vocht" by Ciaran Carson. Nuala Ní Dhomhnaill, *Pharaoh's Daughter* (rev. ed.; Winston-Salem, N.C.: Wake Forest University Press, 1993), 131.

75. The closeness in conception of *The Secret Rose* and *The Wind Among the Reeds* is apparent in the fact that three of the four personages in the 1899 *Wind Among the Reeds*—Aedh, Michael Robartes, and Owen Hanrahan—were taken from *The Secret Rose*, and the title poem of *The Secret Rose* is included among the poems in *The Wind Among the Reeds*.

76. "Rosa Alchemica" is particularly emphatic about the importance of ancient polytheism for the poet or dreamer. Christ is represented as one god among many, and Mary, "the mother of the god of humility," is described as holding "in her hand the rose whose every petal is a god" (*SR*, 235). During the ceremony of initiation, the narrator observes "a pale Christ on a pale cross" in the midst of a floor of green stone and asks Michael Robartes its meaning. Robartes answers, "To trouble His unity with their multitudinous feet" (*SR*, 257). Christianity is included in the specifically Irish occult system that Yeats here designs, but Christ is resituated as one god among many.

The climax of "Rosa Alchemica" poetically reenacts the experience of inspiration, so that the narrator feels the terror and exhilaration of "great imponderable beings" sweeping through his mind (*SR*, 240). The narrator is taught that "all minds are constantly giving birth to such beings," who are "what men call the moods" (*SR*, 252): all great events are accomplished by "a mood, a divinity or a demon, first descending like a faint sigh into men's minds and then changing their thoughts and actions" (*SR*, 253). The experience of inspiration is so intense that the narrator dreams he is just a mask that various divinities try on their faces in an Eastern shop (*SR*, 255). The final rose-shaped dance, where mortals dance with immortals "until all the winds of the world seemed to have awakened under our feet" (*SR*, 258), and the rhythm sets the spirit free and the mortals' eyes reveal "the brightness of uttermost desire" (*SR*, 259), is described as an almost unendurable ecstasy. The terror of such inspiration is emphasized when the narrator feels that the immortal beside him was drinking up his soul and he faints, and again later when he carries a rosary around his neck to protect him from the "many voices of exultation and lamentation" (*SR*, 261, 264).

77. It is generally agreed that Michael Robartes was based on MacGregor Mathers, Owen Aherne on Lionel Johnson, and Red Hanrahan on the eighteenth-century poet and rake Owen Roe O'Sullivan (Eoghan Rua Ó'Súilleabháin). See Michael J. Sidnell, "Mr. Yeats, Michael Robartes, and Their Circle," Warwick Gould, "'Lionel Johnson comes the first to mind': Sources for Owen Aherne," and Laurence W. Fennelly, "W. B. Yeats and S. L. MacGregor Mathers," in *Yeats and the Occult*, ed. George Mills Harper (New York: Macmillan, 1975), 225–306.

78. The interdependence of the foolish, powerless lover-poet and the image of bodily perfection who is his antiself and counterpart is also the theme of "The Cap and Bells" in *The Wind Among the Reeds*, and Yeats returns to it many years later in *The King of the Great Clock Tower* (1934). In the 1934 version of the play, the king tells his queen, who is looking at the decapitated head of the stranger who claimed to love her, "Dance! Dance! If you are nothing to him but an image, a body in his head, he is nothing to you but a head without a body. What is the good of a lover without a body? Dance! (*VPl*, 1002). As the Queen dances, the dead lips begin to sing, as they did in "The Binding of the Hair": "Images ride . . . / Out of the grave."

79. "I will arise and go now, for always night and day / I hear lake water lapping with low sounds by the shore; / While I stand on the roadway, or on the pavements grey, / I hear it in the deep heart's core." A related later treatment of the heart as a lake may be found in George Moore's novel, *The Lake*, in the first (1905) edition of which the beloved was named "Rose." See Moore, *The Lake*, afterword by Richard Cave (Gerrards Cross: Colin Smythe, 1980), esp. 241–58.

In *The Wind Among the Reeds*, it is worth noting how many poems are addressed to or concerned with the heart: "To His Heart, Bidding it Have no Fear" (originally "The Windle-Straws / II. Out of the Old days," packaged with "O'Sullivan Rua to the Curlew" as part I); "The Lover tells of the Rose in his Heart"; "Into the Twilight"; "The Heart of the Woman"; "The Lover mourns for the Loss of Love"; "A Poet to his Beloved"; "He Gives His Beloved Certain Rhymes" ("I bade my heart build these poor rhymes . . . / You need but lift a pearl-pale hand, . . . / And all men's hearts must burn and beat"); "The Lover asks Forgiveness because of his Many Moods" (originally "The Twilight of Forgiveness," then "Michael Robartes Asks . . ."); "The Travail of Passion"; and "The Lover speaks to the Hearers of his Songs in Coming Days."

80. *The Metamorphoses of Ovid*, trans. Mary M. Innes (Harmondsworth: Penguin, 1955), 47–48. I am grateful to Lauren Richards for drawing my attention to this connection.

81. Ella Young, *Flowering Dusk: Things Remembered Accurately and Inaccurately* (New York: Longmans, 1945), 62.

82. *Scattering Branches: Tributes to the Memory of W. B. Yeats*, ed. Stephen Gwynn (New York: Macmillan, 1940), 20.

83. *A*, 131; in Gwynn, ed., *Scattering Branches*, Gonne uses "polytheism" instead of "mythology" in quoting this passage (21).

84. Although the *sidhe* are certainly associated with the wind, most people trace the *word* "sidhe" to "hillside." See Peter Berresford Ellis, *A Dictionary of Irish Mythology* (Oxford: Oxford University Press, 1991), 209.

85. It is interesting to note that Villiers de L'Isle-Adam uses the same metaphor in part III of *Axël*, where Axel refers to himself as a mere "reed of a single day" (*Axël*, 135).

86. The beautiful Edain was the second wife of Midhir, a king of the *sidhe*. Midhir's first wife was jealous and drove Edain away, whereupon she was taken in and cared for by Aengus, who took her wherever he went. As Lady Gregory recounts, "wherever they rested, he made a sunny house for her, and put sweet-smelling flowers in it, and he made invisible walls about it, that no one could see through and that could not be seen" (*Gods and Fighting Men*, 89), which Yeats calls the "tower of glass." Midhir's wife was jealous even of Edain's happiness with Aengus, so she changed Edain into a purple fly who was swept out of the house of glass by a blast of wind. For seven years Edain "was blown to and fro through Ireland in great misery" (Lady Gregory, *Gods*, 89). Aengus made a harp to communicate his sorrow to her as she flew through the winds.

87. W. B. Yeats, *The Wind Among the Reeds: Manuscript Materials*, ed. Carolyn Holdsworth (Ithaca: Cornell University Press, 1993), 99.

88. Joyce's *Chamber Music* is deeply indebted to *The Wind Among the Reeds*, which Joyce called "poetry of the highest order" ("The Day of the Rabblement," *CW*, 71). Like Yeats, whose early symbols are invariably symbols of the heart, Joyce addresses his "chamber music" to the chambers of the heart (although he also evokes several other kinds of chambers; see VI and XXIII, in particular). Again emulating Yeats in *The Wind Among the Reeds*, Joyce uses wind as the main corollary to music (there are fifteen references to wind alone, without counting the numerous references to air, sighs, and breath). The relationship between his poetry and air is much more explicit in Yeats's poems than in *Chamber Music*; in "Aedh Thinks of Those Who Have Spoken Evil of his Beloved," he challenges his beloved to resist the rumors that circulate about her with "this song": "I made it out of a mouthful of air, / Their children's children shall say they have lied." (Compare *Chamber Music* XIX: "Be not sad because all men / Prefer a lying clamour before you.") The russet hood of Maid Quiet in "Hanrahan Laments because of his Wanderings" is imported into XII to furnish the cowl of moon and Capuchin; the image of folk dancing "like a wave of the sea" from "The Fiddler of Dooney" informs the image of the "Winds of May, that dance on the sea, / Dancing a ring-around in glee" of *Chamber Music* IX, and the indebtedness of the plunging horses of XXXVI to the "Shadowy Horses" of "Michael Robartes Bids his Beloved Be at Peace," who also "plunge" in the heavy clay, has frequently been noted. Yeats's repeated imprecations to his beloved to "loosen your hair" ("Aedh Thinks of Those Who Have Spoken Evil of his Beloved") is echoed in XI, where Joyce's speaker tells his beloved "softly to undo the snood / That is the sign of maidenhood."

William York Tindall long ago indicated that many of the poems in *Chamber Music* echoed *The Wind Among the Reeds* in local ways, but the correspondences between *Chamber Music* and *The Wind Among the Reeds* go far beyond the official record of what Joyce owes to Yeats. At the same time, a new assessment of Joyce's debt inspires an equally new appreciation of what differentiates his volume from that of his countryman. First, and most noticeably, Joyce pares down the cast of his volume to two unnamed lovers and one equally anonymous rival, which contrasts sharply with the characters of Aodh, Michael Robartes, Hanrahan, and Mongan, who represent varying states of mind in the 1899 version of *The Wind Among the Reeds*. Secondly, he severely restricts his use of color, paring away the crimson that for Yeats represents sensual passion in conventional contrast to the white purity of the spirit. The "Lilies of death-pale hope, [and] roses of passionate dream" ("The Travail of Passion") that Yeats imported from Tennyson via pre-Raphaelite art are conspicuously absent from *Chamber Music*, as is Yeats's energetic and excessive expectation of apocalypse. Joyce has reduced the scale of desire, placing it more simply between the hidden womb and narrow tomb, between alternate yearnings for light ("sunrise") and darkness, daydream, and nightmare.

89. Donald R. Pearce, "The Systematic Rose," *Yeats Studies Annual*, No. 4, ed. Warwick Gould (London: Macmillan, 1986), 195–200.

90. Michael Robartes tells the story of his adoration of a ballet dancer "who had not an idea in her head" in "Stories of Michael Robartes and his Friends," *A Vision* (New York: Macmillan, 1965), 37–38. Robartes relates that "I adored in body what I hated in will," and as a result he kept trying to change the dancer, and in the process his judgmental tendencies threatened to behead himself: "judgement is a Judith and drives steel into what has stirred its flesh."

91. In a note to "Parting" (*The Winding Stair*) Yeats also suggests that he associates the love of women with darkness, which gives it an erotic as well as a destructive dimension: "I have symbolised a woman's love as the struggle of the darkness to keep the sun from rising from its earthly bed" (*VP*, 830). See also David R. Clark, ed., *The Winding Stair (1929): Manuscript Materials*, (Ithaca: Cornell University Press, 1995), xxiv.

92. Cited by Richard Ellmann, *The Identity of Yeats*, 147.

93. For an extended treatment of Yeats's fascist tendencies in the 1930s, see "The Blueshirt Episode and its Background" in Paul Scott Stanfield, *Yeats and Politics in the 1930s* (New York: St. Martin's, 1988), 40–77, and Elizabeth Cullingford, *Yeats, Ireland and Fascism* (New York: New York University Press, 1981).

4 Joyful Desire

1. Jacques Mercanton, "The Hours of James Joyce," in Willard Potts, ed., *Portraits of the Artist in Exile: Recollections of James Joyce by Europeans* (Seattle: University of Washington Press, 1979), 249.

2. See Margot Norris, "Not the Girl She Was at All: Women in 'The Dead'" in *James Joyce: The Dead*, ed. Daniel R. Schwarz (Boston: St. Martin's 1994), 190–205.

3. This argument is similar to the implied argument about etymology illustrated in the discussion of "status" earlier in the chapter. Meaning resides not only in the current usage of a term, but in the interplay between a word's current usage and its metaphorical root, an interplay that changes over time.

4. Despite the fact that Bloom is a Jew, or that—at least—his father was Jewish, he appears eager to tell the stereotypically anti-Semitic story of Reuben J. Dodd in "Hades." And Stephen, despite the fact that he has been befriended by a man whom he believes to be a Jew, sings him an anti-Semitic song in "Ithaca." See Mahaffey, "Male Refractions and Malefactions in 'Ithaca,'" *James Joyce: Engendered Perspectives*, ed. Kimberly Devlin and Marilyn Reizbaum (forthcoming, 1998).

5. For an account of the advertising campaign promoting *Giacomo Joyce* and its reception, see my "*Giacomo Joyce*," in *A Companion to Joyce Studies*, ed. Zack Bowen and James F. Carens (Westport, Conn.: Greenwood Press, 1984), 388–90.

6. Two important exceptions are Henriette Power, "Incorporating *Giacomo Joyce*," *James Joyce Quarterly* 28 (Spring 1991): 623–30, and Joseph Valente, "Dread Desire: Imperialist Abjection in *Giacomo Joyce*," in *James Joyce and the Problem of Justice: Negotiating Sexual and Colonial Difference* (Cambridge: Cambridge University Press, 1995), 67–131.

7. See Paul Wunderlich, *Giacomo Joyce: Vorzeichnungen zu der Mappe "Giacomo Joyce"* (Stuttgart, 1976). Hermann Lenz's essay "Wunderlichs Joyce" is included in this work.

8. Wunderlich was mobilized only a few weeks before the cessation of hostilities and was freed in Denmark without having fought. See Octave Négru, "La Mort et l'eros," *Paul Wunderlich* (Paris, 1979), 23.

9. Edouard Roditi, "Paul Wunderlich: An Introduction," in *Werk-Verzeichnis der Lithographien von 1949–1965*, ed. Dieter Brusberg (Hamburg, 1966), 120.

10. Wunderlich, whose name in German means "peculiar," "eccentric," "curious," "bizarre," and "fanciful," is best known as a technically brilliant lithographer, but he has also done work in oils and in sculpture, as well as collaborative work with his wife, the photographer Karin Székessy. He is often identified as a surrealist, although he has vehemently denied the appropriateness of the classification on several occasions. Alfred Werner, for example, compares him with the older German neosurrealists Hans Bellmer and Horst Janssen; see Alfred Werner, "Macabre Universe: Paul Wunderlich at Staempfli," *Arts* 44 (May 1970): 39–41. For Wunderlich's explanations of why he isn't a surrealist, see Négru, "La Mort et l'eros," 11. Heinz Spielmann writes that although the association of Wunderlich with surrealism is "understandable in view of the imagination and fantasy in his art, the work can be described just as well if not more accurately as an analysis of political involvement." Spielmann, "Paul Wunderlich," in *Contemporary Artists*, 3d. ed., ed. Colin Naylor (Chicago, 1989), 1039. See also Frank Whitford, "Paul Wunderlich: A Grand Dandy," *Studio* 175 (May 1968): 248–51; and Fritz J. Raddatz, "Der böse Blick des gläsernen Auges," *Paul Wunderlich und Karin Székessy: Correspondenzen* (Zurich, 1977).

11. See Lenz, "Wunderlichs Joyce": "Die herabfallende Lorgnette, die rechts unten zu sehen ist, weist auf viele angedeutete Brillen hin, die durcheinanderliegen wie auf den Brillenhaufen, die in den Konzentrationslagern gefunden wurden."

12. See the photo of *Der gelbe Stern*, 1960, reproduced in Raddatz, *Paul Wunderlich und Karin Székessy: Correspondenzen*, 23.

13. Compare Wunderlich's *Monster Traum*, in which a photograph of a nude woman on a desk/drawing table with a man sitting next to her (as in *Giacomo Joyce VIII*) has been altered, so that the man in Joyce's position wears the face of a monster (reproduced in Raddatz, *Paul Wunderlich und Karin Székessy: Correspondenzen*, 118).

14. Wunderlich seemed to develop this into *Vis à vis* (1978), in which Amalia and Wunderlich have changed places, and the Amalia figure has wings; the Wunderlich figure, in contrast, is represented as a skull with flash-cube eyes. Reproduced in exhibition catalogue, "Paul Wunderlich," Staempfli Gallery, New York, 31 March–2 May 1981, back cover.

15. Lenz, "Wunderlichs Joyce: Der Gesang Paul Wunderlichs an die Jüdin. Eine Totenklage."

16. Whitford, "Paul Wunderlich: A Grand Dandy," 249. Although Whitford does not identify his source, this passage seems to be a translation of something Wunderlich wrote in *Wegzeichen im Unbekannten* (*Road-Signs into the Unknown*) (Heidelberg, 1962), an extract from which is reprinted in Wunderlich, *Werk-Verzeichnis*, 130. I am grateful to David Herman for translating the extract.

17. She is also the model for Beatrice Justice in *Exiles* and seems to have influenced the figure of Issy in *Finnegans Wake* as well, especially in her relation to Shaun the Postman. According to Willard Potts, Joyce told Herbert Gorman to add this footnote to Gorman's discussion of the models for Molly Bloom: "There was also a second major model for Penelope, an Italian, much handsomer than her Dublin rival. Her correspondence during wartime passed through my hands. There was nothing political in it but I wonder what the Austrian censor thought of it. That did not perturb her." Potts, "Notes on the Gorman Biography," *ICarbS* 4 (Spring–Summer 1981):86. In a letter written in 1934 authorizing Popper's translation of *Dubliners*, Joyce alluded to having handled her letters during the war: "I would like to forget that I was also your postman!" Quoted by Michele Risolo, "Mia Moglie e Joyce," *Corriere della Sera*, 27 February 1969, 11.

Joyce refers once again to his role as Popper's postman, a role charged with erotic overtones, as in the children's game of "postman's knock" or "post office" (*FW*, 27.07, 430.9–10), through Shaun's function as postman in *Finnegans Wake*. As in Dion Boucicault's melodrama *Arrah-na-Pogue*, one of the many intertexts for *Finnegans Wake*, a political communiqué can be concealed in a kiss; the sexual and the political are oddly interchangeable codes. In III.1, Shaun, as the bearer of "these open letter," is asked to "Speak to us of Emailia" (*FW*, 410.23), where the spelling of "Amalia" is changed to accent the pun on "mail."

In his recent biography, *James Joyce: The Years of Growth, 1882–1915* (New York: Pantheon Books, 1992), Peter Costello briefly contests Richard Ellmann's identification of the figure in *Giacomo Joyce* with Popper by commenting that "even the evidence [Ellmann] adduces in support of his case undermines it; the dates simply do not fit" (p. 308). A footnote suggests that Costello has drawn his inference from "the devastating critique by Helen Barolini"—see "The Curious Case of Amalia Popper," *New York Review of Books*, 20 November 1969, 44–48. Further references will be cited parenthetically in the text as Barolini. In one sense, Costello is right; the dates of Joyce's tutelage of Popper do not coincide with the dates when parts of *Giacomo Joyce* were composed and written down: Joyce seems to have tutored her in 1908–09, and she moved to Florence in 1910, became engaged at Easter 1913, and was married in December 1914, whereas *Giacomo Joyce* seems to have been composed from 1911–14, with the final version completed in July or August 1914. For the arguments concerning the composition dates of *Giacomo Joyce*, see Ellmann, "Introduction," *GJ*, p. xvi.

What neither Ellmann nor Costello seems to have registered, though, is that Joyce continued to see the Popper family (frequently visited by Popper herself) from 1910 through World War I; more importantly, the Easter betrayal that forms the climactic turning-point of *Giacomo Joyce* (*GJ* 10) coincides with the date of Popper's engagement to Risolo (Easter 1913). In his private papers, Ellmann shows the same kind of uneasiness about the identification of Amalia Popper with the woman in *Giacomo Joyce* that Costello expresses, but he overcomes it at the insistence of Ottocaro Weiss and Stanislaus Joyce; however, he can never make the dates "fit" either, largely because of the gaps in his knowledge of Joyce's relation to the Popper family.

18. I am indebted to several people for their help in the preparation of this sec-

tion of the chapter. First and foremost I would like to thank Elisabetta Pellegrini Sayiner, who translated several articles, corresponded with Stelio Crise in Trieste, and obtained the address of Silvia Risolo in England. Her research assistance was invaluable. Patricia Chu and Jonathan Max Gilbert were very helpful in the early stages of the project.

19. See Valente, "Dread Desire," in *James Joyce and the Problem of Justice*.

20. Postscript to a letter from Risolo to Ellmann, 21 April 1968. Located in the Richard Ellmann Papers, Department of Special Collections, McFarlin Library, University of Tulsa. In an earlier letter, dated 24 November 1967, Risolo had written that the friendship between the Poppers and the Joyces grew out of the reciprocal liking between Leopoldo and James.

21. Bruno Cherslica, *È tornato Joyce: iconografia triestina per Zois*, con una prefazione di Giancarlo Vigorelli e un commentario di Stelio Crise (Milano: Nuova Rivista Europea, 1982), "Leopoldo Popper."

22. Silvia Risolo seems to be suggesting that her grandmother was a Sephardic Jew (from Spain and Portugal), rather than an Eastern European Ashkenazi. See Ira Nadel, *Joyce and the Jews* (London: Macmillan, 1989), 194, and especially the section on the Jewish community in Trieste, 198–207.

23. In "Una Nota," appended to the recent reprint of Popper's translation of *Araby* (Empoli: Ibiskos Editrice, 1991), Stelio Crise writes that the lessons began in October 1906, when Popper was only fifteen (95). Risolo's account is from a letter to Ellmann of 24 November 1967, located in the Richard Ellmann Papers at the University of Tulsa. In a response to an article in *L'Espresso* by Elio Chinol, "Casanova senza qualità" ("Casanova without qualities"), Risolo is more specific: he argues that Popper took lessons from Joyce for four months in 1908 and two months in 1909. Risolo's response was published one year later than his letter to Ellmann in *L'Espresso* (24 November 1968).

24. Response to "Casanova senza qualità," *L'Espresso* (24 November 1968), 3. Earlier, in a letter to Ellmann dated 21 April 1968, Risolo wrote that he and his wife met in late October.

25. The news of Popper's engagement to Risolo, coming as it did during the Easter holiday of 1913, may well have prompted the description of Giacomo's "passion" as he listens to *Tenebrae* and feels himself crucified. He describes his student beside him: "pale and chill, clothed with the shadows of the sindark nave, her thin elbow at my arm. Her flesh recalls the thrill of that raw mist-veiled morning, hurrying torches, cruel eyes. Her soul is sorrowful, trembles and would weep. Weep not for me, O daughter of Jerusalem!" (*Giacomo Joyce*, 10). The fact that this scene is set in Paris not only evokes the adulterous desire of the mythological Paris but also recalls the service Joyce attended at Notre Dame on April 10, 1903, a few hours before he learned his mother was dying. See Mahaffey, "*Giacomo Joyce*," 398–401.

26. Boito is known primarily for the libretti he wrote for Verdi—*Otello* and *Falstaff*—as well as the libretto for Ponchielli's *La Gioconda*. *Mefistofele* caused a riot when it was first performed at La Scala but later became very popular and influential. Boito had been influenced by Wagner's music dramas, and *Mefistofele* is credited with helping to introduce a new operatic style into Italy.

27. Roberto Curci, "Chi? Quella 'fiamma' triestina," *Il Piccolo* di Trieste, 13 January 1991.

28. It is interesting to note that Rainer Maria Rilke was also a resident of Trieste, his sojourn partly overlapping that of Joyce. He lived in the modern castle adjacent to the ruins of Duino, where he wrote the *Duino Elegies*. See Ellmann, *JJ* II, 195.

29. Curci, "Chi? Quella 'fiamma' triestina." See also Curci's recent book, *Tutto è sciolto: L'amore triestino di Giacomo Joyce* (Trieste: Edizioni LINT, 1996).

30. Helen Barolini, "The Curious Case of Amalia Popper," *New York Review of Books*, 20 November 1969, 46.

31. Richard Ellmann, response to Helen Barolini, *New York Review of Books*, 20 November 1969, 49.

32. Michele Risolo, quoted by Ellmann, ibid.

33. Ibid.

34. Most writers agree that it was Giorgio who made the corrections under his father's direction, since Joyce was suffering from one of his periods of blindness. Roberto Curci, following Bruno Cherslica, asserts that Joyce did *not* review the "Essential Biography," but neither Curci nor Cherslica gives evidence to support this claim, suggesting only that Joyce's involvement was "unlikely."

35. Letter from Risolo to Ellmann, 24 November 1967, Ellmann Papers, University of Tulsa.

36. Barolini, "The Curious Case," *NYRB*, 20 November 1969.

37. Letter from Risolo to Ellmann, 24 November 1967. It is tempting to speculate about the discrepancies in Risolo's accounts of the translation and publication process, especially since both of his conflicting versions are quite detailed. What the stories have in common is their insistence that his wife was merely a passive instrument in the process, which, of course, raises the question of whether she was quite so uninvolved and pliable as Risolo presents her as being.

38. Cherslica, *È tornato Joyce*, "Amalia Popper."

39. For a translation of the biography, see Mahaffey, "Fascism and Silence: The Coded History of Amalia Popper," *James Joyce Quarterly*, 32 (Spring/Summer 1995): 514–17.

40. Quoted by Curci, "Chi? Quella 'fiamma' triestina."

41. Published in *Letteratura*, Florence, vol. 5, no. 3 (July/September 1941): 3, 26–35 and vol. 5, no. 4 (October/December 1941): 23–35. Translated into English by Ellsworth Mason, *Recollections of James Joyce* (New York: The James Joyce Society, 1950).

42. Crise, "Una Nota," *Araby* (1991), 95.

43. Mary Colum, *Life and the Dream* (London: Macmillan, 1947), 383, cited by Ellmann, *JJ* II, 389. Joyce's opinion of Austria-Hungary had been somewhat different earlier, when he was living in Pola; on New Year's Eve 1904, he wrote to Mrs. William Murray, "I hate this Catholic country with its hundred races and thousand languages, governed by a parliament which can transact no business and sits for a week at the most and by the most physically corrupt royal house in Europe." *Letters* I, 57.

44. Alessandro Francini Bruni, *Joyce intimo spogliato in piazza*, translated and quoted by Ellmann, *JJ* II, 218. Interestingly, Joyce's socialist skepticism of patriotic fervor is remarkably close to that of Mussolini in his socialist phase. According to Denis Mack Smith, *Mussolini: A Biography* (New York: Random House, 1982), in 1910–12, when Mussolini was editing the socialist weekly *La Lotta di Classe* (The Class Struggle), "He thought it ridiculous to fight to win Trent and Trieste from the Austrians so long as most Italians were illiterate. Proletarians had no fatherland and should refuse to fight for purely patriotic reasons: 'the national flag is for us a rag to plant on a dunghill.'" (15). Mussolini's lack of patriotism became more emphatic in his condemnation of Italy's early war on Libya in 1911–12, when he argued that no socialist could be a patriot, because "we socialists are not Italians but

Europeans." He argued that patriotism inevitably grew into militarism, which was certainly true for the later *fascisti* (19). Mussolini gave up what by that time he was calling the "pretence" of socialism in 1918.

45. Letter from O. Weiss to Ellmann, 10 June 1967.

46. Stelio Crise, "Una Nota," *Araby* (1991), 97–99. According to Roberto Curci, Stanislaus said that "between the very young pupil and the bizarre teacher . . . a frail and ambiguous love sprung" ("Chi? Quella 'fiamma' triestina.") It is possible that not only Joyce, but also Stanislaus was attracted to Amalia Popper; in 1962, Ellmann wrote to Weiss that he had met a Triestine woman at Bread Loaf who had been a pupil of Joyce's. According to this woman, Amalia had named Stanislaus rather than James as the one who was interested in her. Weiss replied that he was certain Amalia was the person referred to in *Giacomo Joyce*. See letter from Ellmann to Weiss, 14 September 1962.

47. Crise, "Una Nota," *Araby*, 97–99. According to Ellmann, in a letter to Weiss dated 16 September 1967, Weiss had purchased the manuscript from Nellie Joyce at Ellmann's suggestion.

48. Ellmann Papers, box 10: *Giacomo Joyce* correspondence.

49. In the first edition of his biography, Ellmann denied in a footnote that Popper ever translated *Dubliners* (*JJ* I, 359 n.); he changed the note in *JJ* II (348n).

50. The meaning of this strangely coded communication via *Dubliners* changes, of course, if we see her as predominantly passive, with Joyce choosing the stories. Then the particular selection becomes a vehicle for him to convey certain interpretations of her past to *her*, none of them very complimentary.

51. Woolf's manuscript notes for a speech given before the London/National Society for Women's Service, 21 January 1931, printed in the appendix to *The Pargiters: The Novel-Essay Portion of* The Years, ed. Mitchell A. Leaska (New York: Harcourt Brace Jovanovich, 1977), 164.

52. Alwyn and Brinley Rees, *Celtic Heritage: Ancient Tradition in Ireland and Wales* (London: Thames and Hudson, 1961), 62. The discussion of the differences between the Ulster and Fenian cycles is based on the Rees's excellent account.

53. *James Joyce's Scribbledehobble: The Ur-Workbook for* Finnegans Wake, ed. Thomas E. Connolly (Evanston: Northwestern University Press, 1961), 86. This notation comes under the heading of "Telemachos."

54. The parallel between the Buckley episode and the Phoenix Park murders is strengthened by the resemblance between the Russian general and Nikolai Bobrikov, the governor general of Finland who was assassinated in 1904 in what Joyce saw as a kind of reprise of the Phoenix Park murders.

55. Joyce records a version of the often-denied love letter between males in III.3, 488.19–489.34, which he identifies as "That letter selfpenned to one's other, that neverperfect everplanned" (*FW*, 489.33–34). In this never-completed letter, the Shaunlike author confesses, "I wronged you . . . I am no scholar but I loved that man who has africot lupps with the moonshane in his profile, my shemblable! My freer!"

56. See also the reference to "History as *her* is harped" (*FW*, 486.6) (my emphasis), which rhythmically echoes "Storiella as she is syung" (*FW*, 267.7–8). "Storia" is "history" in Italian, although it suggests "story" or narrative fiction in English. The parallel between the two phrases about history in *Finnegans Wake* suggests not only a revisionary insistence on history as female, but also a view of history and story as having common roots in song (reading "syung" as "sung"—as well as "sighing," "lying" and "young").

57. Peter Berresford Ellis, *A Dictionary of Irish Mythology* (Oxford: Oxford University Press, 1991), 154.

58. W. B. Yeats, preface, in Lady Gregory, *Gods and Fighting Men: The Story of the Tuatha De Danaan and of the Fianna of Ireland* (1904; Gerrards Cross: Colin Smythe, 1970), 12.

59. The phrase is taken from Yeats's preface to Gregory's *Gods and Fighting Men*, where he talks of the fianna and their gods, whom we know "from fragments of mythology picked out with trouble from a fantastic history running backward to Adam and Eve" (16). Yeats explains the uncanny conjunction of myth and history in the tales of the fianna by arguing that medieval chroniclers confused the heroic kings of Tara with the half-divine kings of Almhuin (the Hill of Allen in Leinster, where Finn and the fianna lived). It is this confusion, he argues, that gives "the stories of the fianna, although the impossible has thrust its proud finger into them all, a curious air of precise history" 11–12).

60. Yeats, preface to Lady Gregory's *Gods and Fighting Men*, 14. See also Lady Gregory's note on "The Age and Origin of the Stories of the Fianna," in which she writes, "I found it impossible to arrange the stories in a coherrent [sic] form so long as I considered them a part of history. I tried to work on the foundations of the Annalists, and fit the Fianna into a definite historical epoch, but the whole story seemed trivial and incoherrent until I began to think of them as almost contemporaneous with the battle of Magh Tuireadh, which even the Annalists put back into mythical ages. In this I have only followed some of the story-tellers, who have made the mother of Lugh of the Long Hand the grandmother of Finn" (360).

61. See Giambattista Vico, *The New Science*, 3d ed. (1744), trans. Thomas Goddard Bergin and Max Harold Fisch, rev. and abridged (1961; Ithaca: Cornell University Press, 1970), 75–76; 127–28. Hereafter cited in the text as *NS*.

62. In *Dublin* (London: Granada, 1979), Peter Somerville-Large recounts how archeologists discovered the layers of civilization buried beneath present-day Dublin. Discussing the four major sites that have been investigated, Somerville-Large tells how the sites had been covered by late seventeenth- and eighteenth-century houses with cellars,

> whose foundations were sunk deep into the rubble of earlier buildings. Beneath these foundations was a layer, averaging six feet in thickness, of a dark compact substance resembling turf. This had been known about for a long time, and used to be considered as evidence that Dublin was built on a bog. Now it was identified as the compressed core of Norse and medieval refuse that had accumulated since the tenth century. . . . Since it had accumulated on boulder clay which is impervious to damp, it became waterlogged, a process that helped to preserve much fragile organic material. This powdery black compost concealed a mass of objects discarded during the city's early existence. (31)

63. For an excellent early summary of Vico's influence on *Finnegans Wake*, see James Atherton, *The Books at the Wake: A Study of Literary Allusions in James Joyce's Finnegans Wake* (New York: Viking, 1960), 29–34. Most Joyce scholars agree that Joyce uses Vico's four-part structure not only as a model of history, but also as a way of categorizing the different generations in an individual family.

Divine Period	Heroic Period	Human Period	Ricorso
Power of the parents (*FW,* I)	Play of young children (*FW,* II)	Maturation of the children (*FW,* III)	Transformation of the children into a new generation of parents, while mourning the passing of the old (*FW,* IV)
Birth (Religion)	Marriage	Death/Burial	Resurrection

My point is simply that Irish history is also compatible with a Viconian structure:

Ancient Irish gods (Tuatha Dé Danaan)	Historical Irish kings on Hill of Tara	"Modern" period of colonial rule (800 years)	Construction of new Free State out of bloodshed of 1916–22

A superb recent reading that rightly highlights the inadequacy of merely schematic treatments of Joyce and Vico may be found in "Vico's 'Night of Darkness': *The New Science* and *Finnegans Wake*" in John Bishop, *Joyce's Book of the Dark:* Finnegans Wake (Madison, University of Wisconsin Press, 1986), 174–215.

64. See Bishop, *Joyce's Book of the Dark,* 184: "In Vico's 'gentile history,' man creates over generations his own human nature—and exactly as he also creates human nations. Since human nature and nations evolve interdependently with language, Vico conveys their commutual coming-to-be" by weaving together words that originate from the same root, *gen* (to come to be). See chart, 186–87.

65. "Performance" derives from the Old French *per* (thoroughly) + *fournir* (to complete, to supply what is lacking). My argument is that performance works two ways: as we supply what is lacking in a text by "performing" it, it simultaneously supplies—for the moment—something lacking in us, which is what I mean when I say we *become Finnegans Wake* instead of appropriating it.

John Bishop reads what Vico calls "poetic wisdom" and "ignorance" somewhat differently than I do here; he sees it as an apprehension of what we would now call the unconscious, which, he argues, Vico lacked the psychoanalytic terminology to name (*Joyce's Book of the Dark,* 182). Although I am sympathetic to Bishop's argument, I hesitate to equate ignorance with the unconscious, since the state that Vico describes seems to me to be a conscious one; it is simply uninformed and un*self*-conscious; properties of the self are projected outward onto nature.

66. A particularly appropriate example of a word to be read right to left occurs at the beginning of I.2, where the narrator explains that "the Dumlat . . . has it that it was this way" (*FW,* 30.10). The "Dumlat" is the "Talmud," which must be read in English as it would be read in Hebrew.

67. Gilles Deleuze and Félix Guattari, *A Thousand Plateaus: Capitalism and Schizophrenia,* trans. Brian Massumi (Minneapolis: University of Minnesota Press, 1987), esp. chaps. 1, 10, and 12.

68. See Yeats's description of Red Hanrahan's patriotic poems in "Kathleen the

Daughter of Hoolihan and Hanrahan the Red" in the first version of *The Secret Rose*, illus. J. B. Yeats (New York: Dodd, Mead, 1897), 159. Yeats discloses that some of Hanrahan's poems disguised "a passionate patriotism under the form of a love-song addressed to the Little Black Rose or Kathleen the Daughter of Hoolihan or some other personification of Ireland."

69. Anne Chambers, *Granuaile: The Life and Times of Grace O'Malley, c. 1530–1603* (Dublin: Wolfhound Press, 1988), 52, 101, 173. Compare Archibald Hamilton Rowan, after whom Richard Rowan's son Archie was named in *Exiles*; he, too, was labeled a traitor by both the Irish and the British, because he did not take sides unilaterally but made individual judgments about which side he would take in different disputes.

70. The Grania link explains the repetition of the name "dermot" in the Prankquean episode of *Finnegans Wake* (21.14; "redtom" 21.31; "dom ter" 22.18), as well as the reference to Dermot's love spot ("she washed the blessings of the lovespots off the jiminy with soap sulliver suddles," 21.27–28). For the story of "How Diarmuid Got His Love-Spot," see Lady Gregory, *Gods and Fighting Men*, 251–52. Dermot tries to go over to a beautiful young girl who is Youth, but she says to him, "'I belonged to you once, and I can never belong to you again; but come over here to me, Diarmuid,' she said, 'and I will put a love-spot on you, that no woman will ever see without giving you her love.'" What the prankquean washes off the Dermot-like jiminy is precisely his irresistibility to women.

For a particularly fine exploration of how the Dermot-Grania-Finn love triangle inflects the Prankquean episode, see Bernard Benstock, *Joyce-Again's Wake: An Analysis of* Finnegans Wake (Seattle: University of Washington Press, 1965), 267–69.

71. In I.3, Joyce returns to the relation between HCE/Jarl van Hoother and ALP/queen of pranks, relating that she teases him (yet another reference to "tea," one that conjoins joking and sexual stimulation) and that he then misbrands her: "did not she, come leinster's even, true dotter of a dearmud [Diarmuid] . . . with so valkirry a licence as sent many a poor pucker packing to perdition, again and again, ay, and again sfidare him, tease fido, eh tease fido, eh eh tease fido" (*FW*, 68.13–17). "And did not he, like Arcoforty [It. Strongbow], farfar off Bissavolo, missbrand her behaveyous with iridescent huecry of down right mean false sop lap sick dope [do re mi fa so la ti do; musical scale and colors of the rainbow]? Tawfulsdreck! A reine of the shee [queen of women; queen of fairies], a shebeen quean [frequenter of an illicit tavern], a queen of pranks" (*FW*, 68.19–22). She, prankster, pirate, temptress, fairy, is also the babble and music of history: "He hear her voi of day gon by" (*FW*, 68.26–27).

One of the complicating aspects of the Prankquean story is that there are two Dermots, the Diarmuid of the Fianna who ran off with Grania, and Dermot MacMurrough, the king of Leinster who initiated the Norman conquest in 1172 by asking Henry II to send Strongbow and his forces to Ireland. The Prankquean is not only Grania, who abducts Dermots and takes them away, but also Eve, the daughter of Dermot MacMurrough, niece of St Laurence O'Toole, and eventually the wife of Strongbow. The marriage of Eve and Strongbow represents the eventual convergence of extremes attended by massive destruction and nascent hope; see Adaline Glasheen, *Third Census of* Finnegans Wake: *An Index of the Characters and their Roles* (Berkeley: University of California Press, 1977), q.v. "MacMurrough."

72. Chambers has transcribed Granuaile's petition to Queen Elizabeth, Eliza-

beth's eighteen articles of interrogatory, and Grany Ny Mally's answers to the articles in a supplement to the 1988 edition of *Granuaile*, 203–10.

73. "P" and "Q" also suggest "me" and "you," and "P" by itself is often juxtaposed with "T" (as "pea" is with "tea"). My thanks to the Penn *Finnegans Wake* study group, Kathryn Conrad, Marian Eide, Barbara Lonnquist, Nick Miller, and Joseph Valente, for long and illuminating discussions about the associative meanings of "t" and "p," which are often found together in repeating motifs such as "tip" and "pet," but which also constitute different kinds of relief through wetting (the social reconciliation figured by wetting the tea, the sexual overtones of wetting the tea to make three, and the eliminatory relief of pee). Peas and tea also serve as peculiarly Irish synecdoches for food and drink, a whimsical translation of the communality expressed in Christian terms through bread and wine.

74. Joyce underscores the links between the Prankquean episode and the Norwegian captain episode by repeating a version of this phrase in book II, where he refers to "the wreak of Wormans' Noe" (the wreck of woman's no? war-man's no? Norman's woe, 387.20–21).

75. Lewis Carroll: *The Complete Illustrated Works* (New York: Random House, 1982), 210.

76. Maud Gonne MacBride, *A Servant of the Queen: Reminiscences* (1938; Suffolk: The Boydell Press, 1983), 9.

77. Deleuze and Parnet, *Dialogues*, 101. Hereafter cited parenthetically in the text.

78. Judith Butler, *Gender Trouble: Feminism and the Subversion of Identity* (New York: Routledge, 1990).

Conclusion

1. Samuel Beckett, *Murphy* (1938; New York: Grove Wiedenfeld, 1957), 280.

Selected Bibliography

Ahl, Frederick. "Ars Est Caelare Artem." In *On Puns: The Foundation of Letters*. Ed. Jonathan Culler, 17–43. Oxford: Basil Blackwell, 1988.

Alighieri, Dante. *The Divine Comedy*. Trans. with commentary by Charles S. Singleton. 3 vols. Princeton: Princeton University Press, 1975.

Anna, Comtesse de Brémont. *Oscar Wilde and His Mother: A Memoir*. London: Everett, 1911.

Atherton, James. *The Books at the Wake: A Study of Literary Allusions in James Joyce's* Finnegans Wake. New York: Viking, 1960.

Attridge, Derek. *Peculiar Language: Literature as Difference from the Renaissance to James Joyce*. Ithaca: Cornell University Press, 1988.

Barolini, Helen. "The Curious Case of Amalia Popper." *The New York Review of Books*, 20 November 1969.

Baudelaire, Charles. *Les Fleurs du Mal*. Trans. Richard Howard. Boston: David R. Godine, 1982.

Beckett, Samuel. *Endgame*. New York: Grove Press, 1958.

———. *Murphy*. 1934; New York: Grove Wiedenfeld, 1957.

———. *Waiting for Godot: A Tragicomedy in Two Acts*. New York: Grove, 1954.

Benstock, Bernard. *Joyce-Again's Wake: An Analysis of* Finnegans Wake. Seattle: University of Washington Press, 1965.

Bishop, John. *The Book of the Dark*: Finnegans Wake. Madison: University of Wisconsin Press, 1986.

Blake, William. *The Works of William Blake: Poetic, Symbolic, and Critical*. Ed. William Butler Yeats and Edwin John Ellis. 3 vols, 1893; reprint AMS Press, 1973.

Blavatsky, H. P. *The Secret Doctrine: The Synthesis of Science, Religion, and Philosophy*. 2 vols. London: The Theosophical Publishing Company, 1888.

Bonwick, James. *Irish Druids and Old Irish Religions*. 1894; reprint, Dorset Press, 1986.

Bornstein, George. *Yeats and Shelley*. Chicago: University of Chicago Press, 1970.

Bornstein, George, and Warwick Gould. "'To a Sister of the Cross & the Rose': An Unpublished Early Poem." *Yeats Studies Annual* 7 (1990): 179–83.

Bottigheimer, Karl S. *Ireland and the Irish: A Short History*. New York: Columbia University Press, 1982.

Butler, Judith. *Gender Trouble: Feminism and the Subversion of Identity*. New York: Routledge, 1990.

Carter, Angela. *The Bloody Chamber*. New York: Penguin, 1979.

Chambers, Anne. *Granuaile: The Life and Times of Grace O'Malley, c. 1530–1603*. Dublin: Wolfhound Press, 1988.

Cherslica, Bruno. *É tornato Joyce: iconografia triestina per Zois*. Con una prefazione di Giancarlo Vigorelli e un commentario di Stelio Crise. Milano: Nuova Rivista Europea, 1982.

Clark, David R, ed. *The Winding Stair (1929): Manuscript Materials*. Ithaca: Cornell University Press, 1995.

Coakley, Davis. *Oscar Wilde: The Importance of Being Irish*. Dublin: Town House, 1994.

Cohen, Ed. *Talk on the Wilde Side: Toward a Genealogy of a Discourse on Male Sexualities*. New York: Routledge, 1993.

Connolly, Thomas E., ed. *James Joyce's Scribbledehobble: The Ur-Workbook for Finnegans Wake*. Evanston: Northwestern University Press, 1961.

Corkery, Daniel. *The Hidden Ireland: A Study of Gaelic Munster in the Eighteenth Century*. Dublin: M. H. Gill and Son, 1925.

Costigan, Giovanni. *A History of Modern Ireland, with a Sketch of Earlier Times*. New York: Pegasus, 1969.

Coxhead, Elizabeth. *Daughters of Erin: Five Women of the Irish Renascence*. Gerrards Cross: Colin Smythe, 1979.

Craft, Christopher. "Alias Bunbury: Desire and Termination in *The Importance of Being Earnest*." *Representations* 31 (Summer 1990): 19–46.

Cullingford, Elizabeth Butler. *Gender and History in Yeats's Love Poetry*. Cambridge: Cambridge University Press, 1993.

———. *Yeats, Ireland and Fascism*. New York: New York University Press, 1981.

Curci, Roberto. "Chi? Quella 'fiamma' triestina." *Il Piccolo* di Trieste. 13 January 1991.

Deane, Seamus, ed. *The Field Day Anthology of Irish Writing*. 3 vols. Derry: Field Day Publications, 1991.

De Brémont, Countess Anna. *Oscar Wilde and his Mother: A Memoir*. London: Everett 1911.

De Lauretis, Teresa. *Alice Doesn't: Feminism, Semiotics, Cinema*. Bloomington: Indiana University Press, 1984.

Deleuze, Gilles, and Félix Guattari. *Anti-Oedipus: Capitalism and Schizophrenia*. Trans. Robert Hurley, Mark Seem, and Helen R. Lane. Preface by Michel Foucault. 1972, Les Editions de Minuit; Minneapolis: University of Minnesota Press, 1983.

———. *Kafka: Toward a Minor Literature*. Trans. Dana Polan. Foreword Reda Bensmaia. 1975, Les editions de Minuit; Minneapolis: University of Minnesota Press, 1986.

———. *A Thousand Plateaus: Capitalism and Schizophrenia*. Trans. Brian Massumi. 1980, Les editions de Minuit; Minneapolis: University of Minnesota Press, 1987.

Deleuze, Gilles, and Claire Parnet. *Dialogues*. Trans. Hugh Tomlinson and Barbara Habberjam. 1977, Flammarion; New York: Columbia University Press, 1987.

Dhomhnaill, Nuala Ní. *Pharoah's Daughter*. Rev. ed. Winston-Salem, N.C.: Wake Forest University Press, 1993.

———. "Why I Choose to Write in Irish, the Corpse that Sits up and Talks Back." *The New York Times Book Review*, 8 January 1995.

Dollimore, Jonathan. *Sexual Dissidence: Augustine to Wilde, Freud to Foucault*. Oxford: Clarendon Press, 1991.

Ellmann, Richard. *James Joyce*. 2d ed. New York: Oxford University Press, 1982.

————. *The Identity of Yeats*. New York: Oxford University Press, 1964.

————. *Oscar Wilde*. New York: Knopf, 1988.

————. *Yeats: The Man and the Masks*. New York: Macmillan, 1948.

Faulkner, William. *As I Lay Dying*. 1930; New York: Random-Vintage, 1964.

Finneran, Richard, ed. *The Collected Works of W. B. Yeats*, vol. XII. *John Sherman* and *Dhoya*, New York: Macmillan, 1991.

Finneran, Richard. "'Old Lecher with a Love on Every Wind': A Study of Yeats's *Stories of Red Hanrahan*." *Texas Studies in Language and Literature*, 14 (1972): 347–58.

Foster, R. F. *Modern Ireland: 1600–1972*. New York: Viking, 1988.

————. *Yeats: A Life*. I: *The Apprentice Mage, 1865–1914*. Oxford: Oxford University Press, 1997.

Frazer, Sir James. *The New Golden Bough*. Ed. and abridged by Theodor H. Gaster. New York: Criterion Books, 1959.

Freud, Sigmund. *Jokes and their Relation to the Unconscious*. Trans. James Strachey. New York: Norton, 1960.

————. *The Interpretation of Dreams*. Avon reprint. London: Hogarth Press, 1953.

Friel, Brian. *Translations* (1981). In *Modern Irish Drama*. Ed. John P. Harrington. New York: Norton, 1991.

Glasheen, Adaline. *Third Census of* Finnegans Wake: *An Index of Characters and their Roles*. Berkeley: University of California Press, 1977.

Gould, Warwick. "'Lionel Johnson Comes the First to Mind': Sources for Owen Aherne." In *Yeats and the Occult*. Ed. George Mills Harper, 255–84. Yeats Studies Series, ed. Robert O'Driscoll and Lorna Reynolds. New York: Macmillan, 1975.

Gregory, Lady. *Gods and Fighting Men: The Story of the Tuatha De Danaan and of the Fianna of Ireland*. Arr. and trans. Lady Gregory. With a preface by W. B. Yeats. 1904; 2d corr. ed. Gerrards Cross: Colin Smythe, 1976.

Grossman, Allen R. *Poetic Knowledge in the Early Yeats: A Study of* The Wind Among the Reeds. Charlottesville: University Press of Virginia, 1969.

Guattari, Félix. "Everybody Wants to Be a Fascist." *Semiotext(e)* 2, (1977).

Gwynn, Stephen, ed. *Scattering Branches: Tributes to the Memory of W. B. Yeats*. New York: Macmillan, 1940.

Hamilton, Walter. *The Aesthetic Movement in England*. vol. 6 London: Reeves and Turner, 1889.

Harper, George Mills, ed. *Yeats and the Occult*. New York: Macmillan, 1975.

Harris, Frank. *Oscar Wilde*. Including "My Memories of Oscar Wilde" by George Bernard Shaw and an Introductory Note by Lyle Blair. East Lansing: Michigan State University Press, 1959.

Hart-Davis, Rupert, ed. *Selected Letters of Oscar Wilde*. New York: Oxford University Press, 1979.

Harwood, John. *Olivia Shakespear and W. B. Yeats: After Long Silence*. London: Macmillan, 1989.

Hirsch, Edward. "'And I Myself Created Hanrahan': Yeats, Folklore, and Fiction." *ELH* 48 (1981): 880–93.

Holdsworth, Carolyn, ed. *The Wind Among the Reeds: Manuscript Materials*. Ithaca: Cornell University Press, 1993.

Holland, Vyvyan. *Oscar Wilde*. London: Thames and Hudson, 1960; rev. ed. 1966.

Hone, Joseph. *W. B. Yeats: 1865–1939*. New York: Macmillan, 1943.

Howard, Richard. Preface. Roland Barthes. *S/Z*. Trans. Richard Miller. New York: Hill and Wang, 1974.

Hyde, H. Montgomery. *Oscar Wilde: A Biography*. New York: Farrar, Straus & Giroux, 1975.

Jameson, Fredric. *The Political Unconscious: Narrative as a Socially Symbolic Act*. Ithaca, New York: Cornell University Press, 1981.

Jardine, Alice. "Woman in Limbo: Deleuze and His Br(others)." *SubStance* (on Gilles Deleuze) 44/45 (1984): 46–60.

Jeffares, A. Norman, ed. *W. B. Yeats: The Critical Heritage*. London: Routledge and Kegan Paul, 1977.

Jennings, Hargrave. *The Rosicrucians: Their Rites and Mysteries*. 3d ed. London: Routledge, 1887.

Jones, Ernest. *Hamlet and Oedipus*. New York: Norton, 1949.

Joyce, James. *Araby*. Versione dal'inglese di Amalia Risolo. Trieste: Casa Editrice Triestina Carlo Moscheni and Company, 1935. Reprint, Empoli, Ibiskos Editrice, 1991.

———. *Collected Poems*. New York: Viking, 1957.

Joyce, James. *The Critical Writings*. Ed. Ellsworth Mason and Richard Ellmann. New York: Viking, 1959.

———. *Dubliners: Text, Criticism, and Notes*. Ed. Robert Scholes and A. Walton Litz. New York: Viking, 1969.

———. *Exiles: A Play in Three Acts, including Hitherto Unpublished Notes by the Author, Discovered After His Death, and an Introduction by Padraic Colum*. New York: Viking, 1951.

———. *Finnegans Wake*. New York: Viking Press, 1967.

———. *Giacomo Joyce*. Ed. Richard Ellmann. New York: Viking Press, 1968.

———. *Stephen Hero*. Ed. Theodore Spencer. London: Jonathan Cape, 1944.

———. *A Portrait of the Artist as a Young Man*. 1916; New York: Viking Penguin, 1964.

———. *Ulysses, A Critical and Synoptic Edition*. Ed. Hans Walter Gabler with Wolfhard Steppe and Claus Melchior. New York: Random House, 1986.

Joyce, Patrick Weston. *An Illustrated History of Ireland*. London: Longmans, Green, 1923.

———. *A Social History of Ancient Ireland*. 3d ed. 2 vols. Dublin: M. H. Gill & Son, 1920.

Kelly, A. A. ed. *Pillars of the House: An Anthology of Verse by Irish Women from 1690 to the President*. Dublin: Wolfhound Press, 1987.

Lacan, Jacques. *Feminine Sexuality: Jacques Lacan and the ecole freudienne*. Ed. Juliet Mitchell and Jacqueline Rose. Trans. Jacqueline Rose. New York: Norton, 1982.

———. *Television: A Challenge to the Psychoanalytic Establishment*. Ed. Joan Copjec. Trans. Denis Hollier, Rosalind Krauss, Annette Michelson, Jeffrey Mehlman. New York: Norton, 1990.

Laforgue, Jules, *Moral Tales*. Trans. William Jay Smith. 1956; New York: New Directions, 1985.

Lebow, Richard. *White Britain and Black Ireland: The Influence of Stereotypes on Colonial Policy*. Philadelphia: Institute for the Study of Human Issues, 1976.

L'Isle-Adam, Villiers de. *Axël*. Trans. M. Gaddis Rose. London: Soho Book Company, 1936.

MacBride, Maud Gonne. *Dawn.* In *Lost Plays of the Irish Renascence.* Ed. Robert Hogan and James Kilroy, 73–84. Proscenium Press, 1970.

———. *A Servant of the Queen.* 1938; Suffolk: Boydell Press, 1983.

MacDonagh, Oliver. *States of Mind: Two Centuries of Anglo-Irish Conflict, 1780–1980.* London: Pimlico, 1983.

Mahaffey, Vicki. "Giacomo Joyce." In *A Companion to Joyce Studies.* Ed. Zack Bowen and James F. Carens, Westport, Ct.: Greenwood Press, 1984.

———. "Male Refractions and Malefactions in 'Ithaca.'" In *James Joyce: Engendered Perspectives.* Ed. Kimberly Devlin and Marilyn Reizbaum. Forthcoming, 1998.

———. *Reauthorizing Joyce.* Cambridge: Cambridge University Press, 1988; University of Florida Press, 1995.

———. "*Ulysses* and the End of Gender." In Ulysses: *A Case Study.* Ed. Margot Norris. New York: St. Martin's, 1997.

Marks, Elaine, and Isabelle de Courtivron, eds. *New French Feminisms: An Anthology.* New York: Schocken Books, 1980.

McGuckian, Medbh. *Marconi's Cottage.* Winston-Salem, N.C.: Wake Forest University Press, 1991.

———. *On Ballycastle Beach.* Winston-Salem, N.C.: Wake Forest University Press, 1988.

McHugh, Roland. *Annotations to* Finnegans Wake. 1980. Rev. ed., Baltimore, Md: The Johns Hopkins University Press, 1991.

McRae, John, ed. *Teleny.* London: GMP, 1986.

Mercanton, Jacques. "The Hours of James Joyce." In *Portraits of the Artist in Exile: Recollections of James Joyce by Europeans.* Ed. Willard Potts, 205–52. Seattle: University of Washington Press, 1979.

Milgrim, Stanley. *Obedience to Authority: An Experimental View.* New York: Harper and Row, 1974.

Montague, John, ed. *Bitter Harvest: An Anthology of Contemporary Irish Verse.* New York: Charles Scribner's Sons, 1989.

Moore, George. *The Lake.* Afterword by Richard Cave. Gerrards Cross: Colin Smythe, 1980.

Myers, Stephen W. *Yeats's Book of the Nineties: Poetry, Politics, and Rhetoric.* New York: Peter Lang, 1993.

Nadel, Ira. *Joyce and the Jews.* London: Macmillan, 1989.

Négru, Octave. "La Mort et l'eros." In *Paul Wunderlich.* Paris, 1979.

Norman, Charles. *The Genteel Murderer.* New York: Macmillan, 1956.

Norris, Margot. "Not the Girl She Was at All: Women in 'The Dead.'" In *James Joyce: The Dead.* Ed. Daniel R. Schwarz. New York: St. Martin's, 1994.

———. *Joyce's Web: The Social Unravelling of Modernism.* Austin, Tx.: University of Texas Press, 1992.

O'Donnell, William H. "Newly Identified Chapters for *The Speckled Bird,* 1897–98 Version: 'The Lilies of the Lord.'" *Yeats Annual* 7 (1990): 147–75.

Ó Siadhail, Mícheál. *Learning Irish: An Introductory Self-Tutor.* New Haven: Yale University Press, 1988.

Pearce, Donald R. "The Systematic Rose." *Yeats Annual* 4 (1986): 195–200.

Pennick, Nigel. *Celtic Sacred Landscapes.* New York: Thames and Hudson, 1996.

Petrarch. *Petrarch's Lyric Poems: The* Rime sparse *and Other Lyrics.* Trans. and ed. Robert M. Durling. Cambridge: Harvard University Press, 1976.

Pharr, Suzanne. *Homophobia: A Weapon of Sexism*. Inverness, Calif.: Chardon Press, 1988.

Potts, Willard. "Notes on the Gorman Biography." *ICarbs* 4 (Spring–Summer 1981).

Putzel, Steven. *Reconstructing Yeats:* The Secret Rose *and* The Wind Among the Reeds. Dublin: Gill and Macmillan, 1986.

Raddatz, Fritz J. "Der böse Blick des glasernen Auges." *Paul Wunderlich und Karin Székessy: Correspondenzen*. Zurich, 1977.

Rees, Alwyn, and Brinley Rees. *Celtic Heritage: Ancient Tradition in Ireland and Wales*. London: Thames and Hudson, 1961.

Regardie, Israel. *The Golden Dawn*. Vol. 2. Chicago: Aries Press, 1937.

Risolo, Michele. "Mia Moglie e Joyce." *Corriere della Sera,* 27 February 1969, 11.

Roditi, Edouard. "Paul Wunderlich: An Introduction." *Werk-Verzeichnis der Lithographien von 1949–1965*. Ed. Dieter Brusberg. Hamburg, 1966.

Rolleston, T. W. *Celtic Myths and Legends*. 1911; rev. ed. 1917. Reprint New York: Dover, 1990.

Schmidgall, Gary. *The Stranger Wilde: Interpreting Oscar*. New York: Dutton, 1994.

Sedgwick, Eve Kosofsky. *Between Men: English Literature and Male Homosocial Desire*. New York: Columbia, 1985.

———. "Some Binarisms (II): Wilde, Nietzsche and the Sentimental Relations of the Male Body." In *Epistemology of the Closet*. Berkeley: University of California Press, 1990.

Seward, Barbara. *The Symbolic Rose*. New York: Columbia University Press, 1960.

Shakespeare, William. *Hamlet*. Ed. Willard Farnham. New York: Penguin, 1957; rev. ed. 1970.

Sherard, Robert H. *Oscar Wilde: The Story of an Unhappy Friendship*. 1905; New York: Haskell House, 1970.

Smith, Denis Mack. *Mussolini: A Biography*. New York: Vintage-Random House, 1982.

Smith, Peter Alderson. *W. B. Yeats and the Tribes of Danu: Three Views of Ireland's Fairies*. Gerrards Cross: Colin Smythe, 1987.

Smyth, Ailbhe, ed. *Wildish Things: An Anthology of New Irish Women's Writing*. Dublin: Attic Press, 1989.

Spielmann, Heinz. "Paul Wunderlich." *Contemporary Artists*. 3d ed. Ed. Colin Naylor. Chicago, 1989.

Stanfield, Paul Scott. *Yeats and Politics in the 1930s*. New York: St. Martin's, 1988.

Stephens, James. *In the Land of Youth*. New York: Macmillan, 1924.

Symons, Arthur. *The Symbolist Movement in Literature*. 1899; rev. ed. New York: E. P. Dutton, 1919.

Toomey, Deirdre. "Labyrinths: Yeats and Maud Gonne." In *Yeats and Women*. Ed. Deirdre Toomey. *Yeats Annual* 9 (1992).

Unterecker, John. *A Reader's Guide to William Butler Yeats*. New York: Noonday Press, 1959.

Valente, Joseph. *James Joyce and the Problem of Justice: Negotiating Sexual and Colonial Difference*. Cambridge: Cambridge University Press, 1995.

Vico, Giambattista. *The New Science*. 1744, 3d ed. Trans. Thomas Goddard Bergin and Max Harold Fisch; rev. and abridged 1961; Ithaca: Cornell University Press, 1970.

Werner, Alfred. "Macabre Universe: Paul Wunderlich at Staempfli." *Arts 44* (May 1970): 39–41.

Whitaker, Thomas. *Swan and Shadow: Yeats's Dialogue with History*. Chapel Hill: University of North Carolina Press, 1964.

White, Hayden. *The Content of the Form: Narrative Discourse and Historical Representation*. Baltimore: Johns Hopkins University Press, 1987.

White, Terence de Vere. *The Parents of Oscar Wilde: Sir William and Lady Wilde*. London: Hodder and Stoughton, 1967.

Whitford, Frank. "Paul Wunderlich: A Grand Dandy." *Studio* 175 (May 1968): 248–51.

Wilde, Oscar. *The Annotated Oscar Wilde: Poems, Fiction, Plays, Lectures, Essays, and Letters*. Ed. H. Montgomery Hyde. New York: Clarkson N. Potter, 1982.

———. *The Artist as Critic: Critical Writings of Oscar Wilde*. Ed. Richard Ellmann. Chicago: University of Chicago Press, 1969.

———. *The Complete Works of Oscar Wilde*. With an Introduction by Vyvyan Holland. New York: Harper & Row, 1966.

———. *The Picture of Dorian Gray: Authoritative Texts, Backgrounds, Reviews and Reactions, Criticism*. Ed. Donald L. Lawler. New York: Norton, 1988.

———. *Salomé*. French text and English version. Ed. Pascal Aquien. Illus. by Aubrey Beardsley. Paris: Flammarion, 1993.

———. *Selected Letters of Oscar Wilde*. Ed. Rupert Hart-Davis. Oxford: Oxford University Press, 1979.

Wilde, Oscar, and others. *Teleny*. Ed. John McRae. London: GMP, 1986.

Wunderlich, Paul. *Giacomo Joyce: Vorzeichnungen zu der Mappe "Giacomo Joyce."* Stuttgart, 1976.

W. B. Yeats. *The Autobiography of William Butler Yeats*. New York: Macmillan, 1965.

———. *The Collected Works of W. B. Yeats*, 14 vols. General eds. Richard J. Finneran and George Mills Harper. New York: Macmillan, 1989–97.

———. *Essays and Introductions*. New York: Macmillan, 1961.

———. *John Sherman and Dhoya*. Vol. 12, *Collected Works of W. B. Yeats*. Ed. Richard J. Finneran. New York: Macmillan, 1991.

———. *The Letters of W. B. Yeats*. Ed. Allan Wade. New York: Farrar, Straus & Giroux, 1980.

———. *Letters to the New Island*. Vol. 7, *Collected Works of W. B. Yeats*. Ed. George Bornstein and Hugh Witemeyer. New York: Macmillan, 1989.

———. *Memoirs: Autobiography—First Draft Journal*. Ed. Denis Donoghue. New York: Macmillan, 1972.

———. *The Oxford Book of Modern Verse, 1892–1935*. Chosen and with an introduction by W. B. Yeats. Oxford: Clarendon Press, 1936.

———. *The Secret Rose*. Illus. J. B. Yeats. London: Lawrence & Bullen, 1897.

———. *The Secret Rose, Stories by W. B. Yeats: A Variorum Edition*. Ed. Phillip L. Marcus, Warwick Gould, and Michael J. Sidnell. Ithaca: Cornell University Press, 1981.

———. *Uncollected Prose by W. B. Yeats*. Ed. John P. Frayne. New York: Columbia University Press, 1970.

———. *The Variorum Edition of the Plays of W. B. Yeats*. Ed. Russell K. Alspach, assisted by Catharine C. Alspach. New York: Macmillan, 1966.

———. *The Variorum Edition of the Poems of W. B. Yeats*. Ed. Peter Allt and Russell K. Alspach. New York: Macmillan, 1957.

———. *A Vision*. New York: Macmillan, 1965.

———. *The Wind Among the Reeds*. London: John Lane, The Bodley Head, 1899.

————. *The Wind Among the Reeds: Manuscript Materials*. Ed. Carolyn Holdsworth. Ithaca: Cornell University Press, 1993.

————. *The Winding Stair (1929): Manuscript Materials*. Ed. David R. Clark. Ithaca: Cornell University Press, 1995.

W. B. Yeats, ed. *A Book of Irish Verse*. Rev. ed. London: Methuen, 1900.

Yeats, W.B., and Edwin John Ellis, eds. *The Works of William Blake: Poetic, Symbolic, and Critical*. 3 vols. London, 1893; New York: AMS Press, 1973.

Young, Ella. *Flowering Dusk: Things Remembered Accurately and Inaccurately*. New York: Longmans, Green, 1945.

Index